DEAD
RINGER

DEAD RINGER

AN INSIDER'S ACCOUNT OF THE MOB'S COLOMBIAN CONNECTION

WILLIAM GATELY
YVETTE FERNÁNDEZ

DONALD I. FINE, INC.

NEW YORK

Library of Congress Catalogue Card Number: 93-074481

ISBN: 1-55611-396-X

All photographs courtesy of the Federal Bureau of Investigation

Manufactured in the United States of America

10 9 8 7 6 5 4 3 2 1

Designed by Irving Perkins Associates, Inc.

For all the law enforcement officials in the United States, Italy and Colombia who have fallen in the line of fire fighting against the proliferation of the illicit drug trade.
—W. GATELY

To my mother and brothers. Thanks for believing in me.
—Y. FERNÁNDEZ

ACKNOWLEDGEMENTS

We would like to thank Trevor Meldal-Johnsen for policing our grammar and for his mentoring skills.

And Dick Weart for giving his time and serving as our political analyst and consultant.

We are grateful for the participation of the Federal Bureau of Investigation, the United States Attorney's Office for the District of Arizona. And, the Office of the Foreign Minister, Republic of Italy as well as the Colombian National Police.

Thank you to the many officials who were willing to participate in this project, particularly: Giusto Sciacchitano, Assistant Minister for Foreign Affairs, Organized Crime, Drug Trafficking and Terrorism, Republic of Italy; Major General Miguel Antonio Gomez Padilla, Former Comandante of the Colombian National Police; Tom Fink, Assistant United States Attorney, Tucson, Arizona; James Brown, FBI Special Agent, Phoenix, Arizona.

And our thanks to Mariateresa Peca in Rome, Italy for her Italian/English translation services.

FROM THE PERSPECTIVE OF A SMUGGLER:

One of our greatest assets was using the interagency rivalry to our advantage.

We often sent a load of drugs in for the specific purpose of having it seized. We knew that the agents from the various agencies would swarm over each other to get it. Then while they were busy fighting among themselves, we'd come in with another larger load and get it through without a problem.

If the agencies put as much time into fighting the smugglers as they do fighting each other, they'd be a lot better at what they do.

—Leo Fraley

FROM THE PERSPECTIVE OF A PROTECTED WITNESS:

I bargained with the devil when I cut a deal with the Mafia and the cartel.

But the deal I cut with the government only had value as long as I had something to offer. When the trials ended, and my days as a witness were over, the support I counted on from the government was no longer there.

If I had it to do all over again, I would have just done my time.

—Joe Cuffaro

FROM THE PERSPECTIVE OF A LAW-ENFORCEMENT AGENT:

The illicit drug trade . . .

It is a market gone wild, free enterprise out of control.

Within this industry there are no rules and no regulators, just profiteers and a cash flow large enough to affect the economy of many of the nations of the world. It corrupts not only the law-enforcement and justice systems in the countries it touches, but the financial institutions, politicians and the very fabric of these nations.

In Colombia, the country and its government are held hostage by the power, influence and brute force of the cocaine barons who control the cartels. The killing fields that surround narco-terrorism include the graves of thousands of police and military, prosecutors, judges, politicians and even the nation's leading candidate for president. No terrorist organization on any continent has wielded such indiscriminate brutality and consummate power.

It is a market driven by addiction on the demand side and an insatiable greed on the supply side.

—Bill Gately

CONTENTS

Whenever possible, the authors relied upon personal experience or written, official documentation for sources of information. Most of the events in the book were based on the recollections of the main characters.

The events told to the authors by the main characters represent their views and opinions.

The conversation depicted in Chapter 13 was created to present additional information and to summarize the context of individual conversations.

Prologue

America's War on Drugs

ALTHOUGH AMERICA'S RECENT "WAR ON DRUGS" arrived during the Nixon years, it is not the first. In fact, there have been several officially declared "wars" targeting the illicit-drug trade, dating back as far as the late nineteenth century. None have been considered outright victories. The first such effort occurred during the mid-1800s when the British Empire defeated the Chinese and successfully took control of the opium trade. Not only did they win the island city of Hong Kong, they were joined by France, the United States and Russia in the Treaties of Tientsin in 1858, which legalized the international opium trade. Britain's shortest war realized a substantial profit, over $50 million in war indemnity. The Chinese response was an all-out war against the opium traffickers. Untold thousands were killed and those who escaped death fled to what is now known as the Golden Triangle, the pie-shaped slice of geography combining corners of the three countries of Burma, Laos and Thailand. The descendants of the Chinese traffickers of the nineteenth century now pay private armies to protect their poppy crops, and today heroin production in the Golden Triangle is the largest in the world.

While this was taking place in Europe and Asia, hundreds of thousands of Chinese immigrants came to North America to build the transcontinental railroads. With these immigrant workers also came the tentacles of the opium trade. It wasn't until the latter part of the century that the evils of opium abuse were manifested in antidrug legislation. The first such law was passed by the state of Oregon in 1870. However, it only touched the surface, simply making it illegal to smoke the substance. It was not until 1914, when the Harrison Narcotics Act was passed, that legislation outlawed the use of opiates and cocaine in over-the-counter remedies and food products such as Coca-Cola.

In 1922, the first federal laws prohibited the importation of opiates and cocaine without a license from the federal government.

In 1968, drug laws were further amended with the passing of the Controlled Substance Act. At this juncture, President Richard Nixon declared his "war on drugs," a theme used throughout his campaign. It was a political declaration by Nixon and served as a carefully planned, multipronged feather in his cap. Public sentiment was rapidly becoming more conservative. The liberal, free-love, drug-culture/counterculture that prevailed in the late sixties was coming to an end. Nixon also saw the antidrug theme as a vehicle to transfer the focus away from Vietnam to a major domestic issue that appeared solvable. But Nixon's strategy never really unfolded before he was driven from the presidency amid the Watergate scandal.

During the Ford and Carter administrations, drugs were such a low priority the issue seldom surfaced on the national scene, let alone on the agenda of our elected leaders. This trend continued through the first year of the Reagan administration until the volume of public outcry demanded a serious look and a new federal policy. Under the Clinton administration thus far, on a list of twenty priority issues, the drug war is next to last. However, a new wave of public dissatisfaction on the issue of drug abuse is again surfacing. Some experts say it may take another public nudge to get the elected officials to realize that drug abuse and its many associated crimes have reached epidemic proportions.

During the 1980s random drive-by shootings and daytime assassinations in shopping malls of trendy and fashionable communities in Miami and other public places in South Florida had become daily occurrences. Colombian drug lords fought to control their new American drug territory. Floridians became so incensed they banded together, collectively gaining enough clout to become a strong political force, and the government was pressured to act. In 1982, the Reagan administration created the vice president's Florida joint task group headed by then–Vice President George Bush. The FJTG sent 400 federal agents from the U.S. Customs Service and the Drug Enforcement Administration and the Bureau of Alcohol Tobacco and Firearms to augment the existing resources throughout the state of Florida, focusing strictly on drug smuggling. Interestingly, the Florida joint task force is still in operation today, well over a decade later, but with less than one-third the manpower it had in the year it was created.

Unfortunately, during these formative days of the new drug war, the government's "soldiers" were led to war without the legislative or judicial ammunition to match enemy firepower. There were no sophisticated, truly effective drug laws to stop the cartel's onslaught of mari-juana and cocaine. In fact, it wasn't until 1990, when the mandatory sentencing guidelines were implemented, that a real bite was put into the war on drugs. In 1986, the first money-laundering statutes were legislated. Unfortunately, this was six years after the cartels had taken control of the U.S. cocaine and marijuana markets. During the 1980s the only law even slightly affecting the drug lords' cash flow and assets was the Bank Secrecy Act of 1971 (which, incidentally, was a law fought in the Congress and the courts and never enforced until 1976, five years after it appeared on the books). However, this toothless tiger only made it a crime not to report $5,000 in cash or "bearer instruments" such as bonds and traveler's checks as they were physically carried across any U.S. border entering or leaving the country. The law carried only a one-year jail term and/or a $1,000 fine, a misdemeanor. At best, and only if other critical elements could be proven, the sentence would increase to five years or a $10,000 fine. There were also seldom-used civil penalties that allowed for the forfeiture of the money. Oddly, Congress never seriously addressed the strengthening of this law or creating strong money-laundering laws until 1986. Thus, with inadequate laws and high profit margins, the drug lords were not only able to corrupt politicians and elements of law enforcement but, more importantly, members of the banking industry in South Florida. This was systematically accomplished by the Colombian drug traffickers who had infiltrated law enforcement first, buying safety and information about law-enforcement operations with cash. The Colombians targeted prosecutors and judges, as well as federal agents for payoffs. They also used their influence with corrupt prison officials who helped them engineer the release and escape of some of their comrades who had been imprisoned. Sadly, since 1982 dozens of federal, state and local law-enforcement officers have been convicted of serious drug and drug-related money-laundering crimes. Some prosecutors and even judges have also been imprisoned for their unholy alliances with the drug cartels.

In this drug war, as in all others that preceded it, politics continues to play a sinister role. The result is that law-enforcement issues and solu-tions are fluctuating from high to low on the national agenda while political posturing is given top priority to capitalize on an issue of ex-treme importance to the American people. The result is a fragmented and ineffective policy that promotes infighting, confusion and duplicity as it stifles the efforts of dedicated individuals who are truly committed to winning the drug war. Today, the drug problem is stuck in the quag-mire of a bureaucracy: the bureaucrats blunder, the politicians use the issue as their platform for personal and political gain, while law-enforce-ment agencies posture for budgets and scarce resource allocations. In essence, drugs have become the evil empire of the nineties. It is a serious social and law-enforcement problem on a global scale much like the threat of communism was, until recently, to the free world. Like communism the drug problem can be significantly impeded. But we must fight to win.

When Nixon declared a war on drugs in 1968, the mission of controlling drugs fell prey to bureaucratic bickering and turf battles among agencies. As a consequence, many law-enforcement agents at that time regarded Nixon's declaration of war as a purely political move to create a national police force under the Department of Justice and then–attorney general John Mitchell rather than FBI director J. Edgar Hoover, whom Nixon could not control. The result was disastrous because it left the borders of our country virtually unprotected. The idea was sold to Congress that drug interdiction was of little significance at the borders, and drug enforcement should be concentrated in the inner cities, focusing almost exclusively on domestic organizations and street traffickers. This further exacerbated the hostility between agencies and caused more friction than ever before. For example, between 1973 and 1982, the special agents of the Customs Service were virtually forbidden to investigate any drug crime within their *own* jurisdiction at the border, where for two hundred years Customs had been the sole border agency. In short, Nixon's war on drugs was a losing proposition from the start. Not only did the administration turn the country's borders into a virtual playground for the smuggler, it also created a system destined to fail. Local law-enforcement officials, as well as the feds who had worked at the border, believed the new plan was ineffective because it ignored the root of the problem by abandoning the border.

As the drug epidemic grew in the seventies and eighties, so did the infighting. It soon became the focus between Customs and the newly created Drug Enforcement Administration to "outnumber" each other statistically for bigger budgets and more credit. As the problem grew into more of an embarrassment than anything else, a bold plan was developed among the agencies. A group of customs and DEA managers proposed the creation of the Border Management Agency. Such an agency would consolidate resources from Customs, DEA and Border Patrol to focus only on border crimes, the top priority being drug smuggling. It was new, and a complete about-face, but the plan was never put into action. Opponents convinced lawmakers that the enemy was not the source but the inner-city user. They further argued that this plan would not decrease the infighting.

In 1982, the Customs Service reorganized under the leadership of

Commissioner William Von Raab. The first item on the agenda was to phase out the patrol division. It took two years to complete, but proved worthwhile by eliminating duplication of the Border Patrol's efforts while permitting Customs, at least in theory, to pursue its own investigations. During this time, however, the DEA had authored a "memorandum of understanding" with the Border Patrol, again exacerbating the rift between DEA and Customs. DEA's arrangement with the Border Patrol gave DEA exclusive rights to investigate all Border Patrol seizures and forbade the Border Patrol from referring these seizures and arrests to any other agency except DEA. It was an obvious ploy to limit Customs' success, but in reality, their strategies for intervention differed drastically. Customs' highest priority was to take border seizures beyond the simple interdiction and immediate arrests, exploiting cases to their fullest. Today, as in the past, customs officials say the agency has achieved its greatest successes with this technique.

Another new idea was implemented in 1984. Congress legislated Title 21, or drug investigative authority, for the FBI, a first for this agency. This political maneuver was easily passed because it gave the impression that the government was increasing its efforts in the drug war. The publicity, however, was a far cry from reality. The FBI special agent force of over 9,000 initially committed fewer than 10 percent to join this war. Nine years later, the commitment from FBI is still a scant 1,200 special agents. To further exacerbate matters, an intense rivalry developed between the two Department of Justice agencies during the 1980s. On three occasions since 1984, the FBI has threatened to consume DEA. Attorney General Janet Reno recently nixed the most recent takeover attempt, but fears, jealousies and, indeed, hatred between the two agencies is still of great concern to the agents who toil in the trenches every day.

Then in 1986, Congress brought in the military, further complicating the already bureaucratically encumbered war on drugs, hamstringing it with the enormous volume of laws and regulations that came with "military assistance." On the surface, it appeared to be a great idea. It sounded good to the public and it was easy to sell visually by showing off radar, sophisticated aircraft, ships and military hardware. It also provided a new and highly visible mission to the military. Millions of dollars were thus shifted to the military from federal law enforcement to support the new player in the war on drugs. With little experience in law enforcement operations, however, the military was not very effective. Further, since the first Continental Congress convened in 1775, the U.S. military has been forbidden to have any police powers within the boundaries of the United States, a law commonly referred to as *posse comitatus*. Instead of using the money appropriated by Congress to support

law-enforcement operations, much was spent on "intelligence" projects
and self-initiated "interdiction" operations. In short, military assistance
has been inconsistent and of little help in the overall thrust against
illegal drugs.

In 1988, Congress created the Office of National Drug Control Policy
(ONDCP). The "Drug Czar" has been law enforcement's greatest friend
and its unlikely foe. The ONDCP was created to oversee all agency drug/
law enforcement budgets and eliminate infighting and jealousies. Staffed
by political appointees from the private sector, however, it was immediately lobbied by each agency to serve their own agenda. The czar has
never lived up to his star billing. The existing problems that created it
have for the most part become buried in yet another new layer of bureaucracy.

During the past two decades, we have come full circle—twice. President
Nixon's formula of creating a single agency to attack the problem was
replaced by the current multiagency system in the mid 1980s, which
stressed a joint effort with individual agency specialization. In September 1993, the drug czar was mandated to eliminate the duplicity in drug
law enforcement by the reorganization of resources available in all federal drug law enforcement agencies. Again the consolidation option was
nixed in favor of the multiagency drug law enforcement effort.

Even though President Clinton's administration has not directly taken
on the drug problem, he did commission a study through his vice president to address the issue of agency duplicity as part of the "reinvent
government" study. To address these concerns, Attorney General Reno
reduced the drug czar's manpower and duties, then appointed Louis
Freeh the new FBI director to also serve as the head of a new Justice
Department office devoted to mediating the ever-present interagency
disputes between the FBI, DEA, U.S. Customs, the U.S. Marshals Service and the Border Patrol. The departing DEA chief Robert Bonner
has criticized the appointment of Freeh. Bonner said, "Having the director of the FBI call the shots here certainly is not going to create the
perception of impartiality and neutrality that I think is important."
These two recent actions have placed the Office of National Drug Control Policy under the shadow of the attorney general, relegating it to
little more than a funding mechanism for the agencies.

These constant internal battles among agencies vying for jurisdiction
and funding and the constant shift in policy from administration to administration have naturally served to strengthen and encourage the position of their adversaries. The U.S. government's changing policies and
priorities, coupled with the economic instability of third world countries,

has fostered fertile ground for a stronger, more volatile illicit drug market. The drug trade is a global enterprise and directly affects the economic and political structure of drug source and transit countries. In turn, the consumption of illegal drugs in the United States has become a problem out of control.

Drug trafficking is the number-one growth industry in the world. To understand its penetrating force, one need only look at the basic principles of business.

There are three important aspects a business must execute precisely and effectively to maintain its operation. They are: manufacturing (supply); transportation; marketing (distribution). The cocaine trade is no different. The supply equation works like this in the South American countries of Colombia, Peru, Bolivia and Ecuador: All are involved in the crop production of the coca plant. Peru and Bolivia are the world's largest producers of the raw material necessary for the production of cocaine, the coca leaf. Bolivia, one of Latin America's poorest countries, has an unemployment rate of 21 percent and an inflation rate of 18 percent. Half of its work force are farmers, whose main cash crop is coca, which is sold for cocaine processing. In Peru, the unemployment rate stands at 20 percent with underemployment estimated at 60 percent —and a staggering inflation rate of seven thousand percent! It is no wonder that as much as 85 percent of the country's cultivation is for illicit production. Ecuador and Colombia are third and fourth in the agriculture department of the equation. Together, the countries of Peru, Bolivia and Colombia are the principles in the manufacturing of cocaine hydrochloride (HCl). Colombia is by far the leader in this process, and most of the raw materials produced by all these nations are shipped to Colombia for processing by the powerful Cali and Medellín cartels. In Central America, the countries of Belize, Panama, Guatemala and Costa Rica, all Latin American democracies, also serve as part of the transportation element. All have provided safe haven to Colombian drug-laden aircraft including landing facilities, fuel, storage and additional land transportation. The countries of Cuba and Nicaragua, while under communist rule, have aided the Colombian cartels, providing these same services at a "government level" by using military resources and accepting millions for their services. The primary corridor for cocaine smuggling from Colombia is through Central America and Mexico, commonly known as the "cocaine pipeline." The second most heavily used route for smuggling is through the Caribbean to Puerto Rico, due to the vast frontier of the island. The third major smuggling route is through the Bahamas, because of their close proximity to Miami, which has become a mecca for the cartels operating in South Florida. It is quickly giving way, however, to the 440 miles of border between the Mexican state of Sonora and Arizona. Today, Arizona has become known as "cocaine alley."

During the 1980s, Mexico suffered severe economic difficulties. Not coincidentally, during this difficult time when Mexico's unemployment rate reached as high as 18 percent and inflation was as high as 30 percent, the Mexican drug trade became king.

Cocaine is transported from Colombia through Mexico to the United States across the southwest border, which stretches from Brownsville, Texas, to San Diego, California. America's border states are typically the main smuggling routes. The cities of Houston, Los Angeles and Phoenix are major distribution points for cross-border cocaine smuggling. Smugglers use any method imaginable to smuggle drugs across the border, from horseback, hidden compartments in cars and trucks to human "mules" crossing the desert with backpacks. In May 1990, a drug tunnel was discovered running from Agua Prieta, Sonora, Mexico to Douglas, Arizona. Two years later, another tunnel, nearly 1,200 feet long, was discovered beneath the California border between San Ysidro and Tijuana.

In Mexico, the cartels have allied with the organizations that have traditionally controlled the marijuana and heroin trade in that country. Through this partnership the cartels have gained more than 2,000 miles of virtually unprotected border with the U.S. For their part in the transportation element of the equation, the Mexican organizations reap a payment of as much as 40 percent of all the cocaine they smuggle into the U.S. In addition, the cartels use Mexico as a warehouse, to stockpile hundreds of thousands of pounds in drugs, and millions of dollars pass through the country, back into the bank accounts of the cartels. The drug "stashes" are held for months at a time, until stockpiles within the United States are depleted. The drug organizations will "overproduce," allowing some drugs to be confiscated, while they "import" another load somewhere else. It's not unusual for the cartels to give up a one thousand pound load to bring in a ten thousand pound load somewhere else. Another reason for stockpiling is to create a demand in the United States and ultimately raise the price of cocaine. The price of cocaine has in recent years fluctuated drastically from a low of $9,000 per kilo to as much as $35,000 per kilo.

The third and most important element in the drug business equation is the distribution of the product and ultimately the multibillion-dollar payoff for the cartels. In the United States, within the major cities the cartels have established a corporate structure as elaborate as any *Fortune* 500 company. In fact, the late drug kingpin Pablo Escobar of the

Medellín cartel was one of the first to establish an organizational structure along the lines of legitimate corporations. His organization sent representatives, or managers, to cities in the United States to establish regional distribution networks. The distribution networks are serviced by "cells," exclusively engaged in the collection, laundering and transportation of the billions of dollars in drug profits. In the early 1980s, one such cell in Miami collected and laundered more than $30 million a month for Escobar's organization. It is estimated that every day over $9 million in drug profits are shipped in bulk to Colombia by the cells. Today, the distribution system has become so sophisticated and effective that individual cells in cities throughout the country operate independently, yet collectively for their respective cartels. Cell members are treated much like corporate employees, receiving benefits such as bonuses, transfers, promotions, sick leave and vacation time. However, poor performance or lost loads often results in execution.

As a result the United States now has the dubious distinction of being the largest consumer of illicit drugs in the world. More than 1.1 million people are currently being treated for drug addiction. In America 80 percent of all violent crime is directly linked to illegal drug use, sales or distribution.

In South America, the past two decades have marked the emergence of a new organized-crime syndicate—the drug cartels of Medellín and Cali. Their strength comes from the close ties they have established with that portion of the Colombian population that knows only despair. People who are so entrenched in poverty often feel disenfranchised from their government. In poverty-stricken countries, strong forces like the cartels can easily win the hearts and minds of the people by providing the desperately needed economic stimulus.

Meanwhile, in the more traditional organized-crime area, drug trafficking in Italy is well documented. It has been one of the most profitable businesses controlled by the Sicilian Mafia since the 1940s. Ties with organized crime throughout Europe—specifically, the south of France and Corsica—and with the Middle East have helped make the Mafia the foremost trafficking entity in the illicit-heroin trade. Next to the Asian distributors who receive their heroin from the Golden Triangle, Italy is foremost in heroin distribution worldwide.

The Sicilian Mafia has also maintained close ties with Mafia families in New York, Chicago, Miami, Kansas City and New Orleans. Hundreds of investigations since 1980 have established the Palermo/New York Mafia drug connection. The best known is "the Pizza Connection." Although not as famous, perhaps the most interesting example of the Euro-American mafiosi connection is a case originally developed in New York by U.S. authorities six years earlier. This investigation resulted in the seizure of only forty kilograms of heroin in Milan, Italy, but the case was prosecuted in Palermo, Italy, and targeted several members of the Sicilian Mafia. The investigation also identified the first heroin lab within Italian borders, on the island of Sicily. The case is also notable for bringing the Italian and American governments together against the Mafia.

In the drug business, the participants are not only the criminal element; at times the police, military and the very leaders of nations become key players, taking part in drug trafficking.

In the country of Panama, Gen. Manuel Noriega, the leader of the nation for over a decade, offered the country's military and financial institutions to the Medellín cartel. While in power, Noriega provided safe haven for drugs and the traffickers. Noriega allowed Panama's banking system to become a conduit to launder billions of dollars in profits.

The military and police of the "source and transit countries" are threatened every day by the superior forces of the cartels. Yet, these nations do not face the epidemic of crime and addiction that exists in the United States. They are, however, faced with a much different and perhaps more oppressive fight. In Colombia in 1990 alone there were more policemen killed in action directly related to drug enforcement than there were throughout the U.S. during the last decade.

With the increasing influence of these *"narcotraficante"* dollars in the depressed countries of Latin America, many are finding a new and easier way to make a better living through the drug trade. This is a trend that has reached every level of society, from peasant to the highest levels of government. This is a symptom of the "drug epidemic" that is also affecting the United States, albeit to a much lesser degree.

Corruption is like a disease. It recognizes no boundaries of race, nationality or position. It looks for the right vein and then infuses its poison while draining society's wealth, health and self-respect.

The very fabric of the countries of Peru, Bolivia, Colombia, Ecuador, Panama, Costa Rica, Guatemala and Mexico is being threatened by the massive flow of illicit drugs through them. In the poorer countries of Latin America the cartels have not only challenged the governments, they have provided the masses with housing, jobs and even schools the government could not provide. By doing this, the cartels win the hearts, minds and loyalty of the people. Even more importantly they provide a means for survival and a "better life," making it easy to overlook the "source" and justify it as a way of life. Drug kingpin Pablo Escobar built homes, churches and schools, primarily in the rural areas where he also employed peasants for the cultivation and processing of coca.

When there is resistance, options are always available. Drug trafficking is like water in a mountain stream. It takes the path of least resistance. When Noriega's stronghold in Panama collapsed, it created a void in the transportation of vast quantities of illicit drugs, specifically cocaine as a "way station" between Colombia and the United States. The cartels immediately looked past Panama and set their sights on Costa Rica. This country, known as the oldest and purest democracy in the Americas, has no military or real police forces capable of combating a foe like the cartel. The government budget has not been committed to fighting crime and defending the nation's borders, but rather toward education and health care, both guaranteed to every citizen of Costa Rica. Today, the long-standing way of life for the people of Costa Rica is threatened as they witness their country becoming one of the transit points for the cartels.

As the self-proclaimed "defenders of democracy," Americans must also be cognizant of the underlying issues threatened by drug trafficking. Regardless of our political, cultural or economic backgrounds, most Americans still feel that maintaining a free society within our own borders is among the highest priorities in government. As a "superpower," this country may not suffer the perils of Latin America, but the same cancer that has afflicted and crippled those countries is also growing in our society.

Dead Ringer is the story of three men who, during the seventies and eighties, became directly involved in the world of drug trafficking—on both sides of the law. Their stories provide a window into the war on drugs. It is a personal look into a world ruled by greed, power and violence.

Dead Ringer reveals the influence of politics, the corruption of officials, the threat to democracy in the Americas and the effect of the illicit drug trade on everyone caught in its path. It is the story of one man who refused to succumb to corruption, who believed in his oath and mission, and the consequences he paid for believing in what he was doing. It is also the story of two others from different worlds, both of whom eventually succumbed to greed and willingly became part of its corrupting environment. But, more importantly, *Dead Ringer* publicly exposes for the first time the alliance between the Colombian drug cartels and the Mafia, both in the U.S. and Europe.

CHAPTER

1

THE CHAMELEON

THE CANOE WAS TWENTY FEET LONG, three and a half feet wide at the center and carved from the trunk of some tropical tree. The Mercury outboard engine that powered it appeared like an alien attachment to the primitive vessel it pushed along this seemingly endless river. It was the eeriest, most beautiful place Fraley had ever seen. Never in his wildest dreams did he believe he would one day be here, deep within this primitive and unspoiled land, separated from everyone and everything that had been important to him. His life had changed radically, from his eating and sleeping habits to the very way he lived out each new day. Everything was uncertain, except one fact: The possibility of turning back the clock and returning to the life he had left behind was becoming increasingly slimmer. The occupants of the canoe who only a short time ago had been strangers were now his only social circle.

It was, it seemed, a century ago when he took that flight aboard the Cessna 402 from the Boca Raton Municipal Airport. It was his first time outside the U.S. For that matter, the planning of his unscheduled, no-flight-plan, departure had been in the hands of a friend, Bobby DeVitto. A "connected guy," DeVitto had been a member of the Larocca crime family in Pittsburgh for many years, and, for the past two, Leo Fraley's best source for Colombian marijuana.

Fraley had been in no position to call any shots. The week before he had left home in Sharon, Pennsylvania, he was embroiled in a cat-and-mouse game without ever seeing the cat. His last words to his family were, "I'll meet youns tomorrow morning. We'll drive to Pittsburgh and catch the first flight to Wilmington."

He had never intended to make that flight to North Carolina or for that matter even speak to anyone—family or friends—except Albert "Tubby" Figer, who drove him to the Cleveland airport that night.

"Are you sure you know what you're doin'?" Tubby asked with concern, adding, "Why the hell are we standin' in this shithouse whisperin' to each other?"

"Look, Tubby, I've probably got a tail and the minute I get close to that jetway they're gonna pounce down on me. Now, if they see yooz with me you're gonna catch some of da heat. So dis is goodbye here." Figer, whose real name was Albert Vacaro, shook hands, pulled him close and gave him a hug, as if he were losing his brother.

Fraley had always treated Figer like family. When Figer was down and out, blackballed by the Cleveland mob, Fraley was the only one to care enough to give him another break. Things were so bad, Figer was eating Campbell's soup cold from the can. He didn't have enough money to turn on the gas in the house. But when Fraley dropped in and found him in his state of despair, he took him out of Cleveland, gave him a place to stay in Youngstown and even cut him in on all of their scores.

Figer had fallen on bad times after he unintentionally blew the cover during a heist. As wheel man, he had sat outside waiting in the getaway car in downtown Cleveland while the others were inside burglarizing an insurance company. Figer's craving for food superseded his better judgment and even his ability to drive rationally. He had intended to cruise around the block in search of an all-night fast-food establishment, when the next thing he knew he was staring into the flashlight of an Ohio state trooper for driving the wrong way on the freeway. When police searched the car, they found a full inventory of burglary tools, from pry bars to an acetylene torch. They quickly surrounded the area and arrested Figer's partners as they carried out their loot.

Much to his surprise, Fraley had glided right past the security checkpoint, was greeted with a smile by the Delta Airlines ticket agent and boarded the flight to Fort Lauderdale without even the hint of a problem. Bobby DeVitto met him at the airport and reassured him that the cops had no clue about their plans.

"Tomorrow you'll be on your way to South America and livin' the good life," DeVitto said as he shoved another forkful of rigatoni into his already overloaded mouth. They ate dinner at Frank's Restaurant in Pompano Beach and drove to Boca Raton where they spent the night. The next morning they shopped for clothes, loaded up two coolers with sandwiches, candy bars and sodas at a local 7-Eleven, and cut a path directly to the airport.

Fraley was introduced to Harvey, DeVitto's pilot. Harvey was a friendly sort of guy who had a perverted zest for flying. DeVitto had talked about him occasionally and some of their experiences smuggling marijuana into the South Florida area. Harvey was a well-educated, upper-crust guy from Boston and a former Navy fighter pilot. It seemed that after two combat tours in Vietnam flying A-6As off of carriers he had become disenchanted with stateside military life, resigning his commission following a brawl with a superior officer.

They unloaded the provisions and two heavy suitcases that DeVitto insisted on personally carrying from the trunk of his Cadillac Eldorado to the airplane. A few minutes later they were in the air. Without any explanation, Harvey made a radical left turn, a three-g dive and landed the twin prop as if he had a tailhook, or had forgotten something, like the wings. As soon as they touched down Harvey opened the throttles full bore, was nose up and they were in the air again. After two more "touch and goes," combat style, the Cessna leveled off about a hundred feet off the deck and headed due east over the early morning, sun-drenched calm of the Atlantic.

Less than two hours later Fraley was on the Bahamian island of Great Inagua. The airport greeting from the island's governor seemed a little strange for the purpose of his visit. But then again he wasn't completely sure why they had chosen this island. The governor reminded him of the Cosby cartoon character, Fat Albert. He wore white pants, a white *guayabera* and sandals—there wasn't a shoe made to cover that foot.

"He was fat from his toes to his nose and everything in between. Even his ears were fat," Fraley would later say, describing his first encounter with the Bahamian politician. DeVitto had spotted him immediately and was down the three steps of the Cessna's ladder to the tarmac, shaking the fat man's hand, in a matter of seconds. Fraley helped Harvey chock the landing gear, stood by the doorway of the airplane and watched from a distance while the mafioso and the local politician talked. Soon the conversation became heated, growing more and more animated. Their voices grew loud enough for Fraley to hear them from where he stood, about fifty feet away. But the conversation simmered almost as quickly as it had come to a boil, and DeVitto did a quick about-face and marched back to the plane as if he were on a mission.

"Don't worry about it," he said to Fraley waving both his hands in unison over his head, as if about to shoot a foul shot with a basketball. "Hand me one of those suitcases we packed in the plane."

Fraley responded without a word. As he reached through the doorway with the bag, DeVitto grabbed it with both hands, turned it on its side and opened it on the tarmac at the base of the ladder. When he pulled the top flap of the soft leather suitcase to one side exposing its contents, Fraley realized that the trip to Great Inagua was more than just a free ride on his way to South America.

DeVitto reached in, grabbed a stack of fifties from among a virtual sea of green and fanned it with his thumb. He shoved the money into his pocket and walked back toward the fat man. Fraley watched as the conversation now appeared to be a congenial greeting between close friends. In less than a minute, the two parted ways, and Fat Albert walked into the airport building.

An hour later DeVitto was sitting on the airplane's ladder finishing off a ham and cheese sandwich when he looked south in the cloudless sky and spotted the Mitsubishi MUJ2 making its approach. As soon as he recognized it, DeVitto looked around to see Harvey heading at a dead run back toward the Cessna. The defrocked Navy jet-jockey fired up both engines and taxied onto the end of the runway. With the door open, brakes on and both engines at full throttle, Fraley sat inside the Cessna and watched DeVitto as he stood by the doorway at the ready.

"That plane's gonna pull up right next to ours," DeVitto shouted over the roar of the engines. "As soon as it does, you take these two suitcases and set 'em right next to the doorway of his plane." Fraley looked at DeVitto, mesmerized.

The Mitsubishi landed hot, using its brakes and full-power-reversed engines to stop the aircraft, a noisy business. It turned toward the Cessna and the pilot held its twin turbine engines at a steady scream.

Suddenly, the door to the Mitsubishi dropped down, and before it was completely open a huge man appeared. In one sweeping move he took a step down the ladder, onto the tarmac. In the same motion, he reached behind him, grabbed two large duffel bags and simultaneously lifted them to each shoulder. His next step launched him into a full sprint headed directly toward the Cessna, where he tossed both duffel bags inside the cabin through the open doorway.

"Don't just stand there. Grab a couple bags!"

Fraley safely placed the two suitcases filled with cash near the door of the Mitsubishi as instructed, but it took him a couple of seconds to react to the new set of orders. The man before him was an awesome sight. He was in his thirties, six feet-seven if he was an inch and 260 pounds of muscle. His baritone voice reminded Leo of an opera singer, but his attitude was all business—much like the Mafia bosses he knew back home. As Fraley grabbed another of the fifty-pound duffel bags and started his own sprint under the wing of the Mitsubishi, he felt his feet leave the ground as he was pulled back and stopped dead in his tracks. He turned to see what had hold of him, and he found himself at eye level with the chest of this huge man.

"Out to the end of the wing. Always to the end of the wing, then around," said the man, shouting over the four aircraft engines.

Fraley didn't know whether to ask him why he had stopped him so abruptly, to follow the man's directions or to continue scrutinizing his SMUGGLING IS NOT JUST A JOB, IT'S AN ADVENTURE T-shirt. Then it hit him: he had almost sliced and diced himself by walking directly into the Mitsubishi's spinning, port-side prop.

It took six runs to get the duffel bags from one aircraft to the other. As soon as the Cessna was loaded, the big man gave a thumbs-up sign, which was acknowledged by Harvey, sitting at the controls, and DeVitto, standing at the doorway. As the Cessna started rolling down the runway, DeVitto, wearing a big smile, pulled the door shut and waved as Fraley stood and watched the airplane disappear into the horizon.

One thing he knew, those duffel bags had not contained marijuana. Without a word of warning DeVitto had just cut him into a deal without compensation. Fraley had loaded over a thousand pounds of coke and his only payment would be his free ride to Great Inagua. He knew they would have no problem smuggling the load. Harvey was known for his ability to defy the odds and find the radar hole. He would turn on his over-the-counter car radar-detector that he had installed on the dash of the 402's instrument panel and keep the Cessna as close to the Atlantic as possible. The speed and prop wash would churn the sea beneath the aircraft as it literally cut a path for the Florida coast. DeVitto told him once about the pilot's near-collision with a sailboat.

Fraley's attention was drawn from the horizon back toward the Mitsubishi as it taxied to the tie-down area. The deafening sound of the airplane's engines had been replaced with the calm of the gentle wind and the surroundings of this otherwise peaceful island.

The fuel man drove Fraley, the large man and his two pilots to a place known as the "main house," located in the center of town. Across the perfectly manicured courtyard was Government House, from which the island's political pulse emanated.

Nightfall had set in hours ago and sunrise was still a few hours away, but Fraley was wide-awake and dying of thirst. As he lay in bed, he turned his eyes to see the large man sleeping in a nearby bed. The man had a .357 Colt Python under his pillow and a couple of million dollars nearby. Fraley wondered whether, if he got up for water, this son of a bitch would shoot him, thinking he was after the money. It was a chance he decided to take. He headed for the bathroom and got a long drink of water.

"What's the matter, you thirsty?" the large man asked when Fraley returned.

"Yeah, I'm thirsty," Fraley answered. He knew the man was simply sending him a message and he acknowledged it as clearly as he could.

* * *

At breakfast Fraley sat opposite the large man, who had still not introduced himself. Damned if he was going to ask. The man's pilot, who he called César, and the copilot, who said his name was Carlos in perfect English, sat to his right. Fraley was not yet sure who these people were, but he noticed they all had the same eating habits. Fraley watched curiously as they all salted their bread and butter. Two other men, both Bahamian cops, also sat at the table.

"You don't say a word," the large man said as he inconspicuously leaned toward Fraley, then did all the talking. He told the police that Fraley and the pilots were from Cuba. They sat and ate silently while the large man spoke. No sooner had the conversation ended when Jefferson entered the dining room.

"Señor, I have the car ready for you now." He was a tall, thin black man, dressed in khaki shorts and a flowered shirt.

"Excellent, we'll be outside in a minute." Then he turned to Fraley. "Did you enjoy your breakfast?"

"Yeah, it was great. I just wish they had some American cigarettes around here. I'm havin' a nicotine fit."

They walked out of the hotel and climbed into the open-air Jeep. It took them quickly to the airport and directly onto the tarmac where the Mitsubishi was parked. Fraley watched as Jefferson topped off the wing tanks of the aircraft from the fuel truck and then began filling six twenty-five gallon containers with the jet fuel. With the help of two other men, Jefferson began loading the heavy plastic barrels into the aircraft while each was closely inspected by César.

Fraley was the last to enter the plane.

"There's no smoking in here," the large man said to Fraley as he secured the doorway setting the lock. "There's no smoking in any of my planes, especially this one." César was firing up the turbines and within a few minutes, or so it seemed, the aircraft was well above forty thousand feet. The radical climb and thin air made Fraley feel like his chest was caving in.

"Just relax, take a nap," said the large man, witnessing Fraley's obvious discomfort. "Get some rest now. We've got some work to do later."

A couple of hours later Fraley felt a tug on his shoulder and forced his eyes open to see a signal to follow his new acquaintance into the aft section of the cabin. Fraley obeyed like a student on the first day of school. He watched his teacher take two panels off the interior of the fuselage, open one of the fuel barrels with a screwdriver, then attach a clear one-inch reinforced neoprene line between the barrel and a T-connection inside the fuselage.

"Here, just pump it, but pump it steady. Don't try to pump it fast, just pump it steady," he said and pushed a hand pump into the top of the barrel.

About an hour and a half later, Fraley felt the plane descend. He looked out of a window and saw they were a couple thousand feet above what appeared to be the jungle canopy.

"You see that river there. This is where my property starts. We'll land before we get to the other side of my property," boasted the large man. "At ten thousand hectares, this is one of my smallest properties, but it is my home."

Once on the ground the pilot seemed to taxi the aircraft into the thick of the jungle, then somehow turned it around on a dime. When they disembarked, Fraley noticed the plane was well covered from above not only by the natural vegetation, but by a huge camouflage net that was suspended from the trees. Fraley followed the large man into a waiting Toyota Land Cruiser.

They drove to a house shaped like a huge L and surrounded by lush tropical foliage. The "farmhouse," as the large man referred to it, had a Spanish tile roof and a white stucco exterior framed by enormous wood beams carved from a single tree trunk. The interior was exquisite, marble floors everywhere. Crystal chandeliers graced the foyer and dining room and even though it appeared to still be undergoing construction, all the amenities were present. A veranda surrounded the exterior of the house, and nearby there were several wooden 500-gallon barrels on stilts to catch the rainwater. Generators for electricity were uniformly positioned near an outbuilding in the distance. And not far from the farmhouse was a rectangular-shaped bamboo-framed cabana with a thatched roof. There were several workers close by who appeared to be native Indians from the area. The jungle, too, was filled with activity. Fraley could hear animals screaming, barking and bellowing, and just a few yards away, in an aviary near the cabana, dozens of pet parrots added to the racket. Suddenly, Fraley realized that he was also under scrutiny.

"¿Quién es el gringo?" a voice asked.

"He's a killer from the United States," the owner of the jungle estate explained to the workers. "He's down here to make sure I do my job for the American Mafia. So if he's watching me, I'm watching you." Then he turned to Fraley, and happily announced the beginning of a celebration.

"I will see you in a few minutes. Carlos will show you the way." Obediently, Carlos escorted Fraley to the fiesta at another nearby *hacienda.* There were dozens of people. Some were drinking, others smoking marijuana and still others danced while music blared from speakers.

"Do you like to play cards?" asked the copilot Carlos.

"Well, sure. But what kind of game are you talking about," Fraley replied with a smile. By then, he learned that Carlos was Canadian-born and adopted by a Colombian couple. His father was a wealthy man who had become a Colombian congressman.

"It's the same as blackjack," the large man interjected as they took their seats at the table in the cabana.

"Un peso por un dólar," said one man as the others laughed. Fraley did not know much Spanish but he did know that the dollar was worth about two hundred fifty pesos. DeVitto had filled him in on the exchange rate while they were waiting on the tarmac on Great Inagua.

"Tell 'em I'll play one peso for one dollar, as long as I can deal," Fraley said to Carlos. Fraley noticed none of the men wanted to deal, because it was a double deck. Fraley had learned years ago how to manipulate two, even three decks of playing cards. The men agreed to his terms, and in less than four hours Fraley had all their pesos. The only one who caught on to his play after the first hand was César, who pulled out right away. Carlos and the large man may have known his scheme, but they played anyway.

As the cards and pesos stacked in his favor, Fraley made a fatal mistake, indulging in the *aguardiente,* the local firewater. It tasted like a mild after-dinner liqueur, but by midnight the men had turned the tables and recouped their losses, and Fraley, too drunk to think, simply fell off his chair and passed out.

The next morning, Fraley woke up under a mosquito net in his sleeping quarters, his clothes still on, sporting a nuclear-class headache. He looked around and his situation began to sink in.

He grabbed his head with both hands, as if the simple act of thinking intensified the pain, and wondered what he had got himself into. "The closest I've ever been to a goddam jungle is readin' the *National Geographic* in the dentist's office," he said to himself. Talking to himself was a habit he picked up in solitary confinement in Western State Penitentiary years ago after he was busted for a burglary. He continued mentally chastising himself for having let Bobby talk him into chilling out someplace he had never been with someone he had never seen before.

And even if he wanted to leave, Fraley had no idea how he would do that or even which direction to go. What was worse, his biggest drug deal up to that point had been five hundred pounds of marijuana; now he was in the middle of a five hundred kilogram cocaine venture.

"My name is Winces Velasco-Peterson," said the large man as his frame filled the doorway. He had finally introduced himself to Fraley. Fraley politely returned the gesture, introducing himself. "I'm Leo Fraley."

"So who did you kill?" Velasco asked matter-of-factly. It was part of the story DeVitto had cooked up to get Fraley inside.

"Believe it or not, I haven't killed anyone. I just need to cool off while Bobby fixes a few things with the feds in North Carolina," Fraley said, checking for Velasco's reaction before continuing. The big man was silent but attentive. "Besides, Bobby wants me to learn the business from this end. So I guess that's what I'm here to do."

Velasco seemed to show a genuine interest in whatever Fraley talked about that first morning and afternoon together, and he surprised Leo when he revealed that he had acquired his English-language skills and proper British accent from his mother, a native of London. Velasco told Fraley he had spent his high school years in England and later had studied business at Oxford.

At his Los Llanos ranch, Velasco ran a very successful family business raising cattle. He explained that they were considered some of the very best in the world, since they were fed organically and grazed on Bermuda grass. But it was Velasco's more profitable business that brought Fraley to the jungle—marijuana farming and cocaine processing. Fraley's drug-trafficking knowledge was limited to marijuana. It was a crop that Velasco considered unworthy of his attention unless it was a large quantity deal. Typically, his marijuana runs consisted of upwards of a hundred thousand pounds. He told Fraley, he would not even consider transporting less than twenty-five thousand. It was a labor-intensive crop. First, he had to dispatch a half-dozen men with cash on hand to buy the crop from the local Indian farmers. Once they had received permission to harvest it, another army of laborers were needed. From there, it was taken to a central processing area. The processing included cleaning, packing and compressing it into transportable bales. Winces, as Fraley soon called him, preferred the cocaine business.

Velasco sat in the center of the canoe taking up half the boat himself. He gave directions as though the maze of Amazonian forest were his own backyard. Los Llanos was an endless tropical grassland that drained through the Arauca, Meta and Vichada Rivers to the Orinoco, and then flowed across central Venezuela, emptying into the Atlantic Ocean. Most of Los Llanos is typical savanna, a treeless plain with a tropical climate. The lowland, located south of the Guaviare River is the Colombian share of the Amazon basin. Until the 1950s, this area was almost entirely covered with *selvas,* or humid forests. It still is a large natural reserve, but pioneers who settled along the upper Guaviare, Caquetá and Putumayo Rivers rapidly turned the forest into cropland and pastures, albeit sparsely populated and undeveloped.

During the past three months in the jungle Fraley and Velasco had traveled this route several times. But Fraley found that, although he was trained in navigation at the U.S. Navy Submarine School in Connecticut, the dense jungle of the Amazon challenged all logic. He was always amazed at how Velasco seemed to know instinctively which of the many tributaries of the river to take just by looking at the vegetation. He read the flora and fauna like Fraley would read road signs on the interstate.

The three other men in the canoe only referred to him with the greatest of respect, beginning every sentence with *"Perdón, Don Winces, por favor . . . ."* Velasco had not spoken much during the two-hour flight on the Cessna 206 from his oceanfront villa in Cartageña that morning. But when he did speak, there was no question he was in total control. The villa in Cartageña was an exquisite Mediterranean-style structure, right out of *The Lifestyles of the Rich and Famous.* Velasco had casually mentioned that the huge adjoining resort hotel and casino were his as well.

It had been a little more than a year—a very long year—since Fraley had taken more than $4 million in gems, gold and cash from the safe-deposit boxes in the Wilmington, North Carolina, bank. The man who had given him the inside information on the vault and the customer boxes was the chief of neurosurgery at some Ivy League university who owed $1.5 million in gambling debts to the Milea crime family in Toronto. The self-proclaimed underboss, Nick Milea, who had left a lot of bodies behind him, gave the doctor a choice to either pay now with information about the bank vault or pay with his life. Since his youth, Fraley had never respected anyone who gambled away his or her money. To him, this chief of neurosurgery—Dr. Coco by name—was an asshole who had sold his friends and their goods for his debt and a chance to gamble his way into a new one, undoubtedly bigger the next time. Well, the heat was on when the good doctor ran up the tab once more, but this time the little weasel bastard went to the cops and gave up what he knew. And what he knew included the name of the safecracker. Fraley had worked with Dr. Coco twice before. Those "jobs" were gold exchanges, one in Providence, Rhode Island, and the other in Greenwich, Connecticut. Both times the deal was set up by the doctor. Fraley got forty percent of the wholesale price of the loot and Dr. Coco fenced the goods at the New York diamond exchange where he was connected. That last bank burglary, however, kicked off Fraley's biggest streak of bad luck ever. Right after he collected his money from the good doctor, his world started to turn to shit.

He was sitting at home, planning a Saturday afternoon with his family when the Sharon Township police and the Pennsylvania State Troopers surrounded his house as if he were Charlie Manson. A local detective, who had literally stalked Fraley for years, held a warrant for his arrest. Fraley was charged with rape. Seven months later, Fraley was doing hard time, to the tune of twelve years, in Western State Penitentiary, Pennsylvania's big house outside Pittsburgh. He had known the woman well, and had been intimate with her several times before. To this day, Fraley maintains his innocence.

"There was no force or threat of violence, just another roll in the hay about which I had long forgot," Fraley testified in his own behalf. Even though the grand jury failed to return an indictment, the State prosecutor's office took the case to trial and won. It was the Sharon Township cop who told Fraley, "It ain't the rape that we want you for—it's everything you've gotten away with since you settled in Pennsylvania." It was the only thing they could pin on him and the cop knew it.

Fraley, who was doing his second jolt at Western, thought things couldn't get much worse until he learned that Dr. Coco had turned informer and was cooperating with the FBI on the jewelry heist. But, as always, he somehow managed to turn adversity to his advantage.

When the U.S. Attorney in Wilmington indicted him, he knew they had a high-profile case that would splash Mafia headlines all over the North Carolina press. A federal writ temporarily transferred Fraley out of the Western State Penitentiary to federal custody in order to have him arraigned in the U.S. District Court, North Carolina. Fraley now had the magic he needed for his freedom. He called his mentor Dominic Debonis in Youngstown and had a mob attorney assigned to his case. The attorney convinced the judge to allow Fraley to confer with him at his office in Wilmington to prepare his defense. Fraley went shopping for a new suit, shaved his beard, and when he appeared in court no one recognized him, not even the deputy U.S. Marshals who had transported him to North Carolina. The federal magistrate mistakenly granted him bond and released him from custody after his arraignment. Needless to say, the Pennsylvania State Prison Authority was a little upset with their federal pal's "mistake." Two weeks later he was back at home in Sharon when the U.S. Marshal from Wilmington called.

"Mr. Fraley, there seems to have been an error in your release."

"What do you mean an error? The judge granted me a bond," Fraley said confidently.

"Well, that was a mistake also," the deputy marshal continued. "You'll have to make arrangements to return to Raleigh as soon as possible."

Fraley politely agreed to return and when he was sure that the marshal was convinced of his sincerity he hung up. It was then that he knew he could not return to prison.

As the canoe slid through the calm river waters, the constant purr of the outboard motor drowned out the sound of the jungle around him. Fraley began to relax and even dozed off. When he awoke, the equatorial sun was at its noon peak, glaring down at him, closer than ever. The heat and humidity were unbearable. He was drenched in sweat. It made an August day working in the steel foundry seem comfortable. Christ, he thought, I've been sent directly to hell. At least his alternative, prison, was something he was familiar with and a place where he knew how to survive.

"The streets and prison—they're all the same, from the rules to the people. The only thing you can't get all the time inside is pussy." This, the gospel according to the first cellmate who shared his eight-by-ten concrete block home in the Western Penitentiary.

Fraley had spent time in prison repeatedly since he was seventeen. The first occasion was for a bank burglary in Connecticut while he was still in the U.S. Navy. He was given "youthful offender" treatment because the mayor of his home town in Ohio had come to testify in his behalf. A great guy. He had been friendly with Fraley and his family ever since the young Leo began running sandwiches and beer for the mob bosses who played poker with the mayor and cops, who just happened to be on the payroll. Fraley was sure his mob friends had sent the mayor to Connecticut to praise his youthful past. After all, it was the mob bosses in Pittsburgh, Pennsylvania, and Youngstown, Ohio, who gave him his first job stoning scabs at the steel mills when there was a strike.

Dominic Debonis, an original member of "Murder, Inc.," was the head of the Mafia crime family in Ohio. Debonis was known as the "Mad Bomber" because the bomb was his weapon of choice when he took out a contract on someone. When Debonis did the job he ended up killing not only his target, but everyone who stood in the way of the bomb blast. He didn't care. In 1928, when Debonis arrived at his bank and found an IRS agent had opened his safe-deposit box and seized eighty thousand dollars in cash, he shot him in both legs, crippling the agent for life. Debonis served seven years for this shooting and was the third prisoner to do time at the newly constructed Atlanta Federal Penitentiary. It was the last time he would see the inside of a prison. Debonis eventually died of old age at ninety-four.

In the early days, he had taken a twelve-year-old Fraley under his wing. Fraley and his pals would stone the cars going in or coming out of the mills and if some "dumb fuckin' scab" were to get pissed off and get out of his car they would lead him on a merry chase to a predetermined place where the wise guys were lying in wait to beat the living shit out of him. This was good money and even his dad, who was a teamster, thought it was an honorable way to make an honest dollar.

Fraley thought about his dad a lot when he was young, wondering what it would have been like to have known him more than one day a week. His father was a long-distance truck driver and was as honest as the day was long. He would leave home every Sunday night and return on the Friday of the following week, late in the evening. He would sleep until midday on Saturday and then Fraley would see him at his grandmother's house that afternoon. He had lived with his grandmother because his own home was too crowded. His two uncles, five brothers and sisters filled up the four-room mill house. When he was young, Fraley always thought of his mom as sick and fat, when in fact she was just constantly tired and pregnant. After his dad became a local union boss, the teamsters' national boss, Jimmy Hoffa, became a frequent visitor at the house. His father said Hoffa visited with them to be around "his own kind," the working class. Fraley's parents now lived in Ohio. If there was anything he could be proud of it was his parents and the closeness he felt for them. He was always there for them. There was nothing more important than family to him.

"My friend, watch above you for the snakes, they are numerous in this area, and keep your hands out of the water, there are piranha." Fraley's thoughts were interrupted by the deep authoritative voice of Velasco.

"Snakes, why the fuck do there have to be snakes," he mumbled. He would rather be sleeping in the sewer in Youngstown with a thousand rats than come within a hundred yards of one snake.

Except for the streams of sunlight that shot down through the tiny openings like a laser light show, the canopy above was a solid mass of vegetation. The waterway had become so narrow the young kid in the front was cutting away the tree limbs and vines with a machete to make a passage. They spoke in Spanish, but Fraley could tell that the dialogue was about where they were going and that they were giving directions to the man operating the outboard motor on the stern of the canoe.

"Muy despacio," the teenager would say and the helmsman would slow down.

If nothing else, he thought maybe he would learn enough Spanish to make his own deals with these people. As a kid, Fraley had considered school a waste of time. He had learned how to make money in prison. It was there, after a burglary conviction, that Debonis ensured Fraley's continued education via the tutelage of his colleagues. Here he was taught the art of safecracking, an art that was also an "honorable" profession. It required knowledge and skill—a skill for which there was always a demand and would pay a percentage of everything he could steal. He had become one of the best because he had worked with some of the best. Fraley had known some of the most notorious thieves in the country including the infamous jewel thief with the playboy image, Murf the Surf. And he had taken the skills of the steel mill trade, where he had worked for two years, and applied it to the business of cracking safes known to be uncrackable. He designed his own variation of the lance, a molten magnesium rod used in the foundry that could cut through ten inches of hardened steel like butter.

His mob tutors had also taught him everything dishonest about his father's livelihood, the trucking business. "Hijacking" sounded like a harsh term for a business that only flourished with the aid of people gainfully employed in and around it. He learned the mob's motto of success: "Never steal anything that isn't a sure thing." Everyone, from the dispatchers to the owners and the cops, was paid off. The only losers in Fraley's eyes were the insurance companies, but then they were the biggest thieves of all. He drove it all—booze, cigarettes, meat, furs, guns —even a forty-foot container of condoms. This was the load he delivered when he was driving trucks for Meyer Lansky. It was Lansky's way of telling the mob boss who had ripped him off during another hijacking to "get fucked." There wasn't any staple of life the mob didn't steal and sell.

Now those days were gone. Every crime family in Ohio, Pennsylvania and New York, the whole damn country for that matter, had turned to the drug business. This jungle trip wasn't Fraley's first taste. He had dabbled in the LSD business for six months when he learned that he could turn a four hundred percent profit. But when his source went to prison and a bad batch got loose at the University of Pennsylvania, Fraley quickly got out of the LSD game. He had also entered the marijuana business, turning over a pound or two in the mid-seventies. Within a year he had hooked up with DeVitto and had begun moving a hundred pounds at a time between his customers in Pittsburgh and New York. But Fraley had never felt the cocaine business was for him.

"Too many spics carrying Uzis and no control, just chaos," the Mad Bomber Debonis had warned him. Yet here he was in the middle of the Amazon on his way to god knew where with a cocaine kingpin.

They had been in the canoe for more than three hours. The narrow passage had opened up now and the river had widened so much, the opposite shoreline sat on the distant horizon. About twenty yards ahead was a pier and a dozen more canoes pulled up on the shoreline. In stark contrast were a half-dozen Boston Whalers with big Merc outboards.

"Llega el jefe, Don Winces," the kid on the bow shouted out to the people on the pier. All that made sense to Fraley was *Don Winces,* but he knew from the tone that it signaled respect. As they approached, the kid jumped out into the shallow water and walked the canoe to the pier. Velasco stood up and with one small step he was out of the canoe and on dry land. Fraley grabbed his duffel bag and barely kept his balance as he stretched to reach the first piling.

He didn't know quite what he was looking at but his best guess was that this was his first cocaine lab. For the length of what seemed like half of a football field he could see corrals staked off about twenty-feet square. Fifty-five gallon chemical drums were stacked everywhere. There was even a small tower with a windsock on top.

Velasco turned to him as if he could read his thoughts. "The runway, it is ten thousand feet, a caleche surface. It's too wet and muddy for any flights. This is a fairly new operation here. We're waiting on the steel planking your military used to construct their runways in Vietnam. We have tried to make direct purchases from the States but there is too much emphasis by your government on shipping military goods outside the country. So now," he boasted, "what we used to buy in the military-surplus stores in New York and Miami we just buy from our friends in Panama."

Fraley was beginning to change his mind about his early perceptions of the Colombians and the cocaine trade. These guys were running the business all the way from the jungle to the city streets. No wonder his Mafia friends wanted in. He walked alongside Velasco toward the center of the compound and as they approached the first series of buildings, the fumes from the chemicals hit him like a wall. Almost by instinct he pulled up his T-shirt and covered his nose and mouth. Velasco walked on seemingly unaffected by the overwhelming odor.

The work area was completely open, with only a corrugated fiberglass-paneled roof covering the tables and barrels. The men and women who were handling the thick paste wore only bandannas around their faces. The skin on their hands and forearms and their fingernails were blackened from the chemicals, much like the foundry workers in Fraley's home town. As a matter of fact the stench in the air was not that much different.

The entire area was covered with military camouflage-netting to disguise the compound from aerial surveillance. It was an incredible sight. Fraley was taking it all in when suddenly Winces turned to one of the two men who were accompanying them, sternly shouted at him in Spanish and backhanded him, knocking him clean off his feet and into the mud. Fraley's first thought was that Winces had some balls belting a guy who was packing an AK-47. But when the khaki-clad man stayed down like an obedient soldier, Fraley was impressed.

Not a second had lapsed when Velasco turned to him and said, "M-19. Their motivation is political, not monetary. They want to save their country from the elitists who have run it for over four hundred years. He should have covered the fuel trucks."

Fraley could see the two tanker trucks parked adjacent to the runway. Both were painted that military green; one was marked JP4 and the other AVION PETRO.

"Of course every revolution must be financed somewhere. We use their soldiers to guard our locations throughout the country. They're better trained and equipped than the police or the army. We see to that and everyone respects it, even the fuckin' DEA. They're peasants like me," he added proudly. "My mother was from a wealthy British family who made their fortune many times over from tourists visiting their hotels here. She married my father, a peasant from a village near Cartageña." Velasco's gestures were becoming larger with each thought expressed. "I have used both to help build one of the largest cash businesses in the world, and we have only just begun."

Anybody that impressed with himself was dangerous, Fraley thought.

"Well, this accent of mine is inbred, but the poverty isn't," Fraley quipped. "I finished high school in prison and got a college degree in computer science there too. All I ever used that shit for was to impress the parole board. I've never needed either of them to do business with anyone. Just my wits and my word have always been enough. And where I come from if you knock the shit out of someone who packs a machine gun you don't let him up again, ever."

"Good advice, my friend. Next time I'm in your country I'll try to remember it." Velasco looked at him and smiled.

As they stepped onto the porch of the main building the door opened and two young, very beautiful women in their late teens or early twenties greeted Velasco affectionately. Fraley stepped inside and noticed the place was open and clean. There was a kitchen and a large room in the center of the building. The furniture was sparse but comfortable.

"All the comforts of home," Velasco bellowed. He placed an arm over the comparatively tiny shoulders of the two women, grasping a breast in each hand, and laughed aloud. Fraley chuckled at the fact the SOB even knew how to get laid in the middle of the jungle.

Fraley dropped his duffel bag on the floor and flopped on the couch, and muttered, "Man, would a cold beer be great right about now." Before he could imagine the taste, one of the *señoritas* had made his wish her command.

"*¿Quiere una cerveza, señor?*" she said with a sweet smile, an ice-cold Corona in her hand.

"Compliments of our Mexican compadres," Velasco said. "The only thing the Mexicans have superior to Colombia is their beer." Fraley thanked the pretty girl for the quick service and almost sucked the bottle dry in one breath.

He scanned the room in that methodical way he had developed whenever he was in unfamiliar surroundings. In the corner, near the front of the building, was a large table with a stack of high-frequency-band radio equipment. On the wall opposite the table was a series of topographical maps. The floor near the wall was stacked with ammunition crates and several AK-47 assault rifles. There were even a couple of LAAWS rocket launchers. It reminded him of the kind of hardware he had hijacked from an army convoy in Tennessee a few years back. He had done it with the help of the commanding officer's information, on whom the mob just happened to hold some major gambling markers. He had wondered then where the market was for that kind of shit. Now he knew.

It was morning and he was still on the couch where he had passed out from the heat. The crowing rooster awakened him.

"Why the hell would anyone have a fuckin' rooster in this place?" he wondered. He checked his watch. A little after 5:00 A.M. He rolled over slowly and the sound of his own boots hitting the floor startled him. He rubbed the sleep from his eyes and reached for his duffel bag. The only thing he could think of was brushing his teeth. What a horrible taste the Amazon left in your mouth. He found his toothbrush and toothpaste and walked to the only closed door in the building. As he opened it he saw the naked shapes of those two beautiful young women through the mosquito net draped over the largest bed he had ever seen.

"Excuse me," he muttered to himself and slowly backed from the doorway. He shuffled out the front door brushing his teeth and walked toward a large tree in the distance. He had to piss something fierce. There he was, toothbrush in his mouth and dick in his hand under the tree and all he could think of was, "My friend watch above you for the snakes. They are numerous in this area."

As he dared to look up Murphy's Law came into play. He was going to die and a snake was going to do it. The biggest snake he had ever seen.

As a matter of fact, the only other one he had ever seen was in the San Diego Zoo while he was in navy boot camp. The zoo keepers had fed it rats. This one could have snacked on a box of rats, and here he was with his hammer in his hand like it was some kind of tasty bait.

Before he could have another thought, three gunshots rang out, echoing around him. The snake, all fifteen feet of it, fell like a ton of bricks around him.

"My friend, if you need to piss don't do it around the trees. Here we are civilized. Use the *baño*. It is in the main building. Come on in. The women will fix you some breakfast." Velasco's baritone voice broke into laughter.

Fraley was impressed again. Velasco had dropped that snake from about seventy-five feet with that .357 revolver and he had literally scared the piss out of him.

The main building was white, wood framed and shaped like a huge

Ohio farm house. It had a corrugated tin roof and was surrounded by a large wooden fence, as if to keep the help out. A few feet away was a great outdoor oven and barbecue area with a huge cooking table. There was an old woman who was already preparing food.

While they ate, Winces boasted of the "factory," as he called it. It was the first of many like it. No longer would they have to rely on the Bolivians and the Peruvians for the coca leaf. They had planted eighteen hundred hectares of *"coca Colombiana,"* a hybrid coca shrub that grew larger than the Bolivian and Peruvian varieties. It was also well adapted to the lowlands of Los Llanos and the poorer quality soils of the Amazon. Velasco was obviously pleased with the operation. "The plants are yielding enough leaf to produce over three tons of product from each harvest," Velasco said.

As they walked outside, Velasco began showing off his operation to Fraley. Those corrals he saw from the pier were actually pits where the coca leaves were tossed in and soaked with kerosene and acetone while they decomposed.

"Come, my friend, I'll take you up river and show you my other ranch. I have another ten thousand hectares of land there."

They walked down to the pier and, as if by osmosis, the young machete-wielding kid from the canoe the day before ran to meet them, jumped into one of the Boston Whalers and cranked over the two-hundred horsepower Mercury engine. In a flash they were hydroplaning across the calm morning mist that glazed the *Rio Yarí*. About fifteen minutes later, Fraley could see the ranch house near the river's edge up ahead. It was a ranch house all right, but more correctly, he thought, this was another million-dollar villa in the middle of the Amazon.

The kid maneuvered the twenty-foot speedboat into the boathouse at the end of the pier with ease, and Velasco led him toward the house. But before they got to the entrance, he stopped at a cabana and began to pull the camouflaged netting from the top of a Range Rover.

"Get in, I'll take you to the best cocaine lab in all of Colombia. We call it *Tranquilandia*."

They traversed some of the worst road Fraley had ever experienced, and that included the Brooklyn/Queens Expressway after a winter of snowstorms. Fraley could have sworn his kidneys were hemorrhaging when they finally reached the lab.

Again, the entire area was covered with the military camouflage netting. There was a sawmill for cutting their own lumber. The huge *cabañas* had palm-frond roofing and the work areas were filled with tables cut from the nearby trees. Velasco showed him the oversized vats where the raw paste from Bolivia and Peru was transformed into cocaine hydrochloride. There were literally thousands of these kilo-sized balls of paste wrapped in a burlap-type cloth, waiting to be processed. Velasco then took him to the drying tables where he proudly displayed the final product, spread out like fresh pasta in an Italian delicatessen. There were dormitories for the workers, a huge generator supplying electricity and several water towers spread throughout the complex. Velasco bragged how he had developed the final wrapping method using a fiber-glass tape that created a hard shell on each kilo. This shell prevented water damage and kept the package from being pulverized on airdrops into the Caribbean and Atlantic. They had suffered most of their losses in this manner on loads headed for their final phase of the journey to the U.S. marketplace.

Fraley was amazed at the efficiency of the operation. But what he really wanted to know was just how much money was to be made and where he could fit into the deal. Now was not the time to ask. Better to wait and learn as much as he could. After all, there had only been minimal talk about the deal with DeVitto. Velasco had mentioned that he had not received even a fraction of the $9 million owed to him and his partners from the last deal. Velasco didn't seem concerned, however, and Fraley didn't think it was any of his business. He couldn't have been more wrong.

CHAPTER
2

ANOTHER STING

THE HUGHES 500 HOVERED above the small rock ledge, the right skid just a foot above the surface. The left skid was about twenty-five hundred feet above the Mojave Desert floor. The DEA pilot was a Vietnam "dust off" vet. He had been in every hot LZ along the Mekong Delta, protecting the medivacs and troop carriers during the 1968 Tet Offensive. But this was the flight that would make him think twice about his flying career.

The surveillance team was standing by, waiting for his signal to step in, when the airship suddenly lost power and the helicopter started to fall like a rock. His right-seat passenger, customs agent Bill Gately, who was holding on to the open door with his left hand, had his right arm extended to assist the surveillance team making the transition from mountain perch to helicopter. The last experience he had like this was in Vietnam.

Danny Ginero looked at Bill Gately and could only say, "Holy fuckin' shit!" as he strained with his right hand, manipulating the collective in order to keep the rotor speed and blade pitch at the perfect combination to keep the helicopter aloft. Ginero pumped the small red button at the tip of the collective's arm with his thumb trying to restart the turbine powerplant.

Gately struggled to stay inside the helicopter and strained against the wind and g-forces to close the door. He felt as helpless as he had twelve years earlier, two hundred feet over Hill 681—three clicks north of the firebase at Khe San. The Sikorsky 34 he and eight other grunts were in lost power and auto-rotated, rolling into the trees and spitting the Marines out onto the hillside.

This time there was nothing to break the fall. This time, the only thing between the helicopter and the ground was the thin, hot desert air. The fractions of a second it took seemed like forever. Finally the whine and roar of the jet engine jerked the helicopter back toward the sky as the rotor engaged and the heavy piece of machinery suddenly became weightless.

An hour later they were at the Palomar Airport in San Diego. As the rotor blades slowed down, Gately, still feeling a sense of total relief, pushed the door open and planted both feet securely on the ground. The three-man surveillance crew climbed out of the back seat. Slowly, methodically, the pilot began conducting his post flight checks, tying down the blades and securing the skids to the tarmac. As the surveillance crew walked away, Gately approached Ginero who was now silently making his flight log entry for the mechanic.

"Hey, Danny, what are you up to tonight?" They gave each other that subtle look of acknowledgment. They'd just been through an unjustified brush with death.

"Oh, you mean right after I change my shorts," Ginero replied. "I'm up for just about anything."

"How 'bout a beer at the ballpark? The Padres are in town tonight." Baseball was always Gately's feel-good remedy for any malady. Just being in the ballpark made life simple. It was like being a kid again, with no responsibilities.

Ginero and Gately sat in the perfect spot, right over the dugout on the third base line. They had each bought two hot dogs and two beers, which they were consuming with a passion. As the game began, the two agents felt an overwhelming need to heckle, as if on a special mission from God.

"Hey, buddy, why don't you take that appliance off your back," Ginero said, stuffing his hot dog into his mouth, while the base runner was thrown out at second, standing up.

"Give the guy a break, man, at least he's got a real job. He can keep his feet on the ground, play baseball for a living and still collect three hundred thou a year. Unlike us making twenty-five, flying in a broken helicopter and risking our lives over a lousy five hundred pounds of Mexican ditch weed," Gately shot back.

"Gately, this is your case." Ginero looked him in the eye. "You customs guys have been fuckin' a duck on this deal for over two months. It was your idea to put that team up there on that mountain and steal this guy's stash. Lets face it, you've been on this case for four months, on the wires for two, and this big cocaine deal ain't happening. And while I'm in your shit, nobody in DEA thinks it's gonna happen. So far, this guy has been flyin' in weed from Mexico and stashing it in that goddamn hole in the desert we almost made our grave today. You geniuses have been sneaking around stealing his dope so you can light up the wires." Then he added with equal disdain to keep the DEA/Customs rivalry intact, "So you made a big-time marijuana case, I'm not impressed. And, I don't think you're ever going to turn this deal into a cocaine case."

Gately had heard this defeatist talk all too often. He looked derisively at Ginero. "First of all, Ginero, I told you not to be thinking when you don't have the equipment for it. In fact, the only thing you're equipped to do is drive that broken-down helicopter. Besides, I don't care about impressing you. And you can tell your DEA brothers not to expect to be able to come running in through the back door when it comes credit time. Now, shut up already, you're making me miss the ballgame." They both looked at each other trying to maintain their John Wayne act, then burst out laughing.

As Gately looked up at the scoreboard, he drifted back to thoughts of better ballgames and better times.

Baseball was the love of his life as a kid and he longed for the days when he had spent the spring and summer afternoons in Washington's Griffith Stadium. The grand but archaic wooden structure had housed the Senators for over three decades. The stadium named for Clark Griffith the player/manager who took the team to their first pennant and their only World Series with the arm of one of the game's greatest hurlers, Walter Johnson. His favorite games were between the Senators and the Orioles and the Yankees. The Senators were the proverbial underdogs and every play was savored. He could remember seeing some of baseball's greatest players like Mickey Mantle, Harmon Killebrew, Whitey Ford, Yogi Berra, Tony Kubek and Frank Robinson.

Gately had grown up in the nation's capital and was the product of Irish/Italian, Catholic parents and was educated in Washington's parochial school system. Here the discipline he received at home was so graciously reinforced by the Sisters of the Holy Cross in grade school and the Dominican Brothers and Priests who taught him in high school. Gately was without question a chip off the old block who admired and respected his father. After a hitch in the Army Air Corps during the Second World War his dad William Francis Gately Sr. had originally sought a career as a highway engineer. Despite his quick advancement, his yearning to become a police officer was strong enough for him to make a change in vocation. After seven years on the job he gave up his seniority and took a twenty percent cut in pay when he joined the Metropolitan Police Department in Washington, D.C. There had been a long history of policemen and firemen on his family's Irish side and there were some advantages to your dad being a cop. For one, every police-man was your friend. You need only to mention your name. In those days everyone respected the police and the neighborhood beat cop was the symbol of law, order and absolute trust.

As Gately grew a little older and wiser he began to understand life in the big city and the system of government that fueled everything in his home town. The hard part was trying to reconcile the ability of his family to tolerate its own ethnic and cultural differences. His mom was the daughter of Italian immigrants and her only language up until the time she attended her first year of school was Italian. His paternal grandfa-ther, whom he loved dearly, was a burly "black Irishman." His coal black hair and olive skin were certainly attributable to his ancestors who were the descendants of the Spanish Armada defeated by the British off the coast of Ireland in the seventeenth century. He was a master machinist who had worked for the U.S. Navy during both World Wars. He built the sixteen inch guns for the great battleships the *New Jersey* and the *Missouri*. The same guns that provided naval gunfire support to Gately's infantry company in Vietnam's Quang Tri Province during the 1968 Tet Offensive. William Patrick Gately had a love for baseball, motorcycles and the ocean. But he rarely seemed to hold his daughter-in-law or her family in his good graces. Gately's mother told him, that his Irish grand-father would visit her at the maternity ward after the birth of each of her ten children. If the child had blue eyes he or she was held in his favor. Green eyes were acceptable and brown eyes ran a slow dead last.

On the Italian side most members of his mom's family were artistic people. Gately's maternal grandfather was a chef who had learned his culinary skills in his Italian homeland of Tuscany. He made his new home in Washington, D.C. after serving in the Italian Army during the first World War. Here in the land of opportunity he rose to the position of chief chef and for the next thirty-five years Frank Tollata served every president from Franklin Roosevelt to Richard Nixon at Washington's Shoreham Hotel.

Gately's father always preached that no matter what your station in life no one was better than you and you were no better than anyone else. Words he never truly appreciated until he became a police officer him-self. In 1970 after a three year enlistment in the Marines and tour in Vietnam he took the oath of a police officer in the nation's capital. For the next eight years he served as member of the metropolitan police force.

Ken Ingleby took one of those ten-mile drags on his cigarette, cocked his head back as he held the telephone to his ear, then slowly blew the smoke straight up toward the ceiling. He was the youngest customs special agent in charge in the country, but he was without question the brightest and for that matter the ballsiest. The DEA SAC, Dodge Gallanos, was on the line bitching up a storm about this drug case, which he had bought into at Ingleby's request. Gallanos's people had convinced him that it was a waste of taxpayer money. DEA was therefore pulling out. Ingleby politely disagreed, but didn't antagonize Gallanos. His response to the diatribe of complaints was, "So you guys want to pull out? No problem—we'll drive the bus." He put the phone down and regained his everyday charm, "Carmen, find Gately. Tell him to get the fuck in here."

An hour later, Gately arrived at the San Ysidro office. He walked through the parking lot, filled with the sounds and smells of Tijuana, Mexico, just a few feet away. The two very distinct ways of life were separated by the ten-foot-high wall that paralleled the southern boundary of the building. As he opened the front door, four illegals jumped over the wall landing at his feet. They barely gave him a glance before running east through the parking lot. But the border patrol was close behind. They had been watching from their perch on the hill above the office. What a shit job that was. Thank god he wasn't in the border patrol, he thought as he climbed the steps to the main floor.

Gately walked past Carmen's desk and got a warning look. He strolled into Ingleby's office. "Hey, boss, what's the deal? You want to go see the Padres tonight?" Ingleby was a baseball addict, but he wasn't having any of it right now.

"Tell me about this case. Gallanos just gave me his professional, expert opinion on why it won't get any better than a bunch of ex-hippies running weed across the border. Then he quit. He's pulling his agents out today. I guess he thinks we'll quit too, or the U.S. Attorney will lose faith if DEA does." He reached for another cigarette, lit it, then calmly but sternly said, "So," as he took another long drag and pointed a piercing look at Gately, "tell me what's going on in this case. Are we ever going to see any cocaine?"

Gately sat down, "I just told those guys the other day they shouldn't be thinking when they're not used to it. Christ, Ken, not only are we on the right track, about to get these assholes with coke, we've just put them with over seventy gallons of ether and hydrochloric acid. It looks like they're setting up a cocaine lab at that ranch in New Mexico. Late last night they had a meeting at the Fallbrook house and talked about the trip to Bolivia. By the way, the "Brady Bug" is working great. It's as if you're sitting in the asshole's living room listening. And the idea to steal his drugs has worked like a charm. The wire couldn't have gotten hotter if he'd set it on fire himself. I promise you, DEA will be begging to get back in when we take this deal down."

Ingleby didn't mind making DEA look bad—but he wanted to make sure it wasn't going to be him with egg on his face. He quickly got down to the real issue, politics: "Is the U.S. Attorney still with us?"

"Not only is he still with us," Gately said, smiling, "he thinks DEA can't find drugs unless they're buying them. He even told them the other day that if there is any question who's running this show it's Customs. You could have sold tickets to any customs agent just to hear that."

As Gately crossed Front Street to enter the Federal Building in downtown San Diego he looked to his left and saw George Hardy, the assistant U.S. Attorney on the case, taking a lunch-time stroll toward the harbor area. Hardy was all-American male, a Yale Law School graduate, East Coast pedigree. But he wasn't the typical arrogant son of a bitch who sported those credentials. If you didn't know him, you'd think he was a blonde-haired, blue-eyed Clark Kent kind of guy. But if you did get to know him he was a down-to-earth straight-shooter who loved baseball, the beach, and just happened to be a pretty good tennis player. That was in addition to being one hell of a lawyer. Gately ran toward him, shouting, "Hey, George!"

Hardy turned, stopped in his tracks and waited. As Gately approached, he said, "Where the hell were you this morning when DEA swarmed all over the office telling me and my boss what a shit case we have?"

"I'm sorry, George, that was a surprise attack meant to scare the hell out of you. They never said a word to me. Ingleby got a call from Gallanos at about the same time. They pulled out. We have it covered, though. Ken is bringing in twelve agents from Arizona and Texas to replace DEA."

Hardy looked at Gately, smiled and said, "So where are you taking me to lunch? And no, I can't go to the ballpark."

It was after two when Gately finished his daily briefing of Hardy over lunch. They continued talking all the way back to the office. By then, George's boss Pete Nunez, the chief of the criminal division at the U.S. Attorney's office, was waiting for George to brief him. The case had reached his status just because DEA was bad-mouthing it. Gallanos was now calling it "an albatross with a diminishing return."

Now Gately was on I-15, on his way back to the surveillance team at Fallbrook. Gately had probably logged more miles between the wire room and the U.S. Attorney's office than were left in the seized Datsun 210 he was driving. What a change from the undercover assignment he'd had in Vancouver, British Columbia, with the RCMP just six months ago. There he had all the trappings of a successful drug dealer. Right down to the sea-green Porsche 930 Turbo. The car had been assembled in Germany as a special order for a Marin County drug dealer. Little did he know that customs agents had been on his trail for some time and were ready for him the day he tried to smuggle his Porsche into the U.S. When he got to the Blaine, Washington, border-crossing twenty minutes south of Vancouver he calmly told the inspector he had been skiing in Canada and had nothing to declare. The inspector sent him off toward Gately and two other agents who had followed him from the seaport in Vancouver. They were waiting for him a few hundred yards down the road. When Gately pulled him over he could only say rather pompously, "What do you want?"

"Just your car. Step out," Gately told him with the same tone. "You just smuggled it into the country and have pretty much donated it to the government."

"What am I supposed to do, take a bus?"

"No, we'll give you a ride to jail."

Gately had often thought of sending him a thank-you note with a photo of himself driving the Porsche for his unselfish gift to U.S. law enforcement. Maybe the guy could hang it on his cell wall at the McNeill Island Federal Penitentiary. It was, in fact, the car that helped Gately kick the Vancouver case off.

Gately was in Vancouver about to "make a meet" with his RCMP counterpart at the Vancouver Hotel. The hotel was a huge Victorian structure that took up an entire city block, a symbol of the British aristocracy that once ruled Canada. As he stepped out of the car and the valet got in, he heard the friendly tap of a Porsche horn. Gately turned and saw a white 930 Turbo just behind him. The driver gave a wave. Another valet approached the white Turbo, the driver exited and walked over to Gately with a friendly, car-lover kind of smile.

"Great car, eh? Like a bloody rocket on wheels! Best car I've ever owned." He stood about six feet three and carried his 220-pound frame like an athlete.

Gately returned the compliment, "Yeah, it's a great car but a magnet for every cop on the freeway from here to LA."

The friendly stranger introduced himself and extended his hand, "Gary Trudeau, no relation to the prick in Ottawa, and I'm not the cartoonist either."

"No, I didn't think you were," Gately laughed. He introduced himself as Frank Cassera, the undercover name he had used for years. "You look more like a guy lookin' for the right kinda deal," Gately quipped.

His new friend smiled back and laughed. "Takes one to know one, eh?"

"I'm meeting someone here for lunch," Gately said as they walked into the hotel lobby.

"Yeah, I'm meeting two lovelies here myself."

They both smiled and walked toward their meeting places. Gately entered the cafe, spotting his contact immediately, and headed toward the table. After a fifteen-minute meeting the mountie left with a mission. Gately paid the tab for the coffee and began walking out when he noticed Trudeau across the room. He was sitting at a table with two blondes who wore enough spandex to leave absolutely nothing to the imagination. Trudeau made eye contact and waved him over.

"What, no date? Did you get stood up?"

"Well, I guess that's not a problem for you. If one stands you up, you've still got another."

"Why don't you join us," Trudeau said. He introduced him as if he had known Gately for years. "This is Frank Cassera. He's from Los Angeles. He's up here slumming in Canada." Through the conversation Gately found out that Trudeau had been a popular Canadian professional football player. His career ended abruptly when a bone-crushing tackle blew out his left knee. His promising career with the CFL and dreams of joining the NFL were suddenly gone. Gately could tell he still carried a chip on his shoulder about it—and missed the celebrity status, no doubt. Maybe his two companions fulfilled the need for the groupies he had lost. By the end of the lunch, Trudeau had given Gately his phone number, pager number, address and tried to give him one of his nineteen-year-old blondes. He had even invited Gately to go flying with him the next day. Trudeau owned his own Cessna 187 seaplane.

During lunch, Gately's pager had been beeping incessantly. It was Cpl. Karl Waversfeld, his RCMP contact.

"Hey Bill, that's a pretty big fuckin' fish you got there." Gately had asked him to check out Trudeau's license plate when he got back to the office.

"Well, who the hell is he?"

"E Division Drugs has been following him for months. We think he's been flying dope into the islands, in the Strait of Juan De Fuca. He's got this Cessna—"

"Oh, you mean his Cessna 187 seaplane?"

"Yeah, how did you know?"

"This guy Trudeau is really a great guy. So far he's bought me lunch, offered me a blonde and tomorrow he's going to take me for a ride in his plane. That's more than you guys have done for me in the year I've been working for you. I think I'll go to work for Trudeau."

"Low blow, Billy."

"Yeah. So what's the deal, Karl, do you want me to stick with him or do you want me to get out of the way?"

"Fuck no, stay with the prick," Karl said in his usual acerbic manner. "You're closer than anyone's gotten. Maybe he's queer for you."

"Okay. I'm going to meet him at his house tomorrow morning. If you guys want to cover me, I'll meet you at the Aldergrove crossing at nine."

The next morning, Gately pulled up to the elegant yet modest community of Pacific Shores in Vancouver. The white Porsche was parked in the driveway outside the house. Gately parked his sea-green Porsche close by and knocked on Trudeau's door. A beautiful raven-haired woman answered. She had almond-shaped bedroom brown eyes and an athlete's body. Gately stared for a second, her beauty surprising him.

"Can I help you?" she asked with a strong French accent. Before he could answer, Trudeau emerged from the hallway and stood by her side.

"Frank, I see you've met my wife. This is Marie. This is Frank. He's a good friend of mine from Los Angeles. We're going flying out to the islands today."

"Good friend?" she asked sternly. "Why don't I know him?" Her tone told Gately she knew exactly what he was up to. Gately just looked at them. All he could wonder was how Trudeau could even consider fucking around with those bimbos when he had this beautiful woman for his wife?

When they got into his car and headed toward the plane, Gately could only say, "You've got a beautiful wife." Trudeau looked at him as if to say, it's no big deal—doesn't everyone? Trudeau looked over at him, wind playing through their hair.

"So you say you have some friends in LA and San Diego?" Gately asked.

"Yeah, I spend a lot of time down there. That's where I wanted to play pro ball with the NFL, in LA. But, the friends I was telling you about, I've known them for years. They fly too." After a few minutes of small talk about San Diego, LA, the weather, football and women, they arrived at the Delta Airpark. While Trudeau was preflighting the plane, Gately waited outside near the right door. He noticed the back seats had been removed. In their place was a blue plastic tarp stretched over the rear portion of the plane's interior.

As soon as they gained altitude, Trudeau pointed the plane west over the bay toward the islands.

"I'd rather be in Southern California. The weather is perfect. You can fly all the time," Trudeau said as he adjusted the headset and recontacted the flight departure at the airport.

"So what do your friends fly?" asked Gately.

"Mostly green," he replied matter-of-factly with a big smile. Gately couldn't believe he was telling him so much so soon. "Lift that tarp in the back." Underneath were two bales of marijuana. Gately thought there must have been between seventy-five and one hundred pounds. "I got those from my friends," Trudeau said.

"Is that all they do, Mexican weed?" Gately asked.

"How'd you know?" Trudeau laughed.

"I've seen enough of my own to know those bales are from Mexico."

"Well, you're right, they are. But, that's good quality sensimilla. It's going for twenty-five hundred a pound up here." Trudeau gave him a look that said, so don't knock it. Then he said, "So you're interested in cocaine?"

"Isn't everyone?" replied Gately, his heart taking a leap.

"Well, maybe next time I'm down your way, I can introduce you to my friends. They've been talking about branching out."

Less than half an hour later they circled a farmhouse on one of the islands. Gately could see four or five plowed fields scattered over the tiny island. In the distance a man was waving to the plane. The man headed toward the pier, less than a hundred feet from the house. Trudeau landed and taxied the Cessna to within a few feet from the pier. "Throw him the line," Trudeau told Gately as the man waited on the pier to tie off the plane. The man caught the line, wrapped it around the tie-down and helped Trudeau and Gately onto the pier. They started talking while Gately stood back a couple of feet.

"I've got your cargo," Trudeau told the man.

"Great. I'm glad you got it today. You're better than Fed-Ex." Without missing a beat, the man said, "Wait here, I've got something for you, too." He headed toward the house.

While he was inside, Trudeau and Gately unloaded the bales, set them on the pier and wrapped them in the blue tarp. Trudeau walked toward the house to meet the man who handed him a small package, and the men quickly said their goodbyes. A few minutes later the Cessna was airborne, headed back toward the mainland.

"Well, it's a tough job, but somebody's got to do it," Trudeau said to him.

An hour later they were finishing off a beer at the English Harbor Cafe overlooking the bay. Gately was trying to break away to make his contact with Waversfeld, but Trudeau had become his best friend and wanted to go party. "Hey, I got to get goin', I've got a date that I can't break."

"What's she look like, maybe I know her," Trudeau bragged.

Trudeau gave Gately his version of the Vancouver Grand Prix, straining the engine, transmission, brakes and turbo of his 930 through the city streets. He dropped Gately off at his car, then blasted off again. His neighbors must hate this guy, Gately thought, as the Porsche roared away.

Gately drove to the financial area, about ten blocks to the east on the edge of Vancouver's infamous red-light district.

"So, Karl, did you have a problem following us? And speak up—this pay phone sucks."

"No problem, it was a piece of cake."

"Then you saw what happened on the pier?"

"You mean the guy you met?"

"No, I mean we delivered two bales of weed to the Farmer Brown dude."

Waversfeld paused, the Gately could hear him yelling out to his comrades, "Gately and Trudeau delivered a load of marijuana at the farmhouse."

"So you guys gonna hit the farmhouse?"

"Fuckin' aye we are." He added, "Don't worry, we'll keep your cover cool."

"Have fun. I know the queen will appreciate your fine work." As usual, Gately felt the need to throw a dig at the Canadian cop.

"And Jimmy Carter is your answer to leadership?" Waversfeld grumbled. Gately gave him the dial tone.

"Hey, sweet thing, you wanna party?" The voice came from a black, blonde hooker dressed in a spandex micro-mini skirt and stiletto heels.

The call had come early the next morning. Gately rushed downtown to E Division headquarters. Waversfeld's group had been up all night; Karl looked like something the cat dragged in when he met Gately in the lobby.

"You bagged the farmer and Trudeau already?"

"Yeah, the farmer rolled on Trudeau in a heartbeat. He had over five hundred pounds in the house and he put it all on Trudeau. It turns out he's his wife's cousin and Trudeau was paying him to use the place as a stash house."

They headed to the holding room where Trudeau was sitting alone at the bare metal table handcuffed to the chair, head in hand, contemplating his fate.

"Are you sure you want to talk to him? He could blow your cover."

"I'm transferring to San Diego in a month so my days here as a UC are numbered. Besides, I think my good friend Gary can do something for us a lot bigger in sunny California."

Waversfeld opened the door and Gately walked in. Trudeau turned, apparently shocked to see Gately.

"I didn't do it," he said to Gately.

Gately smirked at him. "What do you mean?"

"I didn't give you up, it wasn't me." Obviously Trudeau didn't get it.

"The farmer must have rolled on both of us. The prick is my wife's cousin, too. I thought I could trust him."

Gately reached into his jacket pocket, pulled out his black leather-bound credentials and opened them for Trudeau to see.

"You see, Gary, I did you both. It's my job and you made it so easy. To tell you the truth, though, you did yourself. Too many beers and hosebags." Trudeau couldn't believe what he was hearing. He hung his head in defeat.

The Datsun had no air conditioner and this was San Diego's hottest summer of the century. It had gone over the one-hundred-degree mark several times this month. The ride through the heat in Escondido brought Gately back to reality. Twenty more minutes to the wire room and he could check the logs on the telephones. The informant would be calling soon, too. Despite his confidence in the case, the DEA's pulling out had given some cause to push the informant a little harder. The case had dragged on for about four months. They were on the wire more than sixty days, and were about to go for their third renewal. This was another in a long list of cases where Gately used the now famous sting technique as the main thrust of the investigation. But this case had a new twist. They had combined the sting technique with the use of multiple wire-taps. The combination was bulletproof.

The wire room was set up in an upscale condominium at a tennis resort near the outskirts of Fallbrook. Gately walked in, checked on the status of the operation, then headed to his quarters in another condo two doors down. Within minutes the phone rang. It was his daily call from the informant.

"Bill, it's Gary. What's goin' on?"

"Well, that's what you're supposed to be telling me."

"Hey, I'm bustin' my ass working for you. I'm gettin' it done. I've told you everything."

"You'd be bustin' rocks in Canada for ten years at the B.C. penitentiary if you weren't here playing out this deal." Gately also knew that Trudeau was double-dealing. Trudeau had no idea there was also a bug on the phone between him and the two kingpins, John Ward and Gary

Schmidt. Customs heard everything they said on the phone and in their home. Trudeau was under the mistaken impression that he was the sole source of their information, and had begun to cut his own deals with Ward and Schmidt. Gately had tried to lessen the blow by offering Trudeau this deal, which included not having to testify, but Trudeau did himself in again. He suffered from the unfortunate delusion that he was smarter than the rest. And his ballsy attitude just drove him further into his grave. Had he stayed straight he'd have gotten away with doing absolutely no time, as well as a hefty payment for being an informant. But double-dealing was standard operating procedure for any crook. The only exception Gately ever knew were the original Watergate burglars. Gately was assigned to the Washington, D.C., police tactical unit that surprised the burglars at the Watergate Office Building on June 17, 1972. From the day they were captured until the bitter end, they never gave up their boss, even when the rest of the nation, and for that matter the world, knew exactly who he was. It was a discipline Gately admired, even if they were crooks. He remembered the look G. Gordon Liddy had on his face throughout the trial. Even when Judge Sirica sentenced him, Liddy stuck to his guns. Gately could relate to a man who possessed human attributes like "loyalty, honor and courage." After all, Liddy, too, was a Marine.

It was five o'clock in the morning. Gately walked into a crowded, standing-room-only event. Customs had sent agents from the Los Angeles and San Francisco offices and now DEA was back in, just as Gately had predicted. George Hardy had just finished briefing them on the legal aspects of the takedown, which was an hour away. It was Gately's turn to give the operational briefing. While he was speaking, the agents looked at him with blank stares laced with hatred. He didn't know it at the time, but the agents, even his colleagues in Customs, loathed every aspect of this case. They had never worked so hard before, and had for the most part grown accustomed to leisurely jobs focusing on the mundane crimes of smuggling Mexican cheese wheels, exotic birds and laetrile, the apricot plant extract and "cancer cure." This case had accomplished more in six months to raise the profile of the agency in San Diego than had ten years of the other low-level investigations, and, ironically, the attention was unwanted.

By the end of the day, all twelve of the gang had been arrested, all four of their airplanes seized, and three million dollars in cash, cars, gold bullion and jewelry confiscated. Ward's ranch in Las Vegas, New Mexico, was also seized. It had all the chemicals and hardware necessary for a fully functional cocaine laboratory in one of the outbuildings.

To Gately, the most interesting and bizarre twist was the involvement of Larry Reynolds, Ward's attorney. Reynolds was a Seventh-Day Adventists church leader and community activist. Not only was he laundering drug money, he was also flying his own airplane to decoy Customs radar when Ward crossed the border carrying his loads. During the search of his home, agents found high-tech radio equipment used to coordinate their smuggling ventures. But probably the worst was what they found in his office—not your ordinary pornographic magazines. These showed graphic photographs of animals and women having sex.

The case was a huge success and had gone national on the news. The team had accomplished everything they had set out to do and more. Customs and DEA, as Gately had predicted, jointly claimed credit. Gately treated it as an opportunity to move up the ladder, applying for a supervisor's position. But things began to turn bad almost immediately. Instead of the usual praise and commendations for putting together a great case, the emphasis was on Trudeau and his double-dealing. Trudeau's misconduct had grown into allegations of Gately's mismanagement of an informant and possibly his complicity with Trudeau's drug dealing during the investigation. These assertions, based solely on the supposition of one individual, quickly took on a life of their own, casting a cloud over him and the case. To make matters worse, shortly after the San Diego bust, news broke in Miami about the seizure of over thirty-five hundred pounds of cocaine in one air cargo shipment. This overshadowed Gately's case and gave his detractors the perfect excuse to treat him as if he had done absolutely nothing.

Within a few months, seeking new surroundings and the challenge of South Florida's drug war, Gately transferred to Miami.

CHAPTER

3

THE SICILIANS

THE 340-MILE STRETCH of Interstate 95 along the east coast of Florida is bleached white by the sun. The highway, which spans the eastern seaboard from Miami to Bangor, Maine, connects the residents in the Northeastern U.S. to their "second home" in the Sunshine State. It is also the lifeline of commerce between Florida, New York and the rest of the Northeast, covering every major industry from agriculture to space exploration. But I-95 has also become the pipeline that feeds the seemingly insatiable appetite for cocaine that has infected every facet of society in America.

June 3, 1986, was not unlike any other day in South Florida. The morning climate was balmy, the sun was shining, the air warm, and the lush subtropical greenery and tall pines that line the highway made the long ride through Florida pleasurable. The two men in the Cadillac Fleetwood heading north through Fort Lauderdale made small talk. The driver was Joe Cuffaro. The passenger, his business partner Martin Gladstone.

Both men were as different in culture as they were in stature. Martin Gladstone was a small man, a little overweight from a sedentary lifestyle. He stood about five feet seven inches tall. Joe Cuffaro, a decade younger than Gladstone, was rugged with thick, black curly hair, shoulders a city-block wide, standing six feet six inches and weighing in at about 275 pounds. Even though they were from different worlds, during the last four years they had become close friends and shared an even stronger common bond: the success of their new business.

Martin Gladstone was a CPA. He had lived in New York City and relocated to the predominantly Jewish community of North Miami Beach in the early seventies. Marty, as his friends and neighbors referred to him, was a mild-mannered, devoted family man who had been married to his sweetheart for more than thirty years. In his fifties, his age was beginning to show around his middle, and his dark hair was beginning to turn gray. But foremost Marty Gladstone was a businessman who believed in the American Dream. The right idea, he believed, coupled with hard work, honesty and some determination could bring anyone success and anything else they desired in life.

Giuseppe "Joe" Cuffaro was an Italian immigrant from the island of Sicily, born and raised in the seaport city of Palermo. His parents were well-educated people. Joe's father was a banker by trade, with degrees in business and chemistry. His grandfather had been killed in the "war to end all wars," fighting the kaiser on the German front in 1917. This had left his wife, Joe Cuffaro's paternal grandmother, without the resources to give her son the educational and career opportunities he would have acquired had the war not left him fatherless. In her grief and determination, Joe's grandmother petitioned the Queen of Italy for assistance. To everyone's surprise, the queen had written back and included a personal introduction and recommendation directing the *Banca d'Italia* to consider Joe's father for a position. Thirty years later, Joe's father retired as a senior officer of the bank's regional office in Palermo. But he did not settle into retirement. He set out with the zeal of a much younger man to seek his fortune. It was a move that would soon earn him millions. But just as quickly as good fortune came, he lost not only his new-found wealth but his dignity and even his love for Italy. Driven by a passion for chemistry, he attended university at nights to obtain a second degree. After working for years in a small but professional laboratory he constructed in his home, he perfected a formula and process for producing artificial marble.

The Italian government backed him in his venture, but when his factory began production the infamous Sicilian Mafia began to set off bombs to stall the plant's operation, and to intimidate him and his family. Their plan was to terrorize him into capitulation. He would later tell his son Joe that his competition in the northern regions, where the marble quarries not only supplied Italy but the world markets, was responsible for his reversal of fortune. He believed they hired the Mafia for protection, accused him of fraud and eventually convinced the government of Italy to bring criminal charges against him. Although completely exonerated in a criminal trial, where he was acquitted of all charges, his spirit had been broken.

One of the greatest regrets in life for Joe Cuffaro's father was leaving his beloved Palermo. It was especially painful to him to know that Sicily

—which had been ruled by every civilization in the region from the Phoenicians, the ancient Greeks, the Moors of North Africa, the Spanish, French, Germans and British—had finally won its right to self-rule in the nineteenth century, when it became an autonomous region of the Kingdom of Italy—and was now ruled by the Mafia. In 1969, he immigrated to the United States, never again to return to his homeland. Joe's father came to America penniless, with his wife and youngest son, leaving his two oldest sons in Palermo with his wife's brother. Two years later Joe followed his family and settled in New York's "Little Italy." He was seventeen, had graduated from high school early and completed two years of college, where he had matriculated in engineering. His biggest drawback was that he didn't speak a word of English. His father was a cash-register clerk at a grocery store owned by the infamous Paul Gambino, brother of Carlo Gambino and head of the Gambino crime family, and "godfather" of the American Mafia. To everyone else, Joe Cuffaro's father was just another immigrant who could not speak English. His job in the new country humbled him to be sure. In Italy he had been a man of education and stature in the community, an executive heading the Bank of Italy for the region of Sicily. His comparatively simple duty of commanding one cash register in a grocery store was the only way he could support his wife and family.

The Gambinos were the first people the Cuffaros sought out when they arrived in America. Cuffaro's mom was related by marriage to the Gambinos' cousins in Sicily. The Gambino brothers had been kind, welcoming the Cuffaros as if they were family, first providing them with an apartment and later with a job at one of their markets. The Gambino's provided Joe Cuffaro with a union card—a simple enough favor, since they themselves controlled the union locals. Cuffaro was able to get a job at a construction site at Kennedy Airport that paid about $550 a week, about $160 of which went back to the union and into the Gambinos' pockets. When the job was completed, Joe worked directly for Paul Gambino at the Ferro Cheese Company as a truck driver. Shortly afterward, Paul Gambino arranged for him to "learn a trade that he could always fall back on." Since the Gambinos owned the market and were his sponsors, Cuffaro's apprenticeship as a meat cutter earned him the right to learn the trade without the usual menial labor. He immediately began to learn the basics and soon graduated to the specialty cuts. Cuffaro only had two years on the job, but he had the advantage of working with experienced and knowledgeable teachers who had been in the business for over twenty years. This gave Cuffaro the credentials of master meat cutter in less than half the usual four-year period for an apprenticeship. He owed Paul Gambino a great deal.

* * *

They were only an hour out of North Miami, passing through West Palm Beach and, as predicted, Gladstone was beginning to doze off.

"Watch your speed, Joe. The last thing we need is to be stopped," he said as he shifted around, trying to get comfortable in his seat.

"Okay, Marty," he said politely, only to humor his partner. Cuffaro was well aware of the consequences of drawing unnecessary attention. Within a few minutes Gladstone was out like a light.

Cuffaro knew every dip and turn of the interstate. They had made this trip dozens of times, but more frequently during the last six months. Going to New York was always a bittersweet experience for Cuffaro. His feelings weren't based on fear but on the way things were in the city. New York was where his American roots were. His thoughts turned to his early days delivering cheese for the Gambinos. Cuffaro's job had been to intimidate the customers so they would continue to buy their cheese and supplies from the Gambinos exclusively. His first experience in this subtle but institutionalized form of extortion was accompanying Paul Gambino, younger brother of Carlo, the head of the Banilimo Crime Syndicate, to a pizzeria where the owner, a recent immigrant from Sicily, had complained about the excessive fat and grease from the inferior grade of cheese supplied by the Ferro Cheese Company. Through the Ferro Cheese Company, the Mafia was providing newly arrived immigrants with all the supplies, equipment and even the locations of their new pizzerias. They even "gave" them a loan to buy the business. The exorbitant interest rates always ensured that the owners would be in debt to the Gambinos for years. The newcomer had little choice, however. No bank was willing to provide loans to these immigrants, most of whom lacked collateral for a loan, nor could they communicate well enough to do business in neighborhoods where Italian was not spoken.

On that early spring day in 1975, Paul Gambino took Cuffaro aside on the loading dock and put his hand on his shoulder in a fatherly way. "Joe, tonight I want you to come with me. I'm gonna make the rounds to some of my pizzerias. Wear your best suit."

When they arrived at the complaining pizzeria, Paul Gambino walked in and boisterously asked for a slice of pizza for him and Cuffaro. The owner literally jumped to attention, hastily filling his order. Gambino held the pizza in his hand, grease floating off the top of it and dripping onto the butcher paper, and loudly slurped as he shoved half the slice into his mouth. He turned to Cuffaro: "This is delicious pizza, don't you think so, Joe?"

"Yeah, Uncle Paul, this is the best pizza I ever tasted," Cuffaro said as he took a bite, towering at least a foot over everyone in the pizzeria.

"Didn't we get a complaint from this pizzeria today about the cheese?" Gambino asked.

The owner looked at them with terror in his eyes, acknowledging the presence of this mobster and a companion big enough to pick up most men and break them like a bread stick. And he quickly denied that it was his store that had lodged the complaint. He struggled to regain the good graces needed to stay in business by speaking to his countryman in Sicilian. "No, no, Uncle Paul, everything you send us is the best!"

Then there were the times when the pizzeria owners could not make their payments. Gambino would send Cuffaro in during the middle of the day, with customers present, to confiscate the equipment. The owners could do nothing more than stand with tears in their eyes as they watched their livelihood swiftly and mercilessly carried away.

At the time, Cuffaro was too unsophisticated and indifferent to understand that he was being used as a pawn in the Mafia's extortion racket. But a few years later, he felt for the first time the devastation he helped inflict on others. It became crystal clear when the tables were turned on him.

Paul Gambino helped Cuffaro and Carlo D'Arpa set up a meat market, which they called "Joe's Market," in the predominantly black section of Brooklyn's Bedford-Styvesant neighborhood. D'Arpa was a Sicilian immigrant and a cousin to Gambino who had married Paul Gambino's daughter, Providence. Cuffaro could not understand the inbreeding within the Mafia families. Paul Gambino also had married his first cousin, Paul Castellano's sister. Cuffaro and D'Arpa each put up seven thousand dollars for the market. Paul Castellano supplied the equipment and eventually became sole supplier of the meat, poultry and fish. And soon Castellano began supplying inferior products. On many occasions, Castellano's deliveries included poultry so rancid that when Cuffaro opened the packages, the stench made his head and stomach turn.

"Wash it down in salt water, put it on ice and sell it for thirty-nine cents a pound," was Castellano's typical response to Cuffaro's complaint. Castellano would then follow up with a daily delivery of fat trimmings from the meat they sold in other markets. Cuffaro and his partner would grind up the beef fat, and for every three pounds they mixed in a gallon of blood. It was sold as ground round for a dollar forty-nine a pound.

"Don't worry, Joe, it's just for those *tizzuni*. As long as they come back for more we got no problems." This was Castellano's pearl of wisdom on marketing shit in a pretty package.

With his roots beginning to take hold, Cuffaro approached Paul Gambino for help in gaining U.S. citizenship. Gambino contacted Tomas

Masotto, the Mafia's official liaison with the legal community. Masotto owned the Independent Meat Market where Cuffaro had first learned the meat cutting trade, and he was also the "family" member who arranged fake marriages for the new illegal Sicilian immigrants sanctioned by the Gambinos to become citizens. Masotto told Cuffaro he was a close friend of Elmer Fried, the district director of the Immigration and Naturalization Service in New York, boasting that he and Fried were members of the same country club. That day Masotto and Paul Gambino accompanied Cuffaro to the Brooklyn Italian-American club, a local hangout for mobsters and Gambino associates.

"Hey, we're looking for a wife for big Joe here," Gambino announced to the gamblers and thieves in the room.

"He needs his citizenship," added Masotto.

Three hours later, his wife-to-be was delivered to them. Masotto promptly called Cuffaro at the market and told him, "I want you to come down here right away and meet your future wife."

Cuffaro, anxious to get this over with, rushed down to see Paul Gambino. He couldn't believe his eyes when he walked in the room and met Kathleen Anderson. She was a redheaded, big-boned, pale, white-skinned woman covered with freckles. And she was two inches taller than Cuffaro. His eyes immediately fell to the large gold crucifix that dangled between two obscenely large, flabby and well-exposed breasts. They moved like jello with her slightest motion and reminded him of udders on a cow. To Cuffaro, this Irish ten-dollar hooker was the most vulgar woman he had ever met.

"Where's Joe?" she blurted out in a voice two octaves deeper than Cuffaro's. "I'm supposed to marry him."

Masotto and Gambino were barely able to restrain themselves. "This, Joe, is your future wife. I think you should kiss her," Masotto said, and laughed uncontrollably.

When the men had regained control of themselves they adjourned to Masotto's office to do business with Kathleen Anderson. Besides Masotto and Gambino, several other Gambino family members were present. They explained the rules of the deal to the bride-to-be. She would get a thousand dollars now and another thousand once Joe received his citizenship. "And if you say anything to anybody," they said, "we're gonna break your fuckin' legs!"

Kathleen Anderson simply shrugged her shoulders. "Where's the money?" she asked. "I'll marry him right now. I got things to buy."

Masotto reached into his pocket and pulled out a wad of hundreds. As he grasped the money in his left hand, he ritualistically licked both thumbs and peeled off a thousand dollars from the stack of bills.

The next day, dressed in attire that Cuffaro considered to be "almost like a normal person," Kathleen Anderson and Joe Cuffaro went for a blood test and then to the court house for the marriage license, where Kathleen and Joe walked in on a crowd of lovebirds holding hands and standing impatiently for the paper that would mark the start of their new lives. The instant Kathleen laid eyes on the line before her, her cover was blown.

"Shit! I'm not waitin' in this fuckin' line to get the marriage license! Let's get out of here," she demanded. "I've got clients to meet. We'll come back tomorrow."

With a little finesse and a lot of pleading, Cuffaro convinced her to stay. It was, according to him, the most embarrassing moment in his life.

The next day the wedding ceremony was held. Cuffaro's best man Pete Carini, on Masotto's advice, took pictures, just in case some nosey INS official wanted to see proof of the joyous event. Cuffaro also rented an apartment that he decorated with the wedding pictures. He hung some of his clothes and women's clothing in the closet, occasionally making an appearance there.

Several months later, in January 1976, Joe Cuffaro became a U.S. resident and Kathleen Anderson received her second thousand-dollar payment. A month later his marriage was dissolved through a legal annulment, performed by a judge who Masotto claimed was on the Gambino payroll. Masotto and the judge had developed a seemingly fool-proof system to manipulate the court calendar. These special annulment hearings were conducted late in the afternoon, when the courtroom was cleared of any spectators.

By now Cuffaro's business was doing well. As long as meat prices remained steady, Joe's Market was able to make a great profit and compete with Pasquale "Patsy" Conti's Key Foods grocery store across the street. Conti was a rival of the Gambinos, and would later head the Genovese crime family. But when meat prices shot up in '78, Conti continued to sell his beef at the same price, which forced Cuffaro and his partner to do the same. The loss of a dollar a pound quickly added up to a ten-thousand-dollar debt in less than three months. Castellano was now threatening to close Joe's Market and confiscate their refrigerators, displays and cutters. As threats were exchanged, Castellano asked for a "sit down" with Carlo Gambino to settle the matter. Throughout the discussion, Castellano was defiantly merciless.

"It's my right to take this equipment," he told the old gangster. To his surprise, the senior Gambino ruled in Cuffaro's favor, and with the sweep of his hand and a word to Castellano he erased the debt completely.

"When times were good you made a lot of money with this man," Gambino said thoughtfully. "Times are bad now. You take the good with the bad. Because of this, there is no more debt. Joe Cuffaro owes you nothing, *capisci*?" Castellano considered this a slap in the face from Don Carlo and would never forget the disrespect.

When the old man died a year later, Castellano succeeded him as the Don and immediately came back with a vengeance. His threats now extended beyond Cuffaro to include his family. His wife of three years and his year-old daughter became targets of Castellano's rage. Cuffaro quickly decided to sell everything and move away before there was serious trouble. For months his brother had been telling him about Miami, how it was so much like their hometown of Palermo. He often tried to convince him to leave New York and move south with him. Within a month Cuffaro had sold everything they owned, and with only their clothes and twelve thousand dollars, he and his family moved in with his younger brother in Miami's South Beach.

It took Cuffaro a couple of weeks to find a good job. Browsing through the classified section of the Miami *Herald,* he saw an ad for a "specialty meat cutter." That afternoon he walked in and introduced himself to the manager of the meat department. Immediately they locked eyes. When he said his name was Joe Cuffaro, and that he was applying for the meat cutter position, the response was instantaneous. "You're Italian! You're a meat cutter?"

"Well, yes I am," Cuffaro replied with a smile.

"You're hired!" his new boss said with absolute sincerity. He was hired on the spot, for $275 a week at Miami Beach's famous Epicure Market. Over the next couple of years, he became meat cutter to the rich and famous of Miami Beach. By then, he was earning a salary of $500 a week plus tips, preparing cuts and meats at the personal request of celebrities such as Sophia Loren and her husband Carlo Ponti, Julio Iglesias, Peter Sellers and many others. He even prepared meat especially for President Somoza of Nicaragua, who purchased hundreds of pounds of prime cut beef from the Epicure. Within a short period, Cuffaro was able to purchase a modest home in North Miami Beach.

Just thinking about the Epicure Market made Cuffaro hungry. In St. Augustine, they filled up the tank and ate at a nearby diner.

"This is always a miserable trip, but one good thing about not being in the office today is not having to see that asshole Galatolo." Gladstone usually refrained from using obscenities, but Galatolo had a way of bringing out the worst in everybody.

"Yeah, Marty, I don't like the son of a bitch either, but at the time we needed the cash, and that's why he's our partner. Things were a lot better when Malpica was around." With a rather shamed look, Cuffaro added, "But Malpica would never go for this."

"Joe, it's been two years since we took this guy in. Remember we said we would only do this until we got the business going. We thought that was going to be six months."

Cuffaro politely brushed him off. They had lamented over their business decisions many times before. They were stuck and there was no use discussing it.

When they had returned to the car, Cuffaro flipped the keys to his partner and Gladstone took the wheel of his Cadillac. They adjusted the seat positions, the tiny electric motors whirring as Gladstone moved his seat up and in to accommodate his five-foot-seven-inch frame and Cuffaro moving his back and down as far as it could go. Gladstone may have bought the car as a status symbol, but Cuffaro liked it because it was the only car General Motors built that accommodated his six-foot-six-inch frame comfortably.

Looking out at the scenery once they were back on the road, Cuffaro thought back to his and Gladstone's partner Galatolo. John Galatolo's roots were from Sicily. He had immigrated to the United States over two decades ago. He was exiled to the United States on orders from the Corleonese crime family of Palermo after he ruthlessly settled a forty-year-old dispute between his grandfather and a rival gangster: at the age of eighteen Galatolo had lain in wait for the then-seventy-five-year-old perpetrator of the offense. Perched above, on the old man's balcony outside his front door, with his arms raised above his head, Galatolo caved in the old man's head with a cement block, killing him. This almost began a war between the two families. To appease their rivals, the Corleonese family stopped just short of killing the young Galatolo. In the early sixties, the Corleonese banished Galatolo, shipped him off to New York, and the two families declared a truce to the bloodshed that had already claimed so many of their members.

Upon his arrival in America, Galatolo quickly and firmly established himself as a first-rate asshole. Now in his forties, he was a short man, his small legs out of proportion with his long torso. At five feet two inches and weighing about 200 pounds Galatolo looked decidedly like a bowling ball. His round face was topped by a mostly bald head with only a semicircle of hair from ear to ear. His physique was only surpassed by his natural ability to make himself completely unwelcome—a source of continual embarrassment to both Gladstone and Cuffaro. Everything about him, from his lack of personal hygiene to his foul-smelling, out-of-style clothing and his loud and crude conversation, was obnoxious. Gladstone and Cuffaro had a running gag about his body odor. When he walked past, he left a trail like a skunk. Behind him, his two partners sprayed air freshener in an attempt to clear the stench. His wardrobe favored the gangster movies of the early thirties: black pinstriped double-breasted suit, black silk shirt, white tie and two-tone shoes. Of course, Galatolo was also extremely dangerous, with a volatile temper. Jack Green, an advertising man who frequented Cuffaro's place of business and who later became a good friend of Cuffaro, was continually insulted by Galatolo. Green finally heard one insult too many and told Galatolo that not only was he despicable, but that he dressed like a mafioso. Cuffaro found himself defending Green's life when Galatolo threatened to shoot him in the head and hang him from a meat hook. Had Cuffaro not intervened, Galatolo would certainly have carried out his threat. Galatolo was a definite liability, but for now, Cuffaro and Gladstone were stuck with him. Cuffaro had met Galatolo several years earlier by chance at the Miami International Airport. Cuffaro and his brother were waiting for a friend to arrive from Italy, a man traveling to the United States for a delicate eye operation at the Sloan-Kettering Institute in Miami. As the two brothers spoke to each other in Sicilian, Galatolo overheard their conversation and approached them, speaking Sicilian himself.

After the initial small talk, it dawned on Galatolo that he had met Cuffaro before.

"You used to work for Paul Gambino at the Ferro Cheese Company, didn't you?" Before Cuffaro could respond, Galatolo continued, "You were the only driver who would come to my pizzeria carrying two one-hundred-pound flour sacks on your shoulder at one time. Everyone respected your strength."

SAVANNAH, 27 MILES. The next sign read FOOD-GAS-LODGING-NEXT EXIT. The trip was beginning to wear on both men.

"Marty, you look like you're getting tired. Let's pull over, get some coffee and switch," Cuffaro offered, as Gladstone nodded and yawned.

A half-hour later Cuffaro again took the wheel and headed onto the pitch-black highway. As he engaged the cruise control his thoughts returned to simpler times when he worked for the Thal brothers at the Epicure Market.

Despite his success as a meat cutter for the upper crust of Miami's Venetian Causeway, Cuffaro had grown dissatisfied with his comfortable but apparently dead-end job. He found himself one Sunday looking through the want ads of the Miami *Herald,* when he stumbled on the MANAGEMENT POSITIONS OFFERED portion of the help-wanted section. The ad read: PRODUCTION MANAGER WANTED. APPLY IMMEDIATELY. KEY LARGO FAN COMPANY. Before the day was over Cuffaro was interviewing with Richard Markowitz, owner and president of the company. Cuffaro drove to the interview, finding himself in a very nice area of Hialeah. As he walked up the driveway, he passed a new convertible Mercedes-Benz parked near the entrance. Entering the building was an immediate transition from the industrial park setting. The reception area was furnished with the finest Italian leather chairs and sofa and accented with tropical rosewood tables. The elegant atmosphere was plush yet comfortable. Cuffaro heard a voice calling his name.

"Hey, big Joe, what are you doing here?"

Cuffaro looked up and recognized Markowitz, not by name but as one of his regular customers at the Epicure Market. "I'm here to answer your ad," Cuffaro said.

"You here for a job? But Joe, you're a meat cutter!"

"I'm a meat cutter now, but in Sicily I worked in a company that manufactured oscillating fans," Joe began, lying. Cuffaro had had no experience or knowledge of ceiling fans. It was flat-out bullshit. But he did possess good mechanical skills. And above all he had charm, wit and natural sales instincts.

Markowitz took Cuffaro into the office to show him around and then into the warehouse where hundreds of fans were stacked in boxes.

"Joe, we have the best fans in the country because we use the best parts, but the assembly is where we fall short."

"Why don't you show me one of your fans," Cuffaro asked.

"Well, do you think you could really help me?" Markowitz almost pleaded.

As Cuffaro began looking over one of the fans, Markowitz told him his problems. "Our assembly plant is in Chattanooga, Tennessee. We're having a lot of problems there. We have customers calling from all over the country with complaints about the fans wobbling and falling apart."

"Well, Richard, here are some of your problems. Look at this right here." Cuffaro acted as if he knew exactly what he was talking about. "You need to have lock washers on the domes, and these wires, they need to be stripped at least a quarter of an inch. They're not making good contact." Markowitz was mesmerized. He obviously had little knowledge of the product he sold. Markowitz took the hook and Cuffaro easily reeled him in.

"Joe, you really know what you're talking about. Do you think you can help me?"

"Sure I can help you. But tell me, why is your assembly plant located in Chattanooga, Tennessee?"

"I hired this engineer from Chattanooga and he set up the plant there. I've never been there. See, I'm afraid of flying, but we talk on the phone all the time," he said.

This was going to be a piece of cake, Cuffaro thought. "Why don't you send me to the plant? Let me see what I can do."

Before the day was over, Markowitz offered to double Cuffaro's current salary and give him a company car with a telephone, along with an expense account. The next day Cuffaro gave his two-week notice to the Thal brothers, owners of the Epicure. Because the Thal brothers liked Cuffaro they let him bypass the two-week rule. Although they hated to see him leave, they gave him their blessings and told him the door would always be open for him if things didn't work out in the fan business.

Two weeks later, with the credentials of vice president of production in the Key Largo Fan Company and a letter from Markowitz giving him authority to hire and fire, Cuffaro went to Chattanooga. Cuffaro was greeted with a cold shoulder by the plant manager and the engineer who both blatantly ignored his suggestions to improve the assembly quality, and who even called Markowitz demanding that Cuffaro be returned to Miami.

Cuffaro continued to fend off the attacks as he uncovered not only incompetence but outright theft and fraudulent billings to Markowitz by the Chattanooga plant. Cuffaro let Markowitz know that he had found proof that the engineer and plant manager, who were brothers, routinely marked up equipment purchases by one hundred percent. They had also created a dozen ghost employees who turned out to be relatives. Between the double invoicing and the padded payroll, the French brothers were ripping off Markowitz and pocketing thousands of dollars a week. But what was worse in Cuffaro's mind was the total disregard for quality control in the assembly process. The employees used hand-held tools and damaged more parts than they assembled. Parts were intentionally not packed or deliberately damaged.

Cuffaro devised a plan, informed Markowitz and, with his backing, set it in motion. He issued pink slips and a final paycheck for everyone at the plant. The same day he summarily shut down the factory and announced that Mr. Markowitz was moving the entire plant operation to Miami.

The next morning Cuffaro was met by a gauntlet of the "former employees" who were armed with everything from clubs to shotguns. The ten tractor trailers he ordered from Yellow Freight to move the plant to Miami faced a roadblock of pickup trucks and an angry, defiant mob. Cuffaro's only solution was to call the law for help.

An hour passed before the sheriff, who resembled the character in the Burt Reynolds *Smokey and the Bandit* films, parked himself in the Key Largo Fan Company office with Cuffaro.

"What seems to be the problem here Mr. Kay-fair-ry," the sheriff inquired, in his Tennessee twang.

Cuffaro explained his situation, and no sooner had he finished than the sheriff drew his .357 Magnum revolver from his holster and set it on the table between them.

"Well Mr. Kay-fair-ry, tell you what I'm gonna do. I'm gonna leave my pistol raut heah fer ya. Any of these sons of bitches walk in heah, ya got my permission to blow their gottdamned brains out. Then you call me." Cuffaro couldn't believe his ears. The sheriff added, "That's the way we do things roun' heah." Cuffaro watched through the office door as the sheriff walked outside, took hold of his loudspeaker and announced his decision to the sixty-five former employees of the Key Largo Fan Company. "You see this, it's an empty holster. My gun's with Mr. Kay-fair-ry in there. He has my permission to shoot any one of ya." With that, the sheriff got in his truck and drove off.

Cuffaro called Markowitz, explained the situation and asked him to send people from Miami to help disassemble the factory.

"I can't trust anyone here, everyone's related to the French brothers. You gotta send me ten good, strong men right away," he told Markowitz.

Two days later, six hundred people showed up at the Key Largo Fan Company in response to the ad Markowitz placed looking for ten laborers. The next week, ten men wearing flowered tropical shirts and shiny zipper boots with Cuban heels showed up at the Chattanooga airport. Cuffaro couldn't believe his eyes, but he didn't need introductions to recognize his help from Miami. They were all recent immigrants of the infamous Mariel harbor exodus, engineered by Fidel Castro to rid Cuba of the "dregs" of the revolution. They had not only arrived in a place they had never seen before, but in Tennessee they were speaking a language no one had ever heard. Luckily, Cuffaro had himself become proficient in it, thanks to his wife, whose native tongue was Spanish. Cuffaro's first move was to purchase work clothes and boots for each of them.

For the next three days and nights he and his men worked around the clock, packing up every nut and bolt in the plant. By the end of the week Cuffaro, the *Marielitos* and the ten tractor-trailer trucks were headed to Miami. During these few days, Cuffaro befriended one of the men who had taken the initiative to inventory everything in the plant and help organize the labor-intensive task. Rigo Malpica would soon become Cuffaro's good friend and business partner. Malpica was fluent in English, German and Spanish and had worked for the Cuban government as an official translator. Cuffaro was extremely impressed with Malpica's seeming ability to adapt to any task and to make each project a matter of personal pride. When the work was done, Cuffaro and Malpica took the *Marielitos* to see the historic sights of Chattanooga. There was the Chattanooga Choo Choo and others, but the most impressive sight was the local strip joint. It was something they had never seen in Cuba, which was probably why the owner quickly evicted them all for their uncontrollable behavior. At the end of the evening, he treated them to another Cuban rarity—big, juicy steaks.

With Malpica and a couple of the *Marielitos,* Cuffaro reconstructed the plant at Key Largo headquarters and started an assembly line that would rival some of the best in the country. In less than two months Key Largo was producing over two hundred fans a day. Now their distributors could not fill their orders quickly enough and customer complaints were almost nonexistent.

Cuffaro thought he had finally found his niche. Over the next year and a half he travelled to every major city in the United States, selling Key Largo fans, designing and promoting new products. Cuffaro was the first to develop the pivoting ball assembly that eliminated wobbling. He brought in new designs such as the rattan fan, the stained-glass fan, and was the first to display a variety of colors. He was actively sought after by executives at Hunter Fan Company, and Burton Burton, president of Casa Blanca Fan Company, personally offered him a job, but Cuffaro turned both offers down. By 1982 Key Largo had grown from its initial gross of $300,000 annually to bringing in $6 million a year. He had become the focal point at Key Largo Fan Company for the parts suppliers, sales reps and distributors around the country.

The situation was eating at Markowitz's ego. Instead of rewarding Cuffaro, Markowitz considered him a threat. He began telling him he was a "common Sicilian immigrant," an "uneducated peasant," who still had "mud on his shoes." Markowitz also told Cuffaro he would never be a real engineer. Then Markowitz went a step further, hiring Vladimir Drball, an engineer whose only experience was working for a manufacturer producing pacemakers. Markowitz hired Drball at $70,000 a year and told Cuffaro to report to him.

A few months later Cuffaro witnessed the result of Markowitz's mistreatment of his employees. It was a primitive but effective symbol of their deeply entrenched hatred toward their employer, a day Cuffaro would not soon forget.

"Joe! Joe, you gotta come in here!" Markowitz had been opening his mail and was now screaming for Cuffaro.

When Cuffaro arrived in the office, Markowitz was ashen faced and hyperventilating.

"You gotta get this thing out of here!" Markowitz said excitedly.

A voodoo doll—Markowitz's exact replica—lay among the wrappings on his desk. It was filled with needles.

Cuffaro knew why. A couple of months earlier, Markowitz had dispatched Cuffaro to Port-au-Prince, Haiti, to compile an efficiency report on his leather factory. Markowitz had told him his factory was using cheap Haitian labor to produce belts for the Tandy Corporation. While there, Cuffaro heard endless complaints about Markowitz's mistreatment of the factory workers. There were even horror stories that if he did not like an employee, he would report the troublesome worker to his friend, Jean-Claude Duvalier, "Baby Doc." Duvalier was the son and political heir of the infamous "Papa Doc," the former president and dictator-for-life of the island country. According to accounts given to Cuffaro by the factory workers, "Baby Doc" would order his secret police, the *Tontons Macoutes,* to drag the accused employees out of the factory in full view of their coworkers and execute them in the yard at the rear of the factory. The factory employees quietly retaliated by strategically placing a series of photographs of Markowitz at the base of the twenty-foot-long communal urinal.

It wasn't long before Cuffaro himself suffered his last indignity at the hands of Markowitz. It happened at a distributor party while the company officers celebrated a newly acquired large contract. Markowitz loudly announced that Cuffaro's attendance was not welcome. After the hors d'oeuvres, Markowitz added insult to injury. He announced over the loudspeaker that everyone had eaten and now Cuffaro could come in to eat the leftovers. Joe couldn't believe his ears. Twenty minutes later, Markowitz made the announcement again, and this time Cuffaro stormed in.

"You can take these leftovers and shove them up your ass," Cuffaro told him in front of his guests and walked out. It was the last straw. Cuffaro's only thought now was how to punish him. He decided that Markowitz's business holdings were too valuable to be ruined by the owner's incompetence and that it would be much better to simply exercise his own form of a hostile takeover.

Cuffaro set the first phase of his plan in motion. Through his personal contacts and successful track record, he convinced the suppliers who he worked with at Key Largo to help him as he built his own company. With his direct connections to companies such as General Electric and the parts he had been stealing over the last two months from Markowitz, Cuffaro began assembling fans out of his house every evening after work with help from his old friend Rigo Malpica. Three months later Cuffaro turned in the keys to his car, his company credit card and a resignation letter.

"Joe, what are you doing?" Markowitz asked innocently.

"I'm quitting. It's all over," Cuffaro responded.

Markowitz yelled out to his bookkeeper, "Make out a check for five thousand dollars to Joe Cuffaro."

"What, you think you own me? You can't buy me. Take your five thousand dollars and shove them up your ass. I came here when you were almost bankrupt. I spent a week with my wife this last year, while she was pregnant with our third child, because I was on the road for you. I gave up my family and my life for you and now you're treating me like a dog."

When Markowitz realized his money would not convince Cuffaro to stay, he resorted to his usual abusive behavior. "You're still a peasant. You're nothing. You won't be able to get a job anywhere."

"Richard, I'm walking out of here, and my only purpose in life will be to put you out of business. And when I do, I'm going to buy everything in this warehouse. I'll give you six months before you're bankrupt." With that, Cuffaro walked out on Markowitz for good. Cuffaro took his good friend Rigo Malpica, the real glue of the Key Largo factory, along with him.

About twelve months later, Key Largo Fan Company filed for reorganization under Chapter 11 of the bankruptcy code. A few months later the doors closed and Markowitz's company went into Chapter 7, forfeiting his business to his creditors. The landlord now owned all of Key Largo's inventory. On the eve of a public auction, Cuffaro received a phone call from Harry Hamilwich, the owner of the building.

"Joe, I got a warehouse full of fan parts. I called Casa Blanca, and nobody needs anything. So, I want to let you know about the auction coming up."

Cuffaro knew the warehouse held about five hundred thousand dollars in inventory. At the auction, with Malpica at his side, Cuffaro made the only offer that was accepted. He purchased everything in the warehouse for twenty-five thousand dollars. Richard Markowitz, who attended the auction, couldn't believe his eyes.

"You no-good son of a bitch," he said to Cuffaro. "You Sicilian bastard."

"You're a loser, Richard," Cuffaro told him. "Now get off my property before I have you thrown out."

Cuffaro now had more pressing problems, like getting the twenty-five thousand dollars. He needed thirteen thousand to make up the difference. He couldn't get a loan anywhere until he put up his house as collateral to borrow the money from "some Greek guy" he knew. The Greek's terms were that the loan was due and payable within ninety days, plus interest.

The same day he paid the court and got the keys from Hamilwich, Cuffaro stumbled on a shipment of seventy-five boxes of alligator skins, on their way to the Port-au-Prince factory. He had no idea of their value but he knew he could sell them in Little Havana. Cuffaro struck a deal on his very first try. A local purse manufacturer purchased the illegal skins for twenty-five thousand dollars in cash on the spot. The business-man had come across the deal of a lifetime, so he paid Cuffaro, almost pushing him out of the door before he could change his mind. Cuffaro didn't know the merchandise was worth twice as much, but he was after all only interested in paying off his debt to the Greek and keeping his home and new business.

Orders to the Scirocco Fan Company began coming in from all over the country. Yet in spite of the newly acquired inventory from the Key Largo Fan Company, there were still many items they needed to fill the orders. Cuffaro and Malpica sought another partner with accounting experience who was also willing to invest in the company. Their first thought was Marty Gladstone. Gladstone, who had been keeping the books for Key Largo, enthusiastically came in as the third partner. It was the first time he had had the opportunity to get in on the ground floor and this time there was the added benefit of coming on board as a full partner and coowner.

Cuffaro looked over at Gladstone, who was snoring loudly. Joe was hungry. "Wake up sleeping beauty."

"Jeeze, what time is it? I'm starved."

They had been on the road over twelve hours. The dilemma now was where to get good food in North Carolina in the middle of the night, without letting the car out of their sight. A big part of the problem was that they were in a little shit town called Rocky Mount about a hundred miles northwest of the Marine Corps base at Camp Lejeune. They found an all-night diner on the outskirts of town. The first thing they saw as they walked into the eatery was a sign that read, FREE COFFEE FOR MARINES.

As Cuffaro and Gladstone sat at their table waiting for their food, Cuffaro couldn't help but notice the young marines throughout the res-taurant. The grunts reminded him of his days in Palermo, when the U.S. Navy ships would dock and thousands of marines would descend upon the city's nightspots, pizzerias and brothels. It was just another way the U.S. government contributed to the Mafia cause.

Gladstone, on the other hand, hadn't even noticed the surroundings. He was busy with his pocket calculator. Finally he spoke: "Joe, you know Galatolo owes the business a hundred thousand dollars. He's always short-changing us and he's never really come through on his promises."

As he complained, Cuffaro could only think of Galatolo's words less than a week ago. "Gladstone's just a Jew, he's not even Italian. And, he knows way too much about our business. He's gotta go, too." Galatolo talked as if he were discussing swatting a fly.

Ever since Galatolo's last trip to Sicily, his usual boastful talk was starting to take shape in very real terms to Cuffaro. Galatolo was boasting openly of his Mafia connections in Sicily, names Cuffaro recognized. Real killers. Galatolo even started recounting, in detail, murders he had committed in Miami for the mob. He claimed that he was now "blessed," a "man of honor" who had undergone the secret ritual, taking the oath as a member of *La Cosa Nostra*. And now Galatolo was pressuring Cuffaro to take the same step.

"Look, Marty," Cuffaro said to Gladstone, "we both agreed to take Galatolo in, over the objections of Malpica. And that's probably the worst thing we've done, lose Rigo for Galatolo."

"And he never paid Rigo either. He promised him twenty-five thousand for his share of the business and only paid him seven. So, why should he pay us?" Gladstone responded angrily.

"Like we agreed, as soon as we get the money we need to keep Scirocco in the black, we'll get out. Besides, it's not like we haven't tried other ways to get the cash we need to keep the factory open."

Shortly after they formed Scirocco, Cuffaro read a magazine feature article about the gold-mining operations in Ecuador. A month later he was boarding Ecuatoriana Airlines to Quito to see it firsthand. There, he saw a way to subsidize the Scirocco Fan Company. At first Cuffaro had hired a couple of mules, loaded them up with provisions and traveled the winding mountain paths into the 18,000-foot elevation to the mining town of Nambija. There Cuffaro saw what he believed to be Dante's vision of hell, minus the heat. Deep within the Andes, amidst the gray, cold, wet climate with a constant thirty-degree temperature, Cuffaro found himself standing ankle deep in the thick mud that covered everything. Twenty thousand men lived like animals in the *Cuidad de Plástico*, the Plastic City, weatherproofing their cardboard shelters with thirty-gallon Hefty trash bags.

In Nambija, Cuffaro witnessed what greed would drive men to endure. It was called the Plastic City, but he often thought it should have been called the City of Death. The miners, enveloped in the clouds and debris from the constant explosions, randomly blasted into the side of the mountain as other miners were perched on the narrow ledges nearby. It was not unusual for miners to simultaneously blast tunnels above and below each other without regard. Inevitably, the shafts formed by the blasting would cave in, sending tons of rock tumbling down on the miners below, crushing them to death. The frenzy to gather the gold was so intense, they didn't even take the time to bury the dead. The bodies lay where they fell, bloated and decaying like discarded rubbish. The stench of death was everywhere, rivaled only by the accumulation of human excrement. And the blasting was not their only form of suicide. In their quest to gather the most gold first, the miners used liquid mercury to separate the gold from the ore. The next step was to use a torch to burn away the heavy metal. The lethal gases emitted when the ore reached 180 degrees Fahrenheit would rise up from the pan and silently kill the eager miner as he inhaled. But in this hell, Cuffaro saw an opportunity to make big money.

During his many trips, Cuffaro gradually built his own *rancho* on the side of the mountain. He ingeniously eliminated the transportation burden for these miners by setting up his own assay office, purchasing the gold directly from them. At first it was profitable, because the miners were completely ignorant of the world gold price. Cuffaro was able to purchase the gold between seventy and eighty dollars an ounce for a potential resale at a world market price of approximately four hundred dollars an ounce. There was only one obstacle between him and the three hundred percent profit he could make: the government of Ecuador had made it a criminal offense to remove gold from the country. Once he got to the city of Quito, Cuffaro converted the gold into a more transportable form, smelting it into one-ounce ingots, which he was able to conceal in the compartments he had sewn into his boots. With the help of an Ecuadorian airline pilot, Cuffaro successfully smuggled the gold out of the country. He then sold the gold in either Miami or Milan, Italy.

The system worked well for a while, but two factors soon whittled away his profit margin. First, the government of Ecuador decided to educate the miners in Nambija, providing a satellite dish and radio so they could receive the daily world gold price. Then, because of the frequency of his trips, Ecuadorian officials began shaking him down for their "fair share." With the profit margin significantly reduced, Cuffaro was getting ready to quit his gold-smuggling ventures when he heard that the government of Colombia was offering a twenty-percent incentive over the world gold price for gold mined in Colombia. By buying Ecuadorian gold in Nambija at twenty to thirty percent below world gold value, then smuggling it to Colombia where he could get an additional twenty-percent incentive, Cuffaro was able to maintain a reasonable profit. However, the profit was offset by having to split his twenty percent with the Colombian Minister of Natural Resources, who would falsify the records and pocket ten percent. What's more, the Colombians did not pay him in Colombia; the cash payment was delivered a week or so later to his business in Miami in sealed Monopoly game boxes. The trouble and risk involved had begun to outweigh the profits, and Cuffaro was looking elsewhere to make up for it.

During more profitable times Cuffaro had sold his gold in Miami and in Italy. And during his many trips to Milan he had befriended a jewelry manufacturer. Piero Galeazzi had a past with the criminal world, having served for many years as a fence for the Mafia, buying and selling stolen gold and gems. Now he was a legitimate businessman searching for a way to export his jewelry to the United States. Cuffaro began to serve as middleman and translator between his new friend from Milan and his contacts in Miami's jewelry district, earning a ten-percent commission that brought in a couple of thousand dollars extra each month. This all came to a screeching halt when Galatolo found out about his moonlighting.

"I dropped by your office to see you the other day, Joe, and your Jew friend Marty told me about this guy you're dealin' with," Galatolo said pointedly. "How much jewelry does this guy usually have?"

Cuffaro frowned. Gladstone was faithful and an asset to the company, but he often made the mistake of opening his mouth at the wrong time to the wrong people. Cuffaro looked at Galatolo. "Well, sometimes he has about forty, fifty thousand dollars give or take a little," Cuffaro said, knowing there was more to come.

"And what do you get, Joe? What's your end in the deal?" Before Joe could answer, Galatolo continued, "You're stupid to take a commission. You should just set 'em up. We should rob 'em and take it all."

Cuffaro didn't want to hear what he was hearing so he shrugged it off. "John, this guy is an old man and a friend. I couldn't do that to him."

"Hey, Joe, either you do it with us or we'll do it without you."

It became a daily topic with Galatolo until seven months later Cuffaro finally caved in and agreed to do it.

Cuffaro set up the old man, but at the last minute he convinced Galeazzi to keep the gold locked up in the safe of the hotel and to carry only a small sample to show the buyers at the Diabold Diamond Center in downtown Miami. When Galatolo's men, impersonating police, stopped Cuffaro and Galeazzi in the hotel parking lot, they were only able to steal his samples.

It wasn't long after these initial efforts to raise money for the business that Galatolo made them an offer they couldn't refuse. At first Cuffaro and Gladstone had nothing more to do than make a phone call. Galatolo's people simply dropped off a package, then Cuffaro called a pager number, alerting the courier to pick up the package.

This was Cuffaro and Gladstone's quiet introduction to the cocaine business. Galatolo quickly promised them five hundred dollars for every kilo that passed through Scirocco. At first, it was five and then ten kilos. Then it was fifty and a hundred kilos. Soon, they were moving as much as five hundred kilos at one time through the business. Cuffaro's and Gladstone's personal involvement also increased significantly. They were transporting large quantities not only in the Miami area but also to

Galatolo's Mafia associates, including the Gambino brothers, Joe and John. The brothers, who were distant cousins of Carlo Gambino, worked for John Gotti's Gambino crime syndicate in New York.

Transportation was the mild side of the cocaine business. Joe was not entirely surprised to find that armed robbery, home invasions, rip-offs, firebombings, kidnappings and even murder were in Galatolo's repertoire, and it seemed the cocaine business suited him perfectly. Galatolo had been connected directly to the Colombian suppliers by his attorney Bob Martin, himself a cocaine addict who came in weekly to Scirocco to pick up an ounce to feed his own habit. It was Martin who first introduced Galatolo to Waldo Aponte, a Colombian trafficker from Medellín. Through Aponte, Galatolo was soon getting his drugs directly from the Medellín cartel, thus the ever-increasing volume of drugs.

The many characters with whom Cuffaro and Gladstone came into contact were as interesting as they were despicable. There was Nelson Simeon, one of their "associates" who was also deeply involved in Cuban *santería*, a cross between Catholicism and African voodoo. Several associates used aliases, like David, aka Luis Mejía, a Colombian supplier who worked for Aponte. While it was typical for the Mafia to seek out blacks as customers, it was rare to have a black associate, but Tyrone Walker became a regular and a significant courier, picking up loads weekly from the fan company and carrying them to the Detroit market. Mariela Liggio was the only woman associate. She was one of the first to use the Scirocco fan company as a stash house for her five- and ten-kilo packages. Her partner Luis Miguel was the pick-up man. They were an interesting partnership, she a Colombian with an Italian name, and he a Haitian mulatto with an Hispanic name. Her success was primarily based on her connections with an Eastern Airlines employee who routed the drugs directly to her. The Eastern Airlines drugs were very distinguishable because they were packaged in neat stackable boxes that they dubbed *loncheras,* or "lunch boxes."

Joe Cuffaro had a memorable day when he was sitting in his office just a few feet away from the floor safe that his brother had recently installed in his office. It was filled with money and the *loncheras* for Mariela. He was reading the Miami *Herald*'s headline story about the fifty-four Eastern Airlines and airport employees charged in a drug conspiracy. The article described the many methods used to smuggle the drugs, one of which was lining the interior bulkheads of the aircraft with the *loncheras*. Cuffaro worriedly searched for Mariela's name among the list of people charged. As he read on, he became increasingly upset when he saw that U.S. customs agents had hundreds of hours of video-taped evidence. If he hadn't realized it before, Cuffaro knew then that he had gone too far. Even though his initial intentions were to "get in and get out," he had long since crossed the point of no return—he realized he had become everything he despised, driven not by the "American dream," but by greed. The things he once would never have considered doing he now did almost routinely. It was a bitter thought that made his latest mission to New York even more disheartening.

"Are you listening to me, Joe?" Gladstone had been talking to himself again. "Did you hear me? We gotta find a way to get our money out of Galatolo."

Joe Cuffaro's thoughts exactly.

Cuffaro drove the next three and a half hours through Richmond, the D.C. beltway and north again on I-95 into Baltimore, where they took their next rest. They were both tired and irritable and there was still another three or four hours to go. Cuffaro drove the next two hundred miles as Gladstone brooded about the trip.

Cuffaro genuinely liked Gladstone, although he sometimes had to remind himself of that fact. Gladstone had the irritating habit of going on and on over the same point. The small talk they kept up during this last leg of the trip did little to relieve the tension, however. By the time they reached Newark they had both had enough.

"I think I should go back. I'm really worried about the business with Galatolo there alone. I just don't trust him," Gladstone said to Cuffaro.

"I don't like Galatolo there alone either," Cuffaro said. With that, he drove to Newark International and dropped Gladstone off at the Eastern Airlines terminal.

Cuffaro crossed through the Holland Tunnel, then the Queens Midtown Tunnel connecting to the Long Island Expressway and then headed north on 101 to Port Washington. He drove directly to Galatolo's sister's house to meet her husband, Anthony Corinella. Once he parked the car in the garage, he got out, stretched and searched his pocket for change. The best coin to use was a quarter. With the quarter in his hand, he folded his six-foot-six-inch frame back into the car with his head and shoulders prone on the driver's seat and looked under the dash below the steering column. He reached up with the quarter in his right hand, pressed it against two rivets that were spaced about an inch apart, and he listened for the electronic click. When he heard it, he slid out of the front and walked around to the side where he had good leverage. First he removed the bottom section of the rear seat, then the back part. With the seat removed, the specially built compartment was now in plain view.

The compartment's dimensions were three feet by five feet by eighteen inches. Cuffaro began systematically removing his cargo. With Corinella watching, he pulled out M-16s, AK-47s, Uzis, Ingram MAC-

10s and Ruger pistols all fitted with silencers. Corinella was a gun fanatic, and Cuffaro watched his eyes light up when he saw the weapons.

Corinella quickly picked up one of the Ruger automatic pistols, attached the silencer, stroked the weapon and worked the action. "This one's for me, Joe!" he said emphatically.

Cuffaro simply cut his eyes toward him. He didn't care.

They both repacked the weapons in a large box, then put it in Corinella's station wagon. Once the transfer was made, Cuffaro called Paolo LoDuca. Cuffaro had a standing invitation to drop by any time of the day or night, but he knew proper etiquette required a phone call first, especially when doing business. LoDuca gave him the "all clear" to drive to his house.

LoDuca's house could more accurately be described as a palace or a mansion. It sat prominently in Sands Point, one of the wealthiest sections of Port Washington, New York. His neighbors were the social elite, the rich and famous. Jimmy Connors, the tennis star, lived on the same street. As Cuffaro turned into the grand entranceway, he could see nothing but the huge magnolia trees and the mail box with the LoDuca name proudly printed in gold letters. The ten-thousand-square-foot building looked like a ski lodge adorned with polished granite and marble.

LoDuca, head of the San Lorenzo Mafia family of Sicily in New York, greeted Cuffaro as if they were old buddies, talking to him like a *paisan*. Galatolo had been directed by his godfather Francesco Madonia in Sicily to specifically deal with LoDuca in all matters concerning cocaine trafficking in the city.

Cuffaro and LoDuca pulled the large box of weapons over the tailgate of the station wagon and carried it into the house. At the main entrance two massive oak doors with polished brass hardware swung open and LoDuca's wife greeted them as if they were carrying in the groceries.

They passed through the living room, a tri-level ballroom affair with a solid oak and marble bar that stretched forty feet across the room. On a shelf behind the bar was an enormous gold-plated cappuccino machine. Prominently mounted on top of the machine was a gold eagle ornament, reminiscent of the Italian symbol of ancient Rome.

They carried the box down to the basement—no ordinary basement, to be sure. It was three times the size of most homes. The walls and floors were covered with imported Italian marble. There were several fireplaces and wet bars and big-screen televisions. Cuffaro didn't know it then, but LoDuca, too, was a gun fanatic. He opened the box like a kid at Christmas time, and before Cuffaro's eyes he loaded one of the MAC-10s and fired it, full automatic, into one of his expensive Italian leather sofas.

"Dis is great! Dese are beautiful!" he said in his strong Sicilian accent. Cuffaro watched LoDuca stand there posing with the MAC-10 as if he were a thirties gangster mowing down G-men. LoDuca, a short, potbellied man, looked older than his mid-fifties, and fancied himself a kind of modern-day Napoleon. He had become wealthy beyond most men's dreams over the last twenty years by importing one of Sicily's most profitable exports—heroin.

Cuffaro had met with LoDuca several times before as Galatolo's point man, discussing several big deals. As always, LoDuca was a man of very few words. What was interesting to Cuffaro was that this was the most emotion he had ever seen him show about anything. It was especially pertinent at this time because he had previously been warned by Sal Rina that dealing with LoDuca and his associates, Dominic Mannino and Rosario Naimo, was like playing with dynamite. Rina was a freelancer, moving from family to family, using his talents to make money from all sides. Rina lived in Miami now and was partners with Galatolo in some of his criminal endeavors. Cuffaro had gotten close to Rina and considered him an excellent source of information on the Sicilian gangsters. As Cuffaro watched LoDuca handle the rest of the weapons, Rina's words echoed in his head: "If you make a mistake with these people, they'll come down to Florida and blow your brains out themselves. No questions asked. They won't hire anyone, they'll do it themselves."

Cuffaro spent two days in New York, rested, visited with friends, then headed back to Miami. He missed his family and wondered if Marty had made it home okay and how he was getting along with Galatolo. As the highway stretched into the countryside of Pennsylvania south of Philadelphia, Cuffaro pondered the delivery he had just made to LoDuca. Although it was the first time he had carried weapons to anyone else, guns had become a way of life to him. He was carrying a weapon almost all the time now. Some of his drug runs were in the notorious Liberty City section of Miami where he felt naked without a gun. But this delivery had been altogether different, he knew. It wasn't a matter of self-defense—it was a war between two rival factions of the Mafia in New York and he, Cuffaro, had just delivered the assassins' weapons, a load carefully selected to meet their specific needs. The LAAWS rockets were always favorites with the Mafia. They were easy to obtain, disposable and, best of all, could pass through metal detectors. The .410 and 20-gauge, double-barreled, sawed-off shotguns were custom cut. Short barreled with less kick, they were easy to hold in one hand—perfect with a shoulder sling under a jacket. The Ingram submachine gun had been the easiest to find. Originally made for U.S. law enforcement, the police soon discovered its drawback: when used in fully automatic mode, the rounds spray widely in a rising pattern. Mexican and South American military regimes were not picky, however. They soon became major customers for this lethal weapon.

Men like Galatolo and LoDuca made Cuffaro fearful because of their obvious ruthlessness. But at least he knew that they were driven by greed. He understood their motivation. The man who had supplied him with the guns was a different kind of animal.

The guns had been delivered to Scirocco Fan Company by "Willie the Fireman," a bona fide firefighter who wore his City of Hialeah uniform the day he made the delivery. Willie was Alexander Schwerter's patsy, his gofer. There was no question in Cuffaro's mind that the weapons were from Schwerter. Schwerter came from a wealthy family in Chile. His father had immigrated to Chile from Germany and became a multimillionaire. But when Salvador Allende took power in Chile, Schwerter's father was part of the opposition and was assassinated. Alexander Schwerter claimed he led a group of revolutionaries against Allende, avenging his father's death before immigrating to the United States, bringing with him everything of value his family had, including original art work and an Egyptian mummy. He had lived in Miami since the late 1960s, and was described by everyone who knew him as "brilliant." He was also a linguist, fluent in Spanish, German, English and Italian, and continued to serve as a guest columnist for the Miami *Herald,* writing on the evils of the Allende dictatorship.

Cuffaro had first heard of Schwerter through Galatolo as "the German guy." He did not meet him until a few months after he met Aponte, when Galatolo invited Joe to go with him to Schwerter's house. From the onset, Cuffaro considered Schwerter to be someone who could not be trusted. Among other things, Schwerter claimed to have started the Nazi party in Chile, and that he had hundreds of thousands of followers. He also told Cuffaro his cousin was head of the Nazi party in the United States. His militaristic demeanor was equally disturbing. He wore a .45 automatic in a shoulder holster and a .357 Magnum strapped to his hip. This man, who no doubt attributed his looks to an "Aryan" ancestry, lived in a nice, rather run-of-the-mill townhouse on Land O' Lakes Street in the bedroom community of Miami Gardens, but inside he kept the walls covered with priceless art works. Throughout the house weapons, too, were in plain view. There was also a Doberman, which Schwerter said would attack on his eye command. He also bragged about his special alarm system, which operated on a motion detector, and about his personal bodyguards who lived across the street and who kept a twenty-four hour vigil on his home. Schwerter's largest boast was that he was a contract killer as well as an operative for the CIA.

By the time Cuffaro met Schwerter for the weapons delivery, Galatolo and Schwerter had had a falling out. Galatolo had made a series of promises to Schwerter that never materialized. He began avoiding Schwerter and wouldn't even return his phone calls. But Galatolo needed his help when a thousand-kilo load of cocaine, belonging to Galatolo and Aponte, was confiscated by the Bahamian authorities. Galatolo sent Cuffaro to Schwerter to see if he could find out where the load was and if it could be bought back.

When Cuffaro met with Schwerter he was as militaristic and pompous as he was the first time they had met. Cuffaro relayed only the basic information he had been given. The quantity, the approximate day it was seized and the name of the two pilots. Schwerter told Cuffaro he would return to Scirocco Fan Company in precisely "eighteen hours and thirty minutes" with the information.

In exactly eighteen hours and thirty minutes Schwerter walked into the fan company, carrying with him a spiral notebook. As he stood in front of Cuffaro's desk he flipped it open and began to read off the information he had gathered.

"Your aircraft left Los Llanos in Colombia at precisely zero-eight-o-five. At eleven-fourteen hours the aircraft was sighted on radar and Customs launched two chase aircraft from Guantanamo Bay. They chased your pilots until their Piper Navajo was low on fuel. It landed on the Bahamian island of Eleuthera at thirteen-zero-one hours. The cocaine, exactly nine hundred ninety-eight kilograms, was confiscated by the Bahamian authorities. You can purchase it back for exactly one million dollars. I can handle the transaction if you like." Schwerter tore out the page and dropped it on Cuffaro's desk. With that, Schwerter turned and walked out of Cuffaro's office. He was so matter-of-fact, Cuffaro thought he was full of shit. But an hour later, Cuffaro got the shock of a lifetime.

"¡Puta madre! How did you get this information, Joe?" Aponte was not surprised—he was infuriated, and there was an obvious fear in his eyes. "Whoever gave you this information is an informer or a government agent. No one knows these things but my pilots and the agents who arrested them."

Galatolo sent Cuffaro back to Schwerter several more times. Cuffaro ordered a remote-control bomb on one occasion, and on another bought a lethal syringe filled with poison for twenty-five hundred dollars, for what purpose Cuffaro did not know. During this time Cuffaro learned of another, crueler side to Schwerter. Galatolo told him it was Schwerter's trademark to physically remove the heart from his victims and deliver it to the people who hired him, proof that whatever contract he was working on had been executed. This was the man who was respected in the community as a precious-stones salesman.

CHAPTER

4

OPERATION HIGH HAT

As HE LOOKED OUT over the morning calm of Biscayne Bay, salty sweat began to burn Bill Gately's eyes. The only noise disturbing the silence was the melodic thump of his running shoes on the macadam path that paralleled the length of the eastern shoreline on Key Biscayne. It was four miles from the Key Colony condominium where he lived to the northeastern tip of the island and back. During the last six months, beginning at six every morning, he had made the run a religious ritual.

It was August 2, 1982, and tomorrow he would be thirty-three. The workout helped ease the anger he had carried with him to his new home in Miami. From the outside looking in, Miami really wasn't so bad. In fact, there were a lot of good things about this "Latin-American" city, so lost in the heart of the deep Southern culture of Florida. But, from the inside looking out, this transfer had not been his choice, which made it a sour move. A mandate had been shoved down his throat, and it had left a bad taste in his mouth.

Based on false information that had led to Internal Affairs' opening an investigation on him, Gately had been knocked out of the running for a promotion. The worst part was discovering the source. Less than a week after the trial in the San Diego case had started someone quietly filled the hungry ears over at Internal Affairs with some provocative innuendo. Rumor had it that Gately had given his informant Trudeau "carte blanche" to smuggle as much dope as he could—as long as the information kept coming on John Ward and his gang of "air smugglers." The accusations were investigated despite the fact there was no corroborating evidence. Gately had personally arrested Trudeau for his extracurricular activities, and Trudeau had denied the allegation against Gately during his testimony in court. Yet Trudeau had undeniably played both sides of the street. Like any good rat working against his friends, he was betting on the fact that no one would know he was double-dealing. What he didn't know was that the wiretap that targeted the people he was informing on had also captured his activities. Still, it would have been just as easy for Trudeau to lay blame on Gately in the hope of reducing the potential fifteen-year prison sentence he had hanging over his head. Instead, this crook was honest enough to finally take responsibility for his own actions. Regardless, IA dragged out their "investigation" for six long months, which had effectively eliminated Gately from consideration for any promotions. It was months later that George Hardy, the Assistant U.S. Attorney prosecuting the case, indirectly told Gately who had made the false allegations against him.

"I can't tell you," he said when Gately asked.

"I'm not leaving the room until I read through that file," Gately said, pointing to the "red" file on his desk.

Hardy responded by simply walking out of the room, leaving the file behind.

Gately couldn't believe his eyes. He had often thought the allegations had been spawned by some form of jealousy or competition. As it turned out, only one other person had been competing against Gately for the job, the one person he least expected. John Burns, his partner, driven by ambition and jealousy, had labeled him a drug smuggler. It was of little consequence when Burns later apologized and told Gately he had done it for his family. Gately would have gladly stepped aside if it were really true.

Gately's promotion eventually came, but only after the transfer to Miami. He had been virtually banished from the San Diego office, and the case he had worked so hard to make had become a stepping stone for a man who betrayed him.

Gately checked his watch. It was almost 6:45. He had kept his eight-minute pace and he felt good about that. It was the same time he had been so proud of as a marine almost thirteen years ago. As he approached the pyramid-shaped building that faced the bay, the sun had already risen to the point where the heat was burning his shoulders and back. As soon as he stopped, the sweat began to drench him.

"Buenos días, señor. ¿Cómo está? Hace calor, ¿verdad?" the guard waved and greeted Gately as he walked through the beachfront gate to the private community.

"Sí, pero es bueno," he replied with a smile, hoping he had not mispronounced the few words of Spanish he could speak.

The entrance to the building was grand. Glass, marble and rich tropical wood framed the floors, ceilings and walls. The carpet throughout the hallways was plush and spotless. His only complaint was that the air conditioning was excessive. It was ninety degrees outside, sixty-eight inside. He stared at himself in the mirrored ceiling of the elevator as it carried him to the ninth floor. Then he ran down the hall to his condo, turned the key and escaped from the refrigeration to the cool ocean breeze, which rang the wind chimes on the balcony. He always kept the doors and windows open and only ran the air conditioner when guests were visiting. He washed down a multivitamin with twelve ounces of fresh-squeezed Florida OJ, ate a banana and before he had finished taking a shower the telephone was ringing and his pager was going off. Thus began another in the cycle of eighteen-hour days.

Gately had been assigned to the much-heralded answer to Miami's drug problem, the vice president's Florida joint task group. On the outside it was a grand display by the Reagan administration to win votes not only in Florida but around the country. It symbolized the administration's efforts at taking some "very positive steps" to do something about the Colombian invasion of South Florida. On the inside it was less than one hundred DEA and customs agents reassigned from everywhere else in the nation to Miami to do the impossible.

Cocaine wasn't just a "problem" in South Florida. In reality, it was free enterprise out of control. Miami was the hub of a one hundred billion-dollar-a-year cash market. The only thing between the cartel kingpins and their cash was their own greed. They didn't worry much about the law anywhere in South America—what they couldn't kill they corrupted, or overwhelmed by sheer numbers and a bottomless budget. But in *"El Norte,"* it was a different world. The law was an enemy to be reckoned with, corruption was minimal, and prison terms were a reality.

Gately had spent the majority of his first six months reacting to seizures at the Miami International Airport. A typical day would start with the arrest of some courier carrying a couple of kilos of cocaine in his or her baggage. Others would literally risk their lives swallowing as much as a kilo of cocaine. They would cut the finger cots from surgical gloves, insert one into another, creating a double-thick latex pocket they would then fill with ten to twelve grams of pure cocaine. They would tie off the end with dental floss, roll the excess latex back over the knotted end and tie it off again. This created a tightly rolled ball about an inch and a half in circumference. The "swallowers" would then end their twelve-hour fast by soaking each of these cocaine capsules, enough to stop the heart of a charging bull in a microsecond, in olive oil and load their stomachs and intestinal tracts. All this for five dollars a gram. While the average per capita income in Colombia was less than thirteen hundred dollars per year, this twenty-four hour ordeal was worth between twenty-five hundred and five thousand dollars to the swallower. To Gately, these cases were losers, dead ends. If they were caught, the couriers and swallowers had very little information to give. Usually the drill was a cab ride from the airport to some rundown hotel in Miami's once-trendy South Beach. Here they would check in and wait for a telephone call from someone who would pick up the cocaine and pay them off. Even if a courier cooperated, the best scenario would entail the capture of a low-level local thug. His cooperation might take the law the next step up the ladder to his boss, another low-level thug.

The swallowers couldn't really cooperate even if they wanted to. They were carrying instant death in their digestive tracts. It was a virtual time bomb and their gastrointestinal acids were the fuse. As a law enforcement officer there was a moral and legal obligation to save these people from their own self-destructive conduct and then put them in jail. One of Gately's theories was that the Colombians were sending these couriers and swallowers as human dunnage—and diversions. If they made it through, they made a few bucks. If they didn't, they were at no risk and the loss was simply the cost of doing business. Any way you looked at it, whether by design or coincidence, it was a way of diverting the resources of law enforcement away from the real loads. Gately and the rest of the Florida Joint Task Group (FJTG) could, however, take solace in knowing that somewhere every day some Hollywood executive or Wall Street attorney with a cocaine jones was snorting something that had once passed through the bowels of some impoverished and desperate person and then been collected from the toilet of a hotel room in Miami's seedy South Beach.

The real loads, of which there were plenty, occurred daily at the airport. Cocaine came in every commodity exported by Colombia, from fresh cut flowers to canned mangos. Hundreds of kilos, even thousands, would arrive in a single shipment. Every common carrier operating out of Colombia had become a cocaine transporter. Avianca, the national commercial airline for Colombia, was the most frequent violator. But close behind was Tampa Colombia, a cargo airline whose aircraft were the first to be seized following the discovery of over thirty-five hundred pounds of cocaine in a single cut-flower shipment. Running a close third was ARCA Airlines, another Colombian cargo carrier. Even more amazing were the frequent seizures from Eastern Airlines. Eastern, at the time one of the oldest and most respected transportation companies in the U.S., serviced five cities in Colombia with daily flights from Miami to Bogotá, Cali, Cartegeña, Barranquilla and Medellín. Eastern was a major employer in the Miami community and was headquartered at the Miami International Airport. From Miami, Eastern connected every major city in the continental U.S. with multiple daily flights.

As he dried himself off, Gately walked into the kitchen and picked up the pager. Today wouldn't be any different. It was his partner paging him by phone.

"Hey, Bill, I've got a new one for you," Steve Minas started the conversation. "They got a load in a shipment of tropical fish from the Cartageña flight. I'll pick you up in about ten minutes. Be ready this time." Minas laughed as he hung up. He liked pulling Gately's chain about his never-on-time schedule. Gately, on the other hand, could not see the importance of starting at an exact time when you never knew when quitting time would come.

Gately dressed quickly in cotton twill slacks, a short-sleeve cotton shirt, Dockers, no socks—the uniform of the day for Miami's summer heat and humidity. The only problem was where to carry your gun, badge and credentials. The solution for every fed and local narc was to sport a soft leather zipper handbag, commonly referred to as the "fag bag." Gately grabbed his keys and his fag bag from the kitchen counter and in a minute he was walking outside the guard gate on Key Biscayne's main street—only to see Minas sitting there, engine running, air conditioner roaring, as if he had been waiting forever.

Minas was cut from the same mold as Gately. His father had been a local Texas police detective who became a customs agent in the late fifties and who worked his way through the ranks before heading the New York office. Steve Minas was as dedicated a cop as Gately had ever met. He was smart and gave the job a 100-percent effort, no matter what the task. But above all, Gately trusted Minas more than he had anyone since his days in combat in Vietnam. He considered Minas a true friend. Gately also admired his ability to maintain a life outside the agency. His life was a storybook, a wife and two children at home. Gately was always a little jealous that he had never known the kind of deal Steve had outside the job.

"Geez, its about time. What were you doing in there?" Minas jabbed as Gately opened the passenger door. That was another thing about Minas, Gately had never heard him swear. He wouldn't say the word "shit" if he had a mouthful. So instead of referring to "assholes" and "shitheads," Minas would substitute the mundane and innocuous words of "rascals" and "jerks." Expletives such as "fuck," "shit," "damn," "godammit," "cocksucker" and "motherfucker" came out as "geez," "golly," "holy cow" and "man, I can't believe that guy," etc. Gately smiled, and as he closed the door said, "Let's stop for some *café con leche* before we head for the airport." Gately knew that no matter how hurried or excited Minas was about the next case, he would never turn down coffee in any form.

As they pulled up to the CET team trailer on the far southeastern airport grounds, they spotted the team supervisor waddling toward the car. The CET team, the acronym Gately had learned to loathe, stood for "Contraband Enforcement Team," and it was the brainchild of the team's current supervisor Van Capps. Even the sound of his name irritated Gately. He was an arrogant, overweight, know-it-all whose team had scored more cocaine seizures in Miami than the rest of the agency had throughout the country. That part was okay, but that's where it ended for Gately. Van Capps and his troops were "wanna-bes" playing agents. They never knew where to draw the line. They had long forgotten that they were the inspectors, the finders whose job was to profile the cargo shipments and find the cocaine before it made it through Customs. There was no question his team did that well. It was the long-term surveillances, plainclothes operations and secret-agent complex, which infected each of the CET members that hurt more cases than helped. Simply put, they were not cops and did not have the training, understanding of the law or the experience to pull off serious investigations. Their job was to notify the FJTG agents of any discovery of cocaine and to let them do their job.

"We have a surveillance in place and can do the controlled delivery with Metro Dade if you're too busy." Van Capps was always looking for a way to upstage the agents, and this seizure was no different.

"Let's see the manifest," Gately replied with as much arrogance as he could muster. "And by the way, we haven't got a goddamn thing better to do today than to run this case, so call your men back to the trailer. We've already got Group One in place at the Eastern cooler."

It was almost 3:00 P.M. and Gately and Minas had shared the inside of the surveillance van for more than five hours. They sat side by side operating a camera, which from the inside of the van looked like a periscope in a submarine. On the outside, the camera's eye, mounted on top of the van, could turn 180 degrees. The tricky thing was knowing how to adapt to its limitations, like when a suspect walks too far out to the side and out of the range of the camera.

The industrial park warehouse off Milan Dairy Road had been the first stop for the tropical fish shipment. They had been videotaping the two stooges, dubbed Juan One and Juan Two. They followed them with the camera as they walked past the van carrying Styrofoam containers.

Although the Juans eventually walked out of the view of the camera, Gately and Minas could peek through a back window, camouflaged from the exterior. They watched the two Juans empty the fish-filled Styrofoam containers into the nearby ditch.

"I lost count at two hundred-eighty. This place is going to be ripe tomorrow with all those dead fish rotting back here." Gately stretched and yawned as they watched them dump the styrofoam containers of tropical fish into the ditch behind the warehouse. Then suddenly the monotony changed. The van started rocking as the two Colombians started trying the doors of the van. By now Juan One was on the roof staring dead into the camera lens.

"Puta madre, la policía," Juan One called out to Juan Two.

"Tango units move in. They've made the van. We have one on the roof of the van." Minas was on the radio now calling in the troops from their positions surrounding the warehouse. Within seconds the place was crawling with agents and Metro Dade uniforms.

The two Juans were the first to give up. There were two more in the warehouse sweating up a storm repacking the 294 kilos of cocaine into cardboard moving boxes.

Two hours later Gately and Minas were still processing the paper that accompanied every arrest and seizure. Every FJTG case had to be reported twice to satisfy the bureaucrats in both DEA and Customs.

Gately heard the words almost before Minas began to speak.

"You know, Bill, we've got a meeting set with the guy who works in the enclosure in less than an hour."

"Steve, I hate to tell you this, but I've been spending way too much time with you. I'm beginning to think I can finish your sentences for you," he said.

"I'll page him to this number and let him know that we'll be a little late and where to meet us," Minas said.

It was definitely going to be another eighteen-hour day.

It was 6:15 P.M. and the sun was still hot. The afternoon thunderstorm had blown over and all that remained of the rain now was a steamy ground mist that sizzled under your feet. The employee parking lot at Miami International Airport seemed to spread out forever, but for some reason this guy was right on time and in the exact spot they had agreed on over the telephone. He walked over to Gately and Minas and politely introduced himself.

"Hi, I've been waiting for you. I'm Ray." He extended his hand to Gately and then to Minas.

An hour later Ray was still talking to them across a corner table of a small *café cubano* near Coral Gables. Gately and Minas were almost sitting at attention. Ray wasn't your garden-variety informant. First, he wasn't a crook, which in itself was amazing. Second, this wasn't the first time he had tried to help the cops. It was just that no one had ever believed him before. After all, what could some Dominican mulatto immigrant who wasn't in the dope-smuggling business possibly know that the feds didn't? Ray not only knew what was happening, but he had been eyewitness for the past seven years to one of Miami's smoothest-running smuggling operations. What amazed Gately and Minas were the details, names, dates and places that Ray could recall. He would make a great witness in a historical case against this operation.

The more he talked the more the wheels in Gately's head started to turn. Ray could become the nucleus in a sting that could unravel this conspiracy. Ray told the story of how the skycaps in the U.S. customs enclosure were openly smuggling hundreds of pounds of marijuana and cocaine daily right under the watchful eyes of the agency. He identified the culprits by name and identified the different schemes they employed. But that wasn't all. Ray told the story that would open a Pandora's box at Eastern Airlines. He laid out a dozen ramp-service employees, skycaps and supervisors who were using Eastern Airlines aircraft, communications systems, baggage and cargo controls to smuggle and distribute tons of cocaine into and throughout the country. Ray was not only knowledgeable, he was connected to all these people by virtue of his employment. He was in the perfect position to reach each one of them if he agreed to work undercover.

Ray had not been easy to find. Minas and Gately had spent virtually every spare hour, much of it at home, going over more than a hundred employee records and the "abandoned" drug seizures collected daily in the U.S. customs enclosure. Trying to find a common denominator to the mysterious equation was extremely time-consuming. Nothing seemed to fit or match, the only consistent factor being the seizures of baggage and cargo found first by airline employees as "unclaimed" at the turnstile within the customs area. The drill was, the airline service rep would pull all unclaimed luggage from the turnstile and try to reconcile the baggage claim with the passenger manifest. Once it was determined that no match could be made, the luggage was carried over to the customs supervisor, opened and searched. What was amazing about each of the seizures was that there was no effort to conceal the drugs. The luggage or cargo was simply crammed full of cocaine or marijuana, nothing else. It was as if there was no need to conceal anything.

Gately and Minas had researched the previous two years and had added up a little more than ten thousand pounds of cocaine and eighteen thousand pounds of marijuana, "abandoned" in the customs enclosure. It did not require the intellect of a rocket scientist to conclude that an "internal conspiracy" among the airport and airline employees was in high gear in the customs enclosure. If a customs inspector showed the least bit of interest, the pick-up man would simply walk away from it. The "abandoned" suitcases were the only ones that didn't get through the covert scheme to the waiting marketplace. One could only speculate how many bags full of cocaine had escaped detection.

All they needed was a rat, someone who was part of the seemingly bulletproof scheme who would turn in their friends for the right deal.

Gately and Minas had also discovered that there were more convicted felons and suspected drug traffickers working in the customs area than there were waiting for an initial appearance in Magistrates Court after a major drug bust. Virtually a rogues' gallery. Everything was represented, from rape, sodomy on a minor child, murder, armed robbery, burglary, weapons and drug charges. These and others graced the background of over thirty employees who had unlimited access to the customs area.

Gately and Minas had narrowed the list to three prospects who on the surface appeared to be honest people simply trying to make a living. All three would have potential knowledge of the "internal conspiracy," but it was a crapshoot who, if anyone, would admit anything. Fear of reprisal had to be the first thing that would enter one's mind if one was approached by the law under such circumstances. Gately and Minas had even contemplated approaching one of the rogues they had identified and testing his greed to give up the deal and work against his friends. Then they met Ray, a godsend. In fact, he had been one of the three "honest men," but their first meeting with him was the result of an inadvertent tip. During one of the long afternoons that were all beginning to run together, Gately and Minas walked into the customs enclosure to get a feel for the place. Before they approached anyone, a customs inspector reached out to Gately and Minas, offering to help. He had watched them every day and knew a little about their research on the past "abandoned" drug seizures. Frank Gomez walked by the two agents, slowed his pace, turned back in their direction, leaned close to Gately and whispered Ray's name as a possible informer. This had made it easier. Their first choice turned out to be the best informer any agent could hope to have.

The meeting on August 3, 1982, stretched to over three hours as Ray provided Gately and Minas with enough details to initiate an airtight case. It was a case that would later become one of Customs' most recognized drug-smuggling investigations against an internal conspiracy. But it would not come easily.

*   *   *

By February 8, 1983, much had changed. Gately and Minas had been transferred from the FJTG to the Miami customs office. First stop was the premiere money-laundering group of the eighties, known as Operation Greenback. The next stop was the newly formed NIC (Narcotics Internal Conspiracy) group, "newly formed" being the polite way to describe this group.

Right after their first interview with Ray, they had spent the next two days preparing a Special Operation proposal to fund and support an investigation designed to infiltrate, identify and destroy the conspiracy within the Miami International Airport. Not only was this proposal badly received by the FJTG upper management, but management summarily transferred Gately from the cargo conspiracy group supervisor position to the marine group. His division director, a DEA agent who had spent the last four years in headquarters processing FOIA (Freedom of Information Act) requests, wanted nothing to do with the airport case and openly exhibited intense irritation if he heard Gately mention it to anyone. His expertise seemed to begin in the bootlicking department and end somewhere between talking superficially about police work and black Magic Marker skills retained from his FOIA experience. Matters quickly deteriorated between Gately and Mr. FOIA.

A DEA inspection team was in Miami and wanted to take a look at DEA's drug warehouse, which consisted of fifteen to twenty forty-foot trailers loaded with seized marijuana in a huge underground warehouse. DEA had provided for outside security contracts with off-duty Metro Dade police officers, but had not figured on maintenance of the facility. What no one realized at the inception of this operation was the enormity of the problem of storing several hundred tons of seized marijuana. Nor did they realize that the Miami sewer rat population would acquire a taste for the Colombia-grown herb.

"Hey, Gately, I've got this tasking from division for a work party at the marijuana warehouse," Mr. FOIA began. "I want you to gather up the customs agents in your group, report to the warehouse, issue brooms and square the place away. We've got a full-blown inspection at the division, and the warehouse is on the list for this afternoon." Gately began to smile as if he had been set up for the punchline, but soon realized that Mr. FOIA was incapable of any form of wit or humor. He was serious.

Gately remained seated, looked up at him and with a poker face replied, "My customs guys aren't trained in the fine art of the broom, nor do they have any affection for the DEA mascots living in those trailers. So I suggest that if you want your warehouse to look pretty for your inspection team you round up some DEA agents, issue brooms and square the place away the right way. By the way, don't worry about the rats—they don't eat shit."

Mr. FOIA then made the fatal mistake of letting his anger persuade him he was the better man. As he reached out to inflict corporal punishment he found himself pinned to one of the pillars in the office, with no one to cry to for help.

Gately made two stops that afternoon—the first to the office of FJTG deputy director Jim Schmand, a customs agent who took the DEA position. Schmand had the type of personality that would have driven him to scrub the warehouse floor on his hands and knees with a toothbrush in order to avoid any conflict with DEA.

The second stop was Bill Rosenblatt's carpet. At the time he was the U.S. Customs regional director of investigations, and one of the most respected men—by Gately, too—in the agency. Rosenblatt's baritone voice broke the ice with a complete and accurate rendition of events leading up to Gately's appearance in his office. Known for his ability to cut through the bullshit and find a solution to problems, Rosenblatt transferred Gately to Operation Greenback that afternoon.

Greenback was Rosenblatt's personal creation, the very first money-laundering investigative unit anywhere in Western law enforcement. Greenback was the only unit with vacancies, and it was the perfect spot to relocate Gately to cut the tension at the FJTG.

At the same time, Rosenblatt also reviewed and wholeheartedly supported the proposal for Operation High Hat. The operation was named for the *Luftwaffe*-style hats worn by the skycaps working in the customs enclosure. In fact, Rosenblatt proposed that Gately and Minas be placed in the same group and immediately settle in to develop the investigation. Operation Greenback worked smoothly for a couple of months, but the agents in the group began to grow irritated and jealous of Gately's and Minas's sudden disappearance. This forced Rosenblatt's hand and, in spite of the existing agreement between DEA and Customs to house all of their drug investigative resources at the FJTG, Rosenblatt formed a new drug unit within the Miami customs office.

So came about the NIC group. The title "group" was a little grand for the unit. It was comprised of Gately, Minas and Ed Mederos. Mederos was a former Metro Dade police detective who had joined Customs in 1978, a no-nonsense agent who had an excellent reputation among real cops. A Cuban by birth, he and his family had fled when Castro took power. He became a citizen, educated himself through college and served in the U.S. Army during Vietnam. His goal was to become the customs attaché in Havana, if and when Castro was ousted and democracy restored to his beloved homeland.

Gately came to believe that the friendships formed in this small unit would last all three men a lifetime. They soon developed the kind of relationships that made the eighteen-hour workdays fun. For Gately, it was like working on a project with his brothers. Gately also relished his advantageous position among the threesome. Since Minas was of Mexican descent and Mederos of Cuban descent, Gately never missed an opportunity to yank their chains, playing on the age-old rivalries between the two Latin cultures. He could always count on their falling for it. Of course, they also rarely missed the opportunity to turn the tables on their Irish/Italian partner. And, just to bust his butt, they usually did it in Spanish. Gately could only watch while his partners stood laughing at him.

The two overall-clad, Miami International Airport maintenance men were a little more than they seemed. Gately and Minas knelt on the cinders of the pitch rooftop of Concourse E. It was not the most comfortable place to spend a Saturday afternoon, but what was about to happen would make up for the discomfort.

Among the Eastern Airlines employees whom Ray laid out as drug smugglers were Ruy Martínez, Fernando Tapia and his brother Miguel Tapia. Eastern's Flight 505 from Bogotá was at the gate and the passengers had already entered Customs. The baggage handlers were busily mistreating luggage under the watchful eyes of the customs CET team and were about finished with their task.

"Ed they've got the flight almost completely unloaded and the CET team is about to do their thing."

"Nothing new here in the parking lot. No sign of Miguel," Mederos responded to Minas as he released the talk key on the customs radio and it squelched back at him. Mederos passed the word to the surveillance team in the Concourse C parking area.

The CET crew had been inside the belly of the Boeing 727 for over a minute now, as Gately and Minas watched from their rooftop perch. As the four customs inspectors began to appear at and then exit the cargo door of the aircraft, everything looked routine. There was no sign of anything untoward. It looked as if Ray's information, for the first time in the three months, had not panned out.

"Let's wait awhile and see if they perform some magic down there," Gately said with some confidence and a little anxiety.

This case had started working so well that anything that didn't work on time, exactly as planned, was a total disappointment—the exact opposite of any other drug case. There seemed always to be delays, information that wasn't on the mark and a lot of dress rehearsals. But not in this case so far. Ray had been phenomenal. Not only had all of his information been corroborated, Ray was now working undercover. He took to it like a fish to water. He listened intently to briefings before each meeting and always insisted on instruction in the law. His performance was of Oscar-winning caliber.

In the few months he had been "under," he had been able to lay the groundwork for his cover. He let the others know that he desired to live the good life and wanted into the internal conspiracy. At first Ray sought out assistance from the skycaps to help him bring in small drug loads in passenger baggage. They eagerly jumped in and instructed him on the "proper" way to get his drug shipments through Customs without a hint of a problem, for the right price, of course. What they didn't realize was that Ray was wired and always in full view of the video camera. In the first two months, Ray had roped in a dozen players and established himself as a new and important smuggler in the customs enclosure. The others soon brought him into their deals, seeking his assistance, advice and contacts. Minas and Gately had set Ray up in a waterfront penthouse on Biscayne Bay and their recording studio was established in the adjacent condo. Four microphones and three hidden video cameras fed the studio day and night with some of the best sting footage ever collected by law enforcement. Not only was each of the smuggling ventures preplanned on video, the payoffs, debriefings and celebrations were also captured in stereo and in living color. The preceding week was the first time Ray had been able to establish a real connection with the Eastern Airlines gangsters.

"Ed, we've got some movement up here. There's a supervisor's truck parking by the cargo door." Minas started his blow-by-blow of the action. "Okay, he's out of the truck and headed for the cargo door. He's opening it and going into the belly." Then silence on the radio. Gately and Minas sat speechless and watched. The next two minutes seemed like an eternity.

"What'd he do, get lost in there?" Gately broke the silence and at the same time the supervisor's head appeared in the opening cargo door.

The radio squelch broke the tension even more as Gately and Minas anxiously waited for the next move.

"The surveillance team has Miguel approaching the Concourse C parking lot in a blue Mercury Marquis. Looks like the shit is on, gentlemen." You could hear the hint of excitement in Mederos's voice.

"Do you see what I see?" Gately smiled as he looked to catch Minas's reaction.

"Holy cow," Minas said, as the supervisor started to shove four extra-large and extra-heavy Samsonite hardsided suitcases toward the cargo doorway. There was no question that something wasn't legit about those bags. The supervisor's head was on a swivel, like a pickpocket in a crowded convention hall, and he was working hard to get the bags quickly out of the door into the bed of the pickup and out of sight.

What happened next was as smooth as butter. He secured the cargo door, jumped into the cab of the truck and drove off toward Concourse C. The Eastern Airlines New York flight had recently docked at the jetway and passengers were disembarking. He pulled up to the baggage conveyor belt, climbed over the truck bed in a quick vault, and in the same motion began to change the claim checks on the four bags. In a matter of seconds, the suitcases were on the conveyor belt and on the way into the terminal as domestic luggage from a nonexistent New York passenger.

Minas continued his account of this activity over the radio to Mederos, but it ended abruptly as he felt Gately grab his shoulder.

"Steve, let's get the hell over to Concourse C, I don't want to miss this."

In lightning speed the two "maintenance men" were down the roof access ladder and on their way. The rapid radio squelch was keeping pace with the activity being witnessed by the Hialeah police, who were serving as the surveillance team.

"The bags are still on the belt . . . wait, we've got an Eastern skycap looking hard for something . . . Okay, the bags are on his hand truck and he's headed for the parking lot," said the voice on the radio.

Gately and Minas weren't listening anymore because they were a step behind Mederos as they all watched the next move.

The blue Mercury was in the parking lot about fifty feet from the entrance to the baggage claim area. Miguel Tapia leaned casually on the open trunk lid. The skycap, as if directed by radar, went to him without exchanging a glance or a single word. As the hand truck came to a halt in front of the Mercury's open trunk, Tapia reached down and very routinely began to load 220 pounds of cocaine into the trunk of his car.

And routine it was, indeed. A daily event for Ruy Martínez and the Tapias. It was a no-risk event that allowed four million dollars in cocaine to hit the market each day. The only thing they truly had to rely upon was the efficiency of the airline itself. This was the first cocaine score High Hat would document and it was the key to the unraveling of the Eastern gang.

It was one of many skirmishes that would eventually add up to a success for this operation. But the road to victory was being obstructed by a series of dirty battles for personal credit that were being fought on the inside. The old adage that "everyone hates success in others" was alive and well in this case. On the hit list prepared by Ray were two U.S. customs inspectors who worked in the enclosure. This had forced Gately and Minas to not only notify Internal Affairs of their corrupt activities, but they were forced to work with the epitome of the B-movie IA ass-hole, Special Agent Ken Wagner. Wagner was the kind of guy who would turn in his mother for an "atta boy." Ray's first words to Gately and Minas after his initial meeting with Wagner were: "Man, what the fuck was that 'thing.' No way I'm workin' for *that* asshole."

Wagner tended to remind those who knew him of the James Arness portrayal of the Martian monster in the 1957 version of the sci-fi film, *The Thing.* He resembled the seven-foot (he was only six feet eight but moved like a sloth) blood-sucking, guard dog–eating, vegetable man capable of regenerating himself at will. However, while *The Thing* was fried to a cinder with about one hundred and twenty thousand volts of electricity, Wagner had so effectively insulated himself from any form of responsibility that nothing, not even a massive electrical shock, could even begin to expose his incompetence.

The two customs inspectors represented about 2 percent of the defendants in the investigation and were even less important in the overall scenario. Nevertheless, because of this internal involvement, Wagner and his boss, Assistant Regional Director Vennis "Vince" Moore, sought to steal the case by first attacking the credibility of Mederos and Gately, simultaneously opening cases against both agents. Even Wagner knew the potential for success and career status in the internal affairs division if this case were to succeed. However, when the cases against Gately and Mederos turned out to be unfounded, he went so far as to hide the video-taped evidence they had been collecting. His desperate attempt to control the case by controlling the evidence was thwarted when a letter appeared from the U.S. Attorney mandating that the tapes be maintained by Gately and Minas. The prosecutor, Mark Schnapp, was a fairly new guy on the block, but Wagner's bullshit did not intimidate nor impress him. After this failure, Wagner and Moore began to spread the fairy tale that the two inspectors were out of control and the case had to be shut down to protect the integrity of the agency. This theory was so asinine, even Internal Affairs couldn't find the words to explain it. No one except Wagner believed that the two inspectors had corrupted a hundred Eastern Airlines employees, as opposed to the truth that one hundred employees simply tempted them into their present criminal situation. Yet Internal Affairs had the gall to say that these two "bad apples" would corrupt other customs employees. In fact, the inspectors were involved in less than a tenth of the smuggling activity in the customs enclosure. As one of the skycaps said, this was just giving them enough to make the corrupt inspectors think they were getting their money's worth.

But the *coup de grâce* came when Wagner pushed the envelope by suggesting to his new group supervisor Jimmy O'Brien that there needed to be a meeting between Rosenblatt and the regional director of internal affairs to discuss the future supervision of the investigation. This was to be their frontal assault, to once and for all take the case over and run it their way. It was ironic that O'Brien would be the one to level the charges of corruption against Gately, Minas and Mederos. He had recently been transferred to Miami after being defrocked from his position as regional director of internal affairs in New York. O'Brien was caught with his hand in the proverbial cookie jar—he had been writing himself airline tickets on government travel request forms for his personal use to see his family in Miami. For his twenty-five-thousand-dollar "mistake" he was busted down to a group supervisor position and shipped to Miami—where he wanted to go anyway.

During their meeting, which only Gately and Minas were allowed to attend, because O'Brien had accused Mederos of being corrupt, tempers were flaring.

"Youz guys know dis case is an Internal Affairs case. You know, Bill," O'Brien added with his typical bravado. "We're both from New York, we know about deez things."

"Well, you're right about one thing, we are both from New York," Rosenblatt blasted back. "But, this isn't an Internal Affairs case. Never has been, never will be."

In his best New York style, O'Brien rudely interrupted him. "I'll tell youz why this is an Internal Affairs case. Your agents can't be trusted with this type of information. That's the reason Mederos isn't in the room."

Gately was enjoying the sight of O'Brien trying to match wits with Rosenblatt, who had probably forgotten more in the last minute than O'Brien would ever know. Visually, O'Brien was a man who could easily pass for a rat walking on his hind legs, still sporting his 1960s DJ hairstyle—buzzed-cut short on top, long on the sides, slicked back into a duck tail—except O'Brien's DJ was a little different on the top. He only had three hairs on his forehead, barely visible in bright sunlight.

"What? What do you mean? Who can't be trusted?" Minas stood, with a fist clenched, arm cocked and ready to reorganize O'Brien's face.

Gately reached out and grabbed his arm and Rosenblatt jumped up like a referee.

"Okay," Rosenblatt said, arms outstretched, "I'll handle this. You guys don't have to listen to this." He diplomatically dismissed Gately and Minas from the room.

Despite the emotionally charged expletives being bantered about, the only one that took Gately by surprise, was when he thought he heard Minas say "shit."

As they walked out and the door closed behind them, Gately and

Minas heard the voices become louder. In less than a minute they heard furniture suddenly begin to crash. And by now Rosenblatt's voice could be heard a block away. He had just thrown O'Brien out of his office.

"Hey, man, you said 'shit' in there, didn't you?" Gately asked as if this were the revelation of the century.

They were still both laughing as O'Brien scuttled out of the office. Even his three hairs were disheveled.

Rosenblatt had saved the investigation from being prematurely taken down.

For the next twelve months Gately, Mederos and Minas continued to work the case. With the help of their informant, the three agents racked up a series of successes. They had identified over a hundred airport and airline-industry employees, and had sealed federal indictments against fifty-four.

During that time, Ray had been approached again by Ruy Martínez, but not to smuggle drugs. Martínez had a lot more to offer this time. He had been led to believe that Ray was connected to corrupt officials and asked if he could get information from the customs and DEA computers. Martínez supplied Ray with a steady stream of names to run in the agencies' computers. He paid five thousand dollars for computer runs and up to twenty-five thousand for the investigative file, which they would dummy-up with misinformation. The names helped Gately, Mederos and Minas piece together the Colombian hierarchy. One of the names he furnished the agents was Carlos LaFaurie. This Colombian of French descent was a documented drug smuggler and money launderer who was a high-ranking member of the Medellín cartel. He appeared to be the man in charge of the Eastern Airlines smuggling operation.

But, as their successes surfaced, so did their detractors. Their most formidable was still Internal Affairs.

After nearly eighteen months of infighting, Internal Affairs was pressing even harder to arrest the two corrupt inspectors. The level of resistance was becoming almost nonexistent. The three NIC agents were alone fighting this battle. By now Rosenblatt, content with its success, and weary of the internal struggle, agreed that it was time to shut down Operation High Hat. Gately, Mederos and Minas argued that they had just broken through to the higher echelon of the operation and could now attempt to go after those on the outside and eventually the Colombian connection. The more vocal Gately's resistance to shut down the case became, the more pressure was brought on him.

It was a losing battle. The final meeting was called to discuss how to take down the case. Rosenblatt, his assistant special agent in charge Leon Guinn, who had been Gately's first line supervisor in Miami, Mederos, Minas and Gately were all in the SAC's office. The discussion centered on logistics. How long would it take to shut it down? How many indictments were there? How many people were needed to make the arrests and process the evidence?

Gately tried one last time. "Look, we now have some Colombian connections, and we know this was a lot more organized and bigger than we first thought. As long as Ray's still there and he's still trusted, there's more we can do. IA's just blowing smoke about why they have to arrest these two inspectors. They just want to hang them on a cross for every customs employee to look at. There's still bigger fish to fry."

Rosenblatt cut him off. "Let's get something straight here. This case is over. We've discussed everything we needed to discuss." Everyone stood and followed him out of the room. Gately sat a few seconds, then he himself followed. As he approached Rosenblatt, the SAC turned and said to Gately, "About that transfer we discussed, you've got two weeks to find a home. I hear Phil Bowen, the SAC in Seattle, has a group supervisor job open."

Two weeks after he had transferred to his *de facto* exile in Blaine, Washington, Gately was called back to Miami to help shut down Operation High Hat. For the next six months he flew back and forth between Blaine and Miami to prepare the case for trial and for the many hearings and court appearances that preceded trial.

During this time, DEA had gotten wind of their high-level target, LaFaurie, and the outstanding warrant for his arrest. DEA did the unethically predictable—they quickly arrested LaFaurie. What they did next was despicable, but Gately thought it pure genius. They arrested and "turned" LaFaurie, without even consulting Customs. In exchange for his freedom he eventually gave them every Eastern Airlines employee in New York, Chicago and Los Angeles, as well as his Colombian connection in sworn testimony. Gately watched DEA take credit for the entire case, while nary a word was uttered by anyone in Customs.

Operation High Hat was a matter of personal pride, although in the end it was a professional loss. But High Hat also served as a real education. It was the first time Gately had witnessed the strength and depth of the Colombian cartels. It had also proved they were vulnerable. Even the cartel could be stung. This newly acquired knowledge would serve as an indispensible tool for his next challenge.

CHAPTER

5

THE DOCTOR, THE MEXICAN AND MR. LONG

THE HILL OVERLOOKED a valley that stretched all the way to the coast. They were in the remote region of La Guajira, and the closest thing to modern civilization was the small coastal town of Riohacha. The sun was at its midday peak and the noise from the gasoline generator that ran the compactor was deafening. Leo Fraley was drenched with sweat and covered with the thick resin from the thousands of plants he had been handling. He was working side by side with "Sam," and together they oversaw sixty native Andean Indians. It was the Indians' job to take the harvested plants and separate the buds from the stalks. Fraley and Sam were in charge, with quality control their main concern. They made sure that each bale, when compressed, contained approximately fifty pounds of marijuana and that each was wrapped with seven layers of heavy mill plastic to prevent water damage. Once it was weighed and checked, each bale was marked with its approximate weight. It was an important element in the transportation equation. Weight and balance of any load played a key role, whether the vehicle was a truck, a plane or a ship.

Fraley enjoyed working with Sam because he had a great sense of humor, even with his broken English. Sam's true name wasn't easily pronounced or remembered, so his Colombian friends called him Samuel, the name he had been given by the Catholic missionaries. Sam had received his formal education from these priests, who traveled throughout the northern coastal region of La Guajira bringing the Spanish language and their Christian message to the natives. He later learned English in an environment that contrasted starkly with his earlier education, while working as a seaman onboard the freighters that carried marijuana.

In his own culture, Sam was a *cacique,* or a chief of the Chibcha. Historically, the Chibcha were farmers and weavers, not hunters. The Spanish conquerers exploited them and forced them into servitude as farmers of their traditional European crops. Sam told Fraley that no one really knew their origin for certain, but their ancestry dated back ten thousand years. He said when the first Spaniards arrived the Chibcha were at war with the Caribs, Indians who had invaded the coastal regions and mountain valleys. After more than a century of oppressive European colonization, the indigenous people of Colombia began to resist the Spanish rule. The Spaniards imported millions of African slaves to replace the Chibcha, whom they either slaughtered or drove away from their settlements. Eventually the Chibcha lost their culture and their people. Once the largest tribe in the land, the Chibcha now comprised less than one percent of the total population in Colombia.

In Sam's estimation, their lot in life had not changed much during the past four hundred years. The Chibcha were still farming for the Europeans. But today, marijuana and coca replaced coffee and sugar cane. Velasco befriended him over the years after Sam had helped him gain the rights to harvest tons of marijuana on the land owned by his native people. Most of his youth Sam lived the primitive life of his people, where everything they had, from their food to their clothing, was made from the region's natural resources. But today Sam was a rich man who coveted material things, although he still didn't have his own home. His most prized possession was his new 911 Turbo Porsche.

One day during a recent stay in Velasco's home in Cartageña where Sam kept his car, Sam offered to take Fraley for a ride after observing how he admired the German sportscar. At first Fraley thought Sam was simply showing off by keeping it at a steady cruising speed of ten miles an hour. But he soon discovered that Sam simply didn't know how to shift through the gears—or, for that matter, that there were gears to shift through. After spending most of the afternoon at a local cantina, Fraley suggested to Sam that he was less drunk and that he should be the one to drive. Reluctantly, Sam agreed. Within the first ten seconds, Fraley had the car well in excess of a hundred miles an hour and headed straight out of town toward the coast. Sam's expression was priceless. His face displayed a combination of fear and excitement when he realized just how fast his $200,000 imported automobile could go.

At Sam's request the natives shut down the generator to refuel it. As the roar of the engine sputtered to a halt, Sam and Fraley heard the familiar sound of Velasco's bush plane. The blue and white Cessna 206 was making its approach to the makeshift landing strip about a half mile from the harvest site. In his native language, Sam quickly dispatched a driver to pick up Don Winces.

In a few minutes the Toyota stake bed truck, bouncing and jolting violently as it traversed each new bump and hole, approached the work area. The door opened and Velasco's large body emerged from the cab. Velasco, cutting a path through the workers, whose average height was about five feet, reminded Fraley of a scene from *Gulliver's Travels*. His six-foot-seven-inch frame was never a sight one got used to seeing, but this time the expression on his face was concerned, and Velasco's powerful stride did not inspire the usual calm.

As he watched Velasco come closer, Fraley continued to direct the workers who were preparing the bales to be loaded on the trucks. The closer Velasco got the more Fraley sensed something was wrong. He watched as the Indians backed away, lowered their eyes and their heads as Velasco passed them. Fraley had struggled to comprehend Spanish, but he more importantly had learned to read body language, especially Velasco's, during these past few months. Reading emotions had become necessary for survival. Sensing their anger or discontent had become an intuitive and incisive skill because their display was so subtle when compared to the direct behavior he witnessed almost daily back home.

"We've had a great day here," Fraley said cheerfully. "I think there are over eight thousand bales ready to truck to Barranquilla. This place has been busier than Macy's basement at Christmas time. We damn near processed the entire harvest."

But this effort at good news had no apparent effect on Velasco's mood.

"We must go to Bogotá. There is trouble," Velasco told Fraley. Fraley knew that when he said "we," it didn't mean him necessarily. But he was included, almost by default, because over the past few months Fraley had essentially become Velasco's shadow. Going to Bogotá wasn't a problem anyway. He had learned that their meetings always included the best and most food he had ever had. All the drug traffickers tried to outdo each other. If one had five-course meals, the other had to host a six-course meal. If one had maids the other would hire butlers. If one had a Mercedes-Benz pick up his guests, the other would have a Rolls-Royce. It was a never-ending game of one-upmanship.

"Come. Leave this work to Sam. We will go back to my home in Bogotá."

The following night a dinner meeting was held at Velasco's home. The estatelike structure had a view of the city and the Plaza de Bolívar. The house was decorated like a lavish palace, and expensive original art adorned his walls. To top it off, it was located on Embassy Row. His neighbor on the left was the Cuban ambassador, and on his right was the American ambassador.

As his shadow, Fraley had learned to keep a certain distance and never directly address the others unless he was first spoken to. Although he was not an invited guest and was not introduced, he did share the house with some of the world's most notorious drug lords. And that evening they all attended—not only the Romero brothers, whom he had met in Los Llanos, but José Rodríguez-Gacha and Pablo Escobar, and a half-dozen others. Fraley had heard Velasco talk about their volatile natures, but this time he said they were on the verge of declaring war.

"Esos condenados Cubanos . . . Deberíamos matarlos nosotros mismos . . . Pinchi comunistas!" These were the kinds of hate-filled, emotionally charged words Velasco repeated to Fraley afterward. Fraley didn't know the exact meaning, but what he was able to figure out was that an international political incident had just occurred and they were ready to kill the Cubans over it. What he figured was that a group of M-19 guerrillas had kidnapped some diplomats in Bogotá, hijacked a plane and flown to Havana to seek political asylum. Fraley knew the Cuban ambassador who lived just up the street from Velasco was in deep shit. What he couldn't understand was why in hell all these drug dealers were so worried about political crap, in spite of the importance politics played in Colombian life.

The activities of the numerous guerrilla groups that existed throughout the country were, he discovered, particularly significant. The M-19, or *Movimiento 19 de Abril,* emerged in 1972, taking its name from the 1970 presidential elections, which the group claimed the National Front candidate won through electoral fraud. The real victor, it said, was the former military dictator who was then head of a populist party that maintained a great appeal to the middle and lower classes. The M-19 became the first guerrilla movement in Colombia, its members declaring themselves nationalists, unlike many of the other, more orthodox Marxist groups. Of these, M-19 maintained the closest ties with the Cubans.

Fraley also understood the emergency of the situation due to the recent seizure of the embassy of the Dominican Republic in Bogotá by guerrillas. Fifteen ambassadors were held hostage for several months, including America's diplomatic envoy. A big part of the problem, as these drug traffickers saw it, was that newly elected president Belisario Betancur was leaning toward establishing a more cooperative environment with the guerrilla groups. They were astounded when he offered unconditional amnesty and released more than four hundred political prisoners, including dozens of top guerrilla leaders. In the end, though, Fraley always came back to wondering what any of this had to do with dope. These men had shut down everything and he couldn't see the logic in it.

He soon realized that politics had everything to do with running drugs. He came to see how these drug lords could create a common bond with the Colombian Army by coming to their aid, aid that could be in any form, from manpower to weapons—but principally with money. It was the perfect way to create a situation where not only the military but the entire government seemingly "got in bed" with the big cartels. And of course it became clear that their disdain for these political events was based on purely economic considerations.

The cost of doing business increased astronomically during these political crises. The Colombian government would institute the equivalent of martial law throughout the country. In the capital city and other metropolitan areas such as Medellín and Cali, the cartel utilized the services of "retired" members of the Colombian military intelligence units. These Colombian military officers, who were at one time the counterparts of American CIA agents, frequently performed mercenary services for the cartel. Even though they were "retired," they still had military credentials, vehicles, weapons and access to information concerning troop movements throughout the country. During these lockdown situations the cost of their security services would double, even triple, overnight.

After two months in Bogotá, living in Velasco's shadow in his posh estate, and continuously witnessing the barrage of political rhetoric, Fraley suggested to Velasco that he move out of the main house and live with the workers. His excuse was that it was better for him to spend as much time with them to gain their trust and acquire a better command of the language. In spite of recent inactivity, Fraley had been working with the men, organizing and improving their system. He was a natural with numbers, in assessing a situation and coming up with a solution. But Velasco also helped him develop a business. He told him the key to a successful business was to compartmentalize everything—by which, if one thing were to go wrong it would not have a devastating effect on the others. This also allowed the opportunity to carry on while the broken spoke was mended. Velasco also taught him how to delegate. "One task at a time" was the rule, and of utmost importance was always being around to supervise.

Fraley had moved into an apartment in the most densely populated district of the city, *Centro Internacional*. He spent much of his time becoming familiar with everything the City of Roses had to offer. Bogotá had undergone amazing urban growth, from 500,000 people in the 1950s to more than 5,000,000 in the 1980s. In spite of the crowding, Fraley preferred the eternal spring weather of the city to the humid tropical conditions in Los Llanos. Both areas were located at approximately the same distance from the equator, but it was Bogotá's elevation of over eight thousand feet that influenced its near perfect climate.

On a Saturday afternoon in August 1981, Velasco came to Fraley with news that would certainly change his life forever.

During a card game, as he scanned the room, Fraley noticed the expression on the faces of Rodrigo and the others who were playing suddenly become submissive, which told Fraley that Velasco was nearby. When Velasco entered the room, it was clear there was something wrong. It wasn't just another problem. There was something much deeper.

"Ya know Winces, I should get paid a commission for all I've taught yooz guys about your business," Fraley offered. Velasco stood there stoically, not in the mood for humor.

"Necesito hablar con Leo—en privado, por favor." Velasco's statement brought an uneasy calm to the card game, and in unison Rodrigo and the others dropped their cards to the table and quietly left the apartment.

"My friend, your compadres have not paid," Velasco said bluntly. No further explanation was necessary. Fraley knew this could be a death sentence for him. He felt his heart creep up into his throat. Fraley had thought about what he would do a thousand times if this ever happened to him, but now reality had caught up with him.

"The office is very angry about this situation," Velasco went on. Fraley knew the term "office" meant Escobar and his compadres. "You know that we have sent three loads already, totaling six hundred kilos. They paid for the transportation, but our people never received the merchandise. I have tried to contact DeVitto at all of his numbers," he said as he showed Fraley his phone book. "Some have been disconnected and he is never at the others. No one will put me in touch with him." He leaned closer to Fraley, placing his hand on his shoulder and lowering his voice. "There has been some very desperate talk. Some have suggested killing you to send a message to your friends. They see you as the only contact to DeVitto."

Fraley's first reaction was total disbelief, then anger. What had this to do with him? But he already knew the answer—he was the only connection. The money was missing, the dope was missing and the finger was pointing at him.

"Dead men can't make money for anyone. What good am I to anyone with a bullet in my brain? I've always said as long as Uncle Sam prints money I'll always have my share. I'm worth a hell of a lot more to you alive. Tell your office that."

"My friend," Winces began, "I have been told I do not have a choice. I am supposed to kill you, but I do agree you have been a great partner these past six months and everyone has profited from your ideas."

"Look, I know you got to do what you got to do. Your people made a good deal, they just made it with the wrong man," Fraley said with confidence. He had rehearsed it a thousand times and now it actually sounded convincing. He sure as hell hoped it sounded as convincing to Velasco.

"Let me see what phone numbers you got," Fraley said, pulling out his own pocket phone book to compare numbers.

"You must reach them, my friend, or there will be nothing I can do to help you. You must speak to him." Fraley knew Velasco meant business, and that he truly had no choice—the shipment was not Velasco's; the drugs belonged to the others, Velasco was only the transportation man in this deal. It was a favor. And now, Velasco was being held responsible for either getting the money or sending the proper message.

"If we don't have an answer, we are going to have a war. Now, they either want him, they want the drugs, they want the money or they want you. In any case, they will have something," Winces told Fraley with urgency, then added, "We will return to Los Llanos tomorrow. There is too much pressure for you to remain here."

Fraley spent the night alone in the villa. He had heard Velasco fly over-head in the Mitsubishi hours ago. And Velasco had left with no explana-tion, which added another dose of grief to his already difficult situation. Actually, he wasn't exactly alone—Velasco had left behind his two con-sorts, but they were afraid to speak to Fraley. It was as if they knew he wasn't long for this world.

Christ, Fraley thought, this place was like a palace a million miles from civilization. Why couldn't he just hang out here and run this opera-tion and the one down river, at least until these guys got over being stiffed by DeVitto? That no-good motherfucker had known from the beginning he was going to rip off these Colombians on this deal . . . Fraley was letting his feelings of helplessness get the best of him, but he was unable to fend them off.

He was so goddamn mad now he couldn't think. All he knew was that he was going to survive this thing the same way he had done everything else in life. He had to turn disaster into opportunity. He would convince these rich, jungle-dwelling spics that he was worth more to them alive than dead. He knew he could move their cocaine into the States better than anyone they had. He had met most of their pilots and some of the people they were relying on to get their coke in and their cash back. He could have cut his own deal and gone around these people. They trusted too easily. No wonder DeVitto and others like him had ripped them off. With a little work and a lot of luck, Fraley thought he could become the only honest man in America whose word these Colombians could trust.

It was a long night, but Fraley began the day by racking up a telephone bill for Velasco that would set new standards for a day's calls to the Ohio valley. After several tries, Fraley was able to reach his partner and alleged friend, Bobby Povich.

"Here's the way it is," Fraley spoke sharply into the phone, "I'm here, you're there, I don't know what went down, but you gotta come up with somethin'. If I don't hear from youns in twenty-four hours, these Colombians and me are comin' up there and we're gonna do what we gotta do. I know youns was my partners and all, but the bottom line is, you ain't gonna like me when you see me."

"Calm down! Settle down!" Povich replied.

"What do you mean settle down? I'm sittin' down here in the middle of this goddamn jungle and these people are looking at me for answers. Well, I've called everywhere I know and nobody's answerin' their phones, and you're the only unlucky bastard who was home. So now I'm telling you, I'm giving you the message that somebody better call me. If they don't, I guarantee you, we're on our way up there and I'm gonna show them where every one of you motherfuckers live, including DeVitto."

The next day, all day, Fraley sat by the phone. Velasco had returned with his Colombian partners. The two Romero brothers and even Don Pedro were present. When Don Pedro showed up, Fraley knew this phone call meant his life. Don Pedro was "the heavy," and even Velasco breathed a sigh of relief whenever this man left the room. Velasco had spoken highly of Don Pedro many times and referred to him as the *"general."* He had been a high-ranking officer in the Colombian military. He demanded discipline and perfection even in the drug trade, his new profession. Although less well known than the flamboyant Pablo Escobar or José Rodríguez-Gacha, Don Pedro Ortegón was considered one of the leading drug lords in Colombia. Even before Fraley had been formally introduced to him, he knew he was "the man."

By noon, the phone call came through. It was Bobby Povich. Fraley was told that when DeVitto and his men were on their way to pick up the drugs, DeVitto had an automobile accident. It was explained to Fraley that DeVitto had been hospitalized for the past two and a half months and was practically on his deathbed.

What Povich did not tell Fraley was that they had figured DeVitto was going to die, so Povich and his three partners took off with the load, made their own deals and were holding the profits as well as the nine million dollars that belonged to the "office."

As Fraley relayed the story to Velasco, he gave a simultaneous translation to the Romeros, who immediately started contacting their connections in Miami, New York and, it seemed, every other major city in America. By mid-afternoon, their connections in the U.S. had verified some of the story. But they were still looking to Fraley.

"You must go get the money," Velasco told him.

At least, in America, Fraley thought, if he had to be on the run, he could blend in better and get around easier. But he felt he had to give it a shot. If for nothing else, maybe he could get a cut of it.

Over the next couple of days, Fraley was on the phone again, threatening everyone. "When I get there, shit's gonna be heavy, if yooz don't come up with the dope or the money. Youns all are the ones who put my dumb ass down here, now I'm gettin' even with all you cocksuckers. And, I've got every fuckin' greaseball down here ready to go. I won't have to do anything. All I have to do is aim them at yooz."

"Don't be like that Leo, it wasn't meant to be that way," Povich said, trying to calm Fraley.

"You didn't even tell me the truth, you bastard. I found out you were *already* in the coke business with DeVitto. You were supposed to be *my* partner, you back-stabbin' asshole, and I had to find that out second hand through Bobby. You motherfucker. I ain't makin' two nickles and you're up there livin' high on the hog bringin' in all kinds of cash. Where the fuck's my money from these loads anyway?

"Well don't worry, it's here—"

"Don't tell me not to worry when these people are ready to skin me. Now I'm tellin' yooz we're gonna be right in your fuckin' front door, or wherever we gotta be if that money ain't put together by the time I get there. If it ain't, you better just get to your grave, dig up your goddamn ancestors and jump in, 'cause that's the way it's gonna be."

Fraley hung up and sat shaking his head, steaming. What did he do to make them turn on him like this? First they tell him to go down there, cool off and learn the business—a business he wanted nothing to do with in the first place. He thought to himself, the only reason he was there was because of a beef he had with some cop in North Carolina. "Goddamn!" he said aloud. Now, he thought, they were all out making loads of money while he was down in the jungle walking on pins and needles.

Fraley knew he was in deep shit and he began thinking of those "Colombian neckties" he'd heard the Indians talk about so often, where they don't cut your neck from side to side, but from top to bottom and then pull your tongue out for not keeping your word. What happened to friendship and loyalty? The dope business had brought the worst out in everyone. It was every motherfucker out for themselves.

During the next seven days Fraley took calls from DeVitto's gang, Povich, Big Joe, Little Joe, Tubby and half a dozen other people on the periphery of the deal. They called to give him daily updates, but there was still no money. Meanwhile, the Colombians took their verification of Fraley's findings a step further—they visited DeVitto who was, in fact, in intensive care in a New York City hospital. The combination of these two pieces of information helped Fraley deflect the heat from the Colombians for a little while.

But it was the conversation he had with Velasco's right-hand man, Rodrigo, that really bothered Fraley. Fraley couldn't shake his words: "Sometimes people aren't what they seem." Rodrigo told him how, after he and Velasco were arrested in Florida several years earlier, Velasco was able to whittle down a ten-year sentence to three after he cooperated. That was all he said. Fraley didn't know what to do with this information. He decided the best thing to do was just keep quiet.

The Colombians were now demanding that Fraley return immediately to the United States to retrieve the money. In a matter of a few days Rodrigo delivered a Canadian passport to Fraley with the name Ralph Leavitt. Velasco provided transportation for the first leg of Fraley's journey in the Mitsubishi, and upon arriving in Nassau Fraley checked himself onto an Eastern Airlines flight to Toronto, via Miami.

Before Fraley left Colombia, he made arrangements through Tubby for his wife to meet him in Miami at the airport. When she saw him, she was to make eye contact but not approach him. She was to follow him out of the terminal. If things looked bad he would walk away. If everything looked cool he would approach her first.

His Canadian passport worked like a charm, enabling him to whisk through Customs as if he had a long layover in Miami. Once through the various checkpoints, Fraley walked into the terminal area.

As planned, Fraley and his wife made eye contact. Fraley continued to walk away down the corridor toward the exit as his wife continued to look toward the gate area. After a few minutes Fraley walked back, they made eye contact again, then for the second time he walked away from her. As he turned around, looking over his shoulder to see if she was following him, he noticed her still staring at the gate area. "What the hell's goin' on?" he asked himself. For the third time, Fraley repeated his motions. Again, they made eye contact. But still she continued to wait with her gaze fixed on the gate area. Then he realized that during the last ten months he must have gone through a radical physical metamorphosis. He had trimmed forty pounds off his body; at a hundred and forty-five pounds, he was now a mere portion of his former self.

He walked up behind her and with a smile said, "Are you gonna follow me out of here or what?"

The next day, Fraley set out to accomplish his mission. But in the back of his mind, he just wanted out of the cocaine business and back into the marijuana business. That was something he understood, something he could work with. For the next three days, Fraley was in contact with all his former partners, who were still giving him the runaround. To placate him, however, Bobby Povich sent him a Mercedes and Bobby DeVitto sent a man with a hundred thousand dollars and a Social Security card, New York driver's license, voter's registration card and a birth certificate.

Fraley was now using the name Richard Carbone. DeVitto was recovering from his injuries and had promised to help Fraley resettle his life and make good on the nine million owed to Escobar. With his new ID, the cash from DeVitto and a car to move around town in, Fraley was able to get an apartment in Pompano Beach.

He was on the telephone every day to Velasco, Ortegón and DeVitto, promising the Colombians and threatening his former partners. Before his first month back in Florida, DeVitto had made arrangements to meet with him in Pompano Beach at Frank's Restaurant.

"Leo, I cannot tell you how sorry I am all of this happened. I won't make excuses for Povich and the boys," DeVitto's voice was still strained from his injuries and he was walking with the aid of a crutch.

"You don't have to say anything for those assholes takin' advantage of you while you was dyin' in some hospital." Fraley sat directly across from DeVitto and looked him straight in the eye as he talked. "Bobby, I don't think I've got to explain in any detail what is gonna happen if that money isn't put together soon and sent south."

"Leo, there's something we have to talk about. This is the last thing I'm gonna do in this fuckin' business." Fraley searched for DeVitto's smile and energy. It wasn't there like it had always been before. He looked like a beaten man. DeVitto held his chest and took a deep breath and then continued. "Leo, you never really know who your friends are until some shit like this happens. There's something else—this cocaine business of mine, it's all yours, the customers in New York, Boston, everything. I want you to take it. I'm done with it. I'll have the money together in Miami by tomorrow. Harvey will meet you in Great Inagua. Once it's there it becomes your problem."

WELCOME TO GREAT INAGUA, read the sign at the small airport. Fraley's trip this time brought back the memories of his first experience on this tiny island. He had chartered a flight from Fort Lauderdale with some of the additional ten grand that DeVitto had given him after the dinner at Frank's. He made his way to the Hotel Spanish Cay, where DeVitto told him to wait for a phone call. It was two days before Fraley heard from a man who introduced himself as *"Vivora."*

That night he met the man who called himself "The Snake." He was a mulatto with a heavy New York accent. Leo noticed that the coiled snake tattoo on his forearm and bicep appeared to move as he carried the five oversized suitcases into the hotel room.

"Harvey is waiting for me at the airport. He sends his sympathy to you. I wish you luck with those butchers who work for that fuckin' pig, Don Pedro. I would not bring the *plata* to Colombia for him. I do not wish to die."

Leo paused and contemplated this deal. His thought was: Snakeman thinks Ortegón will kill him if he brings the money to him and I know he will if I don't.

"Yeah, you could get mugged in the subway too, and get run over crossin' the street, hazards of the business. Don't worry about it. It's my problem now."

The mulatto looked at him and said, "Before you get to Colombia you will have to deal with the police chief here on Inagua. He is a petty, greedy man with a large ego and a small brain. He has been on Don Pedro's payroll for the past three years and he knows you are here." Fraley's tattooed friend turned to walk out of the room. *"Buena suerte, mi amigo."*

"Good luck to you, too," Fraley said, then muttered, "asshole."

He was alone. Well, he had five Samsonites with the Burdine's complimentary name-tags still attached. They were filled with nine million dollars in cash. The first thing he did was reach out to Velasco. He tried him at the Los Llanos farmhouse, the villa in Cartageña and the palace in Bogotá. The best he could do was speak to Rodrigo and to Sam. Velasco had either just left or was on his way back. The second day Rodrigo called the hotel room and told Fraley that he had reached Velasco at Los Llanos, passed on the good news, and that Velasco would be on his way to Inagua the following day.

The next three days were filled with the monotony of counting the money—and eating the worst pizzas he had ever had. He had been warned by his mulatto friend that the chief of police would be watching, but there had been no sign of anyone near the room. Fraley had not dared to walk farther than an arm's reach from the door to his room. At least he could see the beach from the walkway outside the room and the breeze from the Caribbean was constant and cool. The maid had become his best friend and brought a beach lounge chair to his room. She delivered cold beer and whatever food she could get from the nearby market. He caught up on South American baseball and soccer and whatever local entertainment he could get on the television. Every other day he could get CNN and catch the news a day late. Fraley was sure of one thing: he might have to wait, but nothing was more certain than that Velasco would come for the money.

Five days passed and still no sign nor even a call came from Velasco. It was about sunset when Fraley, standing in his doorway, spotted out of the corner of his eye the maid talking to a Bahamian cop. She was across the street carrying his grocery order back to him. The cop had her by the arm and was pushing her toward the hotel.

She finally broke away from his grasp, ran toward Fraley, dropped the grocery bag at his feet and sprinted through the parking lot to the bus stop. She had not said a word, but Fraley knew from the terrified look in her eyes that the chief of police had arrived as predicted. Fraley took another drag on his cigarette, picked up the grocery bag and stepped into his room, closing the door and throwing the latch. He had already stashed the suitcases under the bed and in the closet. He pulled the sixer of beer out of the bag, broke them free of the plastic loop and dumped them into the Styrofoam cooler.

He was cracking open the carton of Marlboros when he heard the knock. Fraley opened the door with the safety chain still in place.

"Good afternoon, Mr. Leavitt, I am Chief of Police Ian Stephenstown. I would like to see your passport and travel papers." All Fraley could see were the words HER MAJESTY'S ROYAL BAHAMIAN POLICE FORCE on the brass badge attached to the white pith helmet.

The police chief was a black man, so black he was blue. He was six feet tall and sinewy. The tendons and muscles in his forearms moved with every motion of his hands. His starched white uniform was something from a James Bond movie or the official Bahamas travel brochure. The policeman was articulate and his Caribbean accent was laced with the proper British English of his grandfather's slavemasters who had colonized the islands in the sixteenth century.

Fraley unlatched the door and opened it with a smile. "Can I get you a cold beer, my friend?" he greeted the policeman as he walked into the room.

The policeman pushed the door shut and took off his eighteen-karat gold framed Porsche sunglasses and placed them into his breast pocket. He placed his left hand on the butt of his holstered .45 caliber automatic and politely said, "Just your papers, mon, I'm not a drinker."

Fraley turned to the dresser and picked up the Canadian passport that Winces had given him before he left Colombia. He handed it over, hoping he could remember the information in it. The policeman took the passport into his right hand and opened it with thumb and forefinger, smiled from ear to ear, cutting his eyes from the passport to Fraley and back. He closed it the same way and handed it back without a word. Then Stephenstown walked to the closet, opened the louvered double doors, looked inside, and then cut his eyes back at Fraley. There was no question in Fraley's mind what would come next. This guy was no different than any other corrupt cop. He wanted something and Fraley was caught in the predicament of not having the authority to give it to him. As the possibilities of this problem raced through his head, Fraley contemplated everything from killing this guy to becoming his friend in the next few minutes. No way would he survive if this cop took the cash. It would be the last nail in his coffin.

"You should put your name on your luggage, Mr. Leavitt. Your flight will be here early tomorrow. I will come by and drive you to the airport myself. Be ready by 7:00 A.M., Don Pedro would not understand if you were late." The policeman looked up at him, smiled and walked toward the door, picking up the carton of Marlboros without breaking his stride. He touched them to the brim of his helmet as a salute. "See you in the mornin', mon. Get some rest, and don't worry, you are safe. Her Majesty protects you here."

Despite the assurances of Chief Stephenstown, Fraley spent most of the evening standing guard outside his room. After all, who was this guy that he should take him at his word? How did he know this son of a bitch wouldn't be back to take the money, kill him and take his chances with Ortegón? He wasn't anything to this policeman other than caretaker of the money. This was probably more cash than he would ever earn protecting loads for the Colombians at the Great Inagua Airport.

Seven o'clock took forever to come. Fraley was basking in the early morning ocean breeze when he heard a car approach from the winding street leading up the hill to the marketplace and the hotel. He felt a rush of relief when he saw Velasco's head towering over the windshield of the policeman's Jeep.

They had probably put the top down just to accommodate the big man. He had never thought of it before, but suddenly he realized that Winces had actually become a trusted friend. He wasn't like anyone he had known in the mob. There were not many Oxford business graduates in the Mafia. But then again, there aren't many Colombian drug types with those credentials either.

As the Jeep came to a stop, the chief of police stepped out. "Good mornin', Mr. Leavitt. I trust you slept well. Her Majesty's Royal Bahamian Police Force would have it no other way."

"My friend, it is good to see you are well rested. And how is our cargo? Did you receive the *plata*?" Winces bellowed out to Fraley.

"It's all here." Fraley had barely gotten the words out when he saw a

Nissan pickup truck arrive with the police insignia on the door and a light bar afixed to the roof of the cab. The two Bahamian cops got out and headed directly to his hotel room. They produced their own key, opened the door, went inside and a few seconds later they were carrying the five suitcases through the doorway. The chief of police, smiling from ear to ear, looked Fraley directly in the eyes as if to say, "It was always mine to take, anytime." Fraley had been silent during these two minutes of this cops-and-robbers love-in. He walked over to Velasco, extended his hand and, as he pulled him close to embrace him, Fraley's temper got the best of him.

"You motherfucker, don't you ever leave me hangin' out in the wind like this again. You coulda told me that these assholes were your loyal servants."

Velasco stood silent for a second, nodded his head and said, "You have done a good job here. Don Pedro will be pleased. Come, we have to hurry, there is a weather front approaching."

Fraley walked into the room, grabbed his duffel bag, took a last look at the Spanish Cay Hotel and climbed into the rear seat of the chief's Jeep. Twenty minutes later they were airborne in the Mitsubishi MUJ2. But this ride was a little different than the last one to Los Llanos. Once again the plane was a flying bomb. There were eight twenty-five gallon plastic drums filled with JP4 where the four rear passenger seats were supposed to be.

"If those money-grubbin' Japs only knew the needs of the modern-day smuggler," Fraley said to himself. He was sure they would have designed the aircraft to accommodate them. From the extra fuel, Fraley knew there would be no stops in Aruba or anywhere else. It was back to the Colombian jungle.

As the doors to the plane split open and the steps unfolded, Fraley could see two sets of headlights driving toward them. The halogen lights stopped right under the wing. The light was still blinding him, but he could see the insignia on the grill, RANGE ROVER. They were met by several of the Los Llanos workers, who immediately gathered the five Samsonite suitcases and packed them into one of the all-terrain vehicles, while Winces and Fraley boarded the other.

The jungle ride to the house was beautiful. It was dusk and the sky was aglow with the colors of the passing sunset. As they entered the house, Fraley saw Winces do something he had never seen him do before. Winces walked in, but only after touching the mezuza.

Not only is he a wealthy Colombian educated in England, he's a Jew, Fraley thought.

"Tonight we will eat and rest. Tomorrow we have guests. They are anxious to meet you. You have done well. He will be pleased to see you have brought his money." Fraley watched him leave and walk away with the young women. In the distance he saw him reach over the front of two of the women, put his hands between their legs and carry them off, laughing.

One of the young women stayed with Leo. *"Señor, venga conmigo. Yo le enseño su cuarto."* Leo figured she must have been talking about where he was to sleep. But he really didn't care. She was a joy to look at and he would have followed her anywhere. As he walked into the bedroom he realized it was actually larger than his home in Youngstown that he shared with his uncles, brothers and sisters. The bed was covered with a mosquito net that rose to a point over a bamboo ring ten feet above the bed. The floor was covered with an enormous Persian rug.

"¿Cómo se llama?" Fraley strained to get the accent correct as he addressed the young woman.

"Me llamo Graciela," she purred back to him. Her hair and eyes were so dark and full, her smile so pretty and innocent, Fraley began to feel guilty for looking at her with the absolute lust he felt. She took him by the hand and walked him into the bathroom, started the water in the tub and carefully began to undress him.

"Christ, if they're gonna kill me they sure are being awful nice about it," he muttered under his breath as he watched Graciela move across the room.

Fraley's eyes opened slowly as the morning light pushed through his eyelids. He tried to focus but swore he was caught in a dream when he saw the beautiful brown shape of Graciela next to him.

"Don Pedro, kill me now," he said aloud. He could smell the morning air of the jungle and the sweet scent of the beautiful woman next to him. He rolled over on his back and rubbed his face. To his surprise, his face felt clean and smooth. He smiled as he recalled Graciela had given him the royal treatment, shaving away his beard and neatly trimming his mustache. He felt like the man who had been given his last wish. The sacrificial lamb, he thought, had been properly prepared to meet Ortegón. He could smell the wonderful Colombian coffee brewing. He slipped out of bed and into the *baño,* turned on the shower, stepped inside and began to soak himself awake. His clothes had been carefully hung in the bedroom closet—another good sign. He dressed and walked out into the hallway leading to the great room, feeling the cool breeze of the ceiling fans, which turned silently above.

"Buenos días, amigo." Velasco's voice boomed out, "I trust your evening was filled with Graciela's kindness."

"Where *do* you find these women?" Fraley smiled.

"We have been blessed with all the beauty and wealth the world has to offer, my friend. You gringos know nothing until you experience Colombia. Come, let's have our breakfast." Velasco walked briskly through the great room to the wall covered with beautifully carved teak French doors. He opened two as they walked out onto the veranda circling the entire house. The green hills covered with shimmering coffee plants just beyond the house stretched toward the horizon. They sat at the table that had been prepared for them, adorned with a white linen cloth and set with a gold and silver service. The fresh mangoes and papayas filled a bowl large enough to have fed Fraley's family when he was a kid. The two women who served them moved carefully, as if not to disturb their conversation.

"Don Pedro will be arriving within the next two hours from Bogotá," Velasco predicted. Again he told Fraley how pleased he would be to receive the nine million from New York. "There have been many problems with the New York operation. We have lost some of our best men to the fucking DEA and Customs." Velasco's words were filled with contempt every time he mentioned the American feds. It was ironic how much Velasco sounded like Fraley's mentor, the "Mad Bomber," when he spoke about the problems with the feds. They could always count on buying off the local cops, but it was a crapshoot with the feds which way they would go.

"This marijuana shipment we are preparing is the largest ever. Over two hundred fifty thousand pounds is on the mother ship set to depart next week. We have much work to do to meet this deadline and we must move the product to the seaport in Cartageña."

Velasco ate voraciously as he talked. Fraley listened, intent on continuing to learn all he could from this man, whom he knew could eventually help him cement his niche in this operation. Somehow he would become indispensible to these men—or die trying.

Fraley sat silent as they drove to the runway, contemplating his meeting with Don Pedro, the man who commanded so much respect from Velasco. Or was it fear? If his operation was larger than Velasco's, then he must command a small army, air force and navy, Fraley thought.

The sunlight pressed through the jungle canopy above and the approaching noon hour filled the cab with stifling humidity, despite the rushing air conditioner in this $40,000 Jeep.

"No air conditioner like a Cadillac's," Fraley said to Winces as they both mopped their foreheads. They stopped at the south end of the runway and stepped out into this man-made anomaly in the jungle. The ten-thousand-foot airstrip had been carved into the jungle floor by the enormous road grader and earth mover that were still parked next to the two fuel tanker trucks. The faded red, white and blue of the ESSO insignia was barely visible on the trucks.

"Don Winces, the airplane is approaching from the north," the driver called out to Velasco. The crackle of the HF radio in the Range Rover broke the silence again. *"Aero Comandante mil, a Los Llanos . . ."* Leo assumed the pilot must be asking for landing approach information. Speaking in English, the universal language of air traffic, the driver guided the pilot in. He had a distinct New York accent, Fraley noticed. "Winds are calm from the south, runway is dry. Good afternoon. You are late, we were beginning to worry."

The distinctive shape of the Aero Commander 1000 came into sight at about five thousand feet, a mile south of the runway. The over-wing design, which carries the two turbo-prop jet engines, and the broad fuselage, which sweeps upward to the tail and to a point at the nose of the aircraft, signaled the most popular smuggling plane in the region. It could carry over a ton of cargo, fly at 350 knots and had a range of 2,250 miles, without adding extra fuel tanks. But its most popular feature was its short take-off and landing capabilities. At a cool million dollars a pop, the Aero Commander was an expensive corporate jet, prop airplane. But, to these *nuevo* Colombian aristocrats of the drug cartel, it was another tool of the trade and part of the cost of doing business.

As the aircraft touched down and the dust plumed behind the landing gear, the heat rising up from the runway and the jet exhaust made it look like a mirage moving toward them. The howl of the powerful engines deafened everyone until the pilot began to feather the left propeller.

From the very instant Fraley first set eyes on him, Don Pedro Ortegón commanded an incredible presence. His physique was clearly that of a man who took pride in his appearance. His face reminded Leo of the paintings he'd seen of the Spanish *conquistadores*. He could see his chiseled facial structure despite its being completely covered by a perfectly shaped salt-and-pepper-colored beard. His beard blended into a coal black mane. It was a combination that Fraley found almost stunning.

Winces walked toward Ortegón, both men greeting each other with obvious respect. Even though Velasco stood a head taller and was noticeably larger, Ortegón's aura was without question the grander.

"Don Pedro, gracias por venir. Estamos aquí para servirle."

Ortegón replied with respect, *"El placer es mío."*

These niceties reminded Fraley of the elongated greetings the Mafia wise guys bestowed on the bosses to show their respect and fear. The next man out of the airplane was the bodyguard. He carried a ten millimeter chrome-plated pistol in a shoulder holster. He greeted Velasco with a smile and a firm handshake, then produced a large cigar. He carefully cut the tip, properly preparing it before handing it to Ortegón. As he lit it, Ortegón drew in the flame and puffed a billow of thick white smoke, savoring the flavor.

"Departe de nuestros amigos en Cuba," he bragged to Velasco.

This guy was boasting about his friends in Cuba, Fraley thought, but what he needed were some new friends in the U.S.A. With that Fraley seized the initiative and extended his hand to Ortegón.

"Mucho gusto, Don Pedro. Me llamo Leo Fraley." Ortegón drew on his cigar and stared at Fraley with piercing black eyes. He gripped Leo's outstretched hand, then turned away abruptly, walking to the open passenger door of the Range Rover. Velasco and Fraley climbed into the back seat of the four-by-four as Ortegón turned to the rear seat and looked at Velasco, then in perfect English said, "So this is the man who brought my money from those *pendejos* in New York. We need to clean house there, as they say in America."

Fraley laughed a respectful laugh, one that recognized the wit of Ortegón's statement but also the serious nature of his obvious dislike for the people and problems he was referring to.

"Their man was frightened of you. He would only come as far as the Bahamas," Fraley told him.

Don Pedro smiled again, drawing on his cigar. "The dead need not be frightened."

The next day they were all well rested. They had arrived fairly early and slept until late the next morning. Lunch was a veritable feast—a beautiful presentation of tropical fruits and vegetables to complement a well-seasoned meal. Fraley noticed that everyone acted much more reserved around Don Pedro, an obvious sign of respect. Fraley was only just beginning to understand how important this man was.

As they were eating, Velasco began his soft-sell pitch to Ortegón. It was an uncomfortable position for Fraley, but it was necessary and he knew it could save his life. What drove home the significance of the meeting was that it was being conducted entirely in English, for his benefit.

"Our new lab is operating ahead of schedule, thanks to the help from our new friend. Leo has a gift for organization. He has put everyone on a schedule and has the crew doing twice the work in the same amount of time. The crews are on standby when the planes arrive. They are loaded and fueled in a matter of minutes."

Velasco was doing his best, but Ortegón's reaction remained stoic. His only response was a slight nod of approval. Velasco continued: "We are preparing the plan to transport the two hundred fifty thousand pounds and should be ready by the end of the week. Colonel Vargas's men will begin loading their trucks tomorrow.

"It's very nice of my brother-in-law to assign his battalion to aid us in this endeavor. After all, the military is supposed to look out for the welfare of our country." Ortegón's laugh filled the room as he expressed his amusement. "But your brother-in-law has always been too easy on his men," he said to Velasco. "That is why they lack discipline. That is also why I left the military. There is no resolve left in our government. The people must control the wealth of the nation. It is only through our operation that Colombia grows wealthy on the cocaine and marijuana that we produce. We have become the true government. We rebuild our cities, provide housing and jobs for our people where our government has failed." Then Ortegón turned to direct his next statement at Fraley: "That is why America is also losing its ground. Because its people have no discipline. We are making billions selling marijuana and cocaine to Americans. We don't sell here in our country. We are supplying their weakness." He paused for a moment. No one made a sound. "There are only two kinds of people in America who possess discipline. As a graduate of your military's training I had the opportunity to observe American military men. There is discipline, but I believe not enough." He paused again, then continued: "The others with discipline are the disadvantaged. They have discipline because they must. The lazy Americans should have the great opportunity to struggle."

Silence filled the air. Fraley knew he was expected to say something diplomatic.

"Well, that's how I've always been able to make money," he said. "There's always a demand for something, and I've always made it a point to provide it, as long as the pay is good. It's like I've always said, as long as Uncle Sam's printin' money, I'll have my share."

"Well, since you are a gambling man, let's see how you do at *barajas*," chuckled Don Pedro. Everyone at the table laughed too. They all understood, except Fraley. It was a relief when he saw the table in the other room, and figured that Ortegón simply wanted to play a game of cards. But before they began playing, Ortegón gave Winces a certain look. Winces understood, then turned to his bodyguard. *"Ve por el Coronel Vargas."* The game began and continued for thirty minutes, then Colonel Vargas arrived. When he did, the smiles and jokes came to a halt. Fraley was the only one at the table who did not know what was about to happen.

"Colonel, so nice to see you," Ortegón addressed Colonel Vargas as he entered the room.

Fraley knew something was wrong. His words were friendly, but his tone was piercing. And why would Don Pedro be speaking to him in English? He knew this was at least partially intended for him.

"We have some unfinished business to discuss. Gentlemen, excuse us."

Ortegón rose from the table, placed his cigar in his mouth and motioned for Velasco to follow him. But just before he stepped away from the table he addressed the colonel again.

"Colonel, have you met our new friend Leo Fraley from the American Mafia? He has been our guest here for several months. Mr. Fraley, please join us at the *cabaña*."

"I see Captain Sánchez is with you, Colonel. Good. Please ask him to join us."

Inside the *cabaña*, Ortegón stood at the head of a table while Velasco and Fraley stood on his right waiting for the two soldiers to arrive.

"Please, gentlemen, be seated," Ortegón said as his bodyguard took up a position to his immediate left.

Before the colonel had enough time to get comfortable in his chair, Ortegón began questioning him.

"The last shipment of cocaine I contracted with you arrived in Miami incomplete. Two kilograms were missing."

Fraley couldn't believe he was questioning them about two measly kilos. He knew there were at least five hundred kilos in every load that went out.

"Don Pedro, there have been many people who have handled this merchandise since it left my control." The colonel attempted to maintain his composure, but he was obviously nervous. "I can assure you that every gram you entrusted to me was shipped."

"You are correct, Colonel. Perhaps it is not you I should be addressing. It is Captain Sánchez." As he turned to the captain, he casually took a long draw from his cigar. Captain Sánchez was now obviously uncomfortable. Fraley had seen this look before—guilt masked by surprise. The captain has been caught with his hand in the cookie jar.

"It is Captain Sánchez who has stolen my property," Ortegón continued. "And this is not the first time, is it Captain Sánchez?"

Fraley quickly excused himself and headed for the door. Behind him he could hear the captain pleading for his life.

"Perdóname, por favor, Don Pedro . . ." Sánchez frantically and emphatically begged for his forgiveness.

Ortegón wasn't the slightest bit moved by his plea.

"It is your problem Colonel Vargas. See that you correct it now."

By the time Fraley reached the grand old palm tree a few yards from the entrance, two shots had been fired into Captain Sánchez's forehead.

Fraley had seen plenty of dead bodies before, after the mob finished their business, but he had never before been present at a cold-blooded killing. He wasn't about to watch it happen.

A few minutes later Fraley was summoned back into the *cabaña*. He took a deep breath, finished off his cigarette and headed back. As he opened the door to step inside, two men were carrying out the body of Captain Sánchez. Fraley looked at the colonel, who was still in shock and now covered with the blood and brains of his captain. He looked at Ortegón and Velasco. Velasco made eye contact, giving him a look that told him to say nothing.

"Gentlemen, we have a card game to finish," Ortegón said, taking another drag from his cigar.

They walked back to the main house to continue the game. Fraley knew the killing had been staged for his benefit. It was their message to him. He was receiving a reprieve on his death sentence, but Ortegón had made it clear, those who were disloyal paid with their life.

For the rest of the evening Fraley played Colombian blackjack, drank Mexican beer and smoked Cuban cigars with his new employers.

The report from the Ruger Blackhawk rang out like a cannon, shattering the silence that came over the jungle at dusk. The bobcat dropped in midair as it attempted to flee the cattle corral. The .44-caliber projectile struck it just above the left shoulder. Fraley had killed the cat with one round.

Ortegón, Velasco and the trailing entourage had not even seen the cat in the dimming sunlight. All stood silent as Fraley went to the corral, turned the cat on its side and began to gut and skin the animal. A few minutes later he took the skin to the water trough, wiped his k-bar blade, holstered it and washed the blood from his hands. Fraley had hunted deer with his high-school pals and learned the art of skinning after he discovered there was money selling the pelts and heads. He walked over to Ortegón and offered the pelt to him. Don Pedro smiled and motioned to his bodyguard to take the cat's skin from Fraley.

"You are an excellent marksman. Were you trained in the American military?"

"No, Don Pedro, shooting came second nature to me. My time in the military was with the submariners in the Navy. We didn't do much shooting thirty fathoms under the Atlantic. Most of my time with a gun has been in the hills hunting, or on the streets."

"Tomorrow you will accompany me to Bogotá. You will come to my home and see my gun collection. There I will introduce you to the most important man in Colombia."

*   *   *

The reception at El Dorado Airport came at planeside. Two Mercedes-Benz sedans were waiting at the wing of Ortegón's Aero Commander. At Ortegón's request, Fraley and Velasco parted with him at planeside and were whisked away. As they drove through the city and into the hills, just to the north of the center of Bogotá, Fraley was reminded why it had been named the City of Roses. It was one of the most colorful, beautiful sights he had ever seen.

The driver came to a stop in front of a thirty-foot iron gate, flanked with ten-foot-high Italian marble columns on either side. The driver opened his window. *"Llegamos,"* was all he said into the speaker at the gate. The gate opened and the driver proceeded down the stone driveway onto Velasco's Embassy Row estate property.

Fraley walked into the marble foyer of the house and looked up at the twenty-foot ceiling, lined with mosaic tiles. It was shaped like a dome; at the center hung a huge crystal chandelier from a gold centerpiece.

"Darling, I thought you would be here two days ago. I've missed you so very much." The woman wore an elegant silk robe and high heels, and as far as Fraley could tell that was all she was wearing. She was a beautiful redhead with great legs. Not exactly Velasco's type. First, she was over twenty, and second, she was a *gringa*.

The woman was oblivious to Fraley's presence as she threw herself at Velasco, first pressing up against him and then guiding his hand inside her robe, almost swooning at his touch. Fraley had been to Velasco's home many times in Bogotá, but he had never met his wife.

"Darling, you didn't tell me we were having company. You know we only have this evening," she stopped abruptly as she finally noticed Fraley.

"Katherine, I would like you to meet my friend Leo."

"Nice to meet youns," Fraley said.

"Katherine, I will not be with you this evening. I have an important meeting," Velasco said, without a hint of affection. Speechless, she turned on her heel and left the room.

"You didn't tell me your wife was an American," Fraley said and quickly added, "I think you have probably pissed her off bringing me home."

Velasco broke into laughter, "First, she isn't my wife, she is the neighbor's wife. Second, her moods are of no concern to me. However, her husband is a very important man, so I keep her happy."

"So who's her husband? The Dow Chemical representative in Colombia?"

"No, much better. He's the American ambassador. He is with my wife in Curaçao for two days. It's an excellent arrangement for all of us, don't you think?"

Velasco and Fraley were ushered into the home of Don Pedro Ortegón as if they were dignitaries. They walked through the huge hand-carved rosewood and beveled glass double doors onto the balcony that stretched the length of the house. The view of the city and the surrounding mountains was spectacular. Ortegón greeted both men and graciously introduced them to his guests seated at the circular table in the center of the veranda. Velasco went to the guests immediately, exchanging kind words and embracing each of the three men as if they were best friends.

"Señor Fraley, I would like to introduce you to my *compadres.* This is the honorable senator from our congress, Dr. Pablo Emilio Escobar-Gaviria, José Rodríguez-Gacha . . ." he then introduced him to a host of other very powerful and influential men in the Medellín cartel.

"Mucho gusto. Leo Fraley, a sus órdenes." Fraley had practiced the proper greeting with Velasco. A slight smirk came over his face as he thought about the irony of his predicament. He had finally achieved the status for a formal introduction to the biggest drug lords in the world, including the infamous Pablo Escobar. Although Fraley had been present when these men had met with Velasco in the past, he had never attained the social standing to be introduced. He soon knew them by their nicknames: The Doctor, the Mexican, Mr. Long and dozens of other names that sounded like cartoon-strip characters. Even Fraley was blessed with his nickname—The Chameleon. And to think, all he had to do to meet them, aside from talking them into sparing his life, was to become a hostage.

"Ah, smuggling," he thought, "it's not just a job, it's an adventure!"

CHAPTER

6

IL TRIANGULO

IT WAS THE VACATION they had been wanting to take for years. They were going to get away from it all, relax and enjoy themselves. At least that's what Cuffaro told his wife Rosana about their trip. He had surprised her with the tickets to Aruba only a week earlier.

As they deplaned from the KLM Boeing 727, they could feel the ever present nineteen-mile-an-hour trade wind. It was one of the three constants of this island's climate. Aruba has the most dependable weather on earth, varying no more that ten degrees year round, never lower than seventy-eight degrees overnight and never hotter than ninety-two during the day. The third constant is the neverending sunshine. Even when it rains the trade winds quickly carry the clouds past the island. As they looked around, they saw one of the most visible by-products of Aruba's trade winds, the unusual divi-divi trees, which all grow in the direction of the wind. Their perfectly directed branches all reach out to the west as if pointing to the leeward side of the tiny island.

Aruba's official language is Dutch, but Spanish and English are widely spoken, as is Papiamento, a language found on a few of the Caribbean islands. It is a mixture of Spanish, Portuguese, Dutch and English. Geographically, the island is situated in the Caribbean Sea sixteen miles off the northwest coast of Venezuela, due north of the city of Caracas. Aruba is also within twenty miles of the Colombian peninsula of Santa Marta. Independent from the Netherlands Antilles but still part of the Dutch realm, Aruba has no natural resources apart from its beauty and its climate. It has become a playground for the world's rich and famous, attracting Europeans and Americans. Its number one industry is tourism, then international banking and third is the Esso petroleum refinery, which services the crude oil production of neighboring Venezuela. The refinery is a huge complex that at first appears as a blighted area within the picturesque landscape of the island. But when the true need for the refinery is apparent, it becomes an acceptable trade-off. Since Aruba is almost totally arid, the refinery also serves as a desalination plant. It provides the purest and most potable water in the Caribbean at no cost to every home and business on the island.

The Cuffaros' drive to the hotel seemed to take only a few minutes. They hardly had enough time to finish their conversation with the cab driver. They were impressed with the friendliness of the Arubans. Cuffaro's wife was especially grateful that the inhabitants of this Dutch isle spoke fluent Spanish.

As they checked into the five-star Concorde Hotel on Aruba's internationally known Palm Beach, the open-air lobby allowed a full view of the crystal clear Caribbean Sea. A ribbon of sugar-white beach and coconut palms stretched as far as the eye could see.

"These are the Cuffaros. They are checking in," the bellman announced to the desk clerk. Recognizing his Italian surname, the clerk addressed the Cuffaros in Italian.

"Buona sera, signor Cuffaro. Bienvenuto ad Aruba." Impressed with his language abilities, Cuffaro responded in Italian.

"Molti grazie."

"Muchas gracias," Rosana responded in Spanish.

As they walked through the lobby toward the elevator the pair smiled at each other. The feel of Aruba's friendly people and the beautiful atmosphere had almost made Cuffaro forget about their companions on this trip, and the true purpose of the visit.

"Hey, Joe, what are yoos doin'? Let's have some dinner together," Galatolo yelled across the otherwise serene lobby of the hotel. The cab was far too small to accommodate four passengers, so Galatolo and his wife had decided to rent a car. Galatolo's company during the four-hour flight was enough to make Cuffaro not only wish that he had come on a separate plane, but that they were staying in separate hotels.

"We went for a quick tour of the Palm Beach strip. Dis is definitely the best hotel." Galatolo's irritating voice was audible not only in the lobby but out on the beach. "What d'ya say we get some food?"

"Yeah, good idea, John, we're gonna get a shower and change. We'll meet you two in the lobby in an hour, okay?" Cuffaro was polite, but the thought of eating with this uncouth son of a bitch and his equally foul-smelling wife made him lose his appetite.

"Joe, why do we have to spend time with John? You know how I feel about him and, well, *she's* very nice, but she's still a *cochina*," Rosana pleaded patiently, even while she called Galatolo's wife a pig.

"It's business. I promise we'll have time together as soon as we get this meeting over with." Cuffaro's response was well introduced, but he knew the meeting could potentially consume the entire trip.

Their room was decorated with airy, tropical furniture. It was the perfect place to relax and enjoy the beautiful scenery of Aruba. Cuffaro's wife was doing all those womanly things that usually follow taking a shower and always add at least a thirty-minute wait.

Cuffaro's thoughts drifted back to the many meetings that had led him to this one. Since Galatolo's return from Palermo more than a year ago, Cuffaro had been the point man in making Francesco Madonia's vision a reality. Madonia was the head of the Ressuttana family, and Galatolo's godfather. He had sanctioned Galatolo to crack a deal between the Medellín cartel and four of the Sicilian Mafia families for the direct supply of cocaine to Sicily from Colombia. Madonia's vision structured two divisions of labor to maximize their control of all distribution and profits from sales in the European cocaine market. The Colombians would deal exclusively with the Sicilian Mafia for the bulk shipments of cocaine destined for distribution throughout Italy and their strongholds in Europe. In turn, the Sicilian Mafia agreed to deal solely with the Medellín cartel for the purchase of cocaine.

It was a profitable venture for the cartel, albeit a rather restrictive partnership. Because the Mafia's influence within the existing social, political and financial infrastructure in Italy had become so institutionalized, it was unwilling to relinquish control of any aspect of the drug business to the Colombians. Their only exception to the rule was in the manufacture and transportation end of the business. It was a deviation from their long-standing system in the heroin business, where the Mafia controlled every aspect, including the manufacture, smuggling, distribution and money laundering. On the other hand, the arrangement was an aberration for the Medellín cartel, which had a well-established system of cells, particularly in the United States, that controlled every part of the business. Even though the cartel contracted with the Mexicans to smuggle the cocaine into the United States, they still maintained primary control. This deal with the Mafia meant that no Colombian cocaine could enter Italy without direct permission from the Mafia. It was the single most difficult part of the plan for Cuffaro to sell to the Colombians.

He felt like a pinball, bouncing back and forth between the Colombians in Miami and the Sicilians in New York. The first of these meetings had taken place in September 1987 at the Caffè Paradiso in New York with Dominic Mannino. Since then, Cuffaro had made many trips, trying to hammer out everything from price to the actual logistics of the delivery. He found himself being driven around the city in circles, led through Manhattan's subway stations, to waiting cars, back rooms of restaurants and basements of buildings under construction to avoid the possibility of law enforcement surveillance.

He disliked the position Galatolo had put him in during the negotiations with the Sicilians. To him, these men were important people and Galatolo should have been present. He was even more resentful of Galatolo's lame excuse for not attending the meetings.

"Don't worry Joe, you're only the messenger, and the messenger carries no faults. I am ultimately responsible," Galatolo had told him with his gangster wisdom. Cuffaro simply translated this "Sicilian Proverb" as another manifestation of Galatolo's limited ability and overall cowardice.

Paolo LoDuca was only one of the players who had a role in the U.S. connection to this deal. Rosario Naimo, also in New York, answered directly to Salvatore Riina, in Palermo. Riina, also known as "The Beast," was the head of the Corleonese family, best known for successfully eluding capture by the Italian authorities for almost twenty years. He had been convicted *in absentia* many times for crimes ranging from extortion, to drug trafficking and murder. Then there was Dominic Mannino, head of the Castellammarese family in Philadelphia. Cuffaro was first introduced to these men at a friendly dinner at Frank's Restaurant in Pompano Beach over a year ago.

"Okay, Joe, *estoy lista,*" Rosana said as she proudly modeled her new sun dress.

"You look very beautiful," he said, and kissed her on the cheek as he led her out of the room. As Cuffaro and his wife waited in the hotel lobby, their jaws dropped when they saw Galatolo and his wife approaching. He was dressed in a wrinkled pastel blue *guayabera,* with brown stains in the armpits, which topped long, baggy plaid shorts, black socks and his black and white leather gangster shoes. Cuffaro thought Galatolo's wife was the only woman he had ever seen who could dress worse than Kathleen Anderson. She was wearing a halter top, which did not support her heavy, sagging breasts, and shorts that could never cover enough.

"Mira, vienen los cochinos," Rosana said in a low tone to her husband in disgust.

Cuffaro tried to console her. "I know, but what could I do. He's my business partner. I can't tell him what to wear and I can't choose his women. And besides, who else would have him?"

"They're made for each other," she whispered, and they both chuckled.

Galatolo was motioning Cuffaro to break away from his wife and speak to him alone. He rudely pushed his wife toward Rosana.

"I had a message in my room from Aponte. He and his partner are waiting for us at the Aruba Caribbean," Galatolo said to him. Cuffaro regretted brushing off his wife, but he knew it had to be done. Before he could apologize to her, Galatolo crudely took out a fistful of money and gave it to his wife.

"Yoos two go shopping and have dinner. We got business, Joe and me."

"I'm sorry," Cuffaro apologized to his wife. Her eyes said it all. Cuffaro was going to pay for this.

As they passed through the lobby of the Hotel Aruba Caribbean, they spotted Aponte seated at a table on the terrace of the restaurant. He and his companion were both drinking *San Miguel cervezas* from the bottle. Cuffaro followed Galatolo as they approached the table. Aponte came to his feet quickly in a show of respect for his guests.

"Joe, John, *¿cómo están? Les presento al señor Angel Sánchez."* Aponte was friendly but respectful toward his companion.

"Joe Cuffaro. *Mucho gusto,"* Cuffaro extended his hand to the stranger. *Este es mi jefe, Juan Galatolo,"* he said, almost unaware of his apologetic tone.

Aponte and Cuffaro, the point men, were here to bring their bosses together to solidify the deal. Aponte had earlier revealed to Cuffaro that he was the sole reason this business transaction had come this far, stating in no uncertain terms that he did not like or trust Galatolo.

It was the first time Cuffaro had met Sánchez, and Sánchez's first meeting with any of the Sicilian contacts. It was at Sánchez's request that the meeting was taking place in Aruba. Aponte had told Cuffaro that Sánchez could not travel to the United States, where he was wanted by both U.S. Customs and DEA for drug smuggling. He was a tall, lean, mulatto with thick, black, curly hair and a very prominent mustache. Cuffaro thought he looked like pictures he had seen of the Mexican outlaw, Pancho Villa. He had one feature that stood out more than any other: his eyes. They were deep black pools giving nothing away. Satan could have been his father.

The first part of the meeting was filled with the obligatory niceties common in most cultures, except the American culture. The meeting was conducted in Spanish, the only language common to three of the four people at the table. Everyone was at least bilingual except Sánchez, whose only language was Spanish. Cuffaro served as Galatolo's translator, which placed Galatolo at a disadvantage. His command of Spanish was limited to obscenities, ordering food and soliciting prostitutes on

Miami's Biscayne Boulevard. Not only did he not understand the majority of the conversation, he could not assert himself as the man in charge.

"We are ready to deal with your people immediately," Sánchez said with authority and confidence. "We have made arrangements to provide as much as a thousand kilograms, if we can come to terms on the price." But, first I must tell you that I have not been authorized to contract with your people for less than thirty-five thousand dollars per kilo." Sánchez leaned across the table, eyes to Cuffaro first, then adding emphasis as he looked at Galatolo.

It was the main sticking point. The deal had already been made except for agreement on price, which is why Galatolo and Sánchez were now together. As serious and intense as the back and forth on price became, the conversation was also rather amusing to Cuffaro. It was clearly not a matter of how much each side could afford, but how much Galatolo and Sánchez were going to steal from their partners.

"We won't pay a penny more than twenty-nine thousand," Galatolo blurted out in Sicilian. The Colombians had no idea what he was saying, but they could tell from the tone of his voice he was not in agreement. Cuffaro repeated, in gentlemanly terms, that thirty-five thousand was not acceptable.

Aponte came from a fairly affluent family in Colombia and, like Cuffaro, was well educated. On the other hand, Sánchez, like Galatolo, was from the streets. A thief and a killer from Medellín who had risen in the ranks of the cartel, he was known as the hand of death for leaders like Pablo Escobar and José Rodríguez-Gacha. As is customary in Latin cultures, even in the face of an obvious lie, no insults were traded. Rather, their positions were expressed in the most polite and eloquent language possible. It is important at all times to portray oneself as more dignified than the adversary.

"It is with much regret, my friend, that I inform you our business transaction cannot be made on those terms," Sánchez said in his best Spanish, while Cuffaro translated. It was a firm statement, but one that did not close the door for rebuttal.

The conversation continued in this manner for nearly half an hour, when Sánchez leaned toward his partner Aponte to discuss their next step. The mulatto spoke through his thick mustache. "We have reconsidered, and we will sacrifice the price for a continued relationship with your organization. But we will not go lower than thirty-one thousand. We will also require a million dollars before shipment and a million dollars upon delivery." It was obviously Sánchez's final offer—an offer that would still afford both Sánchez and Galatolo the opportunity to skim several thousand off the top of each kilo. Sánchez needed to keep the price higher than the agreed-upon price he had established with his partners in Medellín. Galatolo needed to keep the price as low as possible, to pocket the difference between the sales price and the price his partners in Sicily would pay.

"We also have reconsidered, and feel it is equally important to establish this partnership with your organization," Cuffaro said, not only translating but reworking Galatolo's awkward acceptance.

With that out of the way, the next hurdle was deciding the quantity of drugs to be delivered. The decision was based on two criteria: logistics and available space. Logistically, the only way to practically transport cocaine across the Atlantic to Italy was by vessel. The size of the specially designed compartment on the vessel the Colombians had chosen had not yet been measured for an accurate load capacity, but they estimated it could hold approximately one thousand kilos. Their decision was to transport at least six hundred kilos.

At $31,000 a kilo, the Sicilians would owe the Colombians $18,600,000. If the true price Galatolo had quoted the Sicilians was actually $29,000, Galatolo stood to make $2,000 a kilo, or approximately $1.2 million. And, if the true price Sánchez quoted to the Colombians was actually $25,000 a kilo, Sánchez could pocket an additional $6,000 a kilo or $3.6 million. In the United States in 1987, the price per kilo fluctuated, like any other commodity, between eighteen and twenty-two thousand. In Europe, the wholesale price per kilo was closer to $60,000. Even if the Sicilians bought it for $29,000, they stood to make a profit of $17.4 million. If they controlled distribution in Italy and Europe they could easily triple their profits.

"By the way, the vessel that will carry the cargo is here in Aruba," Sánchez said, smiling at their surprise. "I invite you to inspect it tomorrow. It is docked at the port of Sint Nichols," he proudly said in his best Dutch accent. "It is called the *Big John*."

"I will take my camera tomorrow to photograph the vessel, so that our people in Sicily will recognize it when it arrives," Cuffaro said, without consulting with his partner.

In the last thirty minutes of the meeting, the four men decided on an approximate date of delivery. The Colombians passed on the code name, "Brito," for Allen Knox, the captain of the vessel. They provided the radio frequencies on which to contact him and determined the longitude and latitude for the pickup, which would take place in the Mediterranean off the coast of Sicily.

Cuffaro hoped the success of this ninety-minute exchange between these two cut-throat organizations would produce enough money for him to walk away from this lifestyle. Although his portion of the deal was only a fraction of what Galatolo would take, Cuffaro stood to make more money than he would ever need to make Scirocco Fan Company a major success.

The next day, Galatolo and Cuffaro chartered a sport fishing boat at the port. Neither caught a fish of any significance, but they took pictures with prized catches just the same. Using this as a cover, Cuffaro also took several pictures of *Big John,* an oceangoing tug with a home port of Concepción, Chile. Cuffaro felt a sense of accomplishment as well as relief. It was not the biggest deal he had been involved with, but it was the first time he held such a front line position in negotiating a deal.

Two days later Cuffaro and his wife were at home in Miami and he was packing once again to go to New York. Galatolo was waiting in Cuffaro's driveway in his black Mercedes, leaning on the horn. Cuffaro grabbed his suit bag and his leather carryon, kissed his wife and kids goodbye and was out the door. Galatolo had insisted on driving him to the airport to catch the flight to LaGuardia. Cuffaro always found the interior of Galatolo's Mercedes almost comical. Red velour was virtually impossible to find except on an old sofa in some fleabag, yet Galatolo had had his fine leather interior removed and reupholstered in blood-red, crushed velour. But the icing on the cake was the small dog whose head bobbed and whose eyes lit up whenever the driver stepped on the brakes. This was hardly the setting for serious conversation, but Galatolo began to unload some pretty heavy facts on Cuffaro as they headed west on the Palmetto Expressway.

"Joe, when I was in Sicily and took the oath, I gave your name to my godfather to put down in our book. I told them that you could be trusted and that you had pulled the trigger for me." Galatolo lowered his voice and looked around as if someone could see or hear him as he drove seventy miles per hour with the windows rolled up. He made a juvenile impression of a man holding a pistol by extending his forefinger, raising his thumb and curling his three lower fingers into a fist, as he spoke in a deadly serious tone.

"What do you mean, you told them I have pulled the trigger? John, I haven't killed anyone, nor will I kill anyone, to join the Mafia." Cuffaro kept his tone matter-of-fact so as not to anger Galatolo.

"That doesn't matter now, Joe, but you must make them believe that you have, if they ask. You don't have to give any details. That's up to me."

As Cuffaro settled into his first-class seat on the Eastern flight to New York, he closed his eyes and tried to collect his thoughts. This was the third time Galatolo brought up the killing business with him. The list became increasingly longer each time he spoke about it. At first he wanted to "do in" Luis Miguel, the Haitian drug dealer who owed Galatolo over three hundred thousand dollars. Then he added his friend and their business partner Martin Gladstone merely because he was a Jew who "knew too much." Galatolo wanted Cuffaro to "off" Tyrone Walker, Mariela Liggio, George Linares and others. Galatolo's solution to all his problems seemed to be murder. He wanted Mariela Liggio dead because he had ripped her off for about two hundred thousand dollars in cocaine. Liggio was a Colombian in her late forties who lived in a gorgeous half-million-dollar home in Coral Gables. Cuffaro thought she was uglier than a horse. Nonetheless, Galatolo had become her lover so he could take advantage of her. But when two Colombians with pistols came looking for their two hundred thousand, Galatolo began to plot Liggio's death. Cuffaro knew he was serious because he had already revealed the details of several murders he had committed.

Galatolo told Cuffaro he had killed two men in Sicily, two in New Jersey and two others in his house in Miami. It was easy to lure the victims to his Miami home because they were lifelong friends. According to Galatolo they were also friends of Tomaso Buscetta. Buscetta had been marked for death by the Mafia because he was a turncoat, the first of the Sicilian Mafia to violate their sacred oath of silence. Buscetta had cooperated with the Sicilian magistrate Giovanni Falcone and provided enough information to jail more than three hundred of his mafiosi brothers. His crime was so massive, the Mafia marked his entire family as well as his friends for elimination.

After they had shared dinner, Galatolo and one of his soldiers, Tony Fasulo, clubbed the two guests unconscious in his kitchen with a baseball bat, shot them several times in the head, wrapped their mangled bodies in sheets and loaded them into the trunk of one of the dead men's cars. They drove north of West Palm Beach near I-95 and tried to sink the car in a lake. But when the rear wheels sank down to the axle in mud, Galatolo and Fasulo simply set it on fire and walked away. This was one of Galatolo's more gruesome stories. It gave Cuffaro good reason to fear him and believe he was as evil as he portrayed himself. Cuffaro still had a vivid memory of the newscast following the incident—the video clearly showed the car partially submerged in the lake and the charred bodies of the victims laid out on the shore as the police investigated the crime scene. Galatolo even bragged to Cuffaro about being questioned as a suspect after one of the victims' family members told the police that he had made threats toward one of the dead men.

"But don't worry," Galatolo began to explain as if he were consoling Cuffaro, "when I first got the order it took me almost a year and a half until I killed these two guys. So take your time, but it needs to be done. Because unless you do, you cannot be blessed."

As the Eastern 727 made its final approach, Cuffaro could see the city lights while dusk settled over the New York skyline. Cuffaro saw his contact as he exited the jetway into the terminal. It was one of Mannino's soldiers. Cuffaro had known Dominic Mannino for many years, since his early days in Brooklyn working for the Ferro Cheese Company. The chemistry had always been bad between them and his contempt for Mannino had grown stronger each time he saw him. As far as Cuffaro was concerned, Mannino was a degenerate and a spineless punk who played the role. His personality was nothing deeper than tough talk and Armani suits that never fit. He was a gutless wimp without his Mafia pals around to provide him with his power and "courage." He was also a compulsive gambler who would let his family go hungry if he could throw the money away playing the horses, poker or craps.

During the ride through the city to the meeting place, Cuffaro sat silent as if Mannino's driver wasn't even alive. He wanted to emphasize that what he had to say was for the ears of those who made the decisions. An hour later, Cuffaro was seated at a large table in Paolo LoDuca's house. LoDuca, Dominic Mannino, Rosario Naimo and their underbosses sat and listened intently to Cuffaro as he repeated the essence of the negotiations during the meeting in Aruba with the Colombians.

"The transportation fee of one million dollars is payable upon delivery to the captain. Payment in full is due in ninety days. The Colombians also want a one million dollar down payment before the ship leaves Colombia," Cuffaro said in Sicilian. But before he could continue, Naimo sprayed half the table with his spit as he swore that the deal was off if the Colombians wanted any front money.

"You tell them that if they want to deal with us, they will have to deliver first—before they are paid."

"This is not a problem," LoDuca said in a calm voice. "These men are in business to make money. Joe can resolve this." LoDuca looked at Cuffaro and said with respect, "Joe, you tell them that we have no problem with the captain's fee. It will be paid. However, the down payment is not acceptable. We will pay no money before delivery. Tell them we will pay one million to them in Italy if they will meet you there after the delivery," LoDuca added with a sense of reasoning as well as confidence in Cuffaro to negotiate this without a problem.

After the meeting, Galatolo told Cuffaro how the money would be divided. "Each of the bosses will get one million, and the underbosses will each get two-fifty." Galatolo would receive one million, and Cuffaro two hundred fifty thousand. In a matter of seconds Mannino had distributed five million dollars.

* * *

It was December 26, 1987, and Galatolo and Cuffaro were again on their way to the Miami Airport. This time Cuffaro was on his way to Palermo. The *Big John* had reportedly been en route from Barranquilla for more than a week. Cuffaro was to appear in Palermo as a relative returning home for a Christmas visit. His flight to New York was just a stop en route to Milan, then on to Palermo. Cuffaro defiantly ignored Galatolo's insistence that he leave for Italy before Christmas in order to spend the holidays with his family. He expected trouble, but instead Galatolo was gracious, acting the understanding family man. Galatolo was conspicuously out of character, far from his normally arrogant demeanor— friendly and accommodating, instead of his usual domineering and demeaning self.

"Tutto va benissimo," Galatolo told him. "In a few days we will all be wealthy men. Joe, I want you to know that LoDuca, Naimo, Mannino and I are all pleased with the outcome of your work." Galatolo then moved on to the business at hand: "My cousin Vincenzo will be waiting for you at the airport in Palermo and will take you to the meeting with the bosses. Joe, you must know how important this meeting is, so remember, if you are asked you must say you have pulled the trigger for me." Galatolo spoke in Sicilian, as if it made his conversation completely confidential.

"John, there is one thing I want to discuss with you," Cuffaro said with total resolve. "These negotiations and this deal have already taken a year out of my life. I often don't see my family for a week at a time. It's been that way for over a year now. I have been the only one up front to the Colombians. If anything goes wrong, it is me who they will come after. They know where my home is and where my family is." Cuffaro added with more emphasis: "Yet when the money was divided, I am to receive the same as the underbosses, like that piece of shit Lorenzo. They have done nothing to make this deal happen. They have no work behind them and no risks ahead."

"You're right, Joe," Galatolo looked serious. "And you have also come up with very creative ideas. Your suggestion to make the delivery on New Year's Day was brilliant. This way we will not have to worry about the Italian National Guard or the American Navy. It's perfect. They'll all be drunk!"

Cuffaro listened with suspicion. Galatolo's words seemed too eloquent, even in Sicilian. Galatolo continued with a pat on the back for Cuffaro, who viewed this more akin to the kiss of death. "The bosses and I have spoken about this, and each of us will put in enough to double your end. And I will personally add another two hundred fifty thousand for you. This way you will get seven fifty." Galatolo was so sincere,

Cuffaro knew he would never see the additional money he was being promised. He only hoped to squeeze as much as he could from these greedy men.

"I will meet you in Palermo," Galatolo said as he waved goodbye.

The next day Cuffaro reached Palermo. After renting a car at the airport, he drove directly to his uncle's house to clean up before the meeting with the four family bosses. It had been several years since Cuffaro had seen his mother's brother, the man with whom he had lived after his parents immigrated to the United States. The few hours he had to get ready and become reacquainted with the family flew by. It was not long before Vincenzo Galatolo was at the door. Cuffaro was beat from the jet lag but was, as always, prepared for the meeting.

When Cuffaro and Vincenzo walked into the back room of the "office" the bosses and their associates were already seated. The office was really the original home of the Galatolo family, built a century and a half earlier when they were tenant farmers of the surrounding orange groves. But as they grew within the Mafia, the land became theirs. It was now their private compound, and among its many improvements was a modern six-story building where they had several luxurious apartments. The old home was kept as a memento of times past and as a meeting place. They began by offering Joe wine, bread and buffalo mozzarella. There was a small amount of idle conversation, but the men were clearly interested in beginning the meeting, when suddenly Raffaele Galatolo entered the room carrying two large shopping bags from an expensive clothing store.

"I've got this week's receipts, about one hundred million lire," the younger Galatolo said, dumping the cash on the table in front of everyone.

Cuffaro quickly did the math and realized that what he saw in front of him was about eighty thousand dollars. The Galatolos controlled the largest and richest area of Palermo, including the seaport. Each week every merchant, from the smallest pizzeria to the grandest hotel in this fifty square block area, had to pay extortion money to survive the next week. The alternative was a bomb, a fire or broken legs, and these were the polite acts that waited for anyone who dared to defy their authority.

Cuffaro was the only one in the room who was not a sworn member of the Mafia. Each of the four families was represented: the Corleonese by Dominic Mannino; the Castellammarese by Alduccio "Salvo" Madonia, Francesco Madonia's son; and Aldo Madonia for the Ressuttana family. After the money was counted, Raffaele began by briefing the meeting on what had transpired during the many meetings in New York, Miami and Aruba.

"The *Big John* will be met by our men, who have already been instructed where to deliver the cargo," Cuffaro explained, holding eye contact with each of the bosses. But before he could continue, his nemesis interrupted.

"What are we talking?" Dominic Mannino began in a boisterous, overbearing voice in broken English. To add emphasis he switched to Sicilian. "Why are we having this conversation in front of Joe? He should not be involved in this."

"Well, I can get up and leave," Cuffaro answered.

"No, no, no. You stay," interjected Salvo Madonia.

"Why should he stay here? He's nobody," Mannino declared defiantly.

"Why should you stay here?" responded Cuffaro. By now, Cuffaro and Mannino were on their feet, pointing at each other, with their voices becoming louder and louder. Cuffaro had had enough. "Who the hell are you?" he said. "You haven't done nothing in this deal. You're only supposed to be here to collect the money, that's it. You're just a fuckin' punk!" Vincenzo Galatolo quickly stepped in, leading Cuffaro out of the room.

"Look, you gotta cool it. You must show respect," he implored Cuffaro.

"What do you mean—he's not showing me any respect. Why should I respect him?"

"Look, I know he's an asshole, but you must show him respect anyway. He is representing the family, Joe."

When they returned to the room, Cuffaro made his diplomatic apology to the bosses, but never looked in Mannino's direction. Cuffaro quickly pulled out a map of the Mediterranean, an architect's triangle, a compass and a pencil, then continued where he left off.

Cuffaro drew lines, first due south from the central southern tip of Corsica, then due west from the city of Trapani in Sicily. Where the lines intersected in the Mediterranean Sea was the location of the prearranged meeting point.

"This is where the exchange will take place, on New Year's Eve," he pointed to the spot. By now all the bosses were crowded around Cuffaro, pushing Mannino to the back, where he had no more than an obstructed view. Cuffaro reached into his breast pocket and pulled out the photographs of the *Big John* and laid them on the table for everyone to see. He reached into his pocket a second time and unfolded a paper. On it were a series of numbers. As they were, they meant nothing. But as Cuffaro decoded the numbers, subtracting or adding the difference with the number ten, before everyone's eyes the HF band radio frequencies given to Cuffaro by Aponte to contact "Brito" appeared.

As Mannino fumed in the background the bosses crowded around Cuffaro and congratulated him. They all knew this would be the first of many such deals with the Colombian cartels. It was a move that would soon allow them to control fully the multibillion dollar cocaine trade in Europe.

The next day, Cuffaro took a reminiscing walk through the central part of the city, which at one time surpassed Rome and Paris as the heart of European culture. Palermo was filled with over ten thousand years of architecture from the ruins of the ancient Greeks and Romans, as well as Moorish palaces and French and Spanish churches. Among Palermo's other distinctive features were its pockets of destruction, which still existed from the bombings of World War II. As Cuffaro walked through the fashionable *Piazzale Ungheria,* built in Palermo's shopping district during the Renaissance, he spotted Mannino walking with an older woman, his wife and their two children. As they approached each other Cuffaro recognized the older woman as Mannino's mother-in-law. But when Mannino looked up and saw Cuffaro nearing, his face turned white with panic and without a word he did a sudden about-face. Cuffaro chuckled as he watched the coward literally run away from his family into the closest store. Cuffaro politely greeted Mannino's mother-in-law, his wife and the two children, then strolled into a nearby cafe for a cappuccino.

The city of Trapani, on Sicily's northwest coast, was famous for being the first place on the European continent where the Virgin Mary is said to have appeared. Catholics from around the world have made pilgrimages to visit the holy sight of the "Madonna of Trapani."

Not far from the site, inside a small beachhouse, two men in their early twenties sat lazily listening to American rock and roll music. The warm light of the setting sun and the cool salt-air breeze filled the room. An open window framed a spectacular view of the aquamarine waters of the Mediterranean. The badly weathered wood shutters occasionally creaked and banged against the stucco exterior of the house as the trade wind quickened and died with the pulse of the sea. On the table near the window were two high-frequency-band radios, a headset/microphone combination, a television and a VCR. On a four-foot-square concrete pad a few feet outside the window, a pyramid-shaped antenna rose thirty-five feet above the ground surface. Both men were in a kind of trance, watching a Madonna music video. But their fascination with the scantily clad rock star was abruptly interrupted by the ringing of the telephone. One of the men immediately lowered the volume of the television with a remote control while the other waited and then answered the phone on the second ring.

"Pronto?" He listened with a serious expression on his face. "We have tried contacting every hour on the half as instructed, but there has been no reply." He paused again, listening intently. "Yes, Don Vincenzo, we will call immediately as soon as there is any contact." He hung up the phone and turned to his partner. "Tonight is the night of the rendezvous. The bosses are nervous because this Brito is not answering our broadcasts."

"He probably found a port to celebrate New Year's Eve," his companion said with a jealous smile. He reached over and raised the volume on the television, turning his attention back to the American girl.

Cuffaro was at his uncle's house preparing his favorite roast of lamb for a family dinner when his uncle entered the kitchen.

"Joe, there is a call for you from a man who says his name is Allen."

Cuffaro lowered the flame on the stove and went into the living room. The voice on the phone was that of Allen Knox, otherwise known as "Brito."

"Buenas noches señor. Estoy en las Islas de Canarias."

Cuffaro listened intently as Brito described the nature of his engine trouble, which had forced him into port in the Canary Islands off the northwest coast of Africa two days earlier. Brito also explained how he encountered bad weather about three hundred miles west of the Netherlands Antilles, which further delayed him. He was four days past the scheduled date of delivery, but Brito showed no symptoms even vaguely resembling anxiety about the current situation.

Cuffaro knew nothing about Brito other than what Aponte had told him. Even though they had seen the *Big John* in Aruba, they had not met its captain. Aponte described him as "a thirty-five-year-old hippie," an Anglo-looking guy, whose father was British and whose mother was Colombian. To further complicate his personality, Brito was born and raised in Chile, received part of his education as a merchant seaman in England and had lived in Baranquilla, working as a smuggler for the Medellín cartel during the past ten years.

"When do you think you will make port?" Cuffaro added a little concern into his tone to bring Brito out of his "I'm-on-a-holiday" attitude.

"I should be in position in less than forty-eight hours." Brito's reply was a little more serious this time. "By the way, Joe, the numbers I gave you for the meeting place are no longer valid. I have passed the new ones on to Aponte. He is in Madrid. He will call you soon. *Hasta luego mi amigo—ciao."* Brito hung up before Cuffaro could reply. Within the hour, Cuffaro received a call from Aponte with the new coordinates for the transfer point. Cuffaro's next move was to meet with Vincenzo Galatolo to ease the tension that had clearly been growing each day without contact from the Colombians.

Two more days passed and Vincenzo Galatolo was hanging tight with Cuffaro. Although his manner was friendly, it was obvious to Cuffaro that the bosses had placed Galatolo's cousin closer to him until the delivery was in their hands. Vincenzo and Cuffaro had just ordered dinner. They sat five hundred feet above downtown Palermo in a fancy restaurant called *Ala D'Oro,* perched on the hillside in the *Aquasante* section of the city. Their table was close to a window overlooking the harbor. As the pasta was served, a teenage boy arrived on a moped, walked over to the window and tapped on it. He looked in the direction of their table and motioned excitedly with his hand. Without a word, Vincenzo disappeared for fifteen minutes. When he returned to the restaurant he went directly to the bartender.

"Dom Perignon for the house," he bellowed loud enough for everyone to turn and look in his direction. He quickly returned to the table and embraced Cuffaro. "We have it, the transfer was made over an hour ago. The cargo is on its way to Palermo. Joe, we owe you a great debt."

The next day Cuffaro was at his uncle's house when he received another call from Brito, the ship's captain.

"Que pasó, hombre. Estoy ahora en Malta. I need to make port in Palermo—can you arrange it?"

Cuffaro took Brito's hotel and fax number and passed on the information to Vincenzo. John Galatolo had often bragged to Cuffaro or anyone who would listen that his family not only controlled all criminal activity within the Port of Palermo, they could move a herd of elephants through it and no one in authority would even take notice. The following day the necessary government papers appeared and were delivered to the proper officials, for the *Big John* to clear the *Guardia di Finanza* and the Port Authority. Within a few hours, via fax, Brito had the documents in hand.

The following day Vincenzo stood by the dock as the *Big John* entered the harbor. As the huge tugboat came closer it turned toward him, and with the apparent ease of parking a small car Brito backed her into the berthing area assigned to her by the harbor master. Vincenzo had never met Brito, but he guessed, correctly, who was who the minute the tall

Anglo with his disheveled red shoulder-length hair—most of which was wrapped in a bandanna—stepped out of the pilot's cabin onto the bridge of the vessel. Brito jabbered briefly with his first mate, then moved quickly down the ladder to the pier. He approached Vincenzo with a big smile and extended his hand.

"*Mucho gusto, señor Galatolo. Soy Allen Knox. ¿Quiere comer?* Come aboard and I'll serve you dinner."

There were many smiles as Vincenzo crossed over the gunwalcs.

The next day Cuffaro received a telephone call at his uncle's house.

"You gotta come down here and help me with this lunatic," Vincenzo's voice was frenzied.

"What lunatic? Who are you talking about?"

"Brito, Brito, that's who I'm talking about. The sonna bitch is a fuckin' wild man. He and some French whore are swimming nude."

The Hotel Villa Igea did not have a modern-day pool, but it was built around a natural lake that lightly caressed the hotel's grounds. It was a five-star hotel. Only the upper-crust of Palermo, wealthy tourists, highly placed politicians frequented it. Even the Popc had bccn known to grace it with a night's stay.

As Cuffaro approached the grand entrance to the Villa Igea he saw Vinccnzo standing in conversation with the hotel's manager. Cuffaro stopped within hearing distance of them and waited for Vincenzo to acknowledge him.

"Don Vincenzo, this hotel has been the cultural hub of Palermo for over a century. We pay you to protect us, and this pig Knox is your guest. I implore you to control his uncivilized behavior." The manager was a complete gentleman as he presented his case to the senior mafioso. At about the same time the hotel valet drove a pearl white Ferrari Mondial onto the semicircular drive at the entrance to the hotel. As the car came to a halt, the manager quickly and elegantly begged Galatolo's pardon and slipped into his one-hundred-thousand-dollar automobile. He winked at the valet, who took a silent step back as Mario the manager drove off into the crowded street.

"Joe, thank you for coming." Vincenzo was obviously distressed. "This Knox is not like anyone I've ever known. These Colombians have no fuckin' culture."

"Hey, he's not a problem. I'll talk to him. I'm sure it's just a language barrier or something." Cuffaro wanted to laugh at the thought that this killer, extortionist and career criminal was making reference to the "un-cultured."

"Listen, Joe—that sonna bitch came into the harbor last night. I personally met with him. He invites me on board his boat and offers me dinner. So I eat the worst garbage in my entire life." Vincenzo began to laugh. "I don't know enough Spanish to tell him he should put a bullet in the cook's head before he dies of food poisoning. Then in the middle of this dinner he tells me in Italian that he wants his money. No respect." He wasn't laughing anymore. "These Colombians don't understand. You never ask for what is already yours. Anyway, I told him we would deliver his cash to him today at his boat. Now, you go talk to him, get him fuckin' dressed and meet me at the dock in an hour." Vincenzo said this last in one breath, with enough hand and arm gestures to make someone think he was leading a symphony orchestra. He left, cursing Cuffaro and wondering how anyone could hope to understand that "wildman."

A minute later Cuffaro was standing outside, surveying the hotel pool area. Sure enough, Brito stood out like a whore in church. Cuffaro watched as the longhaired, bandanna-clad man dove in with a splash. At least Brito was wearing a swimsuit. As for his very attractive feminine friend, she was sunbathing topless in the lounge chair next to his. Their semiprivate lakeside cabana was deserted of other guests, and as Cuffaro approached Brito and his playmate he heard nothing but talk of the two foreigners and their disdainful behavior.

"Señor Knox, Joe Cuffaro. Buenas tardes," he began in Spanish, then switched to Italian, "Come stai?" Cuffaro offered Brito a hand up.

"Bien, bien. ¿Y usted?" Knox's girlfriend tipped her sunglasses to her forehead, exposing her large green eyes. She smiled at Cuffaro as Brito came out of the water.

"I would like to introduce you to my girlfriend. Mr. Cuffaro, this is Antoinette." As Knox spoke, Antoinette raised her tanned body from the lounge with the grace of a model, and extended her perfectly manicured hand.

Cuffaro shook it and explained the need to conduct business. Brito was completely agreeable, laughing.

An hour later Cuffaro was dockside with Brito when Vincenzo and one of his soldiers, carrying a small leather duffel bag, came into view. Without a word all four men climbed the ladder onto the *Big John,* Brito leading the way into the captain's cabin. As they entered the small room, Vincenzo turned to his henchman, took the bag and gave him orders to stand guard outside. Vincenzo pulled back the zipper of the bag and spread it open, exposing the bank-banded, ten-thousand-dollar bundles of brand new U.S. currency.

"One million dollars," Vincenzo proudly exclaimed, smiling. "You should stash it here on the boat where it will be safe, my friend. Palermo is a city of thieves."

The group laughed as Cuffaro translated for both men.

"Yes, I plan to," laughed Brito. "But I will need one hundred thousand for personal expenses while I am in Italy. Can you arrange to take it through the harbor gate past the Customs?"

"The gate I own. The harbor I own. I could pass pink elephants or tanks through the Customs. It is not a problem." Vincenzo could not resist the opportunity to boast of his family's century-long influence over the harbor. Cuffaro had heard it all before.

"Then why did I just risk my life delivering to your vessel in the middle of the storm with fifteen-foot seas? If you control the harbor, I should bring the cocaine directly to Palermo and unload here."

Brito then went on to give an elaborate recap of his bravery when the *Big John* met the Italian vessel in the Mediterranean and the seas had been too high to get close enough to use the cargo hoist to make the transfer. Brito explained how he placed the entire cargo in a zodiac raft and personally carried it to the Italian vessel. After the transfer was complete, he was stranded in the stormy waters for another hour before he could be extracted. When he finished, the cabin was silent.

"Come, let me show you the compartment. There is no way the Customs or their dogs can find it," Brito said.

As they entered the engine room the stench of diesel fuel and fouled sea water filled their nostrils. The engineer, a Panamanian, greeted them as he ate his lunch with blackened hands. Brito stepped down the ladder to the base surrounding the huge engine. He picked up a long wooden-handled flat shovel and began to scrape away a four-inch thick layer of heavy grease from the metal plating. When the corrugated steel surface was exposed, he reached for an acetylene torch, lit it and began cutting away the tack weld that held the plates together. In a few minutes he had broken the bonding, activated the electronic locking device and opened the vaultlike door. This exposed the compartment area, about four feet deep and six feet square, lined in spotless stainless steel.

"It is wrapped in ten inches of foam and the seal is watertight. It cannot leak, and you would virtually have to cut the vessel in half to find it. Even if the ship were to sink the cargo would be safe." Brito smiled brightly as his Italian friends peered in at his pride and joy.

"Well, then," Vincenzo said, impressed. "The next shipment will come directly to Palermo."

Vincenzo was as excited as a kid in a candy store as they returned to Brito's cabin, where Vincenzo began to inquire how much cocaine the compartment on the vessel could hold and how soon Brito could make the journey again. He talked about the possibility of Brito's carrying a load of heroin to the U.S., after delivering the next cocaine shipment, making each trip doubly profitable.

"I can take as much heroin as you want, anywhere in the world you want me to. But I cannot make port in the States. I am not welcome there, if you get my meaning. If you have another vessel meet me anywhere fifty miles off the coast, you have a deal," Brito said with great bravado.

The following morning Cuffaro was scheduled to meet with Brito. As Cuffaro entered the restaurant he immediately spotted Brito seated at one of the window tables overlooking the sea. Antoinette was playfully feeding him slices of papaya. He was wearing faded Levi's, a white tuxedo shirt with sleeves rolled to mid-forearm. The shirt was unbuttoned, exposing his chest and a huge gold rope chain and Mexican gold peso medallion hanging from his neck. With his red hair down over his shoulders and that stupid bandanna around his forehead he stood out like a neon sign in Times Square.

"Buon giorno, signor" Brito smiled, showing off his newly acquired Italian.

"Good morning, I hope you slept well." Cuffaro replied politely in English. He sat down at the table.

"A cappuccino for my friend," Brito said to his attentive waiter.

"Aponte and Sánchez called from Madrid last night. They are anxious to meet with us. They prefer to come to Rome. I told them no problem, but I think we should travel separately. The airport in Rome is crawling with antinarcotics police." Cuffaro was attempting to stay as far away from this lightning rod as he could when it came to exposing himself to the scrutiny of the Italian authorities. "If I may offer a suggestion, when in Rome do as the Romans do or you will attract too much attention to yourself." Brito was listening and occasionally nodding his head as Antoinette continued to feed him from her plate.

"This isn't Colombia, the Mafia does not control the police everywhere as your friends do in Medellín. I have made a reservation at the Excelsior Hotel on Via Veneto. I plan to arrive tomorrow about midday. You should make your own reservation there as well. If you can, take the flight at seven this evening. Take a cab to the hotel. Don't waste your time renting a car. The traffic in Rome is like no other in the world. I'll call you when I arrive."

"Don't worry, Joe, I have a British passport. The police never bother me. They think I'm a musician."

* * *

The Areolineas Iberia flight from Madrid was disembarking at Rome's Fiumicino Airport, agents for the Guardia di Finanza standing by, surveying the passengers as they approached the passport control area. The two agents gave each other a quick look as the two Colombians entered the line to display their passports to the uniformed official. Within minutes Angel Sánchez and Waldo Aponte were in separate rooms disrobing. Their bags had been collected by the Italians and were also in the process of being extensively searched. Sánchez, naked except for the solid-gold Rolex watch with its custom diamond bezel, stood shivering in the room as the uniformed guard sat silently smirking at him. The door swung open and two agents entered.

"Mr. Sánchez, what is the purpose of your visit to Rome?" one agent asked in fluent Spanish.

"I am a tourist," Sánchez answered angrily. "What is the meaning of this search? Why do I have to stand here naked while you question me?"

"You can get dressed now." The taller of the agents smiled and tossed Sánchez's clothing over to him. "Be careful in Rome, Mr. Sánchez. There are many gypsies and other skilled pickpockets in the tourist areas. You have over seventy thousand American dollars with you and could become a victim."

Just then their little party was interrupted by a voice over their radio calling repeatedly for "Pino."

"As soon as you are dressed you may collect your things outside. You are free to go. Enjoy your stay in Rome," the tall agent said.

It was an hour's drive from the airport to Via Veneto in downtown Rome and Aponte spent most of it in the back seat of the cab dealing with Sánchez's heightened paranoia caused by his experience at the airport.

"Did you hear them calling on the radio for 'Pino'? Pino is the fuckin' code name Joe gave us in Aruba. He said when we call him at his uncle's house in Sicily, don't ask for Joe. Ask for Pino. If this fuckin' Joe is an informer or a cop, I swear I'll kill him myself."

Aponte and Sánchez met Cuffaro and Brito in the center of the grand entryway of their exclusive hotel. Cuffaro immediately noticed Aponte's unusually reserved behavior, while Sánchez was not even a part of the conversation.

"What's wrong with Sánchez?" he asked Aponte. He pointed to Sánchez, pacing back and forth apart from the group.

"Joe, don't you know of the problems we had at the airport?" Aponte asked.

"How could I know what problems you had?" Cuffaro responded, becoming more irritated. "What are you talking about?"

"Joe, they took us out of line like they knew who we were, and strip-searched us. They went through everything. I even had to eat your uncle's telephone number. Sánchez thinks you're an informer."

Cuffaro couldn't believe his ears. It was at this time that Sánchez summoned up the courage to confront Cuffaro.

"Do you know what happened to me? If I find out—"

"Look, man, this is a respectable place. I'm not going to talk to you about this here. If you would like to continue this conversation, we can do that outside." Cuffaro looked at him coldly. "Brito and I will walk past the ancient wall toward the park. You and Aponte follow a few minutes later. I'll stop at a place where we can talk." Cuffaro walked along Via Veneto with his friend, trying to calm himself.

Villa Borghese park was just beyond the ancient wall. Villa Borghese is to Rome what Central Park is to New York. About a quarter of a mile inside, along the tree-lined pedestrian walkway on *Paolo del Brasile,* Cuffaro and Knox stopped at a nearby cappuccino bar. Sánchez and Aponte arrived a few minutes later.

Cuffaro walked toward the men, towering above them.

"Now, tell me what happened to you?"

Sánchez jumped in angrily: "While were standing there naked answering their stupid questions, I heard your code name. Pino! Pino! Over and over again. Tell me how the fuck did they know your code name, you sonna bitch—"

"Pino is not my code name, you stupid fuck. It *is* my name. I told you to ask for Pino when you call my uncle's house because that's the name I go by. Giuseppe . . . Giuseppino . . . *Pino* . . . it's my nickname. My uncle does not know me by Joe, he only knows Pino. And what do you expect? You dress like a drug dealer, they're going to treat you like a drug dealer. Look at those fuckin' gold chains around your neck, that Rolex watch on your wrist. And look at your shirt—button it up! This is Rome, the fashion capital of the world. Garbage collectors dress better than you. This is not Medellín!"

Aponte was pulling at Sánchez's sleeve. Obviously there had been a mistake. There was nothing for the Colombians to do but apologize.

"You had to have been there, Joe. I was so upset. I thought for sure I had been pointed out. I'm sorry for what I said," Sánchez said to the big man. Look, I'm a little on edge, I haven't had any cocaine in a couple of days since we left Madrid.

"Yeah, Joe—did you maybe bring an ounce with you from Palermo?" Aponte asked with anticipation.

"What? You mean you people use that shit?" Cuffaro now thought even less of his Colombian associates. "It's a good thing you didn't have any on you at the airport, or you'd be in jail. If I hadda known you two were cocaine addicts, I woulda never worked with you on this deal."

The Colombians persisted. "Well, can you go back to Palermo and pick up an ounce for us?" Aponte asked. Until now Brito had stood by, observing in amusement. But now he joined Aponte and Sánchez in their pleas.

"Why don't you just talk to your friends in Palermo and see if you can't get us a little for our troubles."

"Look, you want cocaine?" Cuffaro stopped them. "Get it yourself. I'm sure you can find it anywhere along the streets of Rome."

"Well, if we can't get any cocaine, let's go get something to eat," Brito suggested, disappointedly.

"Good idea," said Aponte. "Man, I've got to do *something*."

The four men began making their way toward the *Piazza del Popolo.* As they passed the twin churches in the piazza, Cuffaro began suggesting several restaurants within walking distance.

But Sánchez had his own ideas. He had been intrigued by the brightly colored signs directing them to *Piazza di Spagna,* the site of Rome's first McDonald's restaurant. Cuffaro couldn't believe these guys. It almost made him want to laugh. Here in the culinary center of the world, in this cultural mecca, these men wanted to eat at McDonald's.

Joe wanted nothing more than to take a shower, take a nap and relax with his family. He had been gone over three weeks, and in the last eight days had flown back and forth between Rome and Palermo before taking the seven-and-a-half hour flight to Miami. No sooner had he walked in the door than the phone rang.

"Joey, the telephone is for you." His wife handed him the telephone with a tired look in her eyes.

"Hello?"

"Joe, you gotta come over right away." It was Galatolo.

"But I just got home. Why don't I meet you tomorrow?"

"No, Joe, it's very important. You must come right away. I am at the Christine Lee Restaurant in Coral Gables. LoDuca and Naimo are with me and they want to see you."

"Okay," he sighed. "I'll be there as soon as I can." He turned to look over to his wife, but she had left the room.

Two hours later Cuffaro was still sitting in the Chinese restaurant watching these mafiosi gorge themselves on one course after another.

"Joe, what you have accomplished will make all of us wealthy men and open many more opportunities to us," Rosario Naimo said, leading a champagne toast to Cuffaro.

No sooner had the toast ended than LoDuca leaned close to Cuffaro.

"You are a very important man to us. Our work is just beginning. John will give you all of the details. Now you go home, see your wife and children and rest." LoDuca was a little drunk, but he seemed sincere.

"Joe, let me walk you out to the car," Galatolo said, placing his hand on Joe's shoulder as if he were his closest friend. As Joe opened the door to his Mercedes, Galatolo held it open and pulled an envelope from his inside coat pocket. "There's ten thousand dollars here for us. If we both take three we can put four thousand in the kitty."

With that jewel of wisdom Galatolo opened the envelope and, with the skill of a "confidence man," peeled thirty Ben Franklin's off the top and handed them to Cuffaro. "And there's more where that came from."

Cuffaro looked at his partner and then at the wad of money he had in his hand in total disbelief. This was his payment? This was the money he had been promised? This pittance was what he had risked everything for?

The job he had just accomplished was unprecedented. He had connected three of the world's major drug-trafficking centers—New York, Medellín and Palermo. This triangle brought together two of the largest and most violent criminal organizations on the globe. It had taken more than a year out of his life, traveling thousands of miles and spending months away from his family. He easily made more money at the Epicure Market during the holidays and the only risk he had was accidentally cutting himself.

"Joe, next week we want you to return to Palermo. There is another important mission for you to handle."

Cuffaro had had enough. It was time to make his move. Time to devise an escape plan. Little did Cuffaro know then, however, that his knowledge of how this deal was made would be worth more to him than all the money the Medellín Cartel and the Sicilian Mafia could collectively summon.

CHAPTER

7

NEVER SAY NEVER

"BILL, HOW THE HELL ARE YA?"

Although the voice was familiar, Gately could not place it. Then it came to him. It was the soft, Southern drawl of an old friend.

"Blue! *¿Que pasó, amigo?*"

It was the regional commissioner from Houston, William R. Logan or, as he was known to many, "Blue," for the color of his eyes. Despite that, it still seemed contradictory to call a man with very red hair, "Blue." Like Gately, Logan came from a large family with brothers and sisters who had nothing more than each other. Logan began his law enforcement career as a Denver city policeman in Colorado. He had joined the border patrol in 1970 and transferred to U.S. Customs as a special agent in 1973. Gately had worked with him for a few months down in San Diego before Logan transferred to Miami to head Operation Green-back, one year before Gately. Logan had actually been Gately's supervisor during his brief assignment at Greenback, which had followed his falling out with Mr. FOIA over the maintenance of DEA's warehouse at the Florida joint task group. Since then, Logan had changed jobs half a dozen times. Amazingly, he had climbed the ladder from group supervisor to senior executive service rank in three years. His rise had been meteoric, and he had reportedly left a lot of jealous "beltway bureaucrats" lying dead and wounded in his wake. In fact, however, Logan had simply done an incredible job. He truly deserved the rewards he received —and he was lucky enough to get them. Logan was oblivious of the rumors that followed him and would not give his detractors the time of day anyway. Ironically, it was trust in his "friends" that would eventually topple his career, the price all freethinking people pay in government.

On this day he was calling Gately as the southwest regional commissioner, a job where he supervised as many as three thousand customs employees.

"I'm just calling you to say hello—and by the way, you've got the ASAC job in San Antonio. That is, if you want it," he added with a little humor.

It was the call Gately had been waiting for. After two years, his days in exile were finally over.

"Well, Bill, do you want it?"

Gately's excitement over the prospect of getting the job had made the words stick in his throat.

"Yes. I want it. Of course I do. I'll be there tomorrow," Gately replied.

"Well, you don't have to be there tomorrow, but start packing your bags. I'd like to see you there in thirty days."

His old friend had not forgotten him. Logan was going to help him out by making him a part of something new and exciting. Maybe this time Gately would start out with the diplomacy and humility he had reluctantly learned in exile, he thought to himself. Gately had also been offered the ASAC position in San Diego, but had told Ken Ingleby, who was still the SAC in San Diego, that he preferred San Antonio because it was more affordable, an important consideration since he and his new wife were planning to begin a family.

Logan had been newly appointed to the office of regional commissioner, the first time a career special agent had held such a position within the agency. Among his myriad responsibilities as regional commissioner, Logan had been given the additional task of bringing the two thousand miles of border along the southern edge of Texas, New Mexico and Arizona into the twentieth century. This not only meant he had to increase law enforcement resources by fifty percent, he also had to bring the technology on the international trade side of the house into the paperless world of the computer. It seems that the Customs Service Southwest Region was the last government entity still using the typewriter. With the exception of California, the agency had virtually neglected the Mexican border for more than two decades. William Von Raab, Customs' most controversial commissioner, had recognized the problem at once. He had selected Logan to do the impossible and, in the process, was able to get immediate results. Logan and many others that Von Raab picked as his managers were smart, aggressive freethinkers from within the rank and file of the agency, who knew how to get results.

*   *   *

Less than four hours later, Gately's pager went off. He was standing inside the Victoria, British Columbia, airport. When he looked at the digital readout, his heart sank. It was the regional commissioner's number in Houston, Texas. Clearly, he thought, something was wrong. And it was. July 16, 1986, would soon be a day he would never forget. It was the day he got a job, lost it, then got another he never wanted.

"I've got a problem," Logan began the conversation. "It's Neil Lagerman. He's got something against you and he doesn't want you in San Antonio. He didn't have the problem yesterday when we discussed your promotion, but someone has since poisoned him."

It took all the self-discipline Gately could muster not to say what he really believed, that it wasn't Lagerman, the SAC—it was his nemesis Burns who didn't want him to get the promotion. He let Logan continue without a word.

"Bill, this isn't the consolation prize, but I've been thinking for the past week how to get Arizona off its ass. I want you to go to Phoenix—"

"Aw, Blue, Phoenix is a five-man office. My group in Blaine is larger and does ten times the work."

"My point exactly. Bill, I want you to go there and make that office into something." Logan's voice was still friendly, but he was all business. "I'll guarantee you total support. Von Raab wants Arizona to join the rest of the Customs Service. And don't worry about your TO, I've increased Phoenix to three full groups and Yuma to a full group as well. All you have to do is hire everyone, transfer the deadbeats and get to work. Oh, yeah, I also want you to open a three-man office in Flagstaff. Now do you think that will keep you busy for the first three months?"

The news from Logan would not allow Gately to relish the success of his most recent Victoria case. Everything had gone as planned. The Colombians, a few Canadians and a group of smugglers out of West Palm Beach had just made their last payment on a half-million-dollar refurbishing project of a Grumman Albatross seaplane. They had been under surveillance for the last seven months by Gately and his group out of Blaine, Washington, along with the RCMP drug squad. Their plan was to smuggle three thousand kilos of cocaine into South Florida.

Gately sat in the right-hand seat of the Cessna 337 as they flew over the Strait of Juan de Fuca. The pilot took a south-southeast heading toward the San Juan Islands. All Gately could think about was losing the San Antonio job. No matter what Blue had said, Phoenix *was* the consolation prize. And he had a gut feeling that his old "pal" John Burns had been the one to poison Neil Lagerman, the special agent in charge in San Antonio. Burns had been promoted twice in the past three years as well—Ingleby had made him the organized crime drug task force coordinator in San Diego. Now Logan, who considered Burns a good choice and a friend, had selected Burns to be his assistant regional commissioner for enforcement in Houston.

It was mid-February 1987, Gately's second winter in Arizona. He sat in the conference room, waiting for the meeting to begin. His mind was elsewhere as he looked out the window, thinking how easy the winters were here. The mild weather was the only thing that didn't make him feel stressed-out. After his first year in Arizona, the job had become his life once again. Nothing had been easy. His marriage had dissolved and, with it, his hopes to start a family. Gately had then concentrated on rebuilding his office and making Customs a leader in Arizona law enforcement. He had hired over thirty new agents to his staff in Phoenix, Flagstaff and Yuma. Between the three sites there were forty-two agents, less than half of what was needed. To make up for the deficit, Gately was able to accomplish the difficult task of convincing the state and local law enforcement officials in each major city under his jurisdiction to form task forces with Customs, a strategy that increased manpower by a hundred percent. Not an easy job, but it was made harder by his first boss in Arizona, a constant critic and a nonbeliever in any type of change—especially if it wasn't his idea.

Within two months of arriving on the job, the special agent in charge, who did not see eye to eye with Von Raab's or Logan's assessment of what was needed in Arizona, threatened to fire Gately. Two months later that same SAC was on a plane headed to Houston, where he was demoted for openly defying Von Raab. Von Raab quickly replaced him with a much younger and more dynamic personality, Tom McDermott. McDermott was the best choice Von Raab could have made. He was a dedicated agent who had worked his way through every job in the agency, beginning his customs career as a mailroom inspector in 1970. McDermott had been assigned as a special agent in San Francisco, San Diego and Miami. He had served his last three years as the ASAC in his home town, San Francisco. Gately respected McDermott, a real agent who had paid his dues. What's more, he too was a combat infantryman who served in Vietnam during Tet in 1968.

Arizona, known for nineteenth-century Western heroes and villains alike—legends such as Wyatt Earp, Geronimo and Pancho Villa—had a new crop of twentieth-century cops and robbers to add to its collection. The Mexican Mafia and the Colombian cartels of Medellín and Cali had merged in the state of Sonora, creating a cocaine smuggling problem that on any given day rivaled or surpassed that of South Florida. Border county sheriffs in places like Cochise, Yuma and Pima counties had emerged on the frontline of the drug war. Soon local lawmen like Jimmy Judd, John Phipps and Clarence Dupnick appeared in the media and in local and national political arenas to make their case for federal assistance. Their counties shared a largely unpopulated desert area with the Mexican state of Sonora, which was now openly referred to in law enforcement circles and by the media as "Cocaine Alley." In 1986, cocaine seizures for Customs in Arizona totaled a mere 1,200 pounds. By 1988, cocaine seizures surpassed 19,000 pounds.

Gately's attention was drawn away from the window as McDermott, Logan and Dave Hayes, the RAC from Nogales, entered the room. It was the first time they had seen Gately's new office. Since Gately's arrival in August 1986, every customs manager in Arizona had been replaced, except for Rick Ashby, the resident agent in charge in Yuma. The new team was successful, Gately thought, because they all had a similar philosophy. Usually the attitude in law enforcement was "big cases, big problems." But here, their philosophy showed in their personal attitude: "big risks make big cases." Between them there was more than a century of experience from the four corners of the country, as well as both sides of the nation's borders. Best of all was the friendship they shared and the professional respect they had for each other. Despite the difficulties, it was the best working relationship Gately had experienced anywhere.

It was a balmy February afternoon. Hayes was the first to speak up.

"You know, Bill, this confiscated furniture is just a little too nice for you," he said.

Gately's office was furnished with leather chairs, a marble top coffee table and solid mahogany desk with matching credenza. It was top of the line, modern Danish motif, the furthest thing away from the standard post–World War II American government gun-metal gray office environment.

"I think this is SAC quality furniture," Hayes continued. "What do you think, Blue?"

"Definitely, I agree," said Logan.

"Well, that's okay with me," Gately responded. "But you guys realize this is all confiscated and if you take it to Tucson, the government's going to have to pay about four thousand dollars to refurnish this office, and of course that's taxpayer's money." They all laughed. Then Gately added another barb, directed at Logan and Hayes.

"If you guys want to smoke in this office you'll have to go to the smoking section. It's that big open space next to the elevator, just beyond the front door." With that, Gately pulled out two ashtrays for them.

Gately admired how Logan was able to maintain such a positive atti-

44 DEAD RINGER

tude despite the problems that had beset him these last two years. During Gately's first year in Arizona Logan had been under constant investigation by Internal Affairs, based on one false allegation after another. The stress of the job, the continuing investigations and the fact that many in his staff had turned against him had caused Logan to suffer a severe heart attack. Shortly after this life-threatening incident, Logan stepped down as regional commissioner. After his recovery McDermott was the only SAC who would offer Logan a job as his deputy. Ironically, this move put Logan under the supervision of John Burns, who as assistant regional commissioner for enforcement was the supervisor for the five special agents in charge located in the Southwest region. It wasn't long before Logan realized that Burns had used the same tactic on him as he had on Gately. During these two years, Gately, McDermott, Hayes and Logan were dodging a seemingly endless stream of Internal Affairs investigations, which were all later discovered to be attributable to their "friend," John Burns.

Hayes had just finished briefing everyone on his operations in Nogales and Douglas. It was now Gately's turn to bring them up to date on any current significant investigations within his jurisdiction. He went through a list of cases, most of which were in the arrest or indictment stages, a few of which were in the advanced prosecution stages. The last item on the list was a new investigation. Normally, a case in its infancy was not discussed, but Gately had a gut feeling this one had potential.

"We've been on this guy for about a month now. I'll tell you what I know. First, he's using a 'dead baby' ID. He calls himself Dale Peterson, but we know Dale Peterson died a week after birth in Toledo, Ohio, in 1944."

"Is that the crime you're investigating?" Hayes interrupted, taking a drag from his cigarette. "What did he do? Get a phony driver's license? You know, Bill you should probably turn that case over to the DMV." Hayes laughed out loud and the smoke filled the room.

Dave Hayes had been a customs agent for over twenty years. Outwardly he was unimpressed by anything, but inside he still maintained the same zest and excitement for the job he had when he was a rookie in the early seventies in Savannah, Georgia.

Gately returned his fire. "Dave, we send all of our petty and otherwise insignificant cases from Phoenix to Nogales. Isn't that right, Blue?"

It was the perfect response to get Hayes's goat. As the RAC in Nogales, Hayes was about as busy as a one-armed paper hanger. The advent of the official policy of "zero tolerance" forced Hayes to investigate every border drug seizure in Nogales, regardless of quantity. To further exacerbate the situation, he and his agents were run ragged because the state prosecutor in Santa Cruz County refused to file charges in any federal case. This put Hayes's people on the road between Nogales and Tucson three times a day for the processing of prisoners and for initial appearances in federal court.

Logan chimed in without missing a beat: "I think Bill's right, Dave, maybe we should send this DMV case down to you."

"If Dave is done with his assessment, I'll continue," Gately added with a smile. "What I think is significant is that this guy has purchased a $350,000 home, a couple of new cars and to top it off he is casually dropping between eight and ten thousand dollars a day in the night-deposit drop of a local bank. What Mr. Petersen has told the bank is that he is the sole proprieter of a coin-operated vending business. Funny thing is, he hasn't dropped a bag of coins for deposit yet. Just fives, tens, twenties, fifties and hundreds. We've found a neighbor who lives on a hillside overlooking his property who is willing to let us set up a video camera in his living room. That will give us a twenty-four-hour-a-day eye on Peterson's property. We're trying for a pen register on his telephone, but the phone company says he has no service. The irony of that is, we've seen him talking on a mobile phone while sunning himself by his pool. So, he's using a dead baby's name, he has more cash than we can count, and he still feels the need to steal telephone service; and the telephone company doesn't even know how he's doing it. I don't know about you guys but I think we got a good one here."

Leo Fraley had lived in many places throughout his lifetime, from the Ohio Valley and the rolling hills of Western Pennsylvania to the port cities of South and West Florida, to the cities and jungles of Colombia, but he had never considered the Sonoran desert a place to spend his days. Fraley's move to Arizona had come about after a close call with a drug agent from the Florida Department of Law Enforcement in the small town of Floral City, near Clearwater. It all started in the early summer of 1987 during the negotiations and planning of another cocaine venture with his Colombian compadres.

It was his third trip to Belize in two months, and each time there had been a new set of problems with which to contend. The first in this series of near catastrophes was the worst and the most devastating to him personally. Just a few hours before he was to meet Velasco and his Belizian contact at Velasco's hotel room on San Pedro Island, the British Army arrested the Colombian and turned him over to U.S. authorities. Velasco's extradition was swift. He was hustled out to the nearest airport, where a U.S. government plane waited, and in less than four hours he was booked into Houston's Harris County Jail.

The DEA identified Velasco as head of the organization that smuggled over twenty tons of marijuana into the Port of San Diego in 1978. They had a rat who would testify against him. Things looked bad for Fraley's partner. Fraley was still communicating with Velasco through his attorney and, despite his own fugitive status from the bank burglary in North Carolina and his escape from Western State Penitentiary, he brazenly walked into the jail as a registered visitor. A month later, the U.S. Marshals moved Velasco to El Reno, Oklahoma, and a short time later, he was permanently relocated to San Diego's Metropolitan Correction Center, where he, if the feds had their way, would spend the next twenty years. Incredibly, despite his incarceration, Velasco maintained an almost daily contact with Colombia via a third-party conference call arranged by his wife who, with Fraley's help, leased a house on San Diego's prestigious La Jolla coastline. With Velasco behind bars, Fraley, by default, was now the chief of transportation for this branch of Pablo Escobar's cocaine empire. Don Pedro Ortegón, Escobar's CEO for operations, established a direct line of communication with him. It seemed their only concern was to keep the drugs moving. After all, the site in Belize had worked well for them twice before.

The first load of cocaine was only three hundred kilos. They used a Cessna 210 that Fraley had purchased from an airplane broker in Rhode Island to ferry the load from Los Llanos to Belize. Once in Belize, Fraley and his crew carried the cocaine hidden in the transom of a converted "Number One Hull" trailer that Fraley had purchased at a U.S. customs auction in Miami. Two days later he drove the load to Newark and delivered it to a Colombian. At three thousand a kilo, Fraley earned a cool nine hundred thousand dollars. But his partner Velasco got fifty percent of that, and minus his crew expenses Fraley was back down to three hundred thousand in take-home pay.

The success quickly led to another load. This time Escobar shipped a thousand kilos in order to cash in quickly on a new route that skirted around the areostat balloon and Coast Guard patrols via the eastern Caribbean and the Bahamas. Fraley picked a second vessel, also from the customs auction, but this time he found a "Defender Yatch Sportfisherman," with less than eight hundred logged hours. He sent it off to Louisiana to have it overhauled and the engines tweaked to perfection—he did not want to undergo engine failures or mechanical problems during the operation. The new boat was sleeker and fit the role a lot better than the Trawler. But what sold Fraley more than anything were the incredible hidden storage locations that were already custom-built into this vessel. The secret compartments were everywhere: in the internal bulkheads, the forward and aft hulls and the transom. He could carry five tons of cocaine and not have a single kilo anywhere in sight.

Fraley gently maneuvered his newly refurbished eighty thousand dollar, thirty-nine foot Sportfisherman in the San Pedro harbor. This tiny island just off the coast of Belize was a marlin sport fisherman's paradise. The rich and famous coveted their knowledge of the bounty in San Pedro's Honduran Gulf waters, where they came to seek their trophy fish. Of course there were also the Leo Fraley's of the world, the twentieth-century smugglers seeking a haven for their vessels and crews. The businessmen of San Pedro catered to the smugglers as readily as they did to the fishermen. To Fraley it was a safe haven, free of the patrols and hassles in the stretch of water between Central America and Florida's sleepy west coast.

"We'll anchor here and take the skiff into San Pedro for some dinner," Fraley said, cutting the twin six hundred horsepower turbo diesels to an idle. "Ben, you and Barry get ready and come with me. Buck, you take first watch," Fraley addressed his three-man crew from the bridge. They were three men from his old gang back in Ohio. Ben Fannon and John Barry were both as loyal as old dogs. Buck Spicer, the youngest of the three, was the most eager to cash in. Fraley had met him through a mob connection in Ohio. Spicer had been working in a chop shop cannibalizing high-value stolen cars for their expensive parts, or retooling the VIN numbers to put the car back on the road as a "previously owned quality vehicle."

Fraley and two of his crew members were at the Hut on San Pedro's Barrier Reef Drive in less than thirty minutes. Fraley made the Hut a must every time he came to the island. They had the best burgers, sweet potato fries and stone crabs in Belize. While they ate, Fraley's contact Raul Martínez came to the table wearing a smile.

"I see your trip from Florida was uneventful," Martínez said, selecting a stone crab from the center plate. "You'll be pleased to know the cargo is here and you can start loading this evening, as soon as the sun sets."

It was almost midnight when Fraley and his crew finished loading the first thousand kilos into the false bulkheads located in the transom of Fraley's vessel. They had been working nonstop for more than five hours, like a water line in a fire-bucket brigade. The duffel bags were first unloaded from the skiffs carrying the cocaine from the island, then passed across the deck of the vessel to two men loading the bulkheads.

"That's it for tonight," Fraley said. "We'll load the rest tomorrow night." He tossed an M-16 across the deck to Fannon. "I'm gonna take a shower, then I'll take the first watch. Barry, you and Fannon decide who's gonna relieve me."

Just before sunrise, Fannon came up to relieve Fraley, who by now was in real need of rest.

Fraley's deep sleep came to a halt at the sound of the raised voices and scuffling above. "What's going on?" he asked, stumbling up the ladder.

"There's a patrol boat coming up fast," Fannon replied.

They had chosen this area because there would be no patrols here. Martínez swore he had already paid them to stay away.

"Get her ready to go, in case we have to blow out of here in a hurry," Fraley ordered.

In a matter of minutes the twenty-foot Boston Whaler patrol boat, twin hundred-horse outboards rumbling at an idle, was at their side.

"Will the captain of the vessel come on deck? We are with the San Pedro harbor patrol," a voice with a strong Caribbean accent cracked through the loudspeaker. "We must check your papers and inspect your vessel."

"I'm the captain and youns ain't comin' on my boat. You got no reason to board. I'm not even in your goddamn harbor," Fraley responded.

"We must insist on your cooperation immediately," the officer said as the pilot of the police vessel swung his boat around to board Fraley's ship.

Fraley moved back, reached down on the deck near the bench seat and picked up the M-16. He chambered a round, flipped the selector on full-automatic and rested the butt of the rifle on his hip in full view of the harbor policeman.

"I'm telling youns for the last time, youns ain't boardin' my vessel. First of all, your boat has no markings. How the hell do I know if youns are really the harbor police? For all I know you guys are fuckin' pirates. If you get any closer, you're gonna be swimmin' back to the island, cause I'm gonna start fillin' that boat of yours full of holes."

To make sure they understood he meant business, Fraley took the rifle off his hip, brought the gun to bear and fired a burst across the canopy of the Boston Whaler. That was all he had to do. The Boston Whaler virtually stood on its engines as it turned and fled. Within a few seconds the harbor cop was hydroplaning toward the shore as fast as he could.

Fraley's crew was in a panic. They were all trying to convince him to leave, but Fraley would have none of it.

"No way. Martínez says these guys have all been taken care of. These assholes are just lookin' to shake us down for more, and I ain't givin' it up. We're gonna have shifts startin' right now watchin' for that son of a bitch in his Boston Whaler. I want two guys on deck with binoculars, armed at all times."

By midday Fraley's crew was too frightened and intimidated to take on the other thousand kilos. Throughout the day Fraley had been unsuccessful in his attempts to reach Martínez on his ship-to-shore radio, which only added to the already tense situation. By sunset Fraley was beginning to side with his men.

"Leo, we can't be hangin' out here any longer," Fannon pleaded. "If they come back we either gotta shoot it out with 'em or let 'em rip the boat open and take the load. If we go now, at least we'll have the load we got. We can always come back once you fix it with your people down south."

"You're makin' a lot of sense right now, Ben," Fraley replied reluctantly. By now his anger had been subdued by logic. "Okay, hoist anchor, let's get the hell out of here."

The twenty-six hour journey across the four hundred and fifty miles of the Gulf of Mexico was something Fraley would later compare to a sand enema. The daylight hours were filled with Fannon's bad cooking, Spicer's crude jokes and Barry's bouts with seasickness. Fraley passed the time getting a tan, drinking cold beer and listening to the Pirates when he could find the band carrying the broadcast.

Nightfall wasn't as bad. Fraley had the calm of the sea and the panorama of stars painted on the black velvet sky to himself, one of the reasons he always took the first watch. When the rest of the crew went below and crashed, Fraley headed for the bridge. He systematically went through a complete check of all his instruments, testing his radar, sonar and his LORAN Navigator. The forty-five thousand dollars he had invested in his state-of-the-art navigation equipment gave him the peace of mind to kick back in the captain's chair, light up a fresh cigarette, crack open a can of brew and throw his feet up on the dash. It was at times like this when he couldn't help but wonder at the strange ways of fate.

Six years earlier, two months after he had arrived in Florida in the spring of 1981, Fraley had been on his way to Aruba to meet with Velasco to discuss their next deal. Velasco preferred the Holiday Inn on Palm Beach, above the more prestigious Concorde Hotel, simply because he felt it had superior service, a fantastic daily brunch and a better beach. That afternoon they took a drive to the southwest point of the island and indulged in one of their favorite pastimes, Charlie's Bar in Sint Nicolaas Harbor. The bar and restaurant had an interesting decor— it was famous for the thousands of business cards plastered on the walls and hanging on a long fishing line looped from the ceiling, protruding directly over each table. Anyone could unclip the line, pierce a card or note and slide it on for the next patron to read. As he and Velasco worked their way through a burger and half a dozen San Miguels, Fraley noticed a business card that was suspiciously out of place in this establishment.

"Look at this," Fraley said as he pulled off the U.S. government business card. "This guy's got some nerve putting his card in here." He showed Velasco the gold federal badge embossed on the card.

"What's his name? Maybe we should call him for his assistance?" Velasco asked sarcastically.

"William Gately. What an asshole!" Fraley said.

"I want to tell you," Velasco said, changing the tone, "the office is very pleased with you. So, whatever you want to do, we will do. Get a crew together. You do not even have to pay for your transportation needs; the office will front you the cash to purchase a vessel and an aircraft.

"The first thing you must do, however, is purchase an aircraft. I suggest you find a 404 Titan. It is a basic, no-frills twin-engine aircraft, but it has very good range, and best of all it has a huge load capacity. You can transport as much as one and a half tons for as long as two thousand nautical miles."

Velasco could virtually give the specifications on any aircraft, vessel, automobile or truck. He was a walking encyclopedia of transportation. In fact, in the office of his Cartageña home a library contained books, manufacturer's publications, magazines and periodicals on the subject. He had topographical maps, navigational air and sea charts and geographical data on nearly every country on the planet.

After this specific information, there was very little else they spoke of in great detail. But it was all that needed to be discussed. Fraley raised his glass in a toast to Velasco. They had begun a longlasting, extremely profitable business relationship.

Fraley was back in Pompano Beach two days later, and in less than three weeks he had located a Titan. DeVitto had used his connections to help Fraley find it through a Chicago-based broker. With forty thousand dollars Velasco sent to him in airline express packages Fraley made a down payment and agreed to make five more monthly payments of $7,500 each. A week later, his old marijuana partner Bobby Povich found a pilot. It was none other than DeVitto's former wheelman Harvey. Povich bragged to Fraley that Harvey came highly recommended in the street.

"They all say he can fly anything. In fact, Harvey landed a DC-6 Constellation carrying twenty-five thousand pounds of pot on a highway once." Povich went on and on about his great find but Fraley never let on that he and Harvey were old acquaintances.

Shortly afterward, a meeting was scheduled to discuss the planned loads and identify landing areas. They narrowed it down to North Carolina, a couple of spots in Georgia, one on a private island off the coast of Savannah. The island was an undeveloped property for sale, owned by an acquaintance of Povich. The only problem was that the military also used a portion of the island. In an emergency they could also land in

Florida. There was a new community under development, south of Lake Okeechobee right in the middle of the state. It was a perfect location near the seven-hundred-square-mile lake in a sparsely populated area. The development was part of a project for a planned community of homes, schools and high-tech industry in this predominantly agricultural region of Florida. None of the houses had been built, but several roads had recently been completed. If they had problems, and needed to divert to a secondary location, the wide, newly paved streets were a perfect runway for the 404.

As they ironed out the details of their plan, Povich suddenly presented Fraley with an ultimatum: there would be no deal until Povich met the Colombian. Fraley knew that if that happened, he could potentially eliminate him. There was no way he would place himself in that position.

"What the fuck you wanna say to the Colombian when you don't speak Spanish and he don't speak no English?" Fraley said to him, knowing Povich was not aware of Velasco's perfect English and proper Oxford accent.

"I don't know, but I gotta meet him," Povich said defiantly.

"Well, here's the way it is, you ain't gonna meet him. They're sour on gringos as it is, and the only reason I can talk to him is because I brought 'em their money."

It was the answer that killed the entire deal. Povich called off the crew and the pilot. When Fraley tried to go around Povich, not only did he find out that Povich had "put the mouth out" on him, he also learned that the others were double-crossing him. Worst of all, he found out that his protégé and good friend Tubby was also working with Povich.

Fraley didn't let it pass. He flew to Youngstown, Ohio, where the plane was parked at the executive terminal. From there he called Velasco and told him the deal was off, and that eventually he would put together another crew. As soon as he hung up Fraley walked to the plane, opened it and placed two large reinforced plastic trash bags with five gallons of gasoline inside. He took out his packet of cigarettes, lit one and placed it on an open pack of matches near the highly combustible trash bags.

He stood far enough away to watch the crude but effective cigarette fuse ignite the liquid explosive and send flames through the inside of the aircraft.

It was shortly after that incident that Fraley had decided to get out of the drug trafficking business and get on with his life.

The sound of his radar alarm brought Fraley back to his present situation. He could feel his heart rate increase, his eyes open wide and his palms begin to sweat. Who the hell could be out here in the middle of nowhere in the middle of the night, other than the goddamn Coast

Guard? He could see the vessel about ten miles away. As he watched his screen, and calculated its speed, he knew it couldn't be a cutter. It was too small and too slow.

"Must be some fuckin' fool in a sailboat headed for the Yucatán," he muttered to himself. The boat was drifting off the screen.

Fraley's vitals eventually returned to normal. After lighting a cigarette, he locked in his course, rechecked his LORAN, then headed down the ladder to the refrigerator. He grabbed some fruit and another cold beer, then returned to the captain's chair. In a few minutes he had drifted back to the days when he had sworn off the dope business.

In the summer of 1982 he applied for his chauffeur's license and tested for a permit to drive an eighteen-wheeler again. Using his "Richard Carbone" New York driver's license, he traveled to Kansas and immediately tested for his chauffeur's license. The next day he found a job as a truck driver with the Wesport Trucking Company in Kansas City at a salary of seven cents a mile.

Two months later, while pushing his rig at fifty percent over gross through Grants Pass, Oregon, the trucking company filed for Chapter 11 relief. When he returned to the company's headquarters he was told he would not get the eighteen hundred dollars he was owed. Knowing that some of the trucks not repossessed by the banks were the personal property of the owner, Fraley drove directly to the owner's house. He hooked up to one of the owner's trailers and parked it at a mall and secured it with a king-pin lock. From a nearby pay phone, with the trailer in his view, Fraley called the owner.

"If I don't get my money, I'm going to sell your trailer," Fraley calmly threatened.

"You can't do that," the owner said as he looked outside to the empty space where his trailer was once parked.

"The hell I can't. I just did."

When the owner saw that Fraley meant business and was not concerned about the consequences of his threats, the owner agreed to give him a personal check. That same owner, who later joined another trucking business in Cushing, Oklahoma, called Fraley to offer him another job at fifteen cents a mile.

While the trucking business was collapsing during the next two years, Fraley was casually watching the video poker business spring up in every truck stop, tavern and neighborhood grocery store across Ohio and Pennsylvania. He saw dollar signs, so he hooked up with his old burglary pal, Petie Sansone. Over the years, Sansone had become friends with Joe Timanier, who had established some much-needed mob connections in Ohio's Ashtabula County. Timanier's "in" was through his son, who was the city solicitor. With connections on both ends of the equation, Fraley and Sansone eventually had every chief of police in the county on the payroll, including the sheriff. The only official who would not accept their payoffs was a hard-nosed honest cop who was chief in Kingville Township. Their only significant problem was a rival group who were already well established in the numbers business. But Sansone's connections with the Cleveland outfit were all they needed for permission to enter the area. Sansone told Fraley he had gotten permission from the Licavoti boss in Cleveland to do business there. Further, it had been declared "open" because the local mob family was no longer around. Ronnie Carabia was doing time for blowing up Danny Green, and Carabia's brother had recently been "whacked." The youngest brother Willy was so scared he didn't dare come out of the house.

Things were looking good for Sansone and Fraley during the first year they were in business. Other than his fugitive status—and sharing the same geography with some of the cops who would have liked nothing better than to put him away for the rest of his life—Fraley had a fairly low-stress lifestyle. He and Sansone were splitting about eight thousand a week. Fraley had even become the "maintenance/service" man for the machines. This way he could personally rig the payoffs, shifting the percentages as he pleased to maximize their profits. The money wasn't as good as drugs but it was steady, and there was no one out there trying to sell him out behind his back. He made sure that everyone got their share. The way he saw it, as long as the mob got their tribute and the local cops took their piece, everyone was happy with video poker.

As the saying goes, alas, all good things must come to an end, and so did the video poker business in Ohio and Pennsylvania. State legislators passed a bill banning the machines as "gaming devices." Fraley played the same game as everyone in the business and switched out the boards in his machines giving them a new face and format; in reality, however, it was the same thing as poker. The cat-and-mouse game became more and more difficult, and the profits started to diminish. Sansone wanted out, so Fraley bought his end. But even as the sole proprietor Fraley wasn't making enough cash to meet his needs. His father had been diagnosed with cancer, and his mom's health was failing as well. Their medical bills and bills for prescription drugs ran into the thousands of dollars. In one month alone Fraley's father had chemotherapy treatments that cost over eighteen thousand dollars.

He had always kept his ties with Velasco, calling him and keeping his options open, and soon it was as if the past four years hadn't happened as he sat across the table from Velasco, in Aruba once again. It was here that he cut the deal that put him back into the cocaine business as a major player for his Colombian friends. By now the men he had met in Los Llanos and in Bogotá were almost household names. More people recognized Pablo Escobar's name than they did those of heads of state or world leaders. Cocaine had become the drug of choice and it was everywhere, from the crack deals on the street corners of America's worst neighborhoods to the boardrooms of major corporations. It had spread like a virus, infecting virtually every facet of society. Cocaine was like liquor during Prohibition. Everyone wanted it, and the only thing between the people who could supply it and the consumer was the law. There were billions to be made and Fraley was determined to cash in on his share.

Spicer and Fannon were on deck and Barry was on the bridge with Fraley as they entered the cut near Hurricane Pass north of Clearwater and south of Tarpon Springs. The *Return of the Jedi*'s home port was Dunedin Harbor in Clearwater. A huge orange crescent was draped over some low clouds on the horizon as the sun began its ascent over the western shore of Florida. Fannon was putting the last touches on the sport fishing "props" to give the appearance of their four-day trophy-fishing venture to the Yucatán. Spicer was checking the molding along the transom and bulkheads where they had stashed the cocaine for any telltale signs of the false compartments. If there were any detectable flaws it was his job to apply the touch of paint or adhesive to mask anything that would give away their cargo. The customs regulations required all vessels returning from foreign ports to call in ahead of time to make an appointment for their inspection and clearance. What a great rule, Fraley thought: "If you don't call, they don't come."

That night all four men moved the cargo from the boat in Clearwater's harbor to Fraley's farm in Floral City. They packed it into a windowless Chevy van on blocks, just to the north of his property line. He figured if there was any heat and the cops came snooping around, the van wasn't on his property. If the cocaine was found they couldn't justifiably tie it to him. That night he contacted Don Pedro Ortegón in Barranquilla.

"What happened? You left with only half the load, the office is very concerned," Ortegón began his conversation.

That was all Fraley needed to hear. "Tell the office that they have a problem in San Pedro. First Winces gets grabbed on the mainland and now this. These things may be a coincidence, but if I had stayed we could've lost the load I had on board to some nosey harbor cop. Tell them the books are safe. I'll have everything in Miami as planned by tomorrow afternoon."

Ortegón settled down as soon as he heard the story and promised Fraley he would send someone to investigate immediately. Despite Fraley's warning, he still thought Fraley should return as soon as possible to pick up the other thousand kilos, or "books." Within the hour Fraley was passed out in his bed—then his two dogs started making enough noise to wake the entire county. The male and female Rottweilers were ferocious guard dogs.

He got out of bed, pulled on some shorts and grabbed his "deer rifle" with the infrared scope. With the dogs barking and pulling violently at their chains and choking themselves, Fraley put the rifle to his shoulder and scanned the north end of his property through the night-vision scope. Then he saw what he had dreaded. A man stood within a few feet of the Chevy van with a walkie-talkie in his hand. It looked as if he was actually using the van for cover. Then Fraley heard the squelch breaking on the radio in the distance. There was no question in his mind that this guy was a cop and he knew they never traveled alone. He lowered the rifle and thought for a second. What he did next was a gambler's choice. If it was the law, they were either there with a search warrant and about to move in force or they were just snooping, trying to see something they could use against him. Fraley listened to his gut and prayed that it was the latter of the two possibilities.

"Okay, girl, go out there and get that son of a bitch," Fraley whispered to the smallest of the two canines as he freed her from the leash. "You too, boy. Get 'em."

Both Rottweilers were loose and charging across the open field like guided TOW missiles. Fraley leaned back against his porch post, lifted the rifle to his shoulder and through the scope caught a glimpse of the man's silhouette moving at a full sprint through the field toward the state road. There was no time to lose now. With the cops in a retreat he had to move the load as fast as possible. But first he had to test the waters to determine if they were still on his tail. He called Fannon at the Marina.

"Ben, I want you to get over here as soon as you can tomorrow morning. Rent two vans and buy a bunch of empty boxes. Park one of the vans in the Marina and bring one over here with six or seven boxes. Tell Buck and John to stay close to the boat. You got that?"

"Yeah boss, but what the fuck—"

"Ben, just be here as soon as you can."

Fannon was at the house by nine. Fraley had him bring the boxes in and load everything from newspapers to the junk he wanted to throw out but never got around to doing. They carried the boxes out to the van and loaded it.

"Ben, I want you take a drive around Clearwater and then down to St. Petersburg. Take my cell phone. If you grow a tail call me right away."

Fraley wanted to bring the cops to the surface if they were on him. The "heat" runs to Clearwater and St. Pete were designed to do just that. Fraley knew if the cops were watching they didn't have the patience to wait much longer, especially if they saw the rental vans and the activity at his house. The cops would hit Fannon and the house if they were around. If they weren't he was still cool and the cocaine could be moved to Miami with minimal risk.

Fraley was at the poolside bar of the Sheraton Airport Hotel. The Miami River bordered the interior of the property like a moat around an ancient castle. It had been several hours since he had made the delivery to the Miami contact. Now the waiting game for his money was beginning to get on his nerves a little more than usual. Even though Fannon had driven four hours in circles without detecting a tail, Fraley still made a couple of "heat runs" himself before he finally loaded the cocaine into a third rental van and headed south on the Florida Turnpike.

"I'll have another Miller," Fraley said as he checked the dial on his Rolex for the tenth time in ten minutes. As the bartender leaned over to get his beer from the cooler Fraley's pager went off. He reached down, pulled it from his waistband and depressed the tab to initiate the digital readout. He read the coded number, converted it in his head and walked into the lobby to the nearest telephone booth.

"*Bueno,*" the male voice said after one short ring.

"*Este es señor Peterson,*" Fraley began, "*¿Tienes mis papeles?*"

"*Sí, claro. Aquí los tengo.*"

"*Okay, por favor, venga al Hotel Sheraton Aeropuerto. Cuarto cinco-zero-tres,*" Fraley knew his Spanish had been correct when his compadre showed up at the door within thirty minutes.

An hour later Fraley was twenty minutes south of the Fort Lauderdale Airport. The wheels in his head were starting to turn. He knew he could not remain in Florida. He thought he should take the opportunity to get away now, before things heated up more. To do so, he would have to walk away from his two boats, a plane, his home and furniture and all of his cars. Fraley decided his freedom was worth more than all his possessions. As he drove by he decided to pull into the Executive Terminal. Inside, he walked straight to "Executive Jet" private charter service.

"I'd like to charter one of your jets," Fraley told the attendant, very matter-of-factly.

"Where would you like to go, sir?" the young woman replied.

Fraley did not answer right away, trying to decide.

"Sir, where would you like to go?" she asked again politely.

"I think I'd like to go to Phoenix."

"There are several places in the Phoenix metropolitan area, or would you prefer Sky Harbor?" she asked.

"Is there an airport close to Mesa?"

"Yes, we can land at Falcon Field," she replied with a beautiful smile.

Fraley arranged for the aircraft to meet him in St. Petersburg the next morning. With a wink and a smile he paid the young woman twenty-eight hundred dollars in cash for a one-way trip to Phoenix.

It was a cool morning by Florida standards. Fraley was standing at the doorway, trying to keep warm. Beside him were the four duffel bags.

"Are you Mr. Peterson?" asked a middle-aged man wearing a pilot's uniform.

"Yes I am. You must be the pilot."

"Yes, sir. Right this way, sir. We're ready to go." As the pilot reached down to pick up two of the bags he was surprised by their weight.

"Hey, what do you have in here—money?" he asked jokingly.

"Just a couple million," was Fraley's matter-of-fact response.

He spent the next week in Arizona's capital city at the Westcourt Hotel, known as the Buttes. It is one of the city's architectural masterpieces. The hotel is literally carved into the three rocky peaks where it was built. The lobby's far wall located behind the main desk is actually the side of the mountain. It is in its natural state, adorned with saguaro cactus and other desert flora. The designers added a cascading waterfall that drops three floors and empties into a tropical fish pond in one of the restaurants. On the first day Fraley relaxed at the multilevel pool, soaking up the beautiful warm desert sun and flipping through the yellow pages. He had circled seven different banks around the city. During the next three days Fraley opened accounts using a relatively meager deposit of two to three thousand dollars. At each location he purchased a safe-deposit box and on the following day he placed the bulk of his two million dollar Miami payday into two of the safe-deposit boxes.

Life in the desert was good as ever. Actually, for the first time in his life he was happy with his surroundings. The house he purchased in the winter of 1988 for about three hundred thousand dollars was a smuggler's paradise. He had found the home through a broker in the east end of Maricopa County near the city of Mesa. It was in the desert hill country. He had a view for miles around, and in the back of his lot was the side of a mountain rising three thousand feet above the desert floor. The only road that accessed his house was a dead end. Anyone approaching would have to turn around in his driveway. He had a couple of acres surrounding the slump-block construction, ranch-style house. Inside was about thirty-five hundred feet of living space. A huge country kitchen overlooked a great room, where Fraley had a sixty-inch big-screen television and entertainment center. The house had three bedrooms, a master suite with its own bath and an office. Outside, the triple-wide driveway ended at a four-car garage. In the garage was his speedboat, a Harley-Davidson Superglide, a vintage '68 Pontiac Firebird and a replica of an MG Classic he had purchased for twenty-five thousand in cash one day on his way to a local convenience store. Next to it was his pride and joy, a new, sky-blue Cadillac Sedan DeVille. Directly behind the house was a large desert garden with a swimming pool, barbeque and deck area at its center. Fraley had also added a tropical fishpond very similar to the one at the Buttes and stocked it with Japanese poi fish. At the back of the property, or just about anywhere they chose to be, were his faithful Rottweiler dogs. His only concern was the house above him on the hill to the south. Fraley kicked back and relaxed neck-deep on the loveseat of the pool. He looked up at the large, round, decorative thermometer mounted on the veranda fascia board. It read one hundred twelve degrees.

A few months after he moved into the house he was called by Velasco's wife and told to fly to Curaçao to meet her husband, who had been released on an appeal bond. A few days later, as they walked along Breedestraat—Curaçao's Rodeo Drive—Velasco told Fraley that he was able to get the bond because he promised DEA that he would help the agency make a few cases against some high-ranking cartel members. As soon as Velasco got his wings and was a few minutes out of DEA's sight he had jumped bond, fleeing the country.

"That's all he's doing, layin' around the pool all day? What a life," Gately said as he watched excerpts of the last twenty-four hours of video tape.

"Well, not exactly," said Roger Mannhalter, the agent responsible for reviewing the tapes. "Watch this." Mannhalter pressed the fast forward button on the VCR's remote. After stopping and starting the tape a couple of times he cued it to the part he wanted to show Gately. It was a wide shot of the backyard. Gately watched the man known to them as Dale Peterson walk out from under the veranda carrying what looked like an AK-47 assault rifle. The date time recorder on the video screen read JULY 4, 1989. 8:19 P.M. Peterson walked to the back of his lot, raised the rifle to his shoulder and fired off a couple of bursts into the hillside.

"Just celebrating the Fourth. I guess that's what you do when you run fresh out of fireworks," Gately said sarcastically.

Just then the group supervisor Lee Atwood stepped into the room.

"Good news, boss. We know who our man really is. Bailey just called from Ohio. The Dale Peterson from Toledo is truly dead. Bailey tracked down our guy to a small town called Sharon in Western Pennsylvania. When he showed the photos to the locals they went crazy with joy. They say Peterson is really Leo Fraley. According to the local police lieutenant, Fraley is supposed to be doin' hard time for a rape conviction but he escaped about ten years ago. They also said that he is a drug dealer, burglar, the number-one suspect in a ten-year-old homicide and a Mafia member with a rap sheet as long as your arm."

"That still doesn't explain the calls from the Mesa house to Colombia," Gately replied. "What else do we know about his connections in Pennsylvania?"

"Not a whole hell of a lot," Atwood replied. "But we received a call from our Tampa office this morning. They say they may know our guy from an investigation they were working with the Florida Department of Law Enforcement. There's an FDLE agent who says he was on to this guy for smuggling big loads of cocaine into the Clearwater area using fishing vessels."

"Send a photo of Peterson or Fraley what's-his-name to the Tampa office. Let's see if we're talkin' about the same man." Gately started to walk out of the room.

"There's something else," Atwood said, handing Gately a computer printout. "It looks like Fraley also has a federal warrant for failure to appear and bond jumping in North Carolina. The FBI wants him for a bank burglary and the marshals want him for the fugitive warrant."

It all sounded like good news for the agents. A case was finally starting to break after almost seven months. But Gately knew what would come next. They were now dealing with at least five agencies who would like to get their hooks into their target. Between the marshals, the FBI, the local cops in Pennsylvania, the Pennsylvania Department of Corrections and the FDLE, it was going to be a tug of war to maintain control of the investigation.

Gately spent the rest of the day on the telephone with Blue Logan, Tom McDermott, the assistant United States Attorney handling the prosecution of their case, the assistant special agent in charge in the customs office in Tampa, the assistant special agent in charge of the local FBI and with the chief deputy of the U.S. Marshal's Service in Phoenix. There was no question that something was going to happen soon in this case, and it wasn't going to be part of Gately's plan.

No one but Gately's office wanted to allow Fraley one more day of freedom. The plan he presented to everyone was to continue to watch and wait until Fraley made his next move. With the current information about his drug smuggling activities out of Florida and the airplane shopping he had been doing in Phoenix, as well as the daily telephone contact with Colombia, Fraley was ripe to become a candidate for a court-ordered wiretap and caught in the middle of a major cocaine venture.

Now with the exception of the customs officials and the assistant U.S. Attorney in Phoenix, no one else agreed. Fraley was a menace, a career criminal, a rapist, a Mafia hit man, a walking pestilence about to infect all society. He must be arrested and imprisoned immediately or the government would become responsible for his next heinous act. To Gately's way of thinking there was no real evidence of Fraley doing anything other than smuggling major loads of cocaine over the past ten years. The last seven months of video tape suggested that he was fat, dumb and happy to do nothing other than lie around the house, kick back in the pool and talk on the telephone to his Colombian pals. Yet arresting him now surely diminished their chances of getting any higher on the ladder of the Colombian organization he had been working with —and was clearly still contacting. Any news of his arrest would alert his contacts that he could no longer be trusted, and any effort to use him against his friends to build a larger case would be a crapshoot at best.

Nonetheless, on August 12, 1989, the plan to arrest him and search his residence in Mesa was set in motion. There was a sixth contender out for Fraley, the IRS. Not only did they want a piece of this guy, they wanted to walk away with the entire candy store. The basis for their theory of case ownership was that Fraley's night deposits generated the false filing of "Currency Transaction Reports" by the bank receiving the funds. This was a criminal violation of the Bank Secrecy Act, under the jurisdiction of the IRS. Any cash transactions in excess of ten thousand dollars must be reported to the Treasury Department by the financial institution receiving the money. Any willful misfiling is a felony, punishable by five years imprisonment and/or a fine of ten thousand dollars. But it was the pettiest crime Fraley had ever committed, if he even knew he was committing the offense. The IRS did not have a prosecutable case because there had never been any personal contact with anyone at the bank. Even though logic dictated that Fraley was responsible, there was no evidence that he had made the deposits or directed anyone else to make them for him.

"I don't give a flying fuck what that fat bastard's excuse for an agent thinks he has," a frustrated Gately said as he described the IRS group manager. "I don't want his ugly face within a mile of that house or Fraley when we take him down. We'll get one chance to roll him over and I don't want it fucked up because this clown is there for his pound of flesh. Tell him I said to file their CTR case and see if the U.S. Attorney wants to prosecute. Otherwise, stay the hell away from our target." Atwood, as always, would relay Gately's request in the most diplomatic terms.

The surveillance outside Fraley's residence had gone on for more than a week and nerves were getting frazzled. Gately did not want the warrants served unless Fraley was outside the residence. There was no logical reason to assault the house and put this man in a defensive posture. There was evidence that he was heavily armed and what's more, his invalid father, sickly mother, sister and wife were all living in the house as well. As far as Gately was concerned there was no deadlier combination of human characteristics than greed and paranoia, and after years of experience he had learned that every drug merchant and smuggler like Fraley had a large dose of both.

The plan was to give him no chance to arm himself and defend his domain. Their best avenue was to jump him outside the house when he was alone, but so far Fraley wasn't cooperating. He was content to stay at home. On the tenth day of the vigil, on a typical August one-hundred-and-seventeen-degree afternoon, Fraley's wife headed into town in the Cadillac. She drove directly to the Sky Harbor International Airport and went into the terminal one parking lot. While she waited inside at the gate, the agents quickly set upon the car to disable it in the hope that she would call her husband for help. After a brief conversation with Gately and the assistant U.S. Attorney, the agents set out to puncture the right rear tire of the Cadillac. Short of firing a nine-millimeter round point-blank into the sidewall however, it seemed that nothing could flatten the tire. Fraley had prepared for such an occasion by purchasing top-of-the-line tires, the kind manufactured and used by heads of state and his Colombian friends for security on their vehicles. The only way to flatten the tire was to remove the valve stem, which they did.

What happened next could not have been scripted better. As soon as Mrs. Fraley saw the flat tire she went to the nearest pay telephone and called home. That was confirmed by the pen register that traced every call made from or to Fraley's telephone. The surveillance at the house instantly alerted the agents at the airport that Fraley was in his MG convertible headed their way. When he arrived a half-dozen agents descended upon him as he was stepping out of his car.

It all happened in a matter of seconds. It seemed to Fraley that federal agents were dropping out of the sky. There was commotion, a lot of movement and loud voices exhorting him to "Get on the ground!" There was nowhere to run to—they were everywhere. Fraley lay on the ground, his wife next to him. He wasn't exactly sure what to say. Maybe, "Honey, are these your friends?"

An agent stood over him and said "Put your head down," smashing Fraley's head down onto the steaming hot blacktop. Fraley wondered where his gun was so he could shoot the son of a bitch. Then he looked up and recognized him. It was the cop Fraley ran off his property with his two Rottweilers back in Florida. What goes around comes around.

"Put him in the back seat of the car until a uniform car pulls up," Gately ordered.

Fraley was whisked into the back seat of a car. "Oh, well, shit happens," he said out loud. He knew he'd have to wait and see what was going to happen. His family was his first concern and that thought made him panic. He knew the agents were storming his house at that very moment, and he thought about his ambulatory father lying in bed with tubes sticking out of him and his mother who wasn't much stronger. What about his sister? What about his dogs? He couldn't remember if he had tied them up before leaving. If he hadn't he knew his dogs would attack and the agents would kill them.

It was Gately who reassured him. He had already sent a vet out to drug the dogs, he told Fraley. And he had insisted on taking every precaution to protect his family. To him, the only criminal was Fraley. "Don't worry, Mr. Fraley," he said. "The only danger we perceived at your home was you. No harm will come to your family."

As soon as the City of Phoenix police car pulled up, Fraley was transferred into it. Fraley knew his life as he had planned it was over. His only hope for freedom was to do what he swore he would never do.

This is the specially outfitted car used by Joe Cuffaro and his partner Martin Gladstone to transport drugs, money and arms between Miami and New York.

The car's compartment was accessed by the two rivets near the car phone's microphone. When a quarter is touched to the rivets, the locks click open, enabling access to the compartment.

The car's hidden compartment was located between the back seat and the trunk, and was cleverly concealed by using a portion of a Cadillac-manufactured trunk. When the trunk was open or the back seat removed, everything looked just as the manufacturer intended, *left*. Once the padding was removed a compartment approximately five feet long, three feet high and one foot deep is revealed, *right*.

The only photo available of the anti-Mafia Poll (group) of the Italian government, assembled in Palermo in 1985 at the conclusion of the Maxi-trial that resulted in the conviction of over 300 Mafiosi. Judge Guisto Sciacchitano (dark hair) is at the center of the group, in back. Judge Paolo Borsellino is in front of Sciacchitano, to his immediate right. Then head of the Poll, Oscar Luigi Scalfaro, now President of Italy, stands in front of Sciacchitano, to his immediate left. Judge Giovanni Falcone, wearing a beard, is at the far left of the photo. *(Courtesy Guisto Sciacchitano and the Italian Foreign Ministry.)*

The Joint Working Group of the Italian-American Coalition On Organized Crime. Taken in 1985 in Washington, D.C., the photo shows then-Attorney General Edwin Meese on the left, opposite Oscar Luigi Scalfaro (in the gray jacket), head of the Italian delegation. Judge Sciacchitano sits at the head of the table. *(Courtesy Guisto Sciacchitano and the Italian Foreign Ministry.)*

Entryway into the office at Scirocco Fan Company. To the unsuspecting, it looks like any other doorway. Approximately six inches below and sixteen inches above the door jam latch, however, are two small metal contact points.

Judge Sciacchitano, left, is greeted by then-Attorney General Thornburg and FBI Director William Sessions, center. *(Courtesy Guisto Sciacchitano and the Italian Foreign Ministry.)*

When the tile is lifted, the two locks are revealed. By the time the FBI got to it, the safe had been filled with sand and a slab of concrete.

Sal Rina.

Buck Spicer does a little fishing on their way over to Belize to pick up the load.

Ben Fannon on the *Return of the Jedi,* guiding the crew through a shallow passageway. The crew is carrying a thousand kilos of cocaine aboard.

John Galatolo, the "made" Mafia representative of the Sicilian Resuttana family, headed by Francesco Madonia, Galatolo's Godfather. This picture was taken in Aruba, where Galatolo and Cuffaro met with their Colombian cartel contacts Waldo Aponte and Angel Sánchez to finalize the details of the deal between the Medellín cartel and the Sicilian and American Mafia. They posed as tourists on the dock while taking pictures of the boat that was to be used to transport the six hundred kilos of cocaine.

Waldo Aponte. He is currently a fugitive.

Angel Sánchez, currently a fugitive, with his wife Amparo.

The *Big John*. The specially outfitted vessel transported six hundred kilos of cocaine from the Medellín cartel to the Italian Mafia and finally to the American Mafia for distribution in America.

News conference held in Phoenix the night Operation Dead Ringer netted over 5,000 pounds of cocaine. Pictured left to right are Gary S. Phelps, deputy director, Arizona Department of Public Safety; Stephen MacNamee, United States Attorney, District of Arizona; Tom McDermott, special agent in charge, District of Arizona, USCS; James Ahearn, special agent in charge, District of Arizona, FBI; Dave Wood, special agent in charge, District of Arizona, DEA. During the news conference McDermott said: "Operation Dead Ringer represents the largest cocaine seizure in the history of Arizona, the largest interdiction case on the southwest border and the largest controlled-delivery ever completed."

Unloading the drugs upon their arrival at Sky Harbor International Airport in Phoenix.

Stacking the drugs—5,539 lbs. of cocaine—in the rented hangar used by Customs during the undercover operation.

On the sides of the package, one can see the special labels identifying the owner of each kilo. This one says "Centavo," which meant it belonged to José Rodríguez-Gacha.

The cocaine was packaged in one-kilo containers, wrapped in a hard fiberglass resin. The seal says "República de Colombia."

The take from Operation Dead Ringer. The separate kilos have been laid-out, identified, weighed and marked for evidence.

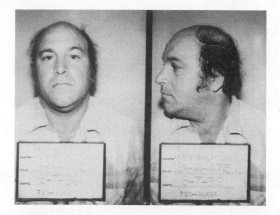

Giovanni "John" Galatolo.

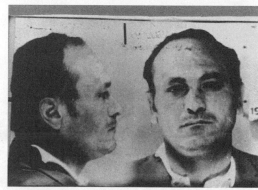

Vincenzo Galatolo.

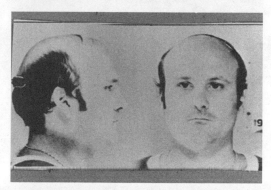

Raffaele Galatolo.

Giuseppe Galatolo.

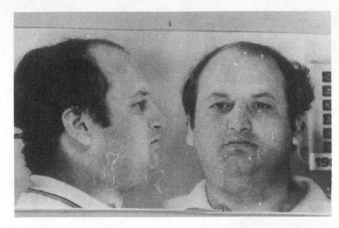

Stefano Fontana, also implicated in Operation Dead Fish.

Antonio Madonia, also implicated in Operation Dead Fish.

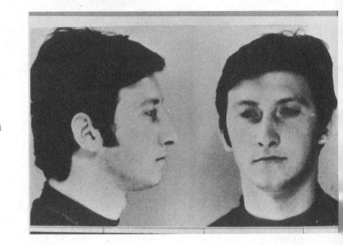

Dominic Mannino. He is currently a fugitive.

This beautiful flower, shown here in full bloom, is the poppy, notorious as the raw material used in all opiates, including heroin.

With the petals removed, the opium easily seeps out through small cuts to the base of the bud.

Shown here are fields of opium poppies in the Colombian mountains. Up until a few years ago, the production of heroin occurred only in Southeast and Southwest Asia, where it has been cultivated for over four thousand years.

Within the last five years the Colombian cartels have branched out from coca/cocaine to poppy/heroin production, hoping to take over the worldwide heroin market. Using their horticultural and chemical skills, the cartels have developed new strains of poppy that can grow in South American climates, including lowland savannas. This new strain is considered just as powerful as the Asian-grown poppy.

Heroin is a very profitable alternative for the cartels. One kilo of cocaine in a fluctuating market can cost between $12,000 and $25,000. Asian heroin sells from $80,000 to $130,000 per kilo. The Colombian cartels are undercutting the heroin market and still making a profit, selling heroin at approximately $60,000/kilo.

CHAPTER

8

OPERATION DEAD FISH

JOE CUFFARO BUTTED THE CIGARETTE in the ashtray, took another sip of coffee and checked his watch. "Where the hell are you, Marty?" he muttered to himself as he lit another Marlboro.

Cuffaro didn't even want to come to this meeting, but Gladstone had been promising him the world. His new contact was loaded, paid cash on delivery, no hassles, and he was a friend of Cuffaro's pal Sal Rina. What more could you ask for? The very best part about this deal was that Galatolo wasn't involved. But something didn't feel right. Gladstone was late and he hadn't seen Rina.

"¿Quiere más café, señor?" the waitress asked as she passed.

"Sí, claro." He checked his watch one more time.

"Hey, Joe, sorry I'm late. It's Sunday and the family all wanted to have a big breakfast at Jerry's," Gladstone said and sat down, across from Cuffaro, nearly knocking the coffee pitcher from the waitress' hand.

"It's okay, Marty, but you know I'm not so sure about this deal with this guy from Philadelphia. How do you know him and why does he want to see us on his boat? Doesn't he have a home?"

"Don't be so skeptical Joe, I've already done business with him. He took five," Gladstone lowered his voice and raised his right hand at table level showing all five fingers for emphasis. "And he paid me on time! That was almost a month ago and everything is okay. Besides, it was Sal who said he could be trusted. Sal's okay. So this guy is okay. Anyway Sal's waitin' for us. Let's go."

It was a thirty-minute drive to the Marriott Hotel near Pier 66 in Fort Lauderdale. There were fast food restaurants, boutiques, nightclubs, hotels and the typical tourist traps surrounding the area. Gladstone led the way from the parking lot to the pier where the sixty-foot sleek-hulled motor yacht was moored. As Cuffaro walked out onto the pier he could see someone on the deck waving in the distance.

The lights were off and the blinds partially closed to cut the glare as silver-haired agent James Brown loaded a tape into the VCR. He pulled off his sports coat and hung it on the gray metal coatrack by the door. He reached down to his waistline and unclipped his holster from his belt, opened his desk drawer and placed his weapon inside, sliding it closed and locking it in the same motion. He picked up the remote control, his notepad and took a seat at his desk. He aimed the remote at the VCR, pushed PLAY and watched as the leader on the tape, FEDERAL BUREAU OF INVESTIGATION MIAMI FIELD OFFICE, appeared on the screen. The scene was the interior of a vessel, a very nicely appointed cabin with two comfortable sofas, a carved oak coffee table and a wet bar. It was an overhead shot and the date and time appeared superimposed on the bottom right corner of the screen. There were two men in the center of the frame seated on one of the sofas. There was another man who moved in and out of the camera's eye. The larger of the two on the sofa was less animated and rarely spoke. It was as if he had his mind on other things. When he did speak it was a simple yes, no or maybe. The smaller man spoke fast, like a used-car salesman about to close on a first-time buyer. The agent was taking notes on portions of the conversation when the door opened and another man walked into the room. It was his partner "Chick," or Special Agent Charles McDevitt, as the name plaque on his desk read.

"Is this yesterday's meet with Kane on the boat?" McDevitt pointed to the video monitor.

"Yeah. The big guy on the sofa is the Sicilian, Cuffaro, and the smaller one is his partner at the fan company, Gladstone. They agreed to deliver another five kilos to us next week. You know, Chick, I keep hearing how the Philly office has a problem with Kane, but he's been a real prince for us."

"Yeah, he's been workin' miracles for the New York office as well," McDevitt said as he kept his eyes on the monitor.

Bob Sweeney and Jim Smith, the Philadelphia agents who handled Kane, had long ago grown tired of his antics. It was not unlike Kane to push the limits with demands, acting like a prima donna. Fed up with Kane's showboating, Sweeney, a former college football player and an intimidating figure, got into Kane's face and reminded him who was boss. His decision to put Kane in his place was to avoid the "surprises" that informants almost always spring on their controlling agency just before a critical moment in the investigation. But they also could not overlook his abilities to move at will among the mafiosi the FBI was targeting.

Bill Kane was an entrepreneur who moved in and out of Mafia circles in New York and Philadelphia, enjoying the company of mafiosi like Joe and John Gambino. Over the years he had become a trusted business associate who also moved freely among their "social elite." What these mob figures didn't know was that they also maintained, by association, a close relationship with the FBI through Kane, who had become a government informant. Many of the meetings that took place in the Gambino-owned restaurant Caffè Giardino on Eighteenth Avenue in Brooklyn's Little Italy were being closely monitored by the FBI. The bureau's New York agents were able to listen in on past secrets and future plans. Their discussions encompassed the full range of the criminal code. The mafiosi who frequented the Giardino for its food and like company were confident that it was impossible to penetrate their private sanctum. It was something the FBI had counted on. Their arrogance, which drove them to speak freely, soon translated into the government's best evidence.

Their sanctity had been covertly invaded through one of Kane's businesses. With Kane's assistance the FBI had planted hidden microphones and transmitters in the vending machines, strategically located inside the restaurant.

Kane had been in on the investigation in Miami from the beginning. It had all started when Sal Rina was released from the federal penitentiary in Springfield, Missouri, in the fall of 1987. Rina was assigned to the federal hospital penal facility where he was being treated for a congenital heart disease. Kane artfully maneuvered himself into meeting Rina at the prison gate and gave him a ride across country to his home in Philadelphia. What Rina didn't realize was that Kane's car was bugged and he had a tail close behind with two bureau agents recording every word, including his past involvement in heroin trafficking. As they cruised into Philly, Rina informed Kane that he was disillusioned with the heroin trade and as soon as he got his feet on the ground he was going to have his parole transferred to Miami—where he was going to move into the cocaine business.

A few weeks later Rina unwittingly led the FBI directly to Giovanni's Pizzeria in Hialeah, where he met with owner John Galatolo. The bureau's Miami agents had been watching the pizzeria and tailing its owner on and off for several months. Among a full array of violent crimes of which he was a prime suspect were a couple of gangland-style murders. But the most enticing information the FBI received was his possible connection to the Sicilian Mafia. When they checked his phone records they found Galatolo was making as many as twenty calls a day to New York. Many of those calls were to known Mafia members. But when Rina walked into Galatolo's pizzeria and became part of the equation, the bureau's case in Miami shifted its focus away from Galatolo. Rina was a known Mafia member and soon became their number-one target. It was Rina who led them to Cuffaro, Gladstone and a number of others connected to their cocaine business. To infiltrate the organization, the Miami office borrowed Kane on a part-time basis from the Philadelphia office. The plan was straightforward: set Kane up as a buyer, have him contact Rina, and whoever Rina brought in also became a target.

"We got a great case, Jim," McDevitt said to his partner. "I think it's coming together well, if we can keep Kane on an even keel," he added. Brown nodded in agreement as McDevitt stood up to leave. "I'll see ya a little later. I've got a dozen 302s to complete."

"Catch up with you later," Brown said as he held his focus on the video. "Don't forget we have a meeting with Kane tonight."

Brown couldn't help cracking a smile as he watched the negotiations for the drug deal coming to a close. He wasn't amused at their conversation nor even that the case was coming together so easily. What was funny was that the setting for their transaction was the same one used a dozen times by the bureau across the country in some very highly publicized cases. In fact this very same yacht was the setting for the demise of many of the U.S. congressmen who had so proudly shoved thousands in cash into their pockets in full view of the video camera. That case was the second sting ever conducted by the FBI, later known to the rest of the world as ABSCAM.

An hour later, having viewed the tape twice, Brown stood at the evidence clerk's window logging the tape back in as evidence.

Jim Brown was living out his dream. His father had spent twenty-five years as a Flint, Michigan, police officer, retiring as a detective lieutenant. In his youth Jim had first aspired to be an attorney, but between high school and college he took a slight detour to follow in his father's footsteps and pursue a career in law enforcement. Before graduating from college Brown began an internship as a clerk with the FBI in Detroit where he endured six long years clerking for the agents. With direct exposure to the agents he supported, Brown began to set his aspirations high, wanting to become an FBI special agent. As soon as the opportunity to make the transition presented itself Brown leaped at the chance. He graduated from the bureau's Quantico Academy in 1974, and was assigned to the Kansas City field office. Nine years later, after a tour in Chicago, he was transferred to Miami on a special detail. A year later, in 1985, that detail became a permanent assignment.

As he walked out of the evidence room he thought about his partner's words, "a great case." Indeed it was, but at the time he had no idea just how great it was to become. What he did know was that it was his first Sicilian Mafia investigation since he had been involved with the FBI and probably his best case since he had left Chicago.

The Miami office had recently reorganized and formed a new squad called the Italian Drug Trafficking Squad. It came on the heels of the famous Pizza Connection. That case best illustrated the powerful ties between Palermo and New York in the Italian organized-crime world. It was suspected that in South Florida members of *La Cosa Nostra* were not only involved in the traditional heroin business but were moving cocaine in conjunction with Colombian traffickers. Brown was looking for a new professional direction when his partner persuaded him to exploit this new, as yet untapped area.

Initially his partner Chick served as mentor. McDevitt had attended the bureau's Italian/Sicilian language school in Monterey, California, where he had been exposed not only to the language but to the intricacies of the unique Sicilian culture. One of the most difficult aspects for Brown to accept was the importance of paying particular attention to the specific birthplace of their targets from the island of Sicily. It was a point that McDevitt preached constantly to Brown and one the younger agent would later use to his advantage. Genealogy and geography were two of the major determining factors in assessing the alliance of suspected Sicilian Mafia members to the crime family with which they were associated.

It was an extremely time-consuming case, with workdays often running late into the evening. It was certainly an imposition on Brown's home life. Yet it was a welcome development in his career. And having McDevitt as a mentor was a plus, too, because he had become a good friend. He shared similar interests, and as a result their families grew close; their teenage children were heavily involved in soccer and the great outdoor sports-oriented lifestyle offered by the South Florida climate; Brown's and McDevitt's wives became very close, and the couples went out and vacationed together in the Florida Keys. One of their favorite trips was to the Hawks Cay Resort, timed to coincide with the local marathon. Even with the long hours and other demands of the case, it was a much better situation than the original assignment that had first brought Brown to Florida, forcing him to commute weekly to Chicago. That case had a heavy personal weight because it was an investigation of one of their own agents. Following that, Brown had recently concluded a similar case involving local government corruption.

In the early eighties, seven Miami police officers began a career in crime by shaking down drug traffickers. They started by stealing drug money, then the drugs. They became even more brazen, orchestrating home invasions and conducting raids under the auspices of their official position. After more than a year of this criminal behavior under cover of their badges, their eventual downfall came when they raided a Panamanian freighter docked on the Miami River. In the process of unloading the cocaine hidden on board the vessel the Colombian *campesinos* jumped ship for fear of being arrested. Unable to swim, three of the workers drowned. The "Miami River Cops," as they became known, were eventually charged with homicide. The then–Florida State's attorney for Dade County, Janet Reno, requested that the U.S. Attorney assume the case. Reno feared that the government's chief witness, Miami's now infamous rogue cop Rudy Arias, would not hold up under the state's long, arduous deposition process. At the same time she believed that the federal drug, corruption and civil rights statutes in existence could more effectively serve to prosecute Arias's compatriots in crime. Jim Brown was the special agent assigned to prepare the case for federal prosecution. The Metro Dade County organized crime unit that had originally investigated the case conducted such a professional and thorough job, the case was handed to Brown essentially ready-made on a silver platter. Brown spent the next year working hand in hand with the OCU, preparing the case for prosecution and developing an excellent working relationship between the two agencies. Despite this, the case resulted in a mistrial. And before defendant Armando García could be brought to trial a second time, he became a fugitive and eventually made it to the FBI's "Top 10 Most Wanted" list.

"Joe, Vincenzo Galatolo's called you several times," Cuffaro's wife said with concern and disdain. "And another man by the name of Dr. Garçón has been calling. He's Colombian, right? I could tell by his accent."

"It's okay, don't worry, it's just business," Cuffaro replied. He was masking his concern. He went to the refrigerator, retrieved a beer, then sat in the living room. He tried flipping through the channels to distract himself but his predicament prevented him from relaxing. Again he was caught in the middle. He was serving two masters. The Sicilians had used him to make the connection with the Medellín cartel and had successfully completed their six-hundred-kilo deal. The Sicilians, who had been relentless in their pursuit of the cocaine, were now not the least bit concerned about paying their debt to their Colombian creditors. Now that the eighteen million dollars was due the Mafia had become deadbeats.

This bothered Cuffaro the most. He knew from past experience that the Colombians were ruthless. Once, Aponte had resisted changing suppliers when he was approached by one of Escobar's top men, "The

Mexican," as he was often called. José Rodríguez-Gacha didn't argue, he simply had Aponte's supplier killed. Gacha then took his competitor's shipment to Aponte and diluted it, reducing its purity to less than half and essentially sending him two hundred kilos of shit. Aponte, unaware of Gacha's treachery, delivered the cocaine to his distributor Cuffaro. Without the slightest thought of checking the integrity of the load, Cuffaro delivered the drugs to the Gambinos in New York, and Tyrone Walker took the bulk of the shipment to Detroit. Within a matter of days Cuffaro was fielding a litany of complaints that rivaled a major department store's receiving unwanted Christmas gift returns on December 26. The entire shipment was returned. Aponte had to make good on the money in order to save his reputation, but he was stuck with four hundred pounds of cocaine he couldn't sell. Within a month Gacha's hostile takeover was in motion and Aponte was no longer an independent. He was now controlled by the Medellín cartel.

Pablo Escobar, using the code name *Doctor Garçón,* had taken a personal interest in this deal and was calling Cuffaro direct two or three times a week. *El Doctor* called Cuffaro at home, at the office and on his car phone. Cuffaro had just talked to Escobar on the phone earlier in the day, trying diplomatically to explain the delay as a simple matter of procedure. Cuffaro told him Italy was not the same as the United States or Colombia, where large sums of money could be easily moved. In his homeland it was a much more difficult process. Cuffaro was simply trying to buy more time, not so much for the Sicilians but for himself. He was the only person both the Sicilians and the Colombians knew and trusted. On one occasion Escobar called Aponte while Cuffaro was meeting with him to discuss payment.

"Buenas tardes, Doctor Garçón. Un momento y se lo paso a Joe," Aponte promptly handed the phone to Cuffaro. Cuffaro sighed and politely listened to Escobar tell him again that his people must pay their debt.

"We had an agreement, Joe. We took care of you and we had a deal," Escobar said in his well-educated and distinctly Colombian Spanish. "Payment was due in ninety days and now we are four months later and have received only a small portion. It is your responsibility to make sure that payment in full is made."

"Sí, claro, Doctor Garçón," Cuffaro replied respectfully. "In fact I am on my way to Palermo tomorrow. You should receive the money shortly."

It was soon after the drugs had been delivered when Escobar personally suggested that Cuffaro contact their associate in Milan to launder the money. The problem for Cuffaro was that he had to physically transport the money from Sicily to the northernmost region of Italy. The banks were closely regulated and all foreign and cash transactions were reported to the Guardia di Finanza. The type of money involved would immediately set off alarms and certainly alert the authorities to his efforts to transfer the funds to Escobar's accounts elsewhere. The entire peninsula was a land of roadblocks, anti-Mafia police, airport checks and any number of other logistical impediments. Nonetheless, Cuffaro traveled to Palermo, where he took control of about one million dollars in lira.

Within a week of his conversation with Escobar, Cuffaro met with Vincenzo Galatolo at the family "office" in Palermo to pressure them to pay.

"Look, Vincenzo, these Colombians are getting very anxious about their payment. And now I've got this *El Doctor* calling me constantly. You must come up with the money. They know where I live. If they're not paid, they're going to come kill me and my family," he said angrily.

"This is not such a problem, Joe," Vincenzo replied matter-of-factly. "We have money here, we can pay," he said, showing him a huge travel trunk full of lira.

"The money must go north and I must turn it over to their man in Milan," Cuffaro explained.

"That's not a problem. We can get it there. As a matter of fact, if you go with me now I can introduce you to the driver."

Cuffaro knew by his words that Vincenzo was telling him the Mafia controlled the trucking industry as well as the fresh produce markets throughout the country. Cuffaro was not about to let Vincenzo out of his sight, and within the hour Cuffaro was accompanying him to meet the driver and look over the truck. The Renault tractor-trailer rig was outfitted with a secret compartment behind the cab and under a false floor. The driver, a Mafia associate, was a personal friend of the Galatolo family, who often transported their goods throughout the country.

After a brief meeting the three men agreed it would be in their best interest to travel separately. That day Vincenzo boarded a boat to Milan, and the same evening the driver, carrying the cash and several tons of fresh Sicilian produce, headed north from Palermo. The next day Cuffaro took the morning Alitalia flight to Milan. On the second day, Vincenzo and Cuffaro met as planned at a hotel in downtown Milan. Together they took a cab to the huge outdoor produce market. The market, which occupied a couple of acres, was known throughout Italy as the largest of its kind. Hundreds of trucks from all over Europe and as far away as Poland and Russia were parked on its perimeter. In the midst of the commotion, and a virtual sea of tractor trailers, Vincenzo and Cuffaro were able to locate their truck and driver. Without a word to Cuffaro, Vincenzo and the driver removed the front seat and headed for the secret compartment to access the trunk with the cash.

"Vincenzo, what are you doing?" Cuffaro asked. "It's broad daylight and the cab driver's watching us. Let's not take it out in front of him. Let's send him away, then take it out and call a new cab."

"Don't worry, Joe. What's he know? It's just a suitcase," Vincenzo replied, undaunted. "Fuck him. I'll tell him it's my clothes."

To Cuffaro there was no logic in this statement but it was too late. Once the transfer was made Cuffaro called Escobar's man Giuseppe Lottussi. Lottussi operated a money exchange brokerage and insurance business in downtown Milan. On their way to the fashionable Piazza Santa Maria Beltrade, where Lottussi's office was located, Vincenzo demanded that he meet the Colombian's Italian money launderer. Cuffaro had no objections—in fact he was more than happy to let Vincenzo make the delivery alone.

While Cuffaro waited outside, leaning against the cab, smoking a cigarette, Vincenzo dragged the trunk into the office building and up the elevator to Lottussi's office. A few minutes later Cuffaro looked up in the direction of where he thought Lottussi's office was located. What he saw was Vincenzo standing in front of a window. He had another man by the collar with his face pushed up against the window. Shortly thereafter, Vincenzo came strutting out of the building, fixing his jacket as if he had just finished a dirty job.

"What's with you and this guy you were cleaning the window with?" Cuffaro asked, fearing Galatolo had done something to harm Escobar's money conduit.

"That short, little bald-headed fuck. He's all primped up in his Armani suit and he tells me he's not taking all the money. He says he can only handle half. He irritated me with his excuses. So I took him by his designer shirt and told him to look down at the big man by the car. If he did not take all the money, I said, I was going to drag him down the stairs and hand him over to you, Joe. So guess what? He took all the money." He turned and raised his fist toward the office window, giving Lottussi the Sicilian "fuck you" sign.

Cuffaro made the trip with Vincenzo four more times. The last time they carried the money in a truck shipping scrap metal. Lottussi moved the money in a variety of ways. Sometimes he called an armored car company and shipped it to a Swiss bank. Once he wired the money to Los Angeles to be converted to U.S. dollars. From Los Angeles the money was wired to Miami and then on to Colombia in the form of the national currency of the cartel, Colombian pesos. Along the way everyone took a piece of the pie, earning between one and four points for simply wiring or converting the currency—that is, everyone except Joe.

He still hadn't seen a penny other than the three thousand dollars—which he used to help cover expenses—that Galatolo had paid him outside Christine Lee's Restaurant in Miami Beach almost five months earlier.

It was another steamy August afternoon in Fort Lauderdale. In the hotel lobby Jim Brown and his partner Chick, with Sweeney and Smith from Philadelphia, met briefly to go over their plan. Soon the four agents were in their room directly across the lobby from the room they had wired for audio. Kane sat patiently in that seemingly private room while Brown and his partners made final adjustments to their technical gear and waited for their star guest to arrive. Meanwhile, outside in the hotel's parking lot Gladstone parked his car alongside another car, driven, unbeknownst to him, by an undercover FBI agent. When Gladstone recognized the car and the young female driver who had earlier been described to him by Kane, he got out of his car, opened the trunk and transferred a package to his contact who was now standing outside her car with the trunk open. When the transfer was made, Gladstone confidently went up to Kane's room, believing that the contact was on her way to deliver the drugs to New York.

"Okay, did she call yet? The transfer was made," Gladstone announced loudly as he walked into Kane's hotel room. "That fifteen went pretty well."

"Fifteen? What do you mean? Our deal was for five," Kane replied.

"But I gave you fifteen. Give it back or you owe me for fifteen," Gladstone insisted.

It was an awkward and unexpected twist for Kane. But he was able to cover himself.

"Well, I'll have to call my people in New York."

Gladstone waited as Kane pretended to call his drug trafficking contacts. In fact, Kane called Brown's room to discuss the situation.

"Yeah, I heard," Brown said on the other end. "There's no way we can give it back."

"What should I do?" asked Kane.

"Punt!" replied Brown. He paused a few seconds. "Stall him awhile. I'll see what I can do."

FBI headquarters had only allocated seventy-five thousand dollars for the purchase of five kilos of cocaine. With the additional ten kilos Brown's case had just taken an unexpected turn. He now had a choice to make. He could bring the case down as-is with the evidence he had gathered to date, or move forward. Moving forward would be costly, not only for the bureau, but for himself and his family. The pressure of the case had begun to take its toll and Brown was feelings its effects. It had become an exhausting case, taking up much of his time, effort and attention, but it was a case that also maintained a high degree of excitement. Then there were the logistical as well as the prosecutorial considerations —in order to continue, he would have to let another hundred fifty thousand dollars walk to pay for the additional ten kilos. He would have to convince his superiors in Miami and FBI headquarters that his case was worth the additional time, effort and risk, not to mention the extended budget. Brown decided to press on.

Fortunately for him, this case had won not only local support, but his desk officer, Special Agent Dennis Buckley, had to this point consistently carried the banner in the J. Edgar Hoover Building to get the necessary backing for Brown's investigation. Now Buckley came through again, in a big way. The bureau authorized the supplemental payment to purchase the "excess evidence" supplied by Gladstone.

Brown was constantly impressed at the response by headquarters throughout the investigation. He knew such smooth waters were not what many agents experienced. He was lucky that headquarters recognized the importance of the case and gave him the support he needed to bring it to fruition without the almost obligatory bureaucratic barriers. Brown's plan was to deliver the cash in three installments of fifty thousand dollars. This would give the Miami agents three more opportunities to follow the cash to its ultimate recipients.

Each one of those meetings was an interesting story in itself. Even Mafia movies couldn't top them for drama and insight. It was that way from the beginning. Kane graphically described how at the very first meeting, held at a well-known seafood restaurant in Martha's Vineyard, Rina ordered a whole fish, plucked its eye out with his finger, popped it into his mouth like an olive and munched it with zest. During the meetings when Kane was wired or when they were videotaped Brown listened and observed. Cuffaro seemed like a man preoccupied, as if attending in body, but not in mind. Gladstone appeared out of place. When he tried to talk like a gangster, he simply didn't fit in. Brown saw him as a man playing a role for which he simply wasn't cut out. As each meeting progressed, the agents watched Gladstone become more and more boisterous. Once he bragged about carrying a gun and sticking it in someone's face, a clear example of grandstanding. Gladstone was an accountant caught up in a world of drug dealers and gangsters—but he still walked, talked and acted like an accountant.

Two weeks later the three installments had been paid in full. Kane was instructed to ask Gladstone for another thirty kilos. It would be the last delivery Gladstone would make, if Brown's plan worked. Not surprisingly, working virtually alone, Gladstone was unable to get his hands on such a vast amount of cocaine. By then, however, another more pressing concern had risen to the forefront for Brown. Cuffaro was making regular trips in and out of the country. If somehow he were to get wind of their investigation, he would certainly not return. Brown and McDevitt decided it was best to act before they lost one of the Sicilians.

On November 30, 1988, the FBI took down the Cuffaro/Gladstone organization based on the "buy/bust" and undercover evidence they had gathered on their fifteen-kilo sale.

Kane and Gladstone had just wrapped up a meeting in the lobby of the Embassy Suites Hotel after the failed thirty-kilo acquisition. As they parted company, Martin Gladstone headed for his car. Before he could even get his foot in the door, Brown and an entourage of other agents arrested him. Gladstone was simply stunned. The confidence he had recently cultivated was stripped to the core. While a search warrant was executed at his home, Gladstone was simultaneously handcuffed and stuffed into the back seat of an FBI car.

On the way to the FBI office, Brown sat next to Gladstone.

"You don't know me and we've never talked before, but some day you're going to understand what I'm about to tell you," Brown said, very matter-of-factly. "That is," he continued, "I have never seen a case more ironclad against an individual than the case we have against you." Brown told him the FBI had a great deal of evidence against him and had been working the case extensively for quite some time. Brown then confronted Gladstone with his only real alternative, presenting it in terms that would easily penetrate the mathematical head of an accountant. It was in his best interest to cooperate—the alternative was to spend the next fifteen years deducting the days one at a time from his calendar in the cell of some federal penitentiary. He wasn't their primary target, Brown explained, but his involvement, no matter how peripheral it may have been, was enough to merit significant time behind bars. It was of course the standard modus operandi for any agent to use or turn a suspect, in hopes of furthering the case. Despite Brown's efforts Gladstone made no admissions. His only response was a request to speak with an attorney.

At the same time another crew of agents was keeping Cuffaro under surveillance. The afternoon of the takedown they had tailed him to Miami International Airport. The agents watched as Cuffaro approached the Ecuatoriana Airlines counter and purchased a ticket with cash. Up until now they had no clue why he was heading south, in particular to Ecuador.

By then Cuffaro had had enough. He had finalized plans to relocate his family and begin a new life in Quito. It was a trip he had anxiously anticipated for several months. Cuffaro was suffocating from the pressure as the payment issue became more and more of a concern to the Colombians, and he was tired of his partner Galatolo's abusiveness and his and his cousin's reckless, lawless natures. He wanted to get as far away as he could from the Galatolos and their Mafia associates. It had been his own greed that had brought them together and it was his decision now to end the relationship before the law could catch up to him. Scirocco Fan Company, the business he had worked so hard to establish, was suffering from his own neglect. It too had become a victim of his greed. And lately he had felt something was not quite right. The meeting he attended on the yacht at Pier 66 kept replaying itself over and over in his mind. Cuffaro's solution was to drop everything and leave. He had already invested in a restaurant in Quito where he could start all over, operating a legitimate business.

With one foot inside the Ecuatoriana Airlines 727 and the ten thousand dollars he had skimmed off the top of a recent load from Galatolo, Cuffaro was poised to disappear into the aircraft. He felt a distinct tap on his shoulder and felt the end crashing down on him.

While he was being arrested, FBI agents were searching his home. His family was told their father had been arrested for the sale and distribution of cocaine and heroin. His wife and children sat in shock as they watched a squad of agents search and sift through everything, including the potted plants.

Cuffaro spent the next few hours contemplating his fate and that of his family. Confronting them with the truth would be one of the most difficult things he would ever do. His most painful admission was to finally tell his wife what he had really been doing these last few years, although she may have suspected. He knew he had placed her and his children in a very dangerous situation and it now had become something he could no longer control. It would not be any easier confessing his sins to his mother, brothers and uncles.

That night at Miami's Federal Metropolitan Corrections Center Brown and McDevitt attempted to question Cuffaro, who they believed had already decided not to break the Mafia code of silence. One of their first questions to Cuffaro was related to his personal weapons. Cuffaro did not hesitate to tell him he had a nine-millimeter Beretta that was registered to him. The FBI agents asked Cuffaro to draw a sketch of the layout of his house and pinpoint the location of the gun. It was a request with which he easily complied. As the meeting began, Cuffaro took out a cigarette.

"Do you have a light?" he asked calmly.

"Yeah, hold on," McDevitt replied. "I'll get you one." A minute later, he arrived with a book of matches in his hand. As McDevitt lit the match and brought it toward Cuffaro's cigarette, Cuffaro's eyes opened wide.

McDevitt was holding a matchbook from Frank's Restaurant in Pompano Beach. That was the first time Cuffaro started to worry about just how long and how often the FBI had been watching him. There were so many meetings at Frank's that had bothered him—but the reality of the matter was that the FBI had no idea just how much Cuffaro knew. During his interrogation Cuffaro could hear Gladstone's voice from a nearby interview room. To Cuffaro, this was a strategic ploy aimed at pressuring him to cooperate. To the agents it became apparent that Cuffaro was willing to accept the minimum mandatory sentence of ten years for his part in the fifteen-kilo cocaine deal. Before the end of the evening the agents allowed Joe to speak to his wife over the phone, with the condition that he respond in English.

A week after his arrest, Cuffaro ran into Galatolo's uncle, who had just been admitted at the correction's center. For days on end the old Sicilian repeatedly told Cuffaro what a despicable person his nephew was and that the best thing for him to do was to cooperate.

Soon Joe's partner Galatolo began sending messages to him in captivity. He initiated his terrorist tactics subtly at first, then moved to more overt threats. It was the Mafia's way of guaranteeing the silence of those less fortunate members who now had only to contemplate their fate in jail. Because Galatolo's cowardice prevented him from meeting face-to-face with Cuffaro, he sent his first message by paying a personal visit to Cuffaro's aging mother, who lived in the Dade County community of North Miami Beach. Galatolo knew this former resident of Palermo, who had lived in fear and in the shadow of the Mafia's threats most of her life and whose husband had been terrorized by them, would be the first to realize that he meant business.

"Whoever betrays me pays the price," Galatolo told Cuffaro's mother in no uncertain terms. He callously told her the story of the fate of his own aunt. "She got out of line, and within three weeks, after moving from Palermo to the mainland of Italy, she was run over by a car. The same accident could happen to you."

He let her know he and his friends were well aware of her activities, down to the very grocery store she frequented. Galatolo counted on the fact that his ability to reach her in her own home would be the most threatening as well as the most painful to Cuffaro. Three days later a muffled message was left on Cuffaro's brother's answering machine. The voice said, "We're going to blow up the whole family, starting with you!" The following week Galatolo called Cuffaro's youngest brother, Ralph. By coincidence, Cuffaro called Ralph within a few minutes of his conversation with Galatolo.

"He wants me to meet him," his brother said.

"Merdoso," Cuffaro said in Italian, followed by *"cobarde"* in Spanish. Galatolo ordered Ralph to leave his mother at home. He knew that the Sicilian Mafia, despite their murderous ways, were prohibited from violence against their target in the presence of family.

About midnight Galatolo took Ralph to a farm he owned in southwestern Dade County. With his hand in his pocket, as if he were concealing a weapon, he ordered Ralph to walk toward a barn.

"Why don't you walk in front of me?" Galatolo said. Ralph Cuffaro was certain Galatolo's next move would be shooting a bullet through the back of his head. But Galatolo wasn't through with his threats. With his hand still in his pocket, he approached Ralph.

"You go see Joe, and you tell him not to even think about cooperating. Because if he does, you'll be back at this barn—in a million pieces."

A day after John Galatolo had delivered this message Cuffaro's brother Ralph was visited by Guy Gambino, a messenger from the New York crime family. It was a short but very direct meeting. Emblazoned in Ralph Cuffaro's memory were the words: "If Joe talks the whole family is going to have a problem."

Galatolo had not given Cuffaro the benefit of trust, nor did he have the courage to communicate his threats to him directly. He was living up to his family's apparently well-earned reputation in Sicily of more than a century of cowardice. Finally the entire Galatolo clan had pleaded with and cajoled Cuffaro. But there was nothing he could do behind bars. And it was apparent he wasn't even going to get a chance—his requests for bond had been denied three times. Cuffaro knew that for all their cowardice the Galatolos, his demented son-in-law/cousin Angelo Fontana and in particular the Gambinos were cold-blooded killers and would not hesitate to obliterate his family.

Four months later, after a deluge of threats by Galatolo and the sustained misery of seeing his family unprotected, Cuffaro made a decision to turn the tide. On the verge of despair, and with great concern for his family, Cuffaro sent a message from his cell in the MCC to his attorney. He had kept silent long enough.

"Joe has information that could be of great interest to you," began the phone call from Cuffaro's attorney Scott Sakin to the federal prosecutor.

To Brown and his fellow agents this kind of phone call was not unlike dozens they had heard before. People in Cuffaro's position almost always said they could do a lot, but very few could actually live up to their promises. Yet Brown had always felt that Cuffaro would make a great witness against Galatolo, if he could get him to turn. He took the news in stride.

CHAPTER

9

OPERATION DEAD RINGER: THE PICK-UP

"YOU ARE TARGETING low-level domestic drug traffickers in the hope that you will make a seizure of a small amount of cocaine. Your request for funding is denied. In addition, the subject Leo Fraley is a career criminal and a danger to the community and should not be allowed to be released on a furlough for the purposes of this investigation."

Gately was reading excerpts from a headquarter's office memo to McDermott over the phone. It was the official response to his request for funding to conduct an undercover sting of Pablo Escobar's organization. Not only had the funding been denied, there would be no further attempts to obtain the assistant commissioner's approval to utilize a federal prisoner in an undercover investigation. This would preclude the possibility of seeking the equivalent and necessary approvals from the Department of Justice.

"Bill, are you sure we covered all our bases in the request that we forwarded?" McDermott slowly and calmly began his conversation following Gately's obvious tense and angry reading of the headquarters memo. McDermott was vacationing at his parents' home in San Francisco.

"Hell, yes, I'm sure. There is no way they even read our request if they respond with this nonsense about pursuing low-level domestic drug traffickers."

McDermott continued to munch on the bag of potato chips. He cleared his throat and took a long pause. Gately waited for his words of wisdom and took the time to calm down.

"Look . . . Rosenblatt's out of the country until next week. Bill Meglen is acting. I want you to call Meglen and run down the facts in this case to him. But before you do, fax him a copy of our request for furlough for Fraley. That way he will have had the opportunity to review it in full if he hasn't already."

Gately took a deep breath, let it out, and before he could respond McDermott came back with a buffer.

"Who signed the memo from headquarters?"

"Some guy named Steve Knoke. He's the acting director in special investigations." As always, Gately was ready to handle the problem himself immediately. "I'm going to give Modrak a call now and find out where his head is and how the hell he arrived at this conclusion."

"Bill, I want you to give Modrak an opportunity to reverse himself. I'm sure he'll see the error in his ways once you tell him how ridiculous his memo sounds, given the facts." McDermott believed most things could be repaired with a few calls to the right people.

Gately hung up and took another deep breath before making the call to Modrak. After five minutes of waiting on hold Gately heard the line clicked on.

"Steve Knoke."

"Steve Knoke? Bill Gately in Phoenix. Just got your memo by fax in reference to the Leo Fraley case. There are some things I think we need to discuss."

"I don't think there's anything we need to discuss," he said defensively.

"Well, you may not think so, but let me go over a few of the facts with you. Do you have your memo handy?"

"I've got it right here in front of me," Knoke said confidently.

"Well, do you have the memo I sent you requesting furlough? Do you have that in front of you as well?"

"No, I don't, but I think I know the facts."

Gately tried to contain himself and speak calmly and diplomatically.

"You do realize that Pablo Escobar is not a low-level domestic drug trafficker. We're not going to argue that, are we?"

There was silence on the other end.

"Well, I'll just continue then. As to your contention that we just hope to seize a small amount of drugs, that doesn't fit anywhere in the scheme of things. We already have audio tapes, as stated in the memo, between Fraley and Escobar's lieutenants, who are willing to give us as much as ten tons of cocaine. I don't think anyone anywhere, not even Pablo Escobar, considers that a small amount of drugs. Now, let's get to the real problem—"

"Yeah, let's talk about the real problem," Knoke broke in with a fervor. "You're talking about releasing a rapist into the community to work undercover for the government. And that isn't all. The guy's an escaped prisoner who has been out for over ten years. What's going to prevent him from escaping again while he's in our custody?"

"What's going to prevent that is what's clearly stated in the memo. Line by line I state specifically how he's chained to the floor. He's locked inside a room with several agents around him at all times. He can't even take a shit without our permission. His entire world is an eight-foot-by-eight-foot room. The only thing he needs is a telephone to pull this off." Gately was steaming.

"You can't guarantee he's not going to try to escape again," Knoke persisted.

"Let's get back to the issue. There's no question Fraley's a goddam criminal. And yes, he's probably done some pretty despicable things. I don't know what rock you've been living under, but he's no different than all the other informants the government uses. To know the kind of people we're trying to put in prison we have to use these people—who else would know how to get to them? Since when did we become so saintly and ethical about informers? Now let's get to the part about releasing a rapist into the community. First of all, he's lived in the community for ten years and hasn't raped anyone. Obviously you didn't read the part where we say we've had him under video surveillance twenty-four hours a day for the past eight months. The most violent thing he's done is playfully throw his wife into the pool. Second, we're not *releasing* him to anybody. It's in the memo if you'd care to read it. And now that I've talked to you, I don't think you have read it. And further, the buck doesn't stop with you. Either you're going to back off and fix it yourself or I'm going to Meglen."

Knoke broke in: "I'll have you know I had a very competent person prepare this memo."

"Who is this competent person?" Gately cut in sarcastically. "Obviously, they're operating on a personal agenda, because they haven't communicated with us."

"It's Sheila Gray. She may not be an agent but she does these things all the time," Knoke proclaimed inanely.

"So I take it you're not going to change your opinion about Fraley's situation," Gately said.

"Well, even if I wanted to it wouldn't change things. Sheila has already talked to the people in main Justice and told them her position." Knoke had dropped the bomb. His "competent associate" had already poisoned the waters and Gately knew his chances were becoming slimmer by the minute. Now he not only had to convince Meglen to reverse Knoke, he also had to try to get Meglen to suffer the humiliation of telling the people at Justice that they had been given bogus information.

"You know, Knoke, there's no question why some people are assigned to headquarters to push paper and why the real agents are still in the field. You found your niche draft-dodging assholes," Gately muttered to himself as he slammed down the phone and hit the intercom in a simultaneous motion.

"Lee, get the hell in here and bring that goddamn memo, that furlough memo we sent to headquarters." As soon as he finished his sentence, Gately knew his emotions were getting the best of him. He was taking it out on one of his best agents. Lee Atwood, the supervisor who had been nurturing the Fraley case for almost a year, walked in as calmly and collectedly as usual.

Atwood was the kind of guy who never let anyone see when he was upset. Gately had recruited Atwood from the Internal Revenue Service where he was a senior special agent. Gately's respect for the IRS as a law enforcement agency was about 2 on a scale of 10. But during the interview Atwood showed he was cut from a different cloth. He was looking for real work, something IRS wasn't interested in unless they were hanging on to the coattails of another agency. Atwood wanted to initiate his own cases and carry his own load. He was smart, methodical and down to earth. What was best was that he understood how to analyze complex situations and he wasn't afraid to tackle problems. Gately also liked him because he had a military background as a company commander in the U.S. Army in Vietnam.

"What's up, boss?" Atwood said with concern and a smile.

"Get that memo faxed to Rosenblatt's office, attention Meglen. We've got a big problem in headquarters." Gately handed Atwood the dreaded Gray/Knoke memo. Atwood read it as he stood in the center of the office. Gately could see his expression changing from disbelief to subdued anger. It was the first time Gately had seen any discernible expression from Atwood.

"I'll get on it right away," he said and headed out of the room.

Gately called out to him quietly. He wanted to stop him before he could speak to anyone else. "Don't tell anyone we're having problems. I especially don't want it to get to Fraley."

But Fraley already knew. He didn't have direct knowledge but he could read the undercurrents. All he could see was that the agents there wanted to do the deal, but clearly they were working with their hands tied. Upper management was barking out orders and restrictions that made it impossible to conduct a successful sting.

Times like this made Gately wonder why he was doing what he was doing, and if it made any difference at all. Why was it that every time someone said, "You can't do this," those simple words incited such a sense of defiance and determination to do exactly what they said he couldn't? Why was the majority so content with mediocrity? What was so wrong with wanting to go after the biggest and the best?

In reality, that wasn't his paramount problem. His problem was that he just didn't want to play the game. He wasn't willing to be politically correct, he wasn't good at ass-kissing and he definitely wasn't good at keeping his mouth shut. No wonder he was so disliked by the wrong people. Then again, he hadn't bowed to pressure easily before, so why start now? Not on this case. He couldn't justify that. Luckily, he knew a lot of people in high places. Then again, maybe it wasn't so lucky—after all, he knew them because, as the saying goes, "big cases, big problems." Over the years, Gately had earned himself the dubious reputation of being a pain in the ass, but at the same time someone who always came through with big cases. Now the only thing standing in the way of this case was a clerk's personal agenda. So what if his informant was a scumbag? It wasn't his place to make personal judgments about his character or his ethical standards. An informant was there to do a job, that's it. If Gately could put aside his judgments, why couldn't the others? There was much more to be gained, and besides, isn't that what they were supposed to do? Wasn't that an agent's job—for the greater good?

Gately spent the next two hours on the phone, first trying to convince the acting assistant commissioner for enforcement to consider the rest of the information, which had been so conveniently omitted by the time it reached him. Gately liked Bill Meglen even though sometimes they disagreed. He respected him because his heart was in the right place. Meglen had an affection for the job and for the agents in the trenches doing the real work. He actually cared and wanted to do things for the right reason. Yet talking to Meglen was often an ordeal. Meglen was one of those cerebral types who too often seem to drift off into an esoteric overanalyzing of issues. The challenge was to keep him on track and get him to react quickly. In this case, Gately provided Meglen with the single piece of information that would make any agent react.

Gately had devised a plan he knew would work, but one that would surely bite him in the ass somewhere down the line. He told Meglen he had invited the FBI to join in on the case, which he had. After all, Fraley was also a fugitive in their bank burglary in North Carolina and it was the politically correct thing to do. Besides that, the FBI had more clout —especially at Justice, their parent department. And in seemingly record time the bureau had not only obtained permission to proceed from their headquarters, they also received the necessary blessings from OEO at main Justice.

"If Customs doesn't get it together right now," Gately told him, "the FBI is going to take our informant and our case right out from under us.

And they'll do that for no better reason than because some clerk has suddenly decided there's a code of ethics our informers have to meet."

This was the information that became the impetus for action. Meglen and Gately moved on to try to smooth out the waters at the DOJ's Office of Enforcement Operations. It took a while, but Gately and his agents finally received the permission they needed. The combined request from Customs and the FBI had been the necessary element that closed the sale at Justice.

Leo Fraley noticed the difference right away. He had watched as the Customs agents tried to overcome the many obstacles put before them, not by the scenario they would have to work with to set up the sting but by the bureaucracy. Fraley could see they were not only up against an unyielding bureaucracy, but his own rap sheet that spanned three decades. Fraley's past had, in essence, come back to haunt him. But worse than that, he was perceived by some within the system to be beyond redemption. This was devastating to his morale. The agents, who had suddenly become the only hope he had to see freedom again, were between a rock and a hard place, and the easiest thing for them to do was to leave him in jail and just say, "Fuck it—who needs the grief?"

During the first week of his cooperation the Department of Justice had refused to release him to the custody of the Customs Service. He couldn't help thinking he was on a sinking ship. By the second week things had changed, however. No longer was Customs attempting to do business with him at the jail in a basement interview room. He was now a permanent guest of the U.S. Customs Service at the downtown Phoenix office. He was surrounded by no fewer than four agents at a time, even while he slept. It was no mystery to him why the radical change had occurred. Two of the agents who had become his roommates were always from the FBI. Fraley knew that the bureau had more muscle. While the rest of law enforcement might disagree, the bureau would get its way.

But there was still one serious nagging issue to overcome. There was no funding granted to carry the investigation. The next move was a conversation with Fraley about creative financing and the next telephone call was to McDermott for an update.

"Okay, Tom, here's what happened. I talked to Meglen, who thank God was forward-thinking in a zig-zag sort of way, but in the right direction anyway. We got permission, but no money. But I've already taken care of that, so don't worry—"

"What do you mean you took care of that?" McDermott interrupted.

"I just sent my guys to get a half-million dollars, which by the way was more than we were asking headquarters for."

"Hmm . . . How'd you do that?" McDermott asked, not sure he wanted to know.

"Leo got on the phone and told Escobar's *segundo* he needed some expense money. He said okay, and that's that."

"Say that again?"

"Just what I said—you heard me right, Tom."

"You're telling me that Pablo Escobar is giving us money to finance a sting aimed at him?"

"What more can I say?"

They both laughed.

As soon as Gately hung up the phone his smile vanished. He knew his ass was severely on the line.

It was a lot more complicated than their brief conversation reflected. The idea of Escobar paying the government's tab was not a new idea or even unprecedented. The only unique aspect about it was the extraordinary expense of the operation. Gately told Fraley to request additional money, above and beyond the normal expenses. The excuse was that they needed money to pay off an air-traffic controller, who they reported would only look the other way for a few days. By using an FAA official in particular they created an urgency and a time period that the agents could control. They told the Colombians that expediency was of utmost importance in taking advantage of the window of opportunity. To give it more credibility Fraley told Velasco that the "official" was scheduled for his Christmas leave after December 18. It was the perfect plan to nail the Colombians—they too wanted the Christmas holiday free from the encumberances of an unfinished smuggling venture.

Gately headed straight for the holding room where Fraley was chained to the floor. First he told the other agents in the room to take a break, hit the john and buy a soda. As soon as they walked out Gately gave Fraley a piercing look.

"Look, Leo, if you decide you're going to suddenly get into an escape mode, you make sure you do it when I'm not around, because I'll shoot you in your head. If there's one thing I can do well, it's shoot straight. I never miss."

Leo looked at him in his usual nonchalant manner. "Dem assholes givin' you some shit, hey? Don't worry. I may be a crook, and you may not like some of the things I've done, but I am a man of my word. That's a fact. I made a deal with you. I gave you my word." Fraley knew actions meant more than words to this agent, and that it wouldn't be long before he'd have to put his words into action.

Gately walked out without replying, but somehow he couldn't help but feel that Fraley was telling the truth.

*   *   *

Special Agent Carlos Salazar stood close to the telephone booth. It was less than three hours ago when he had received his assignment—for the second time. The day before, the communications web between Fraley in Phoenix, his contact José Restrepo in Miami, Velasco in Barranquilla and Ortegón in Bogotá had somehow mixed up the correct meeting time. Salazar's trip the day before had resulted in no more than a practice run.

That meant enduring two roller coaster flights from Phoenix to the John Wayne Airport in Orange County, California, in the customs' King Air. The twin engine turboprop had made record time, but at the expense of the weak-at-heart when it came to flying in fast and low amidst the dense Los Angeles air traffic. Salazar wasn't crazy about flying even in commercial aircraft; as for the customs plane ride, well, he would write it off as one of the many sacrifices he had to make for God and country. The rocky ride over the heat inversions for the first three hundred miles of desert and mountains was mild compared to the twenty minutes circling John Wayne Airport, trying to fit into the landing pattern of the steady stream of scheduled flights. Given the choice, he would gladly have taken the Greyhound back to Phoenix.

Although he expected the call, he was startled at the sudden loud ringing from the pay phone.

"Bueno, me mandó el Doctor. Soy el veterinario. ¿Cómo se llama usted?" Salazar answered with the simple coded phrase given to Fraley during his conversation with Don Pedro Ortegón. Salazar was told to expect to be contacted by the "German" and to identify himself as the "veterinarian."

"Soy el Aleman. Tengo los papeles para usted," said the caller, giving the proper reply.

Salazar turned his head, tucked the receiver under his chin, took off his jacket and held it over his shoulder, signaling his cover team that the "German" had the money and was enroute to the meeting place. Salazar continued to talk, giving the description of his clothing, and listened as the "German" described himself and the car he was driving. Finally he placed the telephone receiver on the hook and walked casually toward the entrance of the parking lot, where he had arranged to meet his new Colombian friend.

Fifteen minutes later a blue Mercury Topaz with a Budget rental sticker pulled into the lot. The cover team watched as Salazar walked toward the car as the driver slowed and parked. *El Alemán* got out of the car, handed Salazar the keys, then headed for another car waiting nearby.

As soon as the "German" was out of sight Salazar signaled the others to walk out of the terminal and join him at the car. Without a word Salazar opened the trunk. Inside was a duffel bag. In one swift motion he pulled back the zipper and spread the canvas bag open.

All three agents stood in silence with eyebrows raised. They had seen their share of large caches of money before, but half a million dollars in twenties, fifties and hundreds is a sight you never really get used to. Salazar broke the tension with his trademark boyish grin and a look that said, "I'm having fun."

For these agents this was more than just money. It was the tell-all sign, the indisputable proof that their informant, chained up in an eight-by-eight-foot holding room back in Phoenix, was telling them the truth. Fraley could deliver. He could cut a deal with the cartel over the phone —he could reach out and touch Pablo Escobar.

"Well, I'll take the money and see you guys back in Phoenix. I may make a quick stop in Switzerland," Salazar said, flashing his ear-to-ear grin.

"No time for a trip this time, Carlos. We're going shopping." Gately's comment surprised them.

The next morning Fraley was on the phone, speaking directly with Ortegón.

"Mi amigo," Ortegón said calmly. "Are the papers in order?" Ortegón was eloquent in both languages, but he made it a habit to continually switch back and forth between English and Spanish. He sounded like a statesman, but Fraley knew this was a ruthless man with ice water running through his veins.

"Claro, Don Pedro. All of the papers are in order," Fraley said confidently and very respectfully. He had learned well the unwritten rule of respect within Latin cultures. Fraley never missed a beat, keeping pace with their well-established code. They never spoke openly about drugs, planes or money. A "book," or a "candy kiss," was a kilogram of cocaine, "girlfriends" were planes, "drivers" were pilots and "papers" meant money.

In the first few weeks Fraley had made dozens of recorded calls to Velasco and Ortegón in Colombia. But there was a new player, Velasco's nephew José Restrepo. The twenty-five-year-old resident of Barranquilla had been sent to Miami by the "Office" shortly after Fraley had gotten out of Florida. His job was to locate Fraley and reestablish the connection. Restrepo had been designated by Velasco to maintain daily contact with Fraley right after he had made his first call to Velasco. Restrepo was in for the long haul on this deal and frequently made the connected Fraley and Ortegón conference through calls between Phoenix, Miami and Bogotá.

In Gately's office Gately and Atwood were discussing their next step. Atwood usually sat in the same seat, the black, soft leather low-back chair to his left as he walked in. Gately sat behind a beautiful Danish mahogany desk placed diagonally in the room. The best part about the office was that three-quarters of the walls were windows. They were the kind one could see out of perfectly, but which no one could see through from the street three floors below.

"Okay, we'll meet you tomorrow," Gately said with a slightly raised voice into the speakerphone as Atwood listened.

"The Executive Terminal at Sky Harbor, at 10:30," said the voice over the speaker.

As he clicked off the phone, Gately said to Atwood with skepticism, "I hope these guys live up to their reputation."

They had just obtained the services of two "contract" pilots known for their smuggling skills. Contract pilots are a slightly higher class of informant, just because they're smugglers who are FAA certified, and can fly a multitude of aircraft. These two had learned their trade in the late seventies and early eighties in South Florida during the smuggling heyday. This was before the aerostat balloon, Customs, The Coast Guard, Marines, Navy and Air Force started taking a hard look at everything entering U.S. airspace on wings coming from a southern, eastern or western heading into the Florida peninsula. These two jet jockeys happened to own a Turbo-Commander—a twin engine, jet-prop that was the preferred smuggling aircraft. It was and is still known for its long-range, high-speed and large-load capacity.

Most contract pilots have smuggled drugs before, though they have not necessarily been arrested, and are now paid informants of the government. They are the mercenaries in the drug war who know all the air routes in and out of Colombia, the Caribbean, Central America and Mexico—all the drug smuggling hot spots. Because they are trusted in those places, where they are known smugglers, they are the perfect solution to the Catch-22 in the drug war. In all wars, the best defense is a good offense. Since the government cannot legally send its own agents into a foreign country to work undercover, which would violate the sovereignty of that nation, it allows its informers and mercenaries to join the ranks of the cartel to get the job done.

"I guess turbine engines are high-ticket items. Fifty thousand dollars seems a little steep," Atwood said, recalling the conversation with the pilot. They had just agreed to replace the starboard engine on the Turbo-Commander to bring it up to peak performance for the high-risk flight they were about to embark upon.

"Fifty grand is a lot of change but Pablo's picking up the freight, so let's spend his money in the right places. The next thing we've got to do is rent a hangar at Sky Harbor," Gately said. He knew that in order to pull off this deal they had to become "Class A" smugglers. That meant the best of everything. It was an exciting feeling, tempered with nervousness. They had four days to acquire the necessary equipment and to travel to their destination in Belize—once again this tiny country serving as middle ground for delivering Escobar's cocaine.

"Hey boss, Leo's on the phone with the contact in Belize," said Special Agent Roger Mannhalter, standing at the doorway to Gately's office.

Gately and the other agents put on the headsets to listen in on the conversation.

". . . Okay, my friend," Fraley was saying to an unidentified voice on the phone.

The voice, with a heavy Caribbean accent, was clearly audible: "I spoke to 'the big man' about your driver and the car. I am to expect them on Sunday. Have him call me at this number when he arrives and Sarge will meet him at the airport."

"Make sure you take him on a tour. He needs to see everything," Fraley responded. "He must see both locations."

Fraley's coded language simply meant his Belizean contact would have the opportunity to speak to his pilot and look over the "car," his airplane. "Both locations" meant either sections of a coastal road or the Pan-American Highway, both of which were often used as landing strips by the cartel.

"Well, there is some construction on one of the roads but I don't think it's a problem. Only if it rains," the Caribbean gentleman replied.

"I'll speak to you tomorrow, and call me at this number or page me if you need me," Fraley added.

"Okay, ciao. 'Bye."

"See ya," Fraley said as he hung up. "Whata fuckin' jerk that Grijales is. I wish there was someone else down there that Winces had for a contact." Fraley added in the same breath.

"Who is this guy?" Gately asked Fraley.

"Armando Grijales. This guy is one of Winces' pals. He's just not very smart. But there's nothin' that goes on in Belize that this guy doesn't know about. That is, except for that time when DEA and the British Army kicked in Velasco's hotel room door and arrested him a few years ago. Grijales was ten minutes late to meet him that time."

"So what's the deal with Grijales?" Gately interrupted.

"He owns a fuckin' island off Belize. It's like a resort for smugglers. Basically that's who goes there. They land, refuel and take a vacation. The place is fuckin' beautiful, let me tell you."

"Leo," Gately simply said his name and gave him that look that told him to get to the point. "Who is this guy connected to."

"I told you, Winces."

"Well, does he know Ortegón?"

"Yeah, but Winces is his point of contact. Still, Grijales does own half the real estate in Belize City. Matter of fact, he owns the land the American embassy sits on."

The expression on everyone's face was a combination of amazement and disbelief. "What the fuck you talkin' about," Gately said. "The State Department pays rent to a smuggler?"

"Yeah, so what's wrong with that?" Fraley replied. To Fraley, it was just another stupid thing the U.S. government did with its money.

Special Agent John Martelli sat in the right seat of the Turbo-Commander as far as Brownsville, Texas. The pilot then continued his journey alone to Belize City, where he met Sarge Reyes at the airport. Reyes had worked with Fraley in the past, "protecting" loads. He was the best person for the job because he had all the resources to protect the drugs in transit from Colombia to the U.S. Reyes was a close friend of Grijales and was the chief of police in Belize City. He had the manpower, equipment and communications network to service the incoming and outgoing drug flights. He would also provide overnight security for the drugs between flights, if there were any delays. Grijales was the cartel's freight forwarder and Reyes was his chief of security and warehouse man. Reyes also had access to the Belizean Defense Forces personnel and equipment if it became necessary. However, this meant additional expenses that Grijales was not always willing to pay.

A day and a half later Martelli and the contract pilot were together on their way back to Phoenix. By mid-afternoon Martelli was in Gately's office briefing him on the outcome of the advance trip. Everything had gone well except for one small detail.

"It's the port engine on the Turbo-Commander," Martelli told Gately. "I think it's gotta be replaced as well."

"The fuck we will," Gately replied. He couldn't believe his ears. It was another in a series of unnecessary setbacks and expenses.

"First have one of our mechanics take a look at it. If they say it needs to be replaced, tell 'em to park it. We can't afford any more delays." With that, Martelli left the room.

Gately turned to Atwood, who had joined the meeting late. "We've gotta get another plane. We don't have time to waste fixing this one. Next they'll want us to replace the wings. Check with our pilots, find out where we can lease a plane that meets the same specs—twenty-five-hundred-mile range, can carry a ton of cargo and extra fuel."

About two hours later Gately received a call from the U.S. Customs aviation unit in Phoenix. Mike Crew, the unit's supervisor, had bad news.

"Forget the Turbo-Commander. The port engine needs to be replaced." Crew had taken the wise initiative to have a solution in-hand before phoning Gately. He had already identified a leasing company in Oklahoma that had a plane that met the specifications.

An hour later Gately phoned Lloyds of London. They insure anything, as long as one can afford it. And with Pablo Escobar's money they could certainly afford this.

"Yes, sir, and how may I help you," said the very polished English voice at the other end of the line.

"I would like to insure an aircraft," Gately told him.

"What sort of aircraft are we speaking of? I'll need manufacturer, model, airframe and engine serial numbers. You can fax that to me later. If you have the year of manufacture, make and model that will be sufficient for now."

"It's a 1989 Cessna 441 Conquest twin."

"And what kind of window do you prefer?"

"Seven days."

"Is this passenger or cargo?"

"Cargo."

"What is the point of departure?"

"Phoenix, Arizona."

"What is your destination?"

"The Yucatán."

There was a moment of silence before the next question. It had clearly been an answer the Lloyds' man did not like, but as an English gentleman a less than cordial reply would not be proper.

"Could you be just a smidgen more specific?"

"You mean, like, a country?" Gately asked, knowing he was ever-so-slightly ruffling those ever-so-proper feathers.

"That would be helpful," the man replied.

"Belize."

"Thank you. One moment." In the background Gately could hear the sound of papers shuffling and a calculator working.

"That will be twenty-nine thousand dollars, sir. We will need to have that by six this evening, London time. Your window for the flight begins today and closes on December 2."

"If I need an extension is that available to me?"

As if already prepared for the eventuality, the underwriter from

Lloyds replied matter-of-factly: "Oh, yes, that is available at a rate of an additional twelve thousand per day."

"Could you give me the bank information and account number where I can wire this transaction?"

It was all so very convenient, Gately thought. They gave him a contact and account information at a Dallas bank, eliminating any problems that could complicate the closing of the deal. What was more amazing was the fact that someone could actually insure a smuggling venture with one of the world's most reputable companies.

"We've got a problem." Grijales was calling to speak with Fraley. Gately and Atwood huddled around the table wearing headsets, listening to the conversation. Grijales seemed in a state of panic. His voice was at a much higher pitch than normal and he was speaking fast.

"Your girlfriend has hurt her leg. The driver ran off the road, now the car's front tire is stuck in the mud. With the books on board, it weighs too much to try to push it. Sarge's men are helping but there are not enough to move it."

In the background the agents could hear him speaking with Reyes over the radio. Grijales was switching back and forth between the handset for the radio and the telephone. In his frenzied state he inadvertently disconnected the telephone conversation twice. The tension in the agents' office was overwhelming. By now every possible insult that could be leveled against Grijales, the two pilots and even their parents had been muttered, shouted and signed by everyone there. After a few minutes that seemed like an eternity they reestablished the telephone linkup.

"We have an additional problem," Grijales began again. His voice was still quaking. "There are many patrols in this area at night. Even the 'white man' is in the area. We will need to take the books out, and I think we should burn the car."

The problem was that the airstrip was really a section of two-lane macadam surface roadway, also known as the Pan-American Highway. The plane's landing gear barely fit within the width—a mere thirty feet —of the roadway. Reyes's people had blocked off about four thousand feet of the highway/runway and lit it with the headlights of police vehicles. Grijales feared retribution from the Army patrols—or worse, that the British Army would come upon their improvised airport. It was no use trying to pay off the British, but Grijales had not even paid off the Belizean Defense Forces, in order to keep more money for himself.

Gately slammed his headsets down on to the table and made a motion for Fraley to cover the receiver.

"You tell him no fuckin' way are they burning that plane. I'll get a customs pilot in here and we'll talk 'em through getting it out of the mud."

Fraley quietly displayed his annoyance with the pilots, rolling his eyes, raising his handcuffed hands to his head, rubbing his face, massaging his eyes and mumbling an elongated, "Mo-ther*fucker.*"

At the same time another agent in the room was on the phone with the customs P-3 Orion radar platform, circling above the crippled aircraft at forty-thousand feet. This extra layer of protection was something Gately insisted on to ensure the integrity of these contract pilots and the operation. They were under radar surveillance from the time they left Phoenix to the time they returned. This prevented the possibility of the pilots double-dealing. There would be no unscheduled airdrops or pit stops along the way, where they could drop drugs to their friends or stash a load for themselves. The P-3 pilot confirmed the plane was in fact where Grijales said it was, stuck at the landing strip.

While they kept Grijales on the phone another twenty minutes a customs pilot rushed over. He had been briefed enroute on everything that had transpired up to this point. The pilot relayed the information to Fraley, who told Grijales, who passed on the directions to the pilots who were stuck in the aircraft. Gately thought Fraley was earning his keep now, but he was also loving every minute of it. He took in every word the pilot said and repeated it verbatim to Grijales. He made him repeat it and would stop Grijales if he changed even one word. Fraley amazingly handled this tense situation with the ease of a veteran air-traffic controller at LAX. They had been on the phone for well over an hour.

Once the plane was out of the mud and one ton of Escobar's cocaine was headed north, Gately told everyone in the room to take a break.

"I'll watch Leo, you guys take a break." As they all exited, Gately thought about the irony of his words. What was he going to do? Leo Fraley was chained to the floor with his legs shackled together and his wrists held together by handcuffs. It was impossible for him to go anywhere. It had become a difficult sight for Gately. It was an inhumane thing to do, even to a criminal. Luckily, Fraley had the kind of personality that could always adapt to adversity. Further, he was able to get along with anybody, even people he didn't like.

"Look, I want to thank you for doing a good job," Gately said to Fraley. He knew he could not force even an informant to give so much of himself. "It's a shame you're going to prison, Leo, because we could make a career out of screwing guys like Escobar."

"Yeah, too fuckin' bad, eh? Now do you think you could take these fuckin' handcuffs off?"

Handcuffed and chained like an animal were the rules handed down from customs headquarters and main Justice. Gately took out his hand-cuff key and unshackled Fraley's hands. He called Atwood over and told him it would no longer be necessary for Fraley to be handcuffed while he was in the holding room. As Gately drove home that night, Fraley's words echoed in his head over and over again.

"I wouldn't hire those two guys to drive a cab in Queens, much less fly these loads out of Belize," Fraley had said. He didn't like the pilots and had made no bones about it.

Gately had written it off as a sign Fraley wanted to hold the reins on this operation like he had a dozen times before. Fraley had always been the boss making all the decisions. But this time the deal was different. The consequences of success and failure were not his. Fraley's only responsibility according to his plea-bargain agreement was to make a "good-faith effort." The goal wasn't the $5.4 million Escobar would pay for this load to get to its destination. This time Fraley was working for "the man." The only goal was to identify and destroy Escobar's operation in the U.S.

Sixteen hours later the sleek, million-dollar airplane taxied closer to the hangar at the southwest end of the Phoenix International Airport. The hangar doors were open and several customs and FBI agents stood by with a sense of excitement and accomplishment as the aircraft came to a halt in the center of the huge hangar. The massive twenty-foot-tall by twenty-foot-wide sections of the sliding hangar doors slowly closed as two agents pushed at opposite ends toward the center.

When the doors were closed and the roar of the two powerful turbine engines had diminished to a quiet whine the back door and stairway combination gently unfolded. John Martelli, who had flown the last leg of the flight from Brownsville, was sandwiched in the tail area of the cabin by the precious cargo. As Martelli stepped down the ladder to the hangar floor a half-dozen agents began to form a fire-bucket brigade to pass the steady stream of duffel bags full of cocaine from the plane's fuselage to make four neat rows along the floor of the hangar. Each kilo was carefully laid out, counted, photographed, individually weighed and secretly marked for identification later.

Gately watched as the FBI and customs agents worked in sync, like a well-oiled machine. FBI case agent Ron Meyers had established the evidence-processing procedure. Meyers was the perfect personality to work a multiagency investigation. He was a consummate professional, extremely proud of his agency and representing the bureau well, but he always left his FBI hat in the office, so to speak. Meyers and customs case agent Rich Bailey worked as a team. And despite the bureaucratic crap surrounding the case in Washington, Gately never heard anything but harmony from Bailey and Meyers. At his own level Gately enjoyed just as much cooperation working with the FBI ASAC.

Four hours had passed and the job was done. It was not uncommon to see a machine gun–toting agent wearing a surgical mask, overalls and latex gloves while standing guard. The cocaine was placed in the original duffel bags and stacked on the floor near the doorway that led to the hangar office. Now the twenty-four-hour-a-day watch would begin. The first load of cocaine, worth over twenty million dollars to the Colombian suppliers, was guarded as if it were a cross between the contents of the vault at Fort Knox and nuclear waste material.

The next flight to Belize was so easy that the plane was back in the air, loaded and headed north before word reached the Phoenix office that it had landed. Now the hangar was the storage facility of more than 5,500 pounds of cocaine, worth over $45 million to Escobar. But what was really mind-boggling was its true retail potential from beginning to end. If this load were to hit the street at $100 a gram to the consumer it could eventually generate $2.2 *billion* in the U.S. and Colombia. This trail of cash represented everyone from the peasant who picked the leaves to the street punk in New York, LA and every other American metropolitan city, to Pablo Escobar himself. Even so, this transaction only represented two percent of the $100 billion-a-year cocaine market in the U.S.

CHAPTER

10

OPERATION DEAD RINGER: THE DELIVERY

TEN DAYS HAD PASSED since the second load arrived in the U.S. and still there were no specific instructions from Ortegón or *El Doctor*. The only news that day came from Winces.

"How are you, my friend," the charming baritone voice of Winces came over Gately's headset as he listened in intently to the conversation with Leo.

"Bien bien," Fraley replied, and quickly added: "Have you had any further contact with *Don Pedro* about the marketplace for the books?"

"Yes, that is why I have called. *El Doctor* has suggested that we ship another eight thousand copies before we open the market."

Gately's face showed signs of disbelief, not in the fact that he thought Winces was exaggerating, but in the prospect that the cartel trusted this Mafia associate from the pits of Ohio with more than a half-billion dollars in product to deliver without a hitch, based on nothing more than his word and past performance. But then again in this business, as Fraley so often said, "Your word is your life."

Winces continued, "Well, what do you think?"

"Well, let me talk it over with my men. I'll get back to you soon." He hung up. Fraley was playing it cool, not committing. In the past weeks he had learned that although Gately had to make the decisions locally, ultimately the bureaucracy was in charge.

After he hung up he looked up at Gately, lit a Marlboro, sat back in his chair and took a long drag. He said, "So what's it gonna be? Do we tell 'em it's a go or do we get the assholes in Washington involved again?"

Gately looked at Fraley, smiled and walked out of the room. Gately knew Fraley had toed the mark and had done a good job. Yet the case had intrinsic problems that were growing, and as each day passed they were more likely to rear up. Simply stated, there were similarities in the people with whom Gately worked and the ones for whom Fraley had been working. Greed, power and glory were the major motivating influences on the cartel's side, but both sides definitely shared the latter two drives, and Gately realized this case was becoming one that could lead even the highest level officials to start grabbing.

The prospect of getting an additional eight thousand kilos was tempting. McDermott liked it, but also knew it meant four more flights to Belize, and if anything went wrong the case could be jeopardized. The logistical nightmare of the eventual controlled delivery of two and a half tons of cocaine was quadrupled by the addition of another eight thousand kilos.

The door slammed shut when DEA informed the customs agents that neither they nor their attaché in Guatemala would run interference with the American ambassador for another flight to Belize. Tom Fink, the assistant U.S. Attorney handling the case, pointed out that the defendants, if convicted, were already facing mandatory life sentences and an additional one hundred tons of cocaine would not make a difference. In the end the decision was made to go with the current load. There would be no more flights to Belize.

Fraley passed the final word to Velasco through his nephew in Miami late that same evening. He told Restrepo that he would not have the resources to adequately protect the balance of the load while he made deliveries. And he added that he would accept the contract for the additional eight thousand after the first load was delivered and he had been paid the five million already owed in transportation fees. On December 18, 1989, Fraley received his final instructions from *El Doctor* through Don Pedro. The load he already had was to be delivered to New York. His point of contact was a prior acquaintance of Fraley's.

Gately's office was crowded. Lee Atwood, the supervisor who would take charge of the cocaine and accompany it to the Teterboro Airport in New Jersey, Rich Bailey, the special agent responsible for preparing the case for prosecution, Gary Pinkava, the supervisor who would accompany and control Fraley to New York, and Tom Fink were discussing the strategy of the investigation and the impending delivery. The atmosphere was intense, but the dialogue was excellent. The supervisors were all careful thinkers and had prepared themselves for the meeting.

Tom Fink was particularly exceptional. The thirty-one-year-old prosecutor was much wiser than his youthful appearance let on. He had nurtured this case from its infancy and was always completely supportive and ready to do whatever was needed to ensure that the U.S. Attorney's office was behind the case one hundred percent. Gately recognized that Fink was not your typical AUSA. For one thing, Fink actually liked agents. He wasn't afraid to share his views over a beer, play a hard game of round ball or just hang out with friends who were not attorneys.

It was especially unusual behavior for a well-educated barrister who came from an affluent Chicago suburb. In Fink's bloodline flowed the legacy of three generations of corporate lawyers. He had maintained the family tradition by sticking with the law as a profession, but he took what his family considered a dramatic detour, first by working for the government, and second by getting his hands dirty with career criminals.

Gately had only met a few rare ones like Fink in the last nineteen years in the six federal judicial districts he had policed. Most AUSAs had the tendency to believe that a law degree made you a superior human being and law enforcement officers were just a step above the people they arrested. This was best illustrated by one AUSA who casually told Gately one day, "All cops are liars."

"Tom, I think there are three things that are very important to us in this case as it progresses to the next phase in New York," Gately said. "First I would like to have indictments—arrest warrants *in hand*—for everyone we have dealt with up to this point. Second, I would like to have your boss' commitment to remove those people arrested in New York back to this district for prosecution." Fink seemed unfazed as Gately spoke. "And last," Gately continued, "I would like you to accompany us to New York to assist us at the New York U.S. Attorney's office with whatever we need."

A smile came over Fink's face. He was getting excited about the trip, which was good. Gately needed his influence and it would add to the control they had over the case once they were in the "other" United States of America, also known as New York. Although Fink had signed off on every move that had been taken up to this point and had every confidence in Gately, his agents and the goals they had set out to accomplish, Fink had no idea what problems existed on the horizon.

Three days later Gately, Fink, Fraley, Atwood, Bailey, his counterpart Meyers, Salazar and Pinkava were in New York to make the deal. Fraley was in the custody of Pinkava and Salazar. They split from the others to maintain the secrecy of the location of their informant. Gately, Fink, Atwood, Bailey and Meyers headed for a meeting that had been scheduled to take place at the FBI offices in Manhattan. The setting was there because, as Gately was told, the customs office could not accommodate the number of people scheduled to attend.

Indeed, the FBI executive conference room held the largest table Gately had ever seen. There were more than thirty people who fit comfortably around it. Gately was scanning the room, searching for familiar customs faces from the New York customs office. There were none. In fact, other than the agents from Arizona and two from the Newark office who accompanied them, there were no other customs agents in attendance. A few minutes before the meeting began, one customs agent from the New York office arrived. It was ASAC John Saladino.

An FBI agent began the meeting by introducing James Fox, the assistant director of the New York office. Fox began by declaring the case "an FBI case." Gately thought, this was just the kind of political rhetoric one could expect from any agency in a situation like this—but Fox was dead serious. During his fifteen-minute diatribe he did not once mention U.S. Customs. At one point Fox revealed that more than eighty FBI agents would be involved in the surveillance. Gately looked at Saladino who was not at all surprised by this. That's when Gately started to worry. He knew something was wrong.

At the same time, Fink looked over to Gately and said, "I think you've got a problem."

Gately then leaned over and whispered to Saladino. "What the hell's he talkin' about? How many customs agents do we have committed?"

Saladino kept his voice low, continued to face Fox, then cut his eyes toward Gately and said, "Rippa cut a deal with Fox. No one in Customs will be involved." He said it casually, as if they were trading baseball cards.

Gately considered this treachery, but he contained himself, for the moment. Gately and Rippa had never seen eye to eye. Rippa had been one of the youngest customs SACs in the history of the agency. Although the SAC position in Cleveland wasn't a sought-after position, Rippa had used it as a stepping stone to his current command position in New York. He was always described to Gately as an up-and-comer, a cerebral kind of guy, but the only impression in Gately's mind was that Rippa was a self-engrossed fat man whose only loyalty was to himself and who, for some ungodly reason that Gately couldn't comprehend, had risen to the position of assistant regional commissioner for enforcement.

David Rippa *was* at one time a lean, mean go-getter. He was probably everything that everyone had ever said about him, once upon a time. But over the years he had become a 450-pound man standing in a five-foot-seven-inch frame. He was a shoo-in for Dick Gregory's fat farm in the Bahamas. He was so heavy he literally could not stand still on both legs. He had to rock back and forth, or the blood would not circulate to his feet. At times, he had even been known to doze off in mid-sentence, as if narcoleptic. Perhaps the blood was not circulating to his head either. Whatever, Gately didn't care about his girth; what made him so despicable to Gately was the utterly, egocentric self-serving bent to everything he did. This was not the first case in which Rippa would totally disregard what was good for his own agency for the sake of ingratiating himself with the head of another agency. Even though they had never seen eye to eye, this case marked the beginning of a serious rift between these two men that would last the better part of their careers together. In Gately's opinion it was also the beginning of Rippa's eventual fall from grace within the agency.

When he wrapped up his speech Fox asked rhetorically if there were any questions. Gately waited no longer than his last syllable to begin: "I have a couple of questions, Mr. Fox. By the way, my name's Bill Gately —I'm the resident agent in charge in Phoenix, Arizona. I did notice during the last fifteen minutes you never mentioned U.S. Customs. I wanna tell you now that this is a U.S. Customs case, always has been, always will be. A few months ago, after we had worked this case for almost a year, we invited the FBI in Phoenix to be our partners in this investigation. I'm not here to argue anything with you. I'm just here to tell you that the informant, the undercover agents and the drugs that are in New York right now are in control of the United States Customs Service, as they will be when we leave New York. Now, my first question is, why aren't there any customs agents involved in the surveillance?"

There was a long, painful silence. Fox gave Gately a hard "fuck you" look, then leaned over to one of his agents and told him something that no one else could hear. Without a word he left the room. He had heard everything Gately said but he never acknowledged a word.

Fink, who sat next to Gately, was just as upset. He could not believe the audacity of the New York FBI agents. The cooperative effort between Customs, DEA and the FBI in Arizona had now become, without notice and with Rippa's sanction, the private domain of Fox and his New York FBI office.

Another agent, whom Fink had been watching chain-smoke cigarettes to the filter, was sweating profusely as he walked to the speaker's post and took the helm.

"Well, I guess we do have a few problems," he said.

A DEA agent from the Newark, New Jersey, office rose to ask why no one from either agency had contacted the Drug Enforcement Administration.

By the end of the meeting everyone involved was aware of the official scenario: the FBI would conduct the surveillance and make the seizures and arrests in New York. Gately still insisted that Customs would control the informant, provide security for their undercover agent, and that the drugs would return to Customs' control after the delivery and arrests were made. The meeting ended at an impasse.

Little did anyone in the room know at the time that behind their backs phone calls were already being made at the highest levels. William Sessions, director of the FBI, was now talking to the commissioner of customs, Carroll Hallett. Hallett then made direct calls to Rippa in New York and to McDermott in Arizona. U.S. Attorneys in the Eastern District in New York and the U.S. Attorney in Arizona, Stephen Mac-Namee, were discussing the case.

In most cases this kind of open, cross-agency communication was something to be applauded, but in this case the communication represented nothing more than a tug of war. In Arizona, Customs, FBI and DEA had up until now worked together well in this case. They had put aside the ever-present interagency rivalries for the good of Operation Dead Ringer. But in New York every law enforcement agency seemed to function as an independent entity.

For Fink the case brought unique problems. Unlike the rivalries between agencies, his colleagues in New York were ready and willing to facilitate. The problems were more a matter of logistics and diplomacy. Within the Justice Department Fink was juggling three different judicial districts: the Arizona District, the Eastern and the Southern Districts of New York. Fink, Gately and his agents had made a huge investment in the case, spending thousands of man-hours during more than twelve months of involvement—and they had an informant who had literally been furloughed from prison. They had a window of opportunity to conduct the agency's most significant drug case targeting the world's most notorious drug trafficker. In the end if anything went wrong it would most certainly be the customs agents from Arizona and Gately in particular who would take the blame for the case's failure. Gately believed he had a right and an obligation to his agents, their informant and to himself to protect the integrity of their plan to bring this case to fruition. It wasn't the proverbial interagency rivalry that stood in the way of total success, it was, as always, the personal agenda of a few bureaucrats in command. This time it had been fueled by the egos of David Rippa and James Fox.

The Colombian contact in New York had picked White Plains as the site of the final transaction. Two hours after the FBI takeover meeting had ended Gately and the Arizona contingent were checking into individual rooms at the White Plains Holiday Inn. Two additional rooms were also rented. One would be center stage for the undercover meeting. The other was an adjoining room, where the cover team could monitor and record Fraley and his partner Carlos Salazar as they met with Escobar's New York "cell" leader. The FBI technicians worked through the night installing the hidden video cameras and microphones.

While the technicians put the finishing touches to the audio/visual system, Gately, Fraley, Fink and the agents discussed the final details of their plan for the early morning sting. They talked over every little detail including specific dialogue, the impending "what-ifs," and above all they agreed not to give up any of the drugs until they received at least half the payment due. That meant the Colombians had to pay at least $2.7 million.

Even though the FBI had declared it their case, the customs agents knew it was still theirs. They all looked to Gately for his assurance that he would defend their case until the bitter end. For Gately it meant what it always meant: he had to be the asshole, if that's what it took. He would have to be the one to come between the case and everyone else, including egomaniacs like Rippa and Fox. Gately knew he would leave New York, having added credence to the reputation that always preceded him.

Fraley's deal would remain the same, regardless of which agency took charge and eventually claimed it as their own. But personally he did not want the FBI to take the case because he knew the loyalty and commitments to him were from Gately and Fink. Until he chose to cooperate Fraley had been facing eighty-five years without parole. Fink had promised to go before the judge himself to have his sentence reduced, and indeed Fink's support helped whittle down Fraley's sentence to somewhere between ten and twenty years. But Fraley would pay dearly for the deal: his payment would include testimony that would mark him for a certain death sentence from the Medellín cartel.

A knocking sound came from the other side of the door. The contacts were right on time. Vicente, Frank Díaz and a Colombian muscleman, unknown to Fraley, arrived at the room where Fraley, Salazar and Salazar's FBI undercover counterpart Prida were waiting. Vicente carried two briefcases. He was dressed like a businessman, wearing a conservative off-the-rack blue suit, white shirt and black tie. Diaz was out of his element. It was twelve degrees outside and he was wearing his Miami tropical attire. He had either borrowed or purchased a leather jacket to throw over his short-sleeved silk shirt and linen slacks.

Vicente had been a go-between for the Colombians several times before with Fraley in Miami. About two weeks into the case, in Phoenix, the Colombians wanted to meet with Fraley in person since they had not seen him in a year. Gately and his agents pulled off a phenomenal scheme. They rented an elegant room at a resort in Phoenix, treated the Colombians to steak dinners and entertainment. At that time, Salazar had been introduced as Fraley's brother-in-law and Prida as one of his "employees."

Now the five men in the Holiday Inn room exchanged small talk and ordered food. In the next room Gately, Fink and the FBI supervisor were all wearing headsets, listening in on the conversation and watching the action on the two video monitors.

Fraley knew that Vicente spoke English with a heavy Colombian accent and very quickly, but during this meeting he spoke mostly in Spanish. His gestures were very jerky and he was ill at ease, something Fraley had not seen before in his two prior encounters with Vicente.

"Quiero ver los libros," Vicente said to Leo as he looked back and forth between him and Salazar.

"He says he wants to see the load, Leo," Salazar interpreted.

"I fuckin' heard what he said. You tell that son of a bitch I wanna see my goddamn money." Fraley was instantly infuriated and insulted. This was not right. In the past, when Fraley had dealt with them the Colombians knew he always had the merchandise and it was always perfect to the gram. He had never shorted anyone. He was a man of his word.

Vicente knew he was wrong in asking for the drugs before showing Fraley the money. His nervous demeanor took on a new dimension. By then, he had gotten out of his chair and started pacing. Salazar was trying to interpret what Fraley said, but Vicente understood perfectly just by the tone of his voice.

"Está bien, está bien. Tengo parte del dinero," Vicente said to Fraley and Salazar, as he turned to Díaz and asked for the smallest of the two briefcases, put it on the table, opened it and proudly displayed the money. He smiled and told Fraley he had $140,000, *"Son ciento cuarenta mil."*

Fraley shot to his feet and was immediately in Vicente's face: "What the fuck is going on here? I don't know whose fuckin' money this is, but I want my money. I want two point seven million. Carlos, you tell 'em two point seven million is not this pile of shit over here. And you tell 'em he better make a phone call right now, or the next call I make is to Don Pedro."

It was all Vicente needed to hear. The name Don Pedro was enough to put the fear of God into anyone. They all knew Ortegón was Escobar's axe man.

Immediately Vicente opened the second suitcase, which held five cellular phones. He began paging people in Miami, New York, Chicago and Houston trying to get the money. He was frantic, using one phone to page people to another phone. Within minutes every phone in his briefcase was ringing. For the next twenty minutes Vicente paced back and forth with at least two phones in his hands going between each in a frenzied attempt to quickly put together $2.7 million in cash. He knew it was his responsibility to have that money there. If he didn't, the drugs would be delayed and that delay would eventually be felt by Escobar himself. It would ultimately be Vicente's fault. He knew Fraley had fulfilled everything in his contract.

Gately and Fink watched, chuckling to themselves in the room next door. Although Fraley was acting out his part, his anger was clearly genuine. This was money that was owed to him even if it wasn't going into his pocket. Fraley was upset because the Colombians were not treating him with the respect he was due. Everyone in the control room was amused—except for the local FBI supervisor, who yanked off his headset in a panic.

"What is he doing? What is he doing?" he said, agitated.

"What do you mean what is he doing?" Gately responded. "He's doing what he's supposed to be doing—not giving up anything until they choke up the money."

"We're not going past this afternoon. If that dope isn't on the street by two o'clock we're shuttin' down this case."

"Oh, yeah, who made that decision?"

"The command center did."

Both Gately and the FBI agent were becoming more and more condescending toward each other with each word.

"And who the fuck's in the command center?"

It was news to Gately that there even was a command center. The proverbial "ivory tower" had been set up in the FBI's Manhattan office to control the case and make all the decisions.

As soon as Gately got the number he called the command center and spoke with the lone customs agent Marty Ficke, assistant special agent in charge of the Newark office.

"Marty, what the hell's going on there? This feeb supervisor here says he's shuttin' this case down at two o'clock, which means putting the dope on the street without the money, even if they can get it together."

"Bill, it doesn't matter what we say. They're puttin' it on the street before two o'clock. They want all the drugs turned over to the Colombians by then. That's their schedule."

In the other room Fraley had the best solution. "Carlos, make it clear to Vicente," he said calmly, "and tell him to take his hundred and forty thousand and come back tomorrow with the rest of it. But tell him to call me on the pager because it's not going to happen here."

The FBI supervisor was now telling Gately he was sick of the case. *Sick* of it? Gately and his agents had been working the case for over a year. Gately knew what he was dealing with. The New York FBI's game plan was to claim the case and reap the reward all within the twenty-four hours it was in the Eastern District of New York.

"Okay, Leo, tengo el dinero," Vicente said.

Carlos began his translation. "He has the money. Part of it will be in

New York the following day and the rest on Monday night from Chi-cago."

"Fuckin' asshole shoulda said that when he came into the room!" Fraley said.

"I don't know about you, Tom," Gately said to Fink, "but I think we should put some pressure on these guys. Why don't you see if you can reach MacNamee and ask him if he'll get hold of the U.S. Attorney in the Eastern District and convince the FBI to shut down for two days until Monday." Fink agreed and went to his room for some privacy to make the call.

Vicente and Fraley had both calmed down considerably. They had come to a gentlemen's agreement. Vicente would pay him half of the fee Monday evening and would pick up half the load.

"Call the room and tell them they have to get it out on the street today," the infuriated FBI agent blurted out in a loud voice.

"I'm not tellin' 'em shit," Gately responded. He left the room to see what progress Fink had made. He knew what the next step would be. It was only a matter of time before Rippa would order Gately to do as he was told.

When Gately got to Fink's room Fink had just spoken with Mac-Namee who said he would do what he could but didn't think he could change the FBI's decisions, even if he could convince his counterpart in New York.

Fink had come around 180 degrees from where he was the first time he had talked with Fraley. Fink's impression of him at the time was that Fraley was displaying the typical behavior of most people caught in his situation. He spoke of grandiose abilities and even named Pablo Esco-bar as a potential target. When Fink heard that he almost lost hope in a good case. Fink perceived Fraley as someone reaching for the stars and, as an extra measure, brought up a name that everyone knew and no one could touch. Fink was now doing his best to support Fraley. Fink firmly believed that if the federal government was ever going to reach into the upper management of the Medellín cartel, it would be through Leo Fraley.

Gately knew that by the time he returned to the monitoring room he would get a phone call, and within seconds of returning he was on the phone with Ficke.

"Bill, it's gonna go on the street and there ain't a goddamn thing we can do about it. You gotta tell the informant to go along with it."

As far as Gately was concerned, Rippa had sold them out. Gately also knew that because he disagreed with the powers that be in New York he had probably come to be known as the agent "out of control."

Gately passed Fraley the order to give the drugs to Vicente, and despite the stupidity of the circumstances, Fraley followed his orders like an obedient soldier. Choking on his words, Fraley told Vicente to go ahead and take everything without giving him any money. It was completely contrary to what he should have done. Vicente should have realized there was something rotten about the deal but his greed got the best of him.

By two o'clock that afternoon Gately could see from his window on the eleventh floor the two sixteen-foot U-Haul vans in the parking lot of the hotel. He felt like a beaten dog. Still, he was determined not to give up. No matter what happened, assuming they didn't lose the load, everyone who took part in the transaction would be turned over to the agents in Arizona for prosecution in federal court in Phoenix. This FBI debacle was high on the list of the stupidest decisions he had ever witnessed.

Over the next hour Gately, Fink and Fraley monitored the movement of the drugs over the radio. A new set of bad guys had been called in to move the load. When they got into a Queens neighborhood they unexpectedly stopped at a bar. While the FBI agents followed them inside, another set of bad guys drove off with the load. Somewhere in New York a ton of cocaine was on the loose with forty some-odd FBI agents frantically trying to find it.

Back in White Plains the FBI supervisor was packing up his audiovisual gear and he and his crew were in the time-to-go-home mode. Gately could see this guy could care less. Really, he just hadn't wanted to be late for dinner.

Fink couldn't believe what he was seeing either. It was just the latest in a string of Keystone Cop antics. When they first arrived, the New York FBI agents had showed up on the scene with a dilapidated U-Haul truck. There was no way anyone would believe that this truck made it cross-country. Then, when Fink was riding in the second car from the Teterboro Airport, within a dozen car caravan following the cocaine-filled truck, he had listened as the radio traffic went crazy. The agents he was riding with were panicking. Fink was never able to really understand the radio talk, but he could tell by the activity and the reaction of the agents in the car that something had just gone very wrong. Even the helicopter pilot was shocked. It turned out that the federal agents driving the truck had decided to make a sudden, unscheduled stop at their favorite hot dog stand. Now the drugs were lost. Fink could have seen it coming.

Two hours later the feds found the load they lost and the cocaine had been delivered to two locations, one in Brooklyn and the other in Queens. The FBI had served their search warrants and arrested everyone—*except* the one who counted the most. Vicente was nowhere to be found.

When Gately heard this back at the Holiday Inn in White Plains he sat down with Fraley and devised a plan to regain control of the case.

"We'll just page the fuckin' asshole," Gately said, and right away Fraley was dialing Vicente's pager. They were bargaining on the chance that he had not yet heard of the bust. If he called back it would be clear that he was still unaware of his own impending misfortune.

"If he calls back, tell him as soon as he gets any more of the money to come meet you at the hotel," Gately told him.

In order to pull this off their crew of six had to do the impossible: they had to operate on their own, their only source of communication being the hand-held radios that they brought from Arizona. The FBI had taken all their equipment. For all they knew, they couldn't even communicate with the FBI if they had wanted to. While the FBI agents were at home having dinner, Gately and his men were standing outside the hotel in below-zero temperatures, waiting for Vicente.

Upstairs, Salazar and Fraley were again on the phone with Vicente, who told them he was enroute to pick up the money and that as soon as he had it he would come meet them at the hotel room. Salazar filled Gately in by radio. Gately contacted Ficke to ask for additional men and cars. While they were waiting, two FBI agents appeared.

"What are you guys doing back here?" Gately asked.

The rookie agent who spoke up was just a kid. "I don't know, they just called us and told us to come here and arrest some guy named Vicente. I don't even know what he looks like."

"Well, you can hang out here, I know what he looks like," Gately told him, amused. "By the way, what are your people doing in the field? Are they looking for him?"

"Yeah, they're lookin' for him." With that, Gately knew that Ficke had folded under pressure. After all, Ficke had to continue to live with these people long after this case was over, and the only thing that really mattered in this sting was arresting Vicente.

Twenty minutes south of White Plains, on State Route 22, and before he had a chance to get to the money, Vicente was found and arrested by the FBI. Gately and the rookie FBI agent were listening to the activity over his radio as it occurred.

The next day the customs contingent and half a dozen FBI agents were in Newark. Although the sting operation was now complete, the competitiveness for the glory had not died down. Gately was told the drugs would remain in FBI custody, despite the fact that they were now in the customs warehouse in New Jersey.

"I don't care if we have to get into a fist fight with them," Gately shouted at Atwood when he got the news. "We're loading the drugs into our trucks and we're going to Teterboro. The P-3's waiting." Customs had a P-3 scheduled to fly surveillance off Puerto Rico the next day. To make the deadline they had to leave Teterboro early that afternoon.

Gately headed straight for the FBI agents who were standing guard. "Do whatever you have to, but I want those drugs returned to Customs on a chain of custody before noon. We have an aircraft standing by at Teterboro that is on a tight schedule."

"I'll call my supervisor," said one of the FBI agents.

"You do that, but make it quick because one way or the other we're leavin' with this shit," he said with the verbal continence of a talking asshole.

Gately sent Atwood to accompany the agent. Atwood returned in less than five minutes. "Okay, I've got it," he said, grinning from ear to ear. "It's signed off."

Leaving New York without the drugs, the single most important piece of evidence in their case, would have been preposterous. Gately would rather have left his family jewels behind than show up in Arizona empty-handed.

Two hours later Gately and his agents had loaded the 5,539 pounds of cocaine and were set to leave. As they were pulling the ladder away from the cargo door a customs agent from the Newark office ran up shouting at the top of his lungs.

"It's Mr. Rippa. He says he's ordering you to remain at Teterboro with the drugs because he's enroute with Mr. Fox to have a press conference."

"Okay. You tell 'em I got the message," Gately yelled back as he pressed himself through the plane's cargo doorway.

"Are we ready to go?" the crew chief shouted over the roar of the four turbine engines.

"Anytime you guys are. Drive this thing out of here," Gately responded with a smile. As the airport was disappearing from view, Gately picked up his cell phone and dialed McDermott.

"Hey, Tom, how you doing?" Gately asked, testing the waters.

"You guys did a fabulous job." McDermott was ecstatic. "But you have got to be back here by six-thirty."

"Thanks. I'm pretty sure we can be back by then."

Gately didn't ask the reason for the deadline—but he was more concerned with the answer to his next question: "Tom, hypothetically, if Rippa and the FBI assistant director wanted to have a press conference here in New York, would that be a problem?"

"Absolutely, it would be a problem. I got a press conference scheduled here at six-thirty. You tell 'em, fuck no. I've scheduled the SACs from the FBI and DEA and MacNamee to be standing by at the hangar with the Arizona press when you arrive. They have to have their tape by seven to be on the air with it by nine.

"Can you handle that one for me?" Gately asked. "You see, Rippa and Fox are on their way to Teterboro. I think they alerted the press they have a couple tons of cocaine to show off. But the dope's with me and we're in the process of climbing to thirty thousand feet, headed due west. I think I may have just screwed up their chances for a press conference."

"Doesn't sound like a problem to me," McDermott said.

CHAPTER

11

PENTITI

"RISE AND SHINE. It's time to get ready. We've got thirty minutes before the van leaves." It was the friendly voice of the deputy U.S. Marshal who had been assigned to him during the course of this trial. Cuffaro had, however, already showered and shaved by the time the deputy knocked on his door.

"Don't worry, they won't leave without me," Cuffaro responded. "Help yourself to some coffee, I just made it." It was the first time since the Galatolo trial that he felt he had a decent place to stay. Since that trial, Cuffaro had become one of the United States government's professional witnesses against the Mafia. He began his new career in the Miami federal grand jury in June 1989. Two months later, in August, Cuffaro was in Philadelphia as the government's expert witness against Francesco Gambino, and Antonino and Salvatore Mannino.

In May 1990, Cuffaro finished his next and, to him, his most significant legal endeavor when he returned as the trial witness in the government's case against John Galatolo, his son-in-law/cousin Angelo Fontana and the Haitian drug dealer Luis Miguel. Since then he had given numerous interviews and depositions involving several investigations conducted by the FBI, the Italian and other European authorities. Throughout all these official proceedings Cuffaro felt like a pinball, bouncing from one forum to another.

The conditions he endured didn't make it any easier. In Collier County, Florida, he was held in a stark, cold cell where he was not even given so much as a cot to sleep on, a towel with which to dry off or, for that matter, toilet paper. Cuffaro wasn't asking for any special treatment, but he thought the very least the government could do was to provide him with humane treatment. The U.S. Marshal's Service had become his keeper when he was not in the custody of the Federal Bureau of Prisons.

Not only had Cuffaro entered the Witness Protection Program, but seventeen members of his family, from his brothers and their families, to his mother, all reluctantly signed on. Even the family's pets were provided for by the U.S. government. When he first entered the program in Miami, the FBI watched over him and his family, under the humane care of Special Agent Jim Brown. Watching this entire family pulled up by the roots had yanked at Brown's heartstrings. They all were suddenly forced to abandon their homes, businesses and friends. Yet none of them had ever had a run-in with the law. It was the price they paid for their blood relationship with Cuffaro.

At first Cuffaro and his family thought the Witness Protection Program was a good deal. They were put up in a hotel complex with full living quarters. They could live as a family, cook their own meals and maintain many of the comforts of home. After Cuffaro was sentenced with a term of ten years, the Marshal's Service took over the responsibility of keeping his family, who were separated and shipped off to various parts of the country. Cuffaro was placed in a special prison, where the government housed their most significant witnesses who had turned against some of the most notorious criminals in the world. Cuffaro affectionately referred to his new home with the name his fellow inmates called it, "The Rat House." Here he met some old Mafia acquaintances, most of whom he had never considered to be friends. He also met new friends, with some of whom he shared a common enemy. One of those men was Leo Fraley, who had also betrayed Pablo Escobar and the Medellín cartel. The Rat House was touted as the safest place for him to be, but those who surrounded him were either members of the Mafia or associates of the Medellín cartel, both of which they had testified against.

With the Galatolo trial over, Cuffaro had fulfilled his obligation to the U.S. government. It was his own decision to continue to testify in numerous courtroom scenes over the next three years. He had decided that if he was to turn his life around, he needed to come full circle. He would work as hard as he could to help the United States and Italian governments put away as many mafiosi as he could.

Cuffaro was fully dressed in his conservative, dark suit. As he was adjusting his tie, the deputy approached the open doorway.

"The van's ready, Joe."

"Okay, I'm ready," Cuffaro said as he extended his hands in unison toward the deputy who was poised, ready to handcuff him. As the cuffs ratcheted around his wrists, he felt the fear and anxiety that had over-whelmed him the previous evening creep back into his mind and body. The two Italian prosecutors, the commissioner of the court and Jim Brown had surprised him at the safe house with a late-night meeting. They began almost in chorus with, "Joe, we have some very bad news." At that instant, Cuffaro's heart sunk. His only thought was that a family member had been killed by the Mafia in retribution for his cooperation. His feelings were only partially right. The Madonia family had murdered again, this time to send a message. But, the person they killed was not related to Cuffaro—he was Palermo's most prominent anti-Mafia judge, Paolo Borsellino. They all knew it was the Mafia's way of warning them not to continue with the trial. Although it was a strong message of deterrence, it only served to enhance their determination to continue.

Each day on his way to court, he traveled in a different vehicle. There was a windowless van, another that resembled a bakery truck, and once he was shuttled in a car with blacked-out windows. He wasn't supposed to know where he was, but he figured he more or less knew his where-abouts. Even though the route was different each time, it usually took about fifteen minutes, and each time they crossed a bridge. Cuffaro thought he was somewhere in Northern Virginia, not far from the south-ern boundary of the District of Columbia. When he arrived at the fed-eral courthouse he entered through the basement level passageway re-served for the judges and the U.S. Marshals.

This stark, granite, six-story building on Third Street and Constitution Avenue, N.W., had seen many famous trials, whose defendants, judges, defense lawyers and prosecutors alike had become part of the nation's history—some had even become household names. The Depression-era structure held within its walls famous cases such as the Watergate bur-glary trial and all the president's men who fell in its wake. Others, like ABSCAM and the Irangate trial of Marine Lt. Col. Oliver North, also echoed in its marbled hallways.

But this case was an example of criminal prosecution not seen since the Nuremberg trials of the Nazi war criminals. It was the first time that two nations had combined their legal arsenals to prosecute a common enemy who refused to recognize the international boundaries or the laws of either nation. Now the governments of the United States and Italy had come together under one of the NATO treaties, known as MLAT, the Mutual Legal Assistance Treaty. It was designed by the signator nations to establish a formal pact, as well as procedures for the purpose of assisting each member nation in the suppression of interna-tional drug trafficking.

Cuffaro was escorted to the same barren underground waiting room where he had spent the previous two days waiting to take the witness stand. But today was different. There were two men and a woman waiting for him as he entered. The deputy removed his handcuffs and left Cuffaro alone with his visitors. By now they were all familiar faces. The two men made up the Italian prosecution team. Giusto Sciacchitano and Carmelo Carrara were magistrates assigned to the anti-Mafia prosecutor's office in Palermo. These two Italian judges were not the first men from his fatherland who had approached Cuffaro seeking his assistance. Within a month of his decision to cooperate, the Italians had reached out to their American counterparts, requesting an opportunity to interview Cuffaro.

The first had been Italy's most revered anti-Mafia magistrate, Giovanni Falcone. Judge Sciacchitano was no stranger to this process either. In fact it was a precedent set by him and his colleague of many years, Judge Falcone. Sciacchitano had worked with Falcone for more than two decades in Palermo prosecuting members of the Sicilian Mafia. It was Falcone and Sciacchitano who in 1980 traveled to New York, seeking the extradition of a Sicilian Mafioso involved in heroin trafficking who had been captured in the U.S. They had approached then–Manhattan United States Attorney Rudolph Giuliani, offering an open exchange of evidence to assist each other in the vigorous prosecution of the Mafia on both continents. Their new alliance with the United States opened the door to cases like the "Pizza Connection" a few years later. Sciacchitano worked hand in hand with attorney Louis Freeh, who many considered one of Giuliani's youngest, brightest and most aggressive prosecutors. At Freeh's invitation, Sciacchitano returned to New York to meet with the American government's golden goose.

With the arrest of Tomaso Buscetta, the Witness Protection Program had added a new member to its fraternity of informers. Drug Enforcement Administration agents in New York had managed to turn this Sicilian mafioso *pentito* against his brothers. There had been several turncoats who had broken the *omertà,* the Mafia's code of silence, sworn by blood oath by every made man. It had been more than three decades, from the time of Joe Valachi's arrest in the fifties, since the government was in possession of current and vital information such as that which Buscetta provided against the Mafia. What followed were some of the most celebrated victories against this thousand-year-old criminal organization. After the Pizza Connection netted two dozen mob members for the distribution of more than $1.5 billion worth of heroin, Falcone and his colleagues in Palermo tried over 300 Mafiosi enmasse at the famous "Maxi-trial." Now these two governments once again shared a valuable informer, Giuseppe "Joe" Cuffaro. What made him such a coveted informer was his knowledge of the Mafia, without him ever becoming a "made member."

"Buon giorno, signor Cuffaro. Come sta'?" Sciacchitano said as he extended his well-manicured hand. He wore a fine virgin-wool Italian tailored suit, silk tie, matching scarf and a crisply pressed cotton shirt. The judge's demeanor and presentation were as impeccable as his attire.

"Bene, grazie, dottore Sciacchitano," Cuffaro politely and respectfully replied in the customary Italian fashion.

"Buon giorno, dottore Carrara," Cuffaro said as he extended his hand to Sciacchitano's partner. Despite their congenial and professional manner, Cuffaro could still sense the despair they felt over the loss of their colleague, Paolo Borsellino. Without missing a beat Cuffaro switched languages and directed his attention to the woman.

"Good morning, Mrs. Fernández."

"Good morning, Joe," Diana Fernández said. "Just to refresh your memory, you'll recall the rules concerning the testimony of U.S. government witnesses state that you must speak in English at all times."

"Yes, ma'am, I do understand. But again, I must tell you that sometimes it may be easier to respond in Italian when the question is asked in Italian." Cuffaro had been through this several times with Fernández. During a meeting at the Rat House, the two judges and Fernández had engaged in a heated debate over the subject. Cuffaro argued that he felt more comfortable speaking in his native tongue, and if the court had simultaneous translation, what difference would it make? He tried to explain that he understood the nuances of the Italian language much better and, unlike English, sometimes the very inflection of the pronounced word had a distinctive and exclusive meaning. Yet he understood that he was also a U.S. witness, thus his testimony should be in English. During the morning meeting, Diana Fernández was, as usual, all business. Although Cuffaro respected her professionally, her rigid demeanor and insipid personality caused him to privately refer to her as the "Iron Lady." In fact, of the three people in the room meeting with him she was the one with whom he had spent the most time. She was a no-nonsense prosecutor from the Fort Lauderdale office of the U.S. Attorney for the Southern District of Florida. She had been a government lawyer for more than a decade, beginning her career in the Manhattan DA's office. Fernández had taken over the Galatolo case in its infancy and presented the government's case in a thorough, always confident manner, which resulted in putting him away for forty-five years. She was a skilled trial attorney, not easily intimidated by anyone, including the Mafia. Fernández was appointed the special United States commissioner to oversee the "Italian American Trial." She was at ease giving commands to Cuffaro, who was at least a foot taller and wider than she. In fact, she could easily disappear in his shadow. Nor was she timid in taking charge of the courtroom proceedings and enforcing the special ground rules that had been established by both governments.

Judge Sciacchitano spoke very little English, but he did understand Commissioner Fernández's direction to Cuffaro. With the skill of a diplomat he told Cuffaro in his native tongue that although they were on American soil, it was still an Italian trial presided over by Italian justices and governed by the rules of Italian courtroom procedure. Sciacchitano reminded Cuffaro that under Italian rules of evidence, a witness could speak to anything about which he had knowledge. This included information that he had acquired directly or indirectly. The magistrate also reminded Cuffaro that Italian rules allowed the witness to express his feelings.

"After the preliminary matters, you will be our first witness today," Sciacchitano told him. With that, the two prosecutors and the court's commissioner left Cuffaro to contemplate his testimony.

The tall, lean, well-groomed prosecutor stood before a packed courtroom and addressed the modern Roman triumvirate.

"Ladies and gentlemen," he began in Italian, "yesterday we were struck by the sad news that came out of Palermo about a massacre involving Judge Paolo Borsellino and the members of his escort." He seemed to make his impromptu speech without hesitation. But it weighed heavily on his heart. It was particularly difficult because just two months earlier his close friend of twenty years, Judge Falcone, had also been slaughtered by the Mafia as he, his wife and bodyguards drove to his home from Palermo's airport. The Corleonese family had lain in wait with over twelve hundred pounds of dynamite stacked under the freeway in a culvert. As the judge's motorcade approached the area at eighty-five miles an hour the assassins detonated the explosives, leaving a hole in the freeway big enough to have been caused by a meteor. By default Sciacchitano was now the most experienced, most visible and the most determined anti-Mafia judge in Italy. Now he had almost certainly become the Mafia's new target and he knew it.

"This crime is seen all over the world and in our country as another act of extreme inequity. Here in America we remember the story of President Kennedy and something he said: 'Do not ask what your country can do for you, but ask what you can do for your country.' Paolo Borsellino and the police of our country have given their response. They did their duty and gave the last full measure to this end. We will remember them with affection."

Sciacchitano then took his seat at the prosecutor's table beside his partner, Carrara.

"The court, notwithstanding the brutal and barbaric act of violence perpetrated against a dear friend of ours and a distinguished colleague, will continue in the administration of justice with impartiality," said the president of the court, Francesco Ingargiola. "Today we invite all present to rise and observe one minute of silence in honor of Judge Borsellino. Together with my colleagues, I am convinced that the prosecution of our work today and in the days to come will be the best way for us to pay our tribute to our colleague and to the members of the National Police who fell in the course of their duties."

The silence was interrupted by President Ingargiola. "The court rules that, concerning today's proceedings, the statements just made should be made a part of the record, and that this part of the record should be conveyed to the members of the families of Judge Borsellino and of the police agents involved. We may now proceed."

"We are going to commence the proceedings this morning with the testimony of Joseph Cuffaro," announced Commissioner Fernández.

As the Italian justice eulogized his comrade, Cuffaro was being ushered up the marshal's elevator to the sixth-floor ceremonial courtroom. The elevator was used only by the marshals and the federal judges to move from floor to floor in the courthouse outside the public's view and access. The elevator door opened and the deputy directed Cuffaro down the narrow mahogany-paneled hallway. The plush, deep blue carpet ensured silence along this corridor leading to the chambers of the chief judge and the ceremonial courtroom. The deputy's pace slowed as they approached the large padded green leather door. When he stopped he turned to Cuffaro, who had already placed his hands in such a manner as to give the deputy easy access to release the handcuffs.

"Good luck, Joe," the deputy said as he opened the door and led his prisoner into the courtroom. Cuffaro stopped directly in front of the three Italian justices who were seated behind the massive hand-carved oak bench perched above the defense and prosecution teams.

Although Cuffaro was an Italian by birth his only real experience in the criminal justice system had been during the last three years as a defendant and witness in the United States.

The scene before him was as alien to him as it was to the predominantly American audience. The most conspicuously missing element associated with an American courtroom was the jury, which in the Italian system did not exist. And although Sciacchitano and Carrara were judges, in this case they served as prosecutors. Heading the proceeding was president of the court, Francesco Ingargiola, and on either side the two judges, Dr. Florestano Cristodaro and Dr. Salvatore Barresi. Near them sat the commissioner of the court, Diana Fernández. There were seven defense attorneys representing a dozen defendants, of which only three were present.

Antonino Mormino represented the defendants associated with the Madonia crime family; Antonino Madonia, Aldo Madonia, Dominic Mannino and Francesco Tagliavia.

Marco Clementi was Mormino's cocounsel to the Madonia gangsters, representing Antonino Madonia and Francesco Madonia. He also served as counsel to Giuseppe Galatolo, Vincenzo Galatolo, Tomaso Farina and Carmelo Cordaro.

Orazio Campo represented Raffaele Galatolo, Stefano Fontana and was also cocounsel for Vincenzo Galatolo.

Giuseppe DiPeri and Giuseppe Giannusa represented Rosario Naimo, Allen "Brito" Knox, Paolo LoDuca, Waldino Aponte, Angel Leon Sánchez and Giuseppe Lottussi, all of whom were being tried in absentia.

The audience did not consist of the usual courthouse groupies and family members of defendants. In fact, seated in the front row of the courtroom behind the prosecution table was the attorney general of the United States, William Barr. The benches throughout the courtroom were filled with judges, Justice Department officials and students from the many prominent law schools surrounding the nation's capital. This was certainly the most closely observed courtroom drama during the summer of 1992.

As a witness, Cuffaro was not allowed in the courtroom to hear the testimony of those who spoke before him. But after so many trials, hearings and depositions there was not much information he had not already heard.

Two days earlier, one of the first witnesses to take the stand was Special Agent Jim Brown. For him the experience as a witness in the Italian trial became one he would never forget. Brown's role as a witness had, after so many years, become fairly routine. As a veteran agent, he could anticipate the attorney's questions and directions. It began that way, answering questions of logistics and chronology, but the questions in this case soon threw him the biggest monkey wrench ever. It came in the form of "hearsay." In the American judicial system, hearsay in criminal cases at the time of trial is generally not allowed, but in the Italian system, hearsay evidence is a tool widely used. It was an uncomfortable feeling, simply because of its newness, but Brown proceeded to explain in detail the nature of the "historical investigation." He described his contact with several foreign law enforcement agencies and the close relationship developed with the Italians in support of their own investigation called "Iron Tower," in which they had charged twenty-four people in a drug trafficking and money-laundering conspiracy surrounding the transatlantic shipment of six hundred kilos of cocaine to the Sicilian coast aboard the *Big John*.

"I obtained information from the Spanish authorities that also served to corroborate the presence of some Colombian individuals in Madrid, Spain, in . . . late December of 1987, early January of 1988, those individuals being Angel Leon Sánchez and his wife, Amparo, and Waldino Jesús Aponte-Romero, and others." As he answered the question, Brown naturally waited for an objection, but it never came.

"Did you also have contact with Italian investigators for the purpose of confirming the presence in Italy at hotels by individuals who were mentioned by Joseph Cuffaro?" asked prosecutor Carrara in Italian. When the translation was complete, Brown answered again a question from which the answers were acquired indirectly.

"Yes, I had provided the information that Mr. Cuffaro had furnished to the FBI legal attaché office in Rome, Italy, and I requested that the local authorities conduct an investigation to corroborate the information Mr. Cuffaro provided." It was a bit more comforting for Brown to add, "I also traveled to Rome myself, personally, and met with some investigators in Dr. DeGennaro's office, of the Italian National Police." He continually checked his own testimony trying to adhere to the new rules. Another difficult aspect was remembering to use the word "we," which under American rules is not acceptable. "We also obtained documents such as hotel records, travel records, that confirmed the travels that were outlined by Mr. Cuffaro during his statements," he replied to Judge Carrara's questions regarding the integrity of Cuffaro's statements.

The judges/prosecutors asked him the preliminary questions laying the foundation of the case, naming the agents and officials who worked with him both in the United States and Italy. In addition to Cuffaro's statements and testimony on various occasions, Brown told the court that Cuffaro also took the agents to various locations himself, pointing out significant events.

"On August of 1989, Agent Gentilcore and I took Mr. Cuffaro to the New York City area, assisted by Agent Clint Guenther of that office. We drove through the Port Washington area of New York, which was where John Galatolo's sister, Giovanna Galatolo, resided with her husband, Anthony Corinella. Mr. Cuffaro pointed out locations, specifically a house that was rented by John Galatolo's group to store cocaine that was to be sent up to New York. Also, he pointed out the residence of Paolo LoDuca in Sands Point, New York." Brown went on to explain how Cuffaro also pointed out several locations where he had participated in drug transactions with Paolo LoDuca at the Saint Francis Hospital parking lot and the Manhasset Bay Marina. "He also accompanied us to New York City, Manhattan, where he pointed out a restaurant called Kenny's Steak [Pub] on Lexington Avenue, about Fifty-first Street." Brown told the court that Cuffaro believed the restaurant was secretly owned by Rosario Naimo. It was at this restaurant where he took part in meetings with LoDuca, Rosario Naimo and Dominic Mannino, which were held in a back room.

Brown continued to explain the events that had taken place since Cuffaro's arrest. Some events to Brown were setbacks, such as Angelo Fontana's acquittal during the Galatolo trial. Others were positive discoveries that helped further their case. He told the court that in June, shortly after Cuffaro began cooperating, an important piece of paper was discovered. The paper had figures that represented the amounts of money that had been collected and brought back to the United States to Galatolo. Cuffaro kept control of the paper when he began to pressure Galatolo for his pay, and Galatolo simply brushed him off with, "We'll talk about it later." That piece of paper had been sitting in his wallet in the evidence room since his arrest months earlier.

It was not long before the spectators saw the emotion that emanated during the Italian trial. And it was not solely between the prosecution and the defense. The president of the court did not hesitate to involve himself with equal vigor.

Under his redirect examination by Sciacchitano, Brown was asked the simple question of how many times had the Italian authorities visited the United States in their Iron Tower case, and of those times how many had included inquiries with Cuffaro.

"I object," exclaimed Mormino, one of the defense attorneys.

"Let's try to elicit the question. The answer to the question," Judge Sciacchitano said sternly.

"Because I have the reports from the Italian police—" Sciacchitano began . . .

"That's provided that the witness is able to respond," President Ingargiola interrupted.

"Objection!" erupted Mormino.

President Ingargiola responded, "We have to see whether the prosecution is entitled to—"

"This can't be turned into an investigation where the prosecution is posing leading questions," interrupted Mormino. "An answer was given to this [question] two or three times. Now, at this point, we can't solicit his recollection to allow for an alternative to the answer that was given, namely saying that it might have been two or three times but without seeing Cuffaro. This is what the question suggests."

President Ingargiola had enough of Mormino. "No, no, no, no, no!"

Mormino interrupted again. "So, in other words, if the prosecution precedes this question by asking how many times Italian investigators came here for contacts with American authorities, this is a reasonable question. This is an appropriate question, but you can't pursue it in this manner."

President Ingargiola tried to pacify the increasingly volatile dialogue. Sciacchitano responded with a conciliatory reframing of the question. "I seem to recall some occasions when they came to the United States where they did not speak with Cuffaro."

"It's possible they did," Brown answered.

"In other words, this in some way modifies your statements? Can we take this to be the case?" asked Sciacchitano.

"He has already answered," interjected President Ingargiola.

Not satisfied, Sciacchitano pressed on. "So in other words, overall, how many times would you say they came to the United States? Two or three times? How many times, how many times?" he said, growing more impatient.

"Please, please. Let's each person speak separately. No chorus. We can't have everybody speaking in unison here. One at a time, please!" demanded President Ingargiola.

This was not the only incident of its kind. Several more times Brown found himself in the crossfire among the officials of the court.

Mormino, who with Clementi represented the Madonias, attempted to punch holes in Brown's testimony. He attempted to show a discrepancy in his testimony regarding the Madonia family's involvement in drug trafficking. In the beginning Mormino told the court that Brown did not include the Madonias as coconspirators. Later, when the name Madonia was brought in Mormino questioned not only the veracity of Brown's testimony, but his source of information.

"These names were provided to me by Joseph Cuffaro," Brown began confidently. He reiterated the names of the four Sicilian families: the Corleonese, the Castellammarese, the Greco family of Bagheria and the Madonia family. "That information was provided to me by Mr. Cuffaro on March 22nd or March 23rd, 1989. And that information is memorialized in my report, dated March 27th, 1989."

"However, you did not mention it with the Italian judge when you were questioned, nor in this court. You didn't mention that before," Mormino shot back.

"I don't recall being specifically asked that question and until the judge refreshed my memory—"

"So, this morning he was not asked for this. I only asked whether those names indicated were just those that Cuffaro had given him. I was extremely clear," Mormino said, addressing the court.

"This is a document we have and it's very clear," Ingargiola pointed out.

"Sure, sure. So you want to tell us exactly what Cuffaro allegedly told you, according to what you are telling us now. In this meeting with Madonia's son in Palermo?"

But before Brown could answer again, President Ingargiola again interrupted. "Well then, we can confirm the contents."

"Please allow me, Your Honor, to ask the question. If we then have to raise objections, we will."

Mormino's cross-examination was an attempt to discredit Brown's testimony and show inconsistencies concerning Brown's prior interviews with the Italian authorities. Mormino was comparing Brown's official reports of statements made to him by Cuffaro with transcripts of the depositions he and Cuffaro gave to Judge Sciacchitano. Brown's reports detailed Cuffaro's meetings with the Madonias in Sicily and some of those details were not in the deposition transcripts.

"So these documents this morning were not the subject of questioning from the prosecution?" President Ingargiola was now opening up another can of worms.

"One cannot oppose it," Sciacchitano interjected. The magistrate was arguing that no witness could recant the statements made to another coconspirator such as those testified to by Brown. Sciacchitano's argument revolved around the fact that the Madonias' statements to Cuffaro were in fact memorialized in Brown's investigative reports even if they did not appear in the transcripts.

Sciacchitano's colleague Dr. Carrara jumped in. "One cannot oppose it because it is still not permitted that the witness would renounce what the defendants have stated. So we have limited ourselves not to ask any questions as others have done on the contents of the statements of the defendants." Carrara was saying that the defense attorneys were not playing by the rules of evidence. They were not asking questions and accepting the answers as given, but instead were attempting to present their own testimony to the court.

"I'm answering the prosecution," said Ingargiola, "and this has been five hours that we think we've talked about Cuffaro's statements. This was accepted by all and there was no objection." But before returning to his question, Mormino felt it necessary to voice his displeasure again. "Still there is a problem that remains," he said. "Now we are acquiring the data for the trial and then we evaluate to say whether it's legitimate or not—what we acquired through the interview—through the questioning of Mr. Brown."

Finally, Brown was allowed to answer. "The information provided by Cuffaro was that following a meeting with Giuseppe Lottussi in Milan, Joe Cuffaro and John Galatolo went to Palermo and they met Domenico 'Mimmo' Mannino there. And Enzo Galatolo was also present at that meeting. And an individual with Mannino was identified as the son of Francesco Madonia who was at that time, as Cuffaro understood it, an Italian fugitive from justice."

Mormino began to ask another question. "If he had talked to you about it and you wrote it in your report—"

"No! This question is not allowed!" Ingargiola admonished Mormino. "Do not answer the question," he said to Brown.

Rephrasing the question Mormino asked, "In your report did you report everything that Cuffaro told you, exactly?"

"The question is allowed," interrupted Ingargiola.

"I believe so," answered Brown.

"No further questions," Mormino replied.

Brown's testimony was significant because he had not only linked Cuffaro's statements with his coconspirators' statements, he had also helped to reveal how the conspiracy unfolded, as well as the roles of the various defendants.

Cuffaro was not allowed to hear the testimony of yet another agent from the Los Angeles area. FBI agent Kevin Petersen supplied the court with another part of the drug trafficking equation. Under questioning by Sciacchitano, Agent Petersen explained his involvement in the money-laundering investigation known as "Operation Polar Cap." It was an investigation that led to several arrests and as he put it, "very, very significant" amounts of money.

The investigation targeted RCG Enterprises, located in downtown Los Angeles on Hill Street—ironically, not far from the U.S. Attorney's office.

"The people that we discovered [to be] the principals behind it were a Giancarlo Formichi Moglia, his wife, Clarissa Meditash, a Michael Meditash, a Rose Kirby and a man by the name of Bruno. I believe his name is pronounced Scopinich." Petersen continued: "According to the records that we reviewed, it was Giancarlo Formichi Moglia and his wife Clarissa Meditash who leased the office from the owners of 550 South Hill." They had claimed to be involved in the gold and jewelry business, but as Petersen told the court, there was no evidence of this during their investigation. There were two other organizations that were connected with RCG, the *Officina de Cambio* and the *Officina de Cambio Internazionale*. They were three companies that appeared to be one and the same.

"How much money was being deposited into these accounts out of the business?" asked Sciacchitano.

"The documents that I reviewed showed over forty-two million dollars, U.S. dollars, that went through the accounts."

"In what time period?"

"That would have been from late in 1986 through late 1988. It was approximately a two year period," the agent responded. "We suspected them of money laundering because of the activities of the business. We could see no legitimate business. And once again, the activities with the large amounts of currency into their bank accounts." Through Polar Cap, the court heard, the FBI was able to connect the activities in Los Angeles to Giuseppe Lottussi, the Colombian's Italian money launderer.

"We requested the assistance of the Italian government through our American embassy in Rome, to tell us the owner or subscriber of that number in Italy," explained Petersen.

Here President Ingargiola asked a question about the July 1988 call. "The court's question: Was it one phone call or more than one?"

"The toll records that I examined only indicated one phone call."

"Was it RCG calling Lottussi or vice versa?"

"It was RCG calling Lottussi," he responded.

With his testimony, the agent helped to build a solid bridge between the Italian money launderer who Vincenzo Galatolo threatened in Milan and Operation Polar Cap, one of the world's largest drug money-laundering investigations.

The defendants sat silently next to their lawyers, but their eyes were fixed upon Cuffaro. The last time these men had met they were partners in the grandest cocaine scheme ever attempted on the European continent. Now Raffaele Galatolo, Antonino "Nino" Madonia and Stefano Fontana faced Cuffaro as their adversary. They knew Cuffaro held their destiny in his words. Cuffaro faced the three-judge panel, took the oath and assumed the witness stand.

"Mr. Cuffaro," began President Ingargiola, "as a defendant of this and connected crimes, you have the right to remain silent in response to any questions. Do you intend to respond or not?"

"Yes," Cuffaro responded simply.

"The court has appointed a defense counsel, Luigi Ligoti, from the Court of Rome. This attorney, although he has been notified, is not present here in the courtroom," the president told him. It was a formality, but to Cuffaro it seemed ridiculous. What did it matter that he was notified, if he was not even going to be present? What other answer could he give than, "I'll waive my rights to have an attorney present."

But before they could begin, Stefano Fontana's attorney Carmelo Cordaro interrupted.

"Mr. President, I want to raise a point. I want to say that Mr. Cuffaro, since he was born in Palermo . . . I would ask that Mr. Cuffaro, perhaps, be examined in the Italian language. This is the appeal that I wanted to formulate," he added delicately.

"This has nothing to do with the court," responded President Ingargiola. "This has been established by the prosecutor and with the commissioner."

"I don't see—" Cordaro began, but he was interrupted by Commissioner Fernández.

"The testimony will be taken in English." Fernández reiterated the rules of the court that she had verbalized the first day of the proceedings. "Because he is in a particular position as a person otherwise implicated in a crime, he is one of the witnesses that we have designated that use-immunity will apply, and that is a condition being imposed during these proceedings."

Fernández had explained earlier that the Italians could question Joseph Cuffaro, Victor Castro, Luis Ferreira, Martin Gladstone, Francesco Madonia, David Sabio and Boris Sánchez, but that their testimony could not be used against them in Italy. The exception to this rule was John Galatolo. "We are not imposing this condition on him since he is a convicted defendant in the United States, presently serving approximately forty-five years." Another condition she imposed was that "while the defendants are here in the court, they are going to remain shackled and handcuffed."

Judge Sciacchitano rose to his position before the tribunal and began his methodical questioning of Cuffaro. Direct examination of a witness in most circumstances was considered to be the smoothest part of any trial. The Italian magistrate's twenty years as a prosecutor and his intimate knowledge of the Mafia's history and methods were clearly evident in his presentation of the government's case. Through Cuffaro's recollection of the events, Sciacchitano carefully elicited the facts of the two years of planning that went into the execution of the transcontinental drug deal. Specifically, he asked for details of the transfer of drugs on the high seas between the Colombian vessel and the Sicilian fishing boat.

"During the beginning of January of 1988, when I met with Allen Knox, or 'Brito,' at the Villa Igea, he described to me how the actual delivery took place off the coast of Sicily. It was during the night, one or two o'clock in the morning, very high seas, maybe four or five meter waves. And the freighter couldn't get close enough to the fishing boat, and that's when Allen Knox decided to inflate the life raft, put the cocaine into the life raft, and his crew members eased them off from his boat to the fishing boat and that's how he was capable to deliver the cocaine to the fishing boat."

Cuffaro held the courtroom's attention with his gestures and animated explanations.

"Another detail he mentioned is that the rope that he was hanging on to broke off and he was left in the middle of the Mediterranean Sea. The fishing boat left, and the freighter had to make a quarter-mile round to pick him up later on."

"Was there any talk in America about other, even larger shipments if this had come to a good conclusion?"

"During the meetings that we had, Rosario Naimo and Paolo LoDuca and Dominic Mannino and especially Rosario Naimo mentioned on several occasions that the ideal thing would be if this first trip would be successful, to follow up with other larger deliveries of cocaine, possibly two or three thousand kilos at a time. And perhaps in the future, if everything would work out smooth, we could ship back heroin from Sicily in the same vessel."

Two hours into Cuffaro's testimony Sciacchitano ceded to his prosecutorial partner. Carrara began his questioning by focusing on Cuffaro's meetings with his Mafia connections as they related to the six-hundred-kilo transaction. Carrara's questions were designed to paint the picture of the interaction between the Sicilian Mafia and John Gotti's Gambino crime family in New York.

"After the six hundred kilos were delivered to Sicily I traveled to the New York area together with Waldo Aponte, the supplier of the six hundred kilos, because part of the original agreement was to pick up a million dollars in the New York area."

Cuffaro explained himself confidently. He had repeated his knowledge of the story numerous times, and each time he explained it, the events became more and more ingrained in his memory.

"It took place around probably February of 1988, when I had a meeting with Mr. Naimo, Mr. Mannino and Mr. LoDuca at Kenny's Steak [Pub] in Manhattan. They told me that the million dollars was not available, but they had a great interest in a large amount of marijuana for John Gotti. I mean, John Gotti had asked them if they could acquire a large quantity of marijuana for the New York area. At that point, I referred the information to Mr. Aponte, who was staying at the Intercontinental Hotel on Lexington Avenue, and he was very upset . . . that the million dollars was not available. But Mr. Aponte made a couple of phone calls to Colombia and assured me that he had no problem supplying half a million pounds of marijuana to the New York area. He just wanted to know what kind of payments, the prices and the details."

Cuffaro continued explaining how the three mafiosi planned this crime while they stuffed their mouths with their forty-dollar steaks.

"Rosario Naimo mentioned that the marijuana could be unloaded right off the coast of Long Island. Also Dominic Mannino said he had no problem to have a freighter of marijuana coming into the Port of

Philadelphia, because he claimed that he had total control of the authorities in the Philadelphia port. There was no problem to smuggle five
hundred thousand pounds of marijuana into the Philadelphia seaport."

The prosecutors led him through the multimillion dollar deal and the
corporate structure of the crime families Cuffaro had dealt with. Then
they shifted their focus to the true nature of the Mafia. Unlike most law-
abiding billion-dollar, multinational corporations, the Mafia settled most
of its problems and eliminated competition and the possibility of "hostile takeovers" by simply pulling the trigger or strategically placing a
bomb.

"To your knowledge, did any of these people want William Kane eliminated?" asked Judge Carrara.

"While detained in MCC [Metropolitan Corrections Center], Miami,
Salvatore Rina confided to me that he was very worried about Bill Kane
being a government informant. He told me that he had several meetings
with Joe Gambino, one particular meeting at the Fountainbleu Hotel in
Miami Beach." Cuffaro told the court their discussion was specifically
about killing Kane. Rina told Cuffaro that although Kane had been a
trusted friend, the Gambinos had suspected a leak and thought that by
eliminating Kane the flow of information would be cut off. It was a
calculated gamble that Kane was the rat, but killing him was certainly
one way to be assured of his silence.

"Joe Gambino gave Salvatore Rina the okay to go ahead and kill Bill
Kane. He also mentioned that he was going to send him a couple of
body bags so that the job could be done."

"Rosario Naimo and Paolo LoDuca—did they assign John Galatolo
to find people who were close to Tomaso Buscetta and Gaetano Badalamenti with the purpose of killing them?" Carrara asked.

Both Badalamenti and Buscetta testified in the Italian "Maxi-trial."
Their testimony was the primary evidence used to convict over three
hundred Mafiosi. Not only had they been marked for death, but their
friends and relatives were as well.

"During one of the meetings in the New York area between myself,
John Galatolo, Dominic Mannino, Rosario Naimo and Paolo LoDuca,
Rosario Naimo asked us if we could ask the Colombians that we were
dealing with if they could find some Italians in Venezuela. They were
friends of Buscetta. And price was no object. Mr. Naimo was willing to
pay any amount for us to ask the Colombians if some Italian individuals
could be located in Venezuela."

Sciacchitano took the helm, continuing in the same line of questioning.

"Did John Galatolo tell you about having committed murders during
the time he was in Florida?"

"He talked about several murders that took place in south Florida, particularly the killing of two individuals that happened right in his own residence."

"Did he tell you that these were Mafia-style murders?"

"He explained to me that these murders were ordered by the Sicilian Mafia and he was given the instructions by the Sicilian Mafia to kill these individuals because they were friendly with Tomaso Buscetta."

Carrara then asked a similar question regarding another Mafioso and former associate of Cuffaro. "Did you learn whether Stefano Fontana was involved in serious, bloody crimes?"

Even with Fontana sitting a few feet away, Cuffaro did not hesitate to answer. "The only thing I know is that right after Mr. Stefano Fontana was released from prison in Palermo, his brother Angelo came back from Palermo to Miami, and during a meeting between myself and Angelo Fontana, Angelo confided to me that his brother Stefano was indeed guilty of that particular murder. But the Italian authority was not able to prove his guilt, and he was freed."

The next day, as Sciacchitano was about to continue his direct questioning of Cuffaro, the court proceedings were interrupted by one of the defendants. Without benefit of his attorney, Antonino Madonia rose to his feet asking for acknowledgment.

"What do you want, Mr. Madonia?" asked the president of the court.

"May I speak? If you authorize me, I have something to say."

"Concerning what?" Ingargiola asked impatiently.

"Concerning our defense, if you authorize me?"

"Yes."

"We didn't do it earlier," Madonia began, speaking from his seat while handcuffed, "for delicacy toward you. We didn't want at all to impede the trial. But this suffering is continuing and I want to summarize our history. We have been here nine days, we are kind of buried in a place where we cannot see the sun the whole day—in a room two and a half meters by three meters. There is a cement block and we must sleep on it with a thin plastic mattress just three centimeters thick." Madonia then mustered a higher level of commitment to back his words. "When we came, we were told in the promises they gave us that we had to leave everything at home. At this point it is forty centigrades, there's quite a bit of heat in that place. We cannot close our eyes. There is a hall not far from us and so the custody agent can see us. There is a fan for her and it makes a big noise." He became more animated. "We cannot wash because there is a shower with hot water, pretty hot water, and they haven't been able to repair it after all this time. We can't understand what's happening," he said referring to his fellow defendants, as the group's speaker. "We had taken with us a towel, they took it and they keep them, just lay on the floor, they don't pass them to us. And for today's washing they give us a small towel as small as a handkerchief just to wipe us." By now, Madonia was growing exasperated. "And what else can I say?"

"I think that—" Ingargiola began.

"No, no, no. There's something still more important. For showering, we are naked and watched over while we are showering and with the small towel we don't even have the wherewithal to cover ourselves." Sensing he was trying the patience of the court, Madonia quickly brought his comments to a close. "Anyway, we're here and we want to continue. We will stay here as long as our presence is useful."

Ingargiola's patience had run out long before Madonia had wrapped up his comments. "Before coming here you accepted the conditions imposed by the American government," he began sternly. "Now, if what you said is different from the conditions that the American government had imposed then we want these conditions to be modified. If these are the conditions to those held incarcerated in the United States of America, there is nothing that can be done about it. So, I pass your question to Dr. Fernández to have things ascertained."

Madonia interrupted again. "In the conditions that we read and were translated to us in Italian, it wasn't there—that—"

"Fine, Madonia, fine! You expressed your opinion." Ingargiola now directed his attention to Commissioner Fernández. "Now, I asked Dr. Fernández to ascertain the conditions in which our incarcerated defendants live to see if they correspond to the conditions imposed on all other incarcerated persons in the United States of America, always with respect to security."

"Okay. As I believe you were informed, and you were certainly informed at the time you arrived, you were going to be held in segregation," Commissioner Fernández was stern and unwavering, regardless of Madonia's pleas. "And segregation here in the United States means a lock-down situation."

Madonia and the other defendants were sinking deeper and deeper into their chairs.

"If there are specific problems that you have, for example you say the shower doesn't operate, I will look into that to try and take care of those matters. But the conditions that the marshals are imposing in your prison are going to be maintained. If you do not wish to remain here in those conditions—as you indicated in Italy before you came that you would abide by the conditions—if you do not wish to remain in those conditions, we will have you returned to Italy. But, it is your choice. But as long as you are here those conditions will remain in place. Is there anything further, then?"

"No." It was the only word left for Madonia.

"Mr. President," began Vincenzo Galatolo's attorney, Orazio Campo, "I ask you to tell Mrs. Fernández that we are very happy with these new arrangements because we do not have any reason to speak with the defendants in places that are not exactly controlled."

Soon the calm of direct examination gave way to the storm of cross-examination—a storm Cuffaro had endured several times before. With blood in their eyes the defense attorneys would seek out their pound of flesh with every question. In the opening volley Cuffaro would undergo the litany of accusations that the defense had to paint to give the judges in this case and the juries in the preceding cases the picture of the government's prize witness as an arsonist, gun-toting drug dealer, thief and, worst of all, liar.

One of the most grueling attacks on his character and credibility came during Galatolo's trial in Miami from his attorney, James Woodward. Woodward had been on a roll, describing twenty years of abuses, beginning with Cuffaro's entry into the United States, his marriage to a street-walker and the numerous prevarications that had been memorialized by official records and by Cuffaro's own admissions.

"Okay, Mr. Cuffaro, you already testified, I believe, that you lied to your lawyer, you lied to the police, you lied to your wife, you lied to the Internal Revenue, you lied to the Immigration and Naturalization Service."

He leaned forward toward Cuffaro and with dramatic emphasis reminiscent of a daytime soap opera, said, "None of these things were for any pecuniary value on your part, were they? These were all gratuitous things, right?"

"Well, I think it is up to the members of the jury to evaluate the amounts of my lying," Cuffaro answered calmly. He had heard this time and time again and he knew it would not be the last.

Attacking his integrity was only one of the tactics used by defense attorneys. Another was painting him as a dangerous and threatening menace to society, more evil than their clients. It was Angelo Fontana's attorney, Lance Stelzer, who masterfully made this point to the jury.

"You understand I have a job to do, and there is nothing personal between you and me here. This is a job," Stelzer began attempting to lead Cuffaro into his trap.

"Of course," Cuffaro replied.

"I want to make sure once you are released from prison in a couple weeks, a couple months, or years, you won't show up mad at me with an Uzi in your hand."

In the midst of objections, Cuffaro remained composed, answering simply, "No, definitely not."

The third and most caustic tactic was attacking Cuffaro's deal with the government.

"Would it be fair to say, Mr. Cuffaro, that you have admitted to the government doing deals that are each punishable by one hundred years, and you admit doing it probably forty times, is that fair?" Stelzer relished his line of questioning. They were facts and could not be disputed.

"That is correct," replied Cuffaro matter-of-factly.

"Now, if my multiplications are correct, that would be four thousand possible maximum penalty years in prison worth of crimes you committed?" His gratification was evident. But Cuffaro remained steady.

"That is correct."

"That is just in the cocaine dealing?"

"Yes."

"Now, with respect to other matters, you admitted tax evasion?

"Correct."

"Can we assume that is a felony in the United States of America?"

"I am not an attorney. I don't know what the charges are." Cuffaro was calm, but he knew the eventual outcome.

"You have been advised it is punishable by five years in jail." Stelzer then walked to the blackboard where he had been tabulating numbers, then added the new figures to the four thousand figure.

"Now, you admitted you were in numerous rip-offs?"

"Yes."

"A rip-off is a polite term for a robbery?" he asked knowingly.

"Correct."

Stelzer continued counting numbers, adding them to his already crowded blackboard. He brought up arson, weapons charges and others.

"Without going into anything else, without reentering whether you did or did not dodge the draft in Italy, would it be fair to say if I total up this column here, another 230 to add to the 4,000, would it be fair to say that in terms of maximum penalties for what you've done over the last several years, the maximum term of years is 4,230?"

There was no way out, but Cuffaro never hedged.

"I would round it off to 4,500 years," Cuffaro said, a twinkle in his eye.

For at least the better part of an hour, Stelzer continued with this line of questioning. Throughout, Cuffaro remained in control of his temper, unfazed by the attorney's verbal bludgeoning. Seeing that he was not gaining ground, Stelzer finally moved on to the facts of the case.

Cuffaro had managed to remain cool throughout the various trials, primarily because U.S. court rules prohibited an emotional response beyond answering the question. But, as Sciacchitano reminded him earlier, under the Italian rules the witnesses were allowed to express opinion and emotion. Cuffaro took full advantage of this after defense attorney Clementi continued to press Cuffaro on minute details of little substance.

"Apparently, you are totally ignorant." Cuffaro's response was tempered with his anger and the stress he felt after four days of cross-examination. The crowd was mesmerized. How could such an answer be tolerated, much less accepted? Yet Cuffaro was determined to fight fire with fire—only smarter.

Marco Clementi, the defense attorney for Vincenzo and Giuseppe Galatolo and the Madonias, Antonino and Francesco, began by politely and methodically confirming factual information concerning events, dates, times, people and places. Then he began testing Cuffaro's memory of the facts and circumstances he had testified to under direct examination by Judges Sciacchitano and Carrara. They had spent the last hour going over the six hundred kilo deal, discussing such mundane details as the distance between ports of entry, and how much money Cuffaro had collected, a question he had been asked and had answered a dozen times. Then Clementi began shuffling the numbers like a con artist with a deck of cards. Cuffaro's patience had run out.

"I feel sorry for your clients. You obviously don't know what you are talking about, unless of course, you are just trying to discredit me."

"What are you talking about?" Clementi yelled back at Cuffaro.

"First of all, don't yell at me," Cuffaro said pointedly. "I am talking to you calmly as a gentlemen, and I expect the same."

But Clementi came back at Cuffaro with a vengeance. With disdain and hatred in his voice, he vented numerous accusations at Cuffaro. Cuffaro would not stand for it.

"You know you're a Mafia attorney. Everybody knows that," Cuffaro, who looked twelve feet tall, had risen to his feet and extended his arm and yelled back at the Sicilian lawyer. The observers took in a collective gasp. "In fact, you were assigned to represent me years ago. You were sent from the Galatolos because you've been on the Galatolos' payroll for years." Cuffaro then sat back down to continue his insults. "As a matter of fact, I never paid you. Why don't you send me a bill through the Marshals Service."

The courtroom was now filled with laughter, even from the judges. Clementi had indeed been hired by the Galatolos in the fall of 1988 to help Cuffaro clear up a legal problem. It was a simple technicality where the Italian government drafted Cuffaro, not knowing he had long ago become a U.S. citizen. But Cuffaro remembered this was a point of contention during his testimony against Galatolo, because the defense tried to use it as a technical advantage, claiming it was a prior conviction.

"I can't understand it. You were brilliant *then*," Cuffaro said, adding salt to the wound.

"You're a liar! You're a liar! You're a liar!" Clementi's face was so red he looked like he was about to burst as he continued to scream at Cuffaro.

Now President Ingargiola interrupted. It was the third time he had warned Clementi. "You are acting like a clown. We are guests of the United States government and you are acting like a clown! You are embarrassing the court and the Italian people. Mr. Cuffaro has been talking to you like a gentleman and you are out of control. The next time you display such outbursts, you will be thrown out of this courtroom!"

The president of the court went on blasting the Italian defense attorney for almost a full ten minutes, or so it seemed to Cuffaro. Cuffaro had held back what he had really wanted to call the short balding barrister: a fucking punk! But Cuffaro knew this was just the beginning. There were six defense attorneys he would have to fend off and over a dozen defendants, including the ones who were being tried in absentia. Luckily for Cuffaro, he had already had some experience as a high-powered defense attorney's punching bag.

The intermittent disciplinary diatribes from the president of the court grew more frequent as Cuffaro's cross-examination continued. On many occasions several attorneys simultaneously fired questions at Cuffaro. One of their tactics for discrediting him was to hit him with a volley of rapid-fire questions. But it only served to raise the ire of President Ingargiola, who also found it necessary to discipline his own prosecutors.

Cuffaro expected more of the same as the next attorney rose to take his shot. Nonetheless, Cuffaro would not ignore the news of defense attorney Antonino Mormino's recent personal tragedy—his father's untimely death.

"Mr. Mormino, first of all, I would like to express my condolences on your loss." Cuffaro had just assumed the witness stand for the sixth day of his cross-examination. But he felt it was important to express empathy, even if Antonino Mormino was Rosario Naimo's attorney and he would undoubtedly begin as most attorneys do, by attacking the government's witness.

"Thank you very much, Mr. Cuffaro," Mormino responded. Cuffaro expected Mormino's demeanor to change next. It seemed to be something intrinsic in attorneys, the ability to express human compassion one minute and immediately undergo a metamorphosis into an uncaring, vengeful, blood-sucking, money-grubbing beast dressed in a $2,000 Armani suit. But it did not happen. In fact, Mormino's questions seemed only to scratch the surface. Perhaps it was his father's sudden death the day before that had dulled the tongue of the beast.

As Mormino's questions fizzled Cuffaro saw Clementi quietly consult with his client Vincenzo Galatolo. Clementi checked his notes and immediately took the floor as Mormino took his seat. Cuffaro imagined he could see horns growing from the fat man's hairless crown and a spear beginning to take shape in his hand.

"Mr. Cuffaro," he began arrogantly, in Italian, as if his question would certainly emerge as the *coup de grâce.* "Are you a man of honor?"

Cuffaro knew where he was heading. It was one of those questions that could potentially backfire no matter what the answer. But Cuffaro did not hesitate.

"Well, Mr. Clementi, there are several ways to answer that question. The way I interpret it is if you make an agreement and you keep your word, even without a handshake, then you are a man of honor." Joe looked around, made eye contact with the defendants and the Italian justices. "The way your clients perceive it is much different," he continued. "They think if you pull the trigger into the back of the head of someone, then you are a man of honor. Any mental retard can do that. That takes no brains at all. That to me does not make him a man of honor. I never did that and never had any intention of doing that."

Clementi had been summarily stopped in his tracks. With his answer, Cuffaro was able to obliterate the next series of questions he had prepared. It was clear he had nowhere to go. So Mr. Clementi returned to his seat.

"Punk," was Cuffaro's only thought.

On the fifth day of the war of words, after court had recessed, Cuffaro was taken back through the marshals elevators, stuffed into the bread truck and whisked away across the bridge to his home away from home.

Left standing alone in the courtroom was Giusto Sciacchitano. The judge took the opportunity to engage in an activity that had become increasingly more difficult to do in Italy—take a walk without an entourage of bodyguards. It was a point of contention with the Marshals Service, especially following the news of Borsellino's assassination, but they reluctantly allowed the judge to have his way. He had visited the United States many times, but he enjoyed Washington, D.C., because unlike many American cities it proudly displayed the country's history. He also enjoyed Washington because of its similarity to Rome. Some of the terminology used in the American government had its roots in the Roman government, which dated back to 200 A.D. The concept of the senate body and even the word itself was derived from Latin, the ancient Roman language, and Roman democratic ideology. Capitol Hill, where his summer evening stroll took him, was another example of Washington's connection with Rome. Rome's Capitoline Hill was the original center of the ancient city and its government. Today it remains modern Rome's government center and the home of the Eternal City's mayor. Sciacchitano walked past the Capitol Building and found his way leading up to the steps of the United States Supreme Court.

The building, constructed of white marble in Greek Revival architecture with eight front-facing Corinthian columns, reminded Sciacchitano of the many historical buildings throughout Italy. The figures in the pediment and the statues on either side of the stairs symbolize justice and the execution of the laws. Above them he read the words, EQUAL JUSTICE UNDER THE LAW. As he stood in admiration of the architecture, he began to reflect on the historical covenant between the two countries. With the death of two of his colleagues, he felt even more alone. It was a consoling feeling, however, to know that in his heart, he carried their friendship and in his mind, he carried their wisdom. He remembered Judge Borsellino's words at Falcone's funeral. He laid his hands on the coffin and told the other anti-Mafia magistrates, "Whoever feels they can't go all the way should feel free to seek a transfer, because this is our destiny."

As he looked at the figures positioned just outside the Supreme Court Building he was reminded of the many philosophical discussions he, Falcone and Borsellino had shared. He thought about the concept of equal justice and the problems that both the United States and Italy now faced in the war against organized crime. It was time for the United States and Italy to assume leadership roles in fighting drug trafficking and corruption. During the past two decades he had witnessed the increasing strength and proliferation of the drug trade. He had seen the steps both countries had taken during the past few years in their legal assault on organized crime to more effectively disrupt and dismantle its thousand-year-old infrastructure. In Italy a variety of new laws had been passed specifically designed to combat money laundering. He thought of his conversation with Cuffaro, who had pressed the Italians to develop a system akin to the American Witness Protection Program. Without it, he told Sciacchitano, ordinary citizens would not feel safe coming forward with the information the government could effectively use against the Cosa Nostra. Sciacchitano thought of the quixotic position both countries faced. The drug trade had brought enormous wealth to the Mafia on both continents, as well as to the Colombian drug cartels, but now the problem was not only combating these criminal organizations but a drug-addicted culture. The illicit drug trade had also created its own global economy, penetrating and corrupting every aspect of society, leaving in its wake a generation of victims.

That afternoon Judge Carrara called the government's next witness, referred to by Cuffaro and others by his first name only, "David." David Sabio, a white Jamaican and former resident of Miami Shores, was an educated and articulate individual. He was serving a fifteen-year sentence for cocaine trafficking and was a onetime friend and business associate of Angel Sánchez.

This was not his first appearance as a government advocate. As a "cooperating individual," for over two and a half years he had proved to be one of the governments' more lethal weapons in their arsenal of turncoats. Sabio had been a witness to John Galatolo's felonious relationship with Sánchez and assisted the Republic of Italy in its "Iron Tower" investigations.

Sabio's uncanny ability to recall dates, times and locations, as well as his ability to recite verbatim conversations with Sánchez and others, proved to be devastating to the defense. Sabio had initiated his cocaine-smuggling ventures in Sánchez's hometown of Barranquilla, shipping their cargo first to South Florida, then Canada and eventually branching out into Portugal and Spain.

The courtroom was silent and all were intently listening to Sabio recalling his profitable adventures in which he had traversed the three continents.

In January 1988, he told the court, Sánchez and his associates, who were in Spain, were awaiting a shipment of cocaine destined for Europe from Colombia. Sabio explained that the ship *Big John* actually contained a load totaling eight hundred kilos of cocaine, two hundred of which were to be off-loaded in Portugal and eventually transported to Canada. The remaining six hundred were destined for Italy and then the United States.

"At that time Mr. Sánchez and Mr. Luis Troncoso were in Madrid at the Mellía Castilla Hotel. Colombia was keeping radio contact with the ship en route," he explained. When they began having trouble with their radio signal, Sabio was asked if he could secure a radio in Europe that could maintain contact. "Before I got the radio, or I was able to get a radio, Colombia [had] restored contact, and it was no longer necessary."

During the various court proceedings the identity of the man Cuffaro described as Dr. Garçón was never really asked directly. Possibly because no one had ever met him. The questions to the nearly dozen witnesses who had some form of contact with "the doctor" were usually limited to, "When did he speak to you?" and, "What did he say?" Only on one occasion was the question asked, "Who was he?" Sabio testified that he had indeed met him personally. He told the court, Dr. Garzón, spelled G-A-R-Z-O-N, was a high-level member of the Medellín cartel known on the streets as "El Pollo."

"In which city did you meet him?" Carrara asked.

"I met him first in Europe when he came to visit with Mr. Troncoso and Mr. Sánchez. Then I met with him on several occasions again in Barranquilla, Colombia."

The mystery of the high-ranking drug lord never seemed to unfold. Agent Brown and his colleagues determined that Dr. Garzón was a high-ranking Medellín cartel drug lord, but believed his true name was Oscar Medina. It seemed that the testimony from other witnesses regarding his identity lacked consensus. No one agreed, but then again, none could disprove another opinion.

Sabio explained that Sánchez and Dr. Garzón discussed with him some of the details surrounding the delivery of the shipment.

"Did these people tell you that the people who were supposed to receive the cocaine in Sicily were under the protection of the Guardia di Finanza or the Coast Guard?" inquired Carrara.

"Mr. Sánchez mentioned that the transshipment, or the delivery of the coke in Italy, was to be surveilled, or supervised, or protected by the local authorities, yes," Sabio confirmed.

He told Carrara that during the summer of 1988, Sánchez, Dr. Garzón and their associates had become very concerned over the delay in payment for their cocaine shipment. While he was in Colombia preparing a container of marijuana to be shipped to Holland, Sánchez contacted him, asking for his assistance.

"Mr. Sánchez asked me if there was any way I had the possibility of receiving Italian lire in Italy and transporting them out of Italy and converting them to international currency," he continued. Sánchez directed Sabio to Milan. Before he could travel to Milan, he still needed to secure his marijuana shipment. In Amsterdam, he began making inquiries regarding the conversion and shipment of the Italian lire for the Colombians.

"I was informed that the money was in cash and it could be packaged properly, that these contacts had the capability of moving it across the border to Lugano and having it exchanged and deposited into international bank accounts. I then traveled to Milan to accomplish this."

Sabio registered himself at the Hilton Hotel in Milan under his alias, Anthony Gannon.

"When I got to Milan, the arrangements were I had to call Colombia and leave my phone number and my room number. I did so, and I was supposed to be contacted by a man by the name of Giuseppe." Sabio called several times, often using the public phones at the *Place de Roma*. He waited there for several days, then at Sánchez's request began calling "Mr. Waldino" in Miami.

He told the court that Waldo Aponte "kept promising me that tomorrow, tomorrow, tomorrow this gentleman will be there. 'Tomorrow someone is coming to see you.' " No one ever showed up to meet Sabio. After a week of waiting he informed his associates in Colombia that he was returning to Amsterdam to take care of his own affairs.

Like most corporations, the Medellín cartel employed its own collection men and even investigators. One of Escobar's investigators was Boris Sánchez. Boris was arrested in May 1988, for participating in a fifty-kilo cocaine deal in Gainesville, Florida. He had been cooperating with the government ever since.

Boris Sánchez, who was Leon "Angel" Sánchez's second cousin, told the court he was assigned to investigate the problems surrounding the payment of the Italian debt. When they first told him about the task, he was summoned to an unlikely meeting area to be briefed on the multi-million dollar debt.

"I met with Amparo, Angel—" he stopped to make himself clear— "[Amparo is] Leon's wife. I met her at the Miami Children's Hospital. Leon Sánchez called Boris Sánchez from his home in Barranquilla. He was then unable to travel to the United States, where he was a fugitive.

"For what reason did you go to the Children's Hospital in Miami?" asked Sciacchitano.

"Angel told me that Amparo, his wife, was at the hospital, that her child was very sick, that I should please go to the hospital and help her as much as I could." Boris explained that his cousin's son was eventually pronounced brain dead.

"Exactly what did Angel Sánchez tell you?

"First he asked me to help Amparo with her child. Then she asked if I would help her collect some money from five hundred kilos of cocaine, from a man called Waldino Aponte."

"So exactly what did you do?"

"First Amparo called Wilmer Salazar and she introduced him to me at the hospital. She told Wilmer that I was a cousin of Angel's and that I would be their representative in the collection of the debt. She also called Waldino Aponte and told him the same thing."

"Why did Amparo call Salazar?"

"I understand that Salazar was already involved in this business, collecting some money for Dr. Garzón in Medellín."

The next ten minutes of questions by Sciacchitano involved details on the agreement reached by Boris Sánchez and Salazar, and their plans for collecting the money. They had ruled out using coercive tactics and outright violence, on direct orders from Dr. Garzón.

"Do you know whether there were also other Colombians, more important than Aponte and Sánchez, involved in this shipment?"

"Amparo told us at the first meeting that the Italians should hurry up and pay because otherwise this *"Sombrerón"* would send people to col-

lect and then they could do nothing. *"El Sombrerón"* was the nickname
. . . of José Rodríguez-Gacha, who also was sometimes called "the
Mexican."

"And who is this person, in rank of importance?"

"He was one of the principal members of the Medellín cartel."

"What was the role played by Garzón, who we already talked about?"

"With regard to Garzón, he had some dealings with Angel. Once
Wilmer told me that a hundred kilos of that cocaine belonged to Dr.
Garzón, that he was also representing Dr. Garzón in this partnership, so
that the collection of the money was for Angel and also for Dr. Garzón."

It was after their third meeting that Boris Sánchez was introduced to
John Galatolo, whom he knew as Giovanni. He told the court that Giovanni had recommended sending his partner to Italy, because neither
Boris Sánchez nor Galatolo could travel at the time. Boris Sánchez
could not travel because he had not yet received the proper documentation, and Galatolo would not leave, "not even if he'd be killed," because
his mother was gravely ill.

"When we said goodbye Giovanni left first. His van was close to the
gate, to the entrance door. Wilmer and I got into Wilmer's car. Wilmer
told me that we were going to follow him. I made a note of the license
plate of the van, and we followed him at a distance. We saw him arrive
ten or fifteen minutes later, at a house near Waldino's." After he entered
the house, Boris told Sciacchitano, "We took down the address of the
house."

"Did you later deliver the license plate number to the FBI?

"Yes."

"Did you meet the person whom Giovanni had called on the telephone?"

"At Waldino's house, three days later."

"Can you describe this person to us? Who was he?"

"He was a big guy, dark skinned. He had a mustache, black hair, if I
remember correctly."

"Did you ever learn this person's name?

"No."

The decision was made that Salazar would travel to Italy, via Spain,
and that Boris Sánchez would remain in Miami to relay messages.
Salazar called him twice from Italy.

"The first time that he called he told me that up to that time he hadn't
seen anybody, and that the number that was given to him, nobody was
answering at the number." Boris then called his cousin Angel and Dr.
Garzón to inform them that no progress had been made.

"How about the substance of the second phone call you got from
Salazar?

"Salazar told me that he had already seen something. I called Angel then, and Dr. Garzón, and I told them what Wilmer had told me."

"Did anything happen after these events?"

"Well, that was when I got involved in picking up fifty kilos of cocaine in Gainesville. And that's why I went to jail."

The court then showed him a photo that he identified as that of the large man that had been called by Galatolo: Joe Cuffaro.

Boris nodded.

President Ingargiola then called on the defense attorneys to cross-examine the witness.

"A little while ago you said that you had phoned this Dr. Garzón. Can you tell me where you called him?" Clementi asked.

"Well, first Amparo called him, and then she passed the phone on to me so that he would know me even if it were only by telephone. And the time that I called him it was from public telephones at the Children's Hospital."

"Where did you find him? Was he in America, Africa, Australia? Where was he?"

"Medellín." His cousin, he told Clementi, was in Barranquilla.

Mormino then asked if Boris Sánchez knew the exact amount of the shipment. Boris explained he had not been given the amount of the shipment but was told to collect on a debt for five hundred kilos.

"That was my job. I don't know anything else."

"What was the debt that was supposed to be paid?" asked Mormino.

"Amparo told me that when the cocaine arrived in Italy they sent one million dollars to Angel in Barranquilla. And that what was still owed was fourteen million dollars."

David Sabio was an important link in the prosecution's case. He had corroborated Cuffaro's story despite the fact he had never met him. Sabio also provided first-hand knowledge of the outstanding millions that the Colombians were trying to collect from the Sicilian Mafia. Sabio also linked the Galatolos, John and Vincenzo, with the six-hundred-kilo cocaine shipment. He had met the elusive Allen "Brito" Knox and confirmed the nature of his cargo as well as the path of the *Big John* between the coasts of Colombia and Sicily.

Although Cuffaro, Sabio and Boris Sánchez provided an incredible amount of information and details, Sciacchitano and Carrara left no stone unturned. The prosecutors called on cooperating witnesses with no more than limited knowledge. Martin Gladstone, who also stood convicted of cocaine trafficking, provided the Italian proceeding with corroborating testimony in support of Cuffaro's earlier statements. The prosecution also called on former friends of Galatolo's. Victor Castro, who had been convicted of selling one kilo of cocaine as well as a second charge of conspiracy to distribute cocaine, testified that he and Galatolo were once as close as brothers. They had shared their vacations, family outings and many leisurely days fishing on Broward County's inland waterways. Castro testified to what could now be considered Galatolo's indiscretion in their former friendship. He provided the court with the intimate details of confidential conversations between him and the Sicilian mafioso. Castro had not only been apprised by Galatolo of his cocaine trafficking, but also of his long-standing association with the Madonia crime family in Palermo.

The next day's proceedings began with Sciacchitano calling John Galatolo as a witness for the government of Italy. Galatolo was an unwilling participant in the prosecution's long list of cooperative former defendants and informers. He entered the courtroom handcuffed, shackled and escorted by two deputy U.S. Marshals. Now the property of the U.S. Department of Corrections for the next forty-five years, Galatolo had been compelled to appear but could not be forced to testify. Unlike the other government witnesses, he had not been given immunity from future prosecution in Italy or elsewhere for any statements he might make.

"We are going to proceed now with the calling of Mr. John Galatolo," announced Commissioner Fernández.

"Mr. Galatolo," President Ingargiola began, "you are a defendant on the same charges for which we are proceeding against the other defendants. Your proceeding, however, was separated because you are legitimately imprisoned in the United States. Therefore we cannot proceed against you in Italy in a legitimately constituted trial. With this respect, a defense attorney was appointed for you in Italy in the person of counsel Barone. Your examination has been requested in this proceeding by the prosecution, Doctors Sciacchitano and Carrara. You will be examined in this proceeding as a defendant in a related crime. Therefore, you have the right to remain silent in response to questions. Do you intend to respond or not to questions that will be asked of you?"

"Upon advice by my counsel, I request to have the American Fifth Amendment and I do not answer to anything because I have nothing to answer," Galatolo said as he stood before the court in shackles and handcuffs. He was doing his best to remain civil, but it was clear he wanted to lash out at somebody.

Both Commissioner Fernández and President Ingargiola asked if he had conferred with his attorneys regarding his decision. Galatolo had decided not to testify, but he would certainly speak his mind.

"With all due respect to the court, you didn't give me that chance, because you yanked me out of the medical, while I'm still in medical. Neither the medical released me. Neither of my lawyers was advised."

"Well, Mr. Galatolo, let me state for the record," Fernández began, "that I have spoken with your attorney Mr. Woodward to inform him both by letter and by telephone concerning your presence here during these proceedings."

"Yes, ma'am," he said.

"He told me that should you wish to confer with him, he would be available by telephone. My only question to you is, have you had enough chance to discuss this matter with him? Is this your decision to refuse to testify?"

"It is my decision to refuse, ma'am. I also answer you that a letter from you said that as long as I was not medically fit I was not going to be moved. And my doctor did not release me."

"Well, Mr. Galatolo, the medical—"

"And I'm being treated very inhumane," he interrupted.

"The medical facility did release you, and that is why you were brought," she responded sternly. "All right. There being nothing further of this witness—"

"There's nothing," Galatolo said.

"He will be released and returned to his facility," Fernández stated.

"The record will reflect the refusal to respond on the part of the witness," exclaimed President Ingargiola.

With that, Galatolo was ushered away by the marshals to begin the rest of his forty-five-year prison sentence, possibly never to be seen outside a federal correction facility again.

The trial to that point had been a success in every way. The testimony from the American and Italian witnesses convicted more than a dozen defendants. Cuffaro saw his words serve as a firing line as each defendant was toppled: Rosario Naimo, Allen "Brito" Knox, Paolo LoDuca, Giuseppe Lottussi, Raffaele Galatolo, Stefano Fontana, Vincenzo Galatolo, Antonino and Aldo Madonia, Dominic Mannino and even the patriarch of the Madonia crime family, Francesco Madonia. But all of them together couldn't bring Cuffaro the satisfaction he felt after he helped put Galatolo away for over forty years. It was a shame that Waldo Aponte and Angel Sánchez got away, and could only be tried and convicted in absentia.

The government had pieced together an enormous puzzle with the testimony of *pentiti* like Joseph Cuffaro, David Sabio, Bill Kane, Martin Gladstone, Boris Sánchez and Victor Castro. The FBI, the United States Attorney, the Italian national police and anti-Mafia magistrates had reconstructed the crime of the century, tracing a complex conspiracy among the world's three most powerful and dangerous criminal organizations. They had secured convictions on the six-hundred-kilogram transaction with nothing more than a few grams of cocaine. It was the only drug evidence the governments of both nations could present. FBI special agent Jim Brown had scraped and vacuumed the residue from the secret compartment in Martin Gladstone's Cadillac.

"Signor Cuffaro! signor Cuffaro! he heard his name being called with the distinct Sicilian dialect. The voice came from down the hall. Cuffaro stood at attention near the deputy who was waiting to handcuff him and transport him back to his holding cell.

It was Judge Sciacchitano and Judge Carrara, smiling and extending their hands.

"Fanti grazie!" "Fanti grazie!" they both seemed to say in unison. In Sicilian, they thanked him for his dynamic performance, his strong recollection, but most of all they expressed their appreciation to him for his bravery and commitment to justice.

Sciacchitano never considered him a mafioso, as many had tried to paint him. He understood Cuffaro was never a made member, but almost miraculously became a high-level associate. Sciacchitano was grateful that Cuffaro had decided to provide assistance in the name of justice. He remembered one of their first meetings with Cuffaro back in June 1990. Sciacchitano, Carrara, the chief of police from Palermo and inspector for the Italian national police, Fernández and Brown had all met with Cuffaro, who provided them with every bit of information they sought. Not only was he a much better witness than they had ever dreamed, Cuffaro disclosed the information they needed to make their case in Europe. Sciacchitano saw Cuffaro as a man who chose the wrong path, realized the error of his ways and made the difficult but honorable decision to try to correct his past mistakes. But his upbringing and professional oath prevented him from considering Cuffaro a hero.

Nevertheless, he let Cuffaro know that he understood his testimony was not mandatory. The judge knew Cuffaro's decision to take on this role was all his own.

Cuffaro watched as the images of the two Italian judges disappeared. He thought about the irony of his situation. He had just taken part in a precedent-setting event, on behalf of the government, and here he was being handcuffed. He had joined up with the good guys but he was still a prisoner. Everyone on the same team as he was preparing to return home to their families; he was on his way back to the Rat House.

CHAPTER

12

THE DEVIL INCARNATE

"YOUR HONOR, OBJECTION." It was another objection raised by Antonio Zuñiga, the federal public defender appointed by the court to represent José Restrepo. The short, slight, and relatively well-dressed attorney was on his feet shouting, adjusting his glasses as he shuffled through his notes.

The legal chess game played by attorneys was always a challenge Tom Fink loved, like a good game of two-on-two. Already, during the first day of Leo Fraley's direct examination, he could tell Zuñiga wasn't going to be a problem he couldn't overlook. But he knew from experience that the attorney would take on the life of a rare fungus—an untreatable, unsightly irritant. Even before the court proceedings began, when they were merely laying down the ground rules, Judge Robert Broomfield, a staunch law-and-order kind of judge, warned Zuñiga that his dramatics would not be tolerated.

"Mr. Zuñiga, let's get things straight now," the judge told him before the jury was brought in. "You have a tendency after I hear everything and rule to jump up and do something else." Judge Broomfield was more than familiar with Zuñiga's repertoire, and he was trying to establish order before chaos ruled his courtroom.

"Your Honor, there has been no information, no knowledge, no testimony from Mr. Fraley that he has any knowledge of what goes on in LA, what goes on in Chicago. And now Mr. Fink, based on some alleged experience on the part of this witness with Mr. Rico-Pinsón, is trying to get this witness to talk about things where there is no foundation for him to allege that he has knowledge."

Fink's trial plan had been to play as many as one-third of the more than three hundred audio tapes recorded during the investigation, plus almost a dozen video tapes, to the jury, with Fraley as one of the participants authenticating the conversation and translating the coded language. Fink had wrapped up his direct examination of U.S. customs' agent Rich Bailey and had just begun to play the tapes for the courtroom, with the intermittent explanations from Fraley.

"I want to expand on Mr. Zuñiga's statements," interjected Robert Moore, the attorney for Lazaro Rico-Pinsón, otherwise known as "Vicente." Fink listened intently.

"I believe that the foundation does not exist simply because the witness says he has a foundation. The mere fact that Mr. Fink claims that Mr. Fraley has a foundation or basis to understand this doesn't mean that he does."

Moore continued making his argument with the skill of a professional boxer. Moore, although portly in appearance, was surprisingly light on his feet, testing his opponent's skills and reaction speed. Then he threw a few light jabs. "My point is, for this witness to explain what my client meant by all that would create a situation where the prejudicial value of this evidence exceeds the probative value." Then, maintaining his articulate speech and distinguished demeanor, he took a body shot, reaching for a kidney. "When you put all the factors together, this witness has inadequate foundation, and the fact that he's not a professional but a—forgive my characterization—a low-life felon who has no real experience testifying as a government witness, I think we're inviting an answer that is based upon his uninformed opinion."

Fink could see it coming. Right now he was trading punches with Moore and Zuñiga. But he knew it was only a matter of time before Fausto "Frank" Díaz's attorney Michael Black would join this tag team. As the sole prosecutor, Fink knew things could be worse. The four other defendants named in the indictment—Pedro Ortegón, Armando Grijales, Sarge Reyes and Winces Velasco-Peterson—were not present. If they had been captured the defense table would have taken on the semblance of a legal "gang of seven."

The sixth-floor courtroom in the downtown Phoenix Federal Building was the legal forum in which Fink hoped to close the last chapter in this lengthy investigation. But Moore was already laying the foundation for the basis of his arguments during the rest of the trial by attacking the character of the government's chief witness.

Fink wasted no time returning a jab. "The witness is being asked to interpret conversation, specifically . . . drug conversation. He's been in the drug business for years. So he's being asked to interpret conversation with which he's extremely familiar based upon his experience in the business and experience with these thousands of conversations. And I believe that is adequate foundation that he's entitled to interpret what's being said."

"Absolutely foolhardy argument!" Zuñiga barged in. "He's saying that Mr. Fraley is now an expert in translating conversations. Your Honor, this man is no expert, number one. Number two, this conversation is going on in Spanish. He doesn't even understand Spanish. He understands a translated English version of what has been stated." Zuñiga followed in his colleagues' footsteps, also taking a jab at Fink's witness. "This man is no expert. He's a slimeball, he's a lot of things, but he's no expert. And for him to try to proffer him as such, Your Honor, is the most ridiculous thing I've ever heard."

Zuñiga and Moore continued making their arguments to the court, with Fink responding to each jab with a counterpunch. Finally Judge Broomfield brought the argument to a halt.

"If there's anyone among those that have testified who has an understanding of the operation involving the defendants named in the indictment and others with whom they're dealing, it's Mr. Fraley. And he may testify to them."

With that decree Fink was given the go-ahead to continue with his tape/translation course of action. Translating from a foreign language to English was typical of a drug trial. But this case was different, with two translations taking place—first from Spanish to English, then with Fraley translating the coded language. For the next several days Fraley deciphered for the court the vernacular of the drug trade from the taped conversations between himself and the defendants, conducted in both English and Spanish and sometimes a combination of the two.

By the end of the week the jury had learned much of the coded language. "Pastrana" was Armando Grijales's code name. "El gordo" was Restrepo's code name—a name his attorney Zuñiga objected to, on the basis of its meaning, "the fat one." "The office" was anywhere Escobar was and "El doctor" was Escobar himself.

However, the rules regarding Escobar and the Medellín cartel had been set early on. Judge Broomfield allowed the introduction of his name only "to the extent that is evidence that is otherwise relevant in the identification of the person referred to as 'the doctor,' it may be covered." He further stated that no reference could be made to the Medellín cartel. In plain English, the judge allowed "the doctor" but not the name Pablo Escobar or the use of the words, Medellín cartel. In essence, the court's rules would only allow vague sentences such as, "I spoke with the doctor."

When Fink first told Fraley about the rules of engagement, Fraley couldn't believe his ears. "Who the hell else would we be talking about?" he said to Fink. "Who else could move that amount of co-caine?"

It was of little consequence to Fink, anyway. He wasn't indicting the cartel or for that matter Escobar, and he didn't have the prosecutorial responsibility to offer a scintilla of proof against them. Besides, Fink never quite believed "El doctor" was really Escobar. He knew the doctor was a high-ranking cartel member, but being an attorney he needed proof beyond a reasonable doubt. Short of a face-to-face meeting with El doctor that Fink could replay to the jury, he was content to let it slide.

The jury also learned the meanings of a variety of words that were essential to their understanding of the substance of the many conversations between Fraley and the defendants. Seemingly innocent words, such as: "Popcorn bags" and "Candy kisses," were translated by Fraley to be duffel bags containing cocaine and kilogram packages of cocaine. They even had their own simplistic yet unique numbering system.

"It's a ten code. It's a code that when I give him a number, you add it up to make ten and you come up with the actual number that I'm sending him. In this case, I was giving him the area code, which is 408. If you add that up to ten, it comes out to 602, which is this area code," Fraley explained. It was a code he and his partners in crime had per-fected, just in case.

During the first three days of the trial Fraley's anxiety level rose; it wasn't until the end of the third day that it began to level off. He began to catch on to the modus operandi of the courtroom proceedings. Each day as he was escorted into the witness stand by deputy marshals he had to walk past the defendants—who were never at a loss for words for their former partner. Fraley felt like a performer surrounded by heck-lers. The three called him names like: *"traidor," "mentiroso,"* and, of course, *"maricón."* It didn't bother him much. Being called a traitor, liar and a faggot didn't really penetrate. Besides, he figured, their attorneys' words would be more piercing.

The jury had just heard a conversation between Fraley and Restrepo on November 25, 1989. Fraley said, "I'm still waiting, but my girlfriend is dancing toward Pastrana." (Fraley explained that this meant that the plane was en route from Phoenix to Belize City, where Grijales was waiting with the load.)

Later in the conversation with Winces Velasco-Peterson they heard more coded language. After the tape was played Fink repeated the words, asking Fraley for clarification.

"Toward the middle," he began, "he says: 'And the other message is that the hotel where they received it the last time, it was destroyed, it does not exist anymore.' And then he says next: 'They had to change everything,' and so forth."

Fink directed his question to Fraley. "What is he referring to when he says the hotel where they received it the last time has been destroyed?"

"He's talking about the sugar cane road to the clandestine airstrip that I used on the first load in Belize. It was destroyed."

"What did you understand him to mean that it was destroyed?" asked Fink.

"Well, that the army had bombed it. They commonly do this when they find a clandestine strip. They blow holes in it."

Fink continued questioning him about the content of the tape as he read from the transcript. "And the next line where he says: 'So that's why Mr. "P" is insisting that it is a must that you send down one of your fellows because he don't know if they changed the area completely and he doesn't know if this guy has the right thing for you.' What did you understand that to mean?"

"I understood that to mean that they changed the airstrip and he wanted either myself or my pilot or copilot to go down and get the exact location and the exact dimensions of the airstrip as far as length and width and type of surface to accommodate the type of aircraft that I was anticipating using in this smuggling operation, sir."

After the noon break, the court reconvened and Fraley took the stand to take up where he had left off. Tape number 252 was played for the jury. A rather agitated Restrepo was saying, "We have a little trouble with your girlfriend." Fraley responded with, "Yeah, I know. I'm supposed to call Mr. Pastrana in about two minutes." As he heard the tape, Fraley could remember that day when he and the agents were in a panic over the plane and its load, stuck on the side of the Pan-American Highway. "Pastrana told Mr. P that your girlfriend, uh, don't want to, to dance, you know," Restrepo said.

"Yeah, I know because, uh, her leg got stuck," Fraley added.

Fraley explained that they had considered unloading the cocaine and burning the aircraft. The tape played for another few seconds before Fink resumed his questioning.

"When you said to Mr. Grijales in this stage, 'Yeah, everything's good,' what were you referring to?"

"That the aircraft had, in fact, taken off," Fraley said. Fraley told Grijales he had spoken with his pilots to confirm this.

"And had you actually done so?"

"No, sir."

"Well, what was the source of your information there?

"From the customs agents," he responded.

"Mr. Grijales said, 'I guess it is only 975 pages,' and then he said he couldn't take everything. What's he referring to there?"

"Nine hundred seventy-five kilos of cocaine, sir. Couldn't take everything, was the rest of the cocaine."

From that tape they proceeded to another conversation conducted in Spanish between Restrepo, Fraley and Don Pedro. In the conversation, Fraley referred to counting and taking inventory. He explained to the court that the cocaine packages were marked with various labels: CENTAVO, YEN, REINA, PALOMA.

"Why was that done?" asked Fink.

"Well, that's standard practice. That's what I was always told to do before in the past, sir."

"Why were you asked to do that?"

"So they can account for the inventory," he replied.

"Would you show the witness government's exhibit 18, please," Fink requested. It was the inventory list of the marked cocaine prepared by Fraley.

"Did you send that inventory by telefax to anyone?"

"Yes, I sent it to José Restrepo, sir."

"Objection, Your Honor," Zuñiga said as he rose to his feet, with one hand in the air and the other on his glasses. Zuñiga then asked to voir dire Fraley. It is a legal term where an attempt is made to determine the competency of the witness. Literally, it means to speak the truth.

"Not yet," said Judge Broomfield.

Fink continued questioning Fraley on the document: "What information did it contain? Who did he fax it to?"

"May I voir dire this witness at this time, Your Honor?" Zuñiga requested for the second time.

"For what purpose?" asked the judge.

"Your Honor, as to the authentication of this document, and as to whether or not he sent it."

"All right," the judge said.

"Your Honor—" Fink began, but Zuñiga jumped in.

"Thank you, Your Honor."

"May I be heard?" asked Fink.

"I'll let him do it this one time," responded the judge reluctantly.

"Mr. Fraley, you've stated that you prepared this document. Is that correct?"

"Yes, sir."

"Did you do the inventory that this document represents?" Zuñiga asked.

"Excuse me, that's not the subject you indicated you wished to inquire," interjected Judge Broomfield.

"Your Honor, I'll move on," Zuñiga said and returned his attention to Fraley. "How was it that you prepared this document?"

"Well, I wrote it up with a pen," Fraley responded sarcastically.

"Were you given any information to put on this document?

"Yes, sir."

"By whom, sir?"

"By various agents, sir."

"So then, this merely represents your copy, or your rendition of information provided to you by others, sir?" Zuñiga asked with his "sirs" becoming more and more pointed. "Yes, sir," Fraley said, then answered Zuñiga's questions regarding the time and date of the production of the document. "November 24th, 1989, around 4:00 P.M." he said.

"And with respect to the preparation of this document, where did you prepare it?"

"Oh, I believe that I prepared that in the customs office, sir," Fraley responded matter-of-factly.

"All right. Where in the customs office, sir? Would you tell the jury, please?" Zuñiga was now laying the foundation for his next battleground. Fink had heard his insinuations before and Fraley was keenly aware of his direction.

"In their lunchroom," he replied.

"And at that time do you recall what agent, if any, was with you when you prepared this document?"

"I believe it was Agent Bailey, sir."

"Were there any other agents with you?"

"Yes, sir."

"Who were they?"

"There were several of them."

Then he made his direction clear. "You got to know the agents pretty well during your visits there, didn't you?"

"Yes, sir."

"Do you have a clear recollection then, based on your fraternization with these agents," he said sternly, "do you have a clear recollection as to which of these agents were with you?"

Fraley gave him the names of various agents with whom he had the majority of contact. He answered Zuñiga's questions regarding where exactly the fax machine was located and if he himself had faxed the document. Suddenly Judge Broomfield interrupted.

"This is cross-examination, it's not voir dire."

"Your Honor, may I, may I please, Your Honor. I just have a couple of other questions." The judge allowed the request and Zuñiga quickly saved face by asking a few more questions before he told the court, "I have no further questions, Your Honor."

Naturally, Fink followed up on Zuñiga's line of questioning.

"Would you explain what you meant, Mr. Fraley, when you said that you couldn't recall whether you yourself had done this, but that you yourself were present when it was done. Can you explain what you meant?"

"Well, I accompanied the agents to the machine and some of the papers—some of the faxes I actually did put in, some of them I didn't put in."

Zuñiga jumped in. "Objection, Your Honor, to this question and this answer. You prohibited me from asking that question and I think that it's improper rehabilitation on the part of the government's counsel to ask a question as a follow-up to a question that you told me not to ask."

"This is appropriate direct examination," responded the judge. "You may cross-examine the witness. You exceeded the office of voir dire."

The clerk changed tapes and began to play number 262. This was a conversation conducted both in English and Spanish among Fraley, Restrepo and Don Pedro. When Ortegon's portion, which was in Spanish, was played, a court translator interpreted.

"Look, please tell him it looks like we have reservations here at the hotel until Monday," Ortegon said.

"Yes, but he says that, what would be wrong with making the reservations for tomorrow night?" said Restrepo.

"Ah, they need to confirm with Pastrana, to reconfirm with Pastrana and we will make them for tomorrow night for lack of time," urged Ortegon.

Another pause, and more questions for Fraley.

"Do you understand, sir, what Don Pedro is saying there about 'put pressure on someone because of the reservation for tomorrow' and 'they charge us for it whether or not we use the reservation?' " Fink asked.

"Yes. He's telling me to apply pressure to Armando to try to hurry up or speed up this process on the other load, sir."

"What's the reference to the 'charge us for the reservation whether we use it or not?' "

"Well, he's talking about, I believe, the schoolmaster, it's paid for the five days, sir."

"Schoolmaster is who?"

"The air-traffic controller in the United States, sir." Fraley had told them he knew of an air-traffic controller who could be paid off to look the other way for a million dollars, but that the window of opportunity would only last five days.

"What was your understanding and your recollection at this time of how many loads of cocaine had been brought back to the United States from Belize?" Fink asked.

"Objection!" Moore interjected. "Hearsay."

"Overruled. You may answer."

"What was the question, Your Honor?" asked Zuñiga without looking up. "I didn't hear it."

"How many loads brought back from—" Moore attempted to repeat the question, but Zuñiga interrupted.

"I didn't hear the question, Your Honor." Zuñiga's pestering worked.

"You want to rephrase it," said Judge Broomfield.

"The question was, what was your understanding," Fink began, "what's your recollection of how many loads of cocaine had been brought back to the United States from Belize, as of this time?"

"One, sir."

"And how many other trips to Belize did you and the agents anticipate would have to occur?"

"One for sure, one more, sir."

"When you say one for sure, are you implying that there might have been more?"

"Yes, sir."

"Why would that have been?"

"Because the man just told me that he possibly might put 940 more kilos in Belize, sir."

"This other 940 additional kilos that were referred to in the prior conversation, is that what you're referring to?"

"Yes, sir."

"And approximately how many kilos of cocaine would that have totaled up to, including the others that have been referred to in the past?"

"It would have been over three thousand, sir."

"How soon did you anticipate that the second trip to Belize for the second would occur? How soon after the first trip?"

"There would be one day of rest and then the second trip would occur, sir."

With more tapes, more exhibits and Fraley's explanations, Fink continued to present the government's evidence. Fraley sat in the witness chair and answered Fink's questions in the proper format, but wished he could tell it like it was.

The first meeting at the Pointe Resort at Tapitio Cliffs in Phoenix with Díaz and Restrepo was the key to proving to the jury that Fraley had a long-standing relationship with the cartel. Fink was preparing for the defense's case ahead of time. He knew Zuñiga, Black and Moore had two avenues by which they could defeat the seemingly bulletproof case against their clients. They would certainly attack Fraley as a liar and try to destroy him in their cross-examination. If that failed, the second half of their frontal assault would come in the form of identifying the government as the real criminals. They would claim that if it hadn't been for the government's actions, no crime would have been committed. Fink's strategy in this adversarial battle of wits was to get the truth to the jury so that no smoke screen could cloud the only real fact—that the defendants were guilty as hell.

Fink's opening statement said it clearly: "The government simply had Mr. Fraley do what he had done before, that is, offer his services, get back in touch with the organization, tell them, 'I'm ready to go back to work.'"

Fink had already entered into evidence the first tape, a call from Fraley to Restrepo. Restrepo was not only happy to hear from Fraley, he offered Velasco's and Ortegón's good wishes and mentioned their eagerness to work with him again. Restrepo told Fraley that the "Office" had sent him from his home in Barranquilla to Florida to find him. They were concerned about his welfare after they heard of his troubles with the harbor police in Belize and the heat that he had encountered near his Gulf Coast home.

Fink began his examination of Fraley by playing the video tape of the Phoenix meeting. The judge, jurors, defense attorneys, the defendants and the prosecution team all donned their headphones one more time and watched as the sixty-inch color "big screen" lit up with Fraley greeting Restrepo and Díaz at the door to the Governor's Suite.

Fraley recognized the television they were all watching this on. It was the same one he had watched the Super Bowl on the previous year in his living room. Like everything else he had owned, it was now the property of the United States government. Part of his plea agreement was the confiscation of not only his house but anything of value generated from the cocaine business.

"Do you recall during the meetings at the Pointe Resort involving Mr. Restrepo and Mr. Díaz and/or the telephone calls that occurred during these meetings, do you recall any discussions about how the cocaine would get to Belize?" Fink fired his first question as soon as the video screen went black.

"Yes, sir."

"What was that discussion?"

"The cocaine would be shipped to Belize in a small aircraft containing possibly 400 kilos per trip."

"Who said that during the meeting?"

"José Restrepo, sir."

Fraley was answering the questions, but what he really wanted to get off his chest was the aggravation he had felt before and during this meeting. It had been his first time outside a jail cell or the customs office and, for that matter, the first time he had not been handcuffed and shackled in over a month. The fact was, he had made a major change in his life and joined the cops to do in a few old friends. There was no way he could turn back. His only chance at freedom, someday, was to work as hard for the government as an informer as he had for the Mafia and the cartel as a career criminal. Fraley had joined the other side, but in spite of this some of his new partners still openly showed their disdain for him.

"Okay, let's get started," Gately began the meeting around the conference table in the Governor's Suite. "Does everyone here know everyone else?" Gately's question was more rhetorical than substantive. He continued by introducing customs agent Carlos Salazar and FBI agent Bob Prida as the two undercover agents who would pose as Fraley's associates and be on hand to meet with the Colombians.

"Just a minute, I don't know you. What agency are you with?" the FBI agent sitting next to Fraley at the table interrupted, directing his question to Fraley.

"I'm not with any agency," Fraley replied in a monotone voice, never looking in the agent's direction.

Gately could see what was coming next. "He's the informant. This is Leo Fraley."

"Well, what's he doing here?" asked the FBI agent.

"Mr. Fraley holds the keys to this operation. The Colombians are coming here to meet with him, not our undercover agents. It is as important to have him at this meeting as it is to have him at the next one." There was no further discussion on the subject, and Gately geared the remainder of the meeting to the logistics of what would take place during the undercover rendezvous with Restrepo and Díaz and the responsibilities of the inside and outside cover teams.

When the meeting was concluded Gately told the agents to make sure everything was in working order, from the video cameras, to the telephone taps, to the hidden microphones. As they were testing the equipment Fraley, Fink, Gately and Atwood continued going over the information they wanted Fraley to draw out of the two Colombians. Salazar, Prida and his supervisor Tom Owens were also listening to the instructions. Then Prida asked Fraley how he should refer to him during the meeting.

Fraley answered, "Just call me 'boss.' "

Fraley was in an untenable situation. On the one hand, he couldn't resist taking a small jab. On the other, although it was not the answer the agent expected, it was realistic.

During this part of the trial Tom Fink also thought about the behind-the-scenes story. He remembered Fraley taking full advantage of his undercover situation to order room service for what seemed to be a top-of-the-line, six-course meal. After being locked up for so many weeks, eating only the fast food the agents brought him, the opportunity to indulge in this simple pleasure must have been extraordinarily tempting.

When the two Colombians had arrived at the hotel their attention was diverted to a news story on CNN about a huge drug bust in Southern California. Díaz and Restrepo began talking about it, and they clearly knew plenty of details—but Fraley, apparently captivated by the feast before him, didn't want to hear it. Fink couldn't believe it. Here they were about to divulge more information about another multimillion dollar drug load, and Fraley wouldn't let them.

Fink had carefully and meticulously presented to the jury many of the over three hundred audio tapes, a dozen video tapes and just as many documents. Now it was time for Fraley to face the defense attorneys in cross-examination. Fink knew Fraley could handle the questions. In fact, at the beginning of the case, when Fink had first visited Fraley in his cell, Fink was astounded not only at his ability to recall times, dates and conversations, but within a half-hour Fink had determined that Fraley would be an extraordinary witness. He never had to conduct any of the typical practice runs through potential questions and answers. Fink simply left Fraley a stack of material to go over to refresh his memory.

And Fink knew he had a strong case. He had presented overwhelming evidence against the defendants, including video and still photographs of the two tons of cocaine. Furthermore, his main witness was their former partner. His concern was focused rather on the inevitable defense tactic of discrediting the witness. With Fraley, the defense attorneys could have a field day. It wouldn't be difficult to attempt to confuse the issue by simply bringing Fraley's mile-long rap sheet to the forefront. And that was exactly what the defense attorneys tried to do.

Probably the strongest interrogation came from Zuñiga, but Fraley wasn't going to make it easy for him to get the answers. In fact, it took the better part of the day just to determine what he was doing in Colombia.

"How were you supporting yourself?" Zuñiga asked.

"Oh, Winces Velasco-Peterson was housing me and feeding me, sir."

"Just doling out the money for you, and you were doing nothing for it," he remarked. "Is that correct?"

"I was there on the farm."

"What were you doing there on the farm," Zuñiga asked, as if he were talking to a child.

"I was living there on the farm, sir," Fraley responded, doe-eyed.

"And for living, breathing, just being there, you were receiving compensation of some sort?"

"You mean a pay?"

"You were receiving pay of some sort?" Zuñiga asked, expecting an obvious answer. But it was not to be.

"No, I didn't get no pay."

"What did you do while you were there?"

"I slept, I ate, I drank, I played cards, I listened to music."

Sensing he was getting nowhere, Zuñiga took a jab. "Did you tell him that you were convicted for rape when you met him?"

"Oh, yes, sir." Fraley was unfazed.

Zuñiga took a step back to his original path of questioning: "Where did you go after you left the farm?"

"To Bogotá."

"Where did you live in Bogotá?"

"In an apartment. In a house, I guess."

"Who paid for this home?" Zuñiga asked, growing slightly impatient. "*Whose* home *was* it?"

"Oh, I don't know whose home that was."

"Was Winces living there?"

"No, Winces didn't live there."

"Why was it that you left the farm to go to Bogotá?"

"Well, he just said, 'Come on, we're going to Bogotá.' "

"How long were you there, sir?"

"I guess four or five months," Fraley replied.

"Just vegetating," quipped Zuñiga.

"I don't know what you mean, vegetating," Leo asked, sincerely. This was an unknown word to him.

"You weren't working, were you?"

"No, I wasn't working."

"You weren't moving any dope anywhere, were you?"

"No, sir."

"You were just drinking, sleeping, getting up, eating. Is that the extent of it, sir?"

"Oh, I went shopping, I went downtown, I went to church, I did everyday normal things, sir. I don't know," Fraley responded casually.

"Did you join the choir?"

"No, I didn't join the choir. I couldn't speak Spanish, sir." Fraley responded without missing a beat. At once, the entire courtroom burst out laughing.

Fraley studied Zuñiga as he paced between the witness stand and the jury. Fraley figured he was about five feet five inches tall, fairly trim, maybe 145 pounds. Fraley guessed he was in his forties, but his jet black hair gave him a slightly youthful look. And he didn't dress too badly, even if his suits looked like they came from an outlet. By then Fraley had summed up his adversary. He was nothing more than a slippery Tijuana ambulance chaser, someone he wouldn't hire to get his dog out of the pound.

"To this day, can you speak Spanish?" Zuñiga was determined to make him trip over his words. He had already tried to disqualify him on this issue despite the fact that Leo spoke a few words in Spanish and understood the Colombians' conversations. Technically, Fraley figured, that superficial knowledge didn't qualify him as a competent bilingual.

"No, I can't speak Spanish," he responded.

"And you did nothing. You did absolutely nothing to earn your keep during these months that you were there," Zuñiga stated, more than asked.

"That's correct, sir."

"After—" Zuñiga stopped. "Where did you go next, after leaving that apartment, if anywhere?"

"I went to Barranquilla, Colombia, sir—no, I'm sorry. I went to Cartageña, Colombia, sir."

"And what did you do there?"

"Vegetating, I guess, sir." Again, the courtroom filled with laughter. Zuñiga was sinking fast. He continued to question Fraley, attempting to get an answer with which he would be satisfied. Fraley's simple answers obviously made quite an impression, but he was infuriating his own attorney Fink.

During a break Fink stormed into the holding room, where Fraley was being watched by a deputy marshal. He asked the deputy to excuse himself for a couple of minutes, and the instant the door closed Fink read Fraley the riot act. In no uncertain terms, Fink told Fraley, the courtroom was not the forum for his comedy act, and if he continued he was going to blow it. It was short, sweet and definitely to the point. Now Fink had to walk back into the courtroom, passing his parents—in particular, his father the corporate attorney—who were in Phoenix visiting him. As it was, his parents couldn't understand how Fink could stand to work in criminal law, where he had to be in close contact with the lowest elements of society.

Fraley's best performance, however, came shortly after he had been put through the ringer by Moore—an attorney who Fraley considered at least slightly smarter than Zuñiga. Fraley wasn't really surprised at the tactic Moore used, he just didn't think it would come from him. Moore attempted to show the jury that the government's witness was a "gutter-dweller." He too asked Fraley to explain what he was doing in Colombia.

"Were you partying?"

"I don't know what you consider partying—" Fraley began to answer.

"Partying," Moore quickly said, "I consider to be getting rip-roaring drunk and getting into promiscuous activity with women and doing drugs like marijuana and cocaine. Now, were you partying in Colombia at all?"

"Oh, I drank."

"Were you partying in Colombia at all, Mr. Fraley?" Moore asked again.

"I drank in Colombia, sir."

Moore was determined to press on. "Did you party? Did you ever use drugs in Colombia?"

"I think I might have smoked marijuana."

"You think you might have smoked marijuana?" Moore asked pointedly. Fraley remembered Fink's telling him not to try to hide or deny his past. He told Fraley, "Just say 'yeah' and that's that." They both knew that an attack on his character was inevitable. To himself, Fraley said, fuck it.

"Okay, I smoked marijuana."

"Okay, that's all you have to do is say it." But Moore quickly moved deeper into the gutter. "Now, let's go back to women and sex for a minute. Do you recall government's exhibit 126-A—you're having a conversation with José Restrepo." He retrieved a document and presented it to Fraley. "This is a transcript, is it not, of a meeting at the Pointe Resort, wasn't it?"

"Yes, sir."

"And this is when you're there with Mr. Prida and Mr. Salazar, and you are pretending to be Leo Fraley the dope dealer, and—"

"I don't believe I was a dope dealer, sir," Fraley interrupted. "I was a dope smuggler."

"Okay. Isn't that a distinction without a difference, Mr. Fraley?"

"I don't know that it is at all, sir. I think there is a big distinction there, sir."

"Let me direct your attention to that meeting. Do you recall during the meeting there was a time when José Restrepo asked you in a very innocent way, he says: 'Gee, how are the girls here?' Do you remember that?"

"Oh, yeah, probably."

"And you said to him," Moore began quoting the transcript, " 'Hah, all the girls are good. All the girls are good, José. I don't want to fuck no girls. I want to fuck, you know, get the big woman.' And then you changed the subject and you introduced Prida and Salazar. Do you remember that conversation?"

Fraley replied that he wasn't sure if that was exactly the way the conversation took place. Then Moore quickly began attacking his memory.

"Let me get this straight. You're saying that's a misprint now?"

"It's possible."

"Aren't you the same Leo Fraley who was on the witness stand here and who told the prosecutor that he's reviewed that transcript, that it's accurate?"

"To the best of my—"

"Aren't you the same guy?" Moore insisted, more agitated than ever.

"To the best of my knowledge, it is, sir."

"Now all of a sudden there's some loss of accuracy, Mr. Fraley?"

"To the best of my knowledge, this is still the same transcript that I reviewed, and to the best of my knowledge, it is accurate, sir."

"Thank you. I thought for a moment you were saying there might be a mistake there. I must have misunderstood you," Moore replied condescendingly, thinking he would have the last word.

"Oh, it's possible, but to the best of my knowledge, this is accurate, sir." Fraley was pushing the issue.

"It either is or isn't, sir." Moore was clearly upset.

"It is. But there is a possibility that there is an inaccuracy here," Fraley replied calmly.

"Would you get that back from the witness, please?" Moore requested, directing the clerk to retrieve the exhibit from Fraley. Moore then moved on to another transcript, where he attempted to do the same. Fink had heard enough. He objected to his line of questioning and asked for a side-bar conference.

"Judge, what we just went through is a series of questions about girls —having sex with girls. And now we're getting into questions involving having sex with young girls. I mean, this is just, this is just information which is classic smoke, which does not go to the witness' credibility, it does not go to any of the issues in the case." Then Fink became even more stern with his objections.

"We didn't ask questions when we, when we played the tapes about Vicente asking about American girls, or José requesting girls or Winces talking about twelve-year-old pussy. This is not proper examination," Fink said, trying to get past the lewd words he had just used in court. "This is solely designed to smear-up the witness and just make him look bad. It is not going to his credibility."

The judge overruled the objection, asking Fink, "Don't you have the upper hand?"

Moore asked more questions about sex and women. Then, he took indirect shots at Fink.

"So your testimony here today is that you never discussed the testimony with Mr. Fink before you testified? Is that what you want us to believe?"

"Repeat that, sir."

"Did you ever discuss your testimony with Mr. Fink before you testified?"

"No, I don't believe I did."

Moore was determined to get the answer he wanted. "And every day" —he began with a tone that said "I don't believe a word you're saying" —"when you were being taken by these marshals up to his office after court, what did you folks talk about?"

"Oh, football."

"You didn't talk about what you were going to testify to?"

"No, I was not coached or—"

"Sir, I didn't—"

"—nothing at all."

"I said, did the lawyer ask you questions? Did he say to you, look, if I ask you this question, what's your answer going to be?"

"No, he never said that."

Moore continued on with this double-whammy badgering. And since Fraley would not give him a simple yes or no answer, Moore began insulting him directly.

"You still can't say no, can you. Did you leave your brain outside the courtroom again, Mr. Fraley?" Fraley and Fink endured a couple hours of Moore's wrath, at the end of which it was no wonder Fraley felt like having a little fun with Zuñiga, an easier target.

Zuñiga couldn't match his colleague. After a frustrating period of question and answer with Fraley, Zuñiga asked for a side-bar conference.

"Your Honor, I think I'm doing the best I can with this witness. He's no dummy. I think it's pretty clear to everyone, and he's taking his answers nice and slow. And, Your Honor, quite frankly I believe that you are interfering with my processing of my cross-examination with your additional comments." Zuñiga's last statement was risky and he wasn't going to push it further.

Fraley couldn't believe this legal "enlisted man" was actually reprimanding his "superior officer." If this was the military, he thought, Judge Broomfield would have court-martialed him.

But Broomfield simply said, "The record will reflect that." He told the attorneys he would continue to interrupt them whenever they began making statements rather than asking questions, and he would continue to instruct the jury to take note of it.

The green digital numbers on the clock were blurred. Fraley strained to focus. He could make out the last two numbers: 59. He pressed his eyelids down and opened them again. Now it was almost clear. The digital readout changed as his vision became focused. It was four o'clock in the morning.

"Leo," the voice said, "time to get ready. You've got twenty minutes before the deputies come."

Four weeks into the trial, and Fraley had learned the drill. The deputies would pick him up at different times each morning. Often, when he was told to be ready at a certain time, their arrival was either much earlier or much later. On the way back and forth between the courthouse and jail, they would take Fraley by a different route. While he rode in the vehicle, a different one each day, a helicopter kept a close watch on their every move. When he arrived at the courtroom extra deputies were stationed on the roof of the building, poised strategically with their high-powered rifles.

One day the deputies spotted a car following them. With precise accuracy and skill the driver turned on a dime and in a split second was heading back the other way, swerving through the city's streets, easily losing the car behind them.

Another day, while in court a Colombian whom Fraley had never seen before entered the courtroom and sat in Fraley's direct line of vision. During Fraley's testimony the man began mouthing threats. It was Fraley's biggest fear—that the cartel had sent an assassin to carry out a suicide mission. Luckily, it didn't take long before the deputy marshals spotted him and forcefully evicted him from the courtroom.

During the past months Fraley had also learned to adjust to the latest set of unspoken rules. Because the defense attorneys had made such a stink about his alleged "fraternization" with the agents and the prosecutor, Fraley had become a leper. The agents and Fink were extra cautious speaking with him about anything—including football.

During the cross-examination, as most prosecutors did, Fink assessed his case as it stacked up against the defense. They attempted to shoot holes in his "expert witness," a DEA chemist who had performed the qualitative analysis of the cocaine. Fink didn't think much of him either, and despite his woefully inadequate skills on the stand, the substance he tested was still cocaine. There were no two ways about it.

They blasted Fink's "other" witness Garrett Benoit, one of the "government contract" pilots who picked up the two loads of cocaine in Belize. Fink didn't have the highest regard for him either, and even Fraley said, "He's so goddamn stupid, I wouldn't hire him to pick up my groceries—much less a ton of cocaine!"

Yet the evidence was overwhelming, and Fink was confident he'd win the case. Still, he couldn't help being concerned over the beating Fraley was taking and the field day the defense attorneys were having as they attempted to steer the issue away from their clients and on to the government's "despicable" witness.

Zuñiga even tried to make an issue over the way Fraley walked and talked. He asked Fraley, "You walk in a certain fashion. How's that? It gives you a certain pitched-forward appearance, correct?"

Then he leaned into Fraley and said, "You are of higher intellect than most people appreciate you to be, yet you've always been able to work on people's perceptions that you are of an inferior intellect. Isn't that true?"

For the first time during these proceedings, Fink thought, Zuñiga had made a fairly accurate assessment. What was also true, however, was that Fraley lacked many of the socially acceptable behavioral skills. That was the downside of a witness with an incredible memory. It was like putting up full-time with the pungent odor of a smooth-tasting, imported cheese.

The last time Fink had to "jump in his shit" was to reprimand him for making "eyes" at a female juror. Everyone noticed it. Even Zuñiga made an issue of it. To Fraley, it was no big deal.

"Did you see the way she is sitting there with her legs open? She's not even wearin' panties." Fraley said.

"Yeah, Leo, you're her fuckin' dream man," Fink's acerbic response was only tempered by his commitment to keep Fraley in line. But by then Fink had observed him in action. He knew crass behavior like standing in front of a hidden camera scratching his ass and breaking wind was just Fraley. He did it because he could.

On October 31, 1990, the government rested its case. The three defense attorneys did not put on one witness. The only pool from which they could draw witnesses were their own clients. But putting the likes of Díaz, Restrepo and Rico-Pinsón on the stand to rebut Fraley would open them up to the very same type of cross-examination they had just put Fraley through.

There were, however, two more critical phases of the trial process before the jury would take the case. Zuñiga, Moore and Black would each take their turn emphasizing the innocence of their clients. Then Fink would grind over the evidence, which he would argue amounted to "proof beyond a reasonable doubt." Judge Broomfield would then instruct the jury on the law and charge them to do their duty—to unanimously agree on the guilt or innocence of each defendant, taking each count of the indictment as a separate issue.

In the federal system the first to present his closing argument is the prosecutor. The defense attorneys take their best shot at arguing their position and then the government gets one more opportunity to argue the merits of the case to the jury, presumably because the government has the burden of proof.

". . . And the theme was simply this: attack the witness Leo Fraley." Fink knew he had to fight fire with fire. He had to show the jury that the defense had no defense. He had to show the jury that their only defense was a classic example of smoke-and-mirrors.

"Attack his character, attack him as a former criminal, as a criminal, as a burglar, as a convicted rapist and as a dope smuggler. They cross-examined Mr. Fraley for days and days at a time. Hundreds and hundreds of questions. Questions about his criminal past and his Mafia connections, burglary activities, the rape conviction, his drug smuggling activities, where he went and how he got there. But in all those questions, there were no more than a handful of questions about the facts and the evidence in this case." In true Perry Mason form, Fink walked from juror to juror, emphasizing his next crucial point.

"And after a while, after the man was up there for a while, after this cross examination, it was almost as if you could forget what you're here to do, and that is, stand in judgment of an indictment brought against these defendants in this case.

"Defense attorneys, in their questioning of Mr. Fraley have tried to turn this into a referendum, or a vote, on Mr. Fraley. Thumbs up," he said motioning, "thumbs down.

"Mr. Fraley is a criminal. He's a convicted burglar. He's a narcotics smuggler, a convicted rapist. He's all of those things, and, to a lesser degree, the pilot Mr. Benoit is the same. The government has never in this case tried to tell you anything to the contrary. We've never tried to indicate that that isn't true. We've never tried to indicate that it's not true because it, in fact, *is* true. But more importantly, I want you to realize that the fact Mr. Fraley is what he is and Mr. Benoit is what he is does not change the facts and evidence in this case against these defendants." Fink asked the jury to recall the hundreds of audio tapes, dozens of video tapes and documents he presented—all of which played out the words and actions of the defendants. He reminded the jury that it was José Restrepo, who represented Don Pedro Ortegón, who had first suggested setting this half billion dollar cocaine deal into motion. It was the first call Fraley made, after he cooperated on September 28, 1989. He told the jury panel that it was Restrepo who had suggested meeting in Phoenix to plan their smuggling operation. And it was Vicente who had suggested sending his right-hand man Frank Díaz to help solidify the plan. Fink continued to go over each step of the investigation, the transfer of funds and the two loads between Phoenix and Belize. During each stage Fink always referred back to the actions and words of the defendants. Most importantly, he told the jury how it was at the defendants' insistence that Fraley became involved in the venture.

"There's a discussion of a third load. Two thousand kilos had been obtained. And there are further calls with defendant Restrepo and Don Pedro Ortegón. The only problem that develops is that Armando Grijales says he's under surveillance down in Belize. Remember when he said, 'the white man is down here,' meaning DEA was watching him? That's the only reason another thousand kilos wasn't seized and obtained in this case. The amount of cocaine was no problem, the interest and the intent of these defendants to get this done was no problem. . . .

"Fraley was instructed to get in touch with the 'worker' who was defendant Rico-Pinsón," he told the jury. "There are calls back and forth with defendants Pinsón and Díaz. Defendant Díaz says, 'We'll meet you in White Plains.' " Fink paused, walked to the podium to check his notes, then returned to his forum before the jury box. "That meeting in White Plains occurs on December 9, 1989." Fink was the proverbial storyteller, describing in detail the events that took place in New York, from the U-Haul trucks carrying their five-hundred-million-dollar cargo to Pinsón's opening up a briefcase full of cellular phones and pagers after Fraley complained about not receiving his cash. He was playacting in this case. But had he not been cooperating and under cover, this measly payment of $140,000 on a balance due of $5.4 million was certainly a basis for anger. In a matter of minutes Rico-Pinsón put together half of his fees with a promise to deliver the rest after the weekend.

What Fink wanted to tell the jury was that were it not for the arrogance and impatience of the New York FBI office, he would have had a $2.7 million exhibit to offer as additional evidence. When he was telling the jury about how the FBI sat and waited at a mall parking lot watching an empty station wagon, where they arrested defendants Díaz and Rico-Pinsón when they arrived to reclaim the car—what he wanted to say was how he almost lost out on the thousands of pounds of cocaine to use as evidence because the FBI lost the load. Luckily they found it, by accident.

"The cocaine is later all recovered," he said, skipping over the background mishaps, "taken back to Phoenix, then to the lab in National City in San Diego. It's all got the same markings on it and it's identified as being the same cocaine taken and used in the operation."

He reminded the jury that defendant Rico-Pinsón, after his arrest, confessed. "He says, I work for Don Pedro. I was sent here to do this deal, to hook up with Fraley, to get the cocaine, to get it distributed. And interestingly enough—and this was brought out most explicitly on cross-examination by Mr. Moore—he had come here eight months ago to do this deal. Eight months ago, before Mr. Fraley was ever arrested or agreed to cooperate, before this operation ever began."

It was their relationship, Fink argued, that was proof of their criminal culpability. "But it's proof of something much bigger and much broader. What these people are a part of, what they were a part of before this investigation ever got going, was a large-scale, ongoing criminal conspiracy involving the importation and distribution of narcotics into this country."

For a little over an hour and a half Fink reiterated, quoted and reminded the jury of every event and every criminal action on the part of the three defendants.

"These three defendants, ladies and gentlemen, [are] not the biggest players in international cocaine trafficking, but [they are] people who are placed in positions of extreme trust, people who are privy to a two-ton cocaine transaction, the kind of people that have to be here, in this country, . . . to get the job done."

Fink thanked the jury and took his seat, ceding to his colleagues.

"Thank you, Mr. Fink," said Judge Broomfield. "Mr. Black."

Black's lead position in the closing argument line-up packed a strong punch.

Throughout the trial it was Michael Black who had refrained from using the smoke-and-mirrors tactic employed by Zuñiga and Moore, and had primarily stuck to the issues. It was Black who worried Fraley and was the one he respected the most. Fink shot Fraley a glance as Fraley watched the clean-shaven, statuesque and impeccably well-dressed attorney eloquently present his case.

"This is my opportunity to speak to you this afternoon, on behalf of Frank Díaz. And it's a difficult task. It's a difficult task because you folks have been bombarded in the media with all sorts of claims about cocaine, Colombians—and you don't even know if Frank Díaz is from Colombia. All you have is a driver's license the government claims is false, where he has an address in New Jersey."

Black told the jury that the government essentially had a two-month trial with one witness and tapes, "That's all," he said, as if hundreds of tapes were nothing. Then Black changed his course. "Now, it really tickles me when the government says that it's their job to keep you from being distracted. 'To keep you focused,' I think the government attorney said. That's his job. Well, let me tell you, the reason those verbs are used is because when the government runs into a problem with the credibility, the believability, of their witnesses, when they are attacked as they should be, when they run into that sort of a problem, they always claim, as Mr. Fink did here, that the defense attorneys are blowing smoke—

they're blowing red herrings. They are trying to cloud the issue when they legitimately attack the credibility of people like Fraley."

Black maintained that Fraley's credibility was an issue. If it wasn't, the government would have put on "character witnesses" to attest to his veracity.

"Hasn't happened in this case. Can you imagine," he said, changing his tone and expression, "Can you imagine," repeating with even more emphasis, "sitting out there this afternoon, you ask whether Leo Fraley was credible to that girl he raped. What do you think she'd say? You know? The government claims that an attack on a witness like Leo Fraley is a distraction, clouding the issue. It's *not*. Because, as the government told you in its opening statement, their case was based upon what Leo Fraley got for them.

"I'm going to get into the evidence to show how they can't prove that Frank Díaz conspired to possess or distribute cocaine. They haven't shown you beyond a reasonable doubt that he conspired to import. Let me tell you why, and I want to pick up precisely where the government left off. You know, Mr. Fink said to you that the proof, the facts, got difficult in New York. You'll remember he made that statement less than fifteen minutes ago. Well, what he means, I submit, is this: when the government says the proof gets difficult, it means there *is* no proof and they have to stretch and heap inference upon inference to bring you to the precipice of reasonable doubt and then give you a little bump to shove you over."

It was as if Black was auditioning to argue this case before the Supreme Court. He told the jury that "the day after Halloween was an appropriate time to give a closing argument in this case," because they had just heard a month's worth of testimony from a "genuinely evil person who is masquerading his sorry ass for your benefit."

He began at this point to plant the seed for his next argument. Not only was Fraley evil, the government that protected him was no better. He even suggested the government had entered into a conspiracy with its witness, calling it a "state-sponsored crime."

Fink watched as this sometime eloquent attorney degenerated quickly into a gutter-speaker.

"I submit that those who don't tell the truth, meaning little sociopaths like Fraley and Benoit, they mean nothing. Because, well, as a matter of modern civility, in an attempt to get along in society, it's kind of nice not to use the word 'fuck.' The only thing, the only thing that Leo Fraley ever used that word for as many times as he did, is that when Leo Fraley used the word fucking, you knew there was a noun somewhere around the corner that went in front of the—that went behind the fucking. His use of that word alone in such a repetitive fashion should tell you something."

It was hard to tell if Black's statements were having an effect. He shifted focus again: "Now, you know that Leo Fraley testified he was no altar boy. I submit he was. I submit Leo Fraley was an altar boy. He was an altar boy to some type of pagan god before whom he genuflected to drugs, duplicities and doing crimes like rape. That's Leo Fraley's god. Fraley is a sly, sly character. He might not be able to quote you Hamlet, and he might not know the quadratic equation, but he sure knows how to get, as he put it, get his 'sorry ass out of a jam.' And Leo Fraley, that unmitigated liar, has the gall to tell you under oath that he moved to Arizona to take care of his family and to retire from the drug business."

Black skimmed over Fraley's testimony regarding the death threats he had received from the Mafia. He said there were only two reasons why the Mafia would threaten Leo Fraley.

"Either he ratted on someone in the Mafia or he took money from them," he paused.

"And you know, there was another thing about Fraley that was just nauseating. The way he stood up there, in deference to you, I suppose, and stood there and watched and looked at you. To think that a guy who lied in front of a jury like this back in Pennsylvania about not having raped a girl stands here and supposedly gives you respect is absolutely nauseating."

Black's closing arguments went on for over two hours, but he was brief compared to Moore, who ranted and raved for the rest of the afternoon.

Moore's first argument centered on the issue of entrapment. Moore tried to tell the jury the same thing every defense attorney has said since the first sting in history—don't believe your lying eyes, what you see in living color is not the truth.

"You have to go beyond what you saw on the TV screen, and that's what Mr. Fink doesn't want you to do. He wants you to focus on what you saw and let the inquiry die there."

Moore then pointed the finger at the government.

"But let us never forget where this plot was born. It was born in the mind of Leo Fraley, nurtured and hatched along with the assistance of agents of the Customs Service here in Phoenix, Arizona. If you remember my opening statement, and one of the things I told you is when Leo Fraley came in here, I asked you to look into his eyes. And I said that for a reason, not because I thought you'd see the incarnation of the devil—although I submit you have. What you saw was an actor, a desperate actor."

Moore attempted to bring up other points, but found himself Fraleybashing once again. "Fraley then, when he gets out of jail in North Carolina, goes back to Ohio and the next thing he does he ends up in South Florida—and who does he contact? A Mafia connection. Now, I want you to begin to see the thread of organized crime running through this, because this is one of the things that the prosecutor doesn't want you to see because it makes a statement and tells a story on its own. He contacts a Mafia connection, someone who's been buying pot from his partner in the used-car business, and who has been selling pot. And they agree to whisk him out of the country. And who does he get taken to? He gets put on a plane and he ends up in Great Inagua, which is an island on the chain somewhere on the way to South America. And there's where he meets Winces Velasco-Peterson.

"Can you imagine a man like Leo Fraley, a resourceful, snake in the grass like him, can you imagine him being literally a prisoner for seven to nine months in Colombia? Well, you want to believe that I've got a bridge in Brooklyn that I want to sell to you, too. Leo Fraley is simply a person who changes color with the scenes, just like a chameleon."

Moore succinctly assessed Fraley's manner of testifying, pointing out the difference in how he answered Fink's questions and how he answered the questions posed to him by himself, Black and Zuñiga. "Leo Fraley's technique was effective because it prevented me and the other lawyers who were seeking to work their way in through the details, it prevented us from making him commit himself to anything. He knew it would work because he is a skilled and resourceful liar."

It wasn't enough for Moore to blast Fraley. His next target was the government's attorney. He retrieved exhibit number 254, and waved it in the air for the jury to see. It was a log of Leo Fraley's visitors.

"They are characterized as 'legal visits,'" he said, then asked: "Why is it that Leo knew the answer to all of Mr. Fink's questions?" He read from the log and said, "Maybe it's because on July 8, 1990, from 10:40 in the morning until 1:35 in the afternoon, Mr. Fink and Leo Fraley were alone together at that prison. Maybe you'll look at other visits where just Mr. Fink and Mr. Fraley were alone. Then you have all the other people from the agencies of the government who were out there seeing him. Just think about the month, the full month that Leo Fraley was living out of the little guest cell in the customs office, removed from the county jail, eating the same food as the agents. Boy, were they talking to him then!"

He went on ad nauseum, becoming more melodramatic as he told the jury that Fraley was a man who would not only "sell his soul, lie and cheat," he would kill you if it meant freedom to him. "He'd put a knife right through your heart if he could."

By the end of the day one would think that Moore had insulted Fraley, the agents and Fink as much as humanly possible, but he reached down one more time to leave the jury with this thought: "This is a case, let me tell you folks, where the case agents in this case got in bed with the devil. And when you lay down with a dog, you come up with some fleas once in a while. And the government laid down with Leo Fraley."

Following his last day of testimony, Fraley returned to the comforts of prison life. At least in prison he didn't have to put up with the pompous sesquipedalian exclamations from attorneys. At least in prison, they told you to fuck off in plain English. He returned to his prison job, immersing himself in his duties, working overtime to earn extra money.

As he walked from the Federal Building in downtown Phoenix, Fink reflected on the events of the case that had consumed the last year of his life. Outside he was met by Gately, who had attended to hear the closing arguments.

"Gee, I don't know if I should be seen with the likes of you, Tom," Gately began jokingly. "The way Moore tells it, you've been laying down with dogs."

"And what about you feeding the devil all those gourmet meals in that luxury suite you call a cell?" Fink replied.

They both gave each other that look, deciding to make a deal right there and then. Intuitively they extended their hands to shake on it and in unison said, "Never again."

As they parted, neither of them could foresee that fate would indeed bring them together once again. Gately was already putting together the case against the individuals responsible for the making of the Arizona/Mexico drug tunnel. And a year later Gately would return to Fink to prosecute an investigation dubbed Operation Rolling Thunder, a case very similar to "Dead Ringer" in which the only elements that changed were the defendants.

On his way home Fink thought that he would have traded all his worldly possessions not to have to sit through Zuñiga's closing arguments the next day.

The early part of Zuñiga's closing argument was filled with the words that had been banned by the judge—the same words Zuñiga had used throughout the trial, causing his defense colleagues to object to his statements.

"The Medellín Cartel—who hasn't heard of them? Who hasn't heard about Ochoa? Who hasn't heard about Pablo Escobar? Who hasn't heard about all of those men?" His colleagues had objected so many times throughout the proceeding, by the time the closing arguments rolled around and Zuñiga spoke the banned words they had given up.

So Zuñiga continued uninterrupted. "I want you to think about it now, because in fact there was no connection in this load with any Medellín Cartel. Mr. Fraley is protecting the Medellín Cartel because he doesn't want to get blown away.

"Mr. Fraley was cunning enough that, when he was arrested, he had time to think. And Mr. Fink got sucked into Mr. Fraley's plan. Fraley had time to reflect and come up with a plan whereby he could throw out some victims to the government and still protect himself, not be afraid that he'd be gunned down by the Cali cartel, the Medellín cartel and the Italian Mafia."

Fink looked at the other two defense attorneys and saw them literally bury their faces in their hands as they listened to their colleague further prejudice the jury against their clients.

Zuñiga went on to espouse the philosophical virtues and demerits of the "war on drugs." Somehow he connected the government's drug war to the *Phantom of the Opera*. It was the biggest stretch of the imagination Fink had ever heard, but he had to give Zuñiga an "A" for creativity. Zuñiga went on to talk about America's promotion of drugs by letting "Manuel Noriega exist for so long." His imagination had taken him beyond left field and out of the ballpark; Fink finally had to object to bring him back on track.

Finally he got around to attacking the credibility of the agents who testified.

"Have you been told the entire truth by the government?" Zuñiga questioned, hoping to inspire doubt as he began his attack on Fink. "Has this shepherd shown you the way to all the facts? This wolf in sheep's clothing has in fact been guiding you down a primrose path. He doesn't want you to ask questions. You're not supposed to look at anything else." He was sounding more and more like a Sunday morning television evangelist. "Don't do what Mr. Fink, the self-anointed shepherd, wants you to do.

"Make no mistake about it. I'm attacking him. No mistake. I don't want to misrepresent myself. I think it's pretty clear. But because he deserves it. He brought it on himself. He attacked us. He tried to plant that seed of skepticism in your mind. Think about what the evidence has been throughout. And, when he tells you, 'Look at the tapes,' just view this idiot box and you will be convinced. But what he's forgetting is that we went through five weeks of torture—all of us."

Zuñiga then bounced back to his allegation of government misconduct. This time he used *Dragnet* as his allegorical metaphor. "We didn't have police back then running around like druggies, giving the appearance that they were something other than what they were."

He decried the government's bargain with Leo Fraley. "Remember, his performance is very important to him. He's not to be sentenced until February of next year. So he's got to do well for the government. The government wants to do well, because, you know what, not one big fish or any fish of any consequence was netted—but they want you to think that." He asked the jury to try to figure out why it was that Winces Velasco-Peterson and Don Pedro were not charged, "when they were clearly willing participants?"

As he got back to characterizing Fraley as a "wise and crafty man" who had duped the government, once again equating the investigation to a theatrical production, which he said was scripted and directed by Leo Fraley, he again brought up the banned words: "He's not going to be killed because he never really snitched anybody off in the Medellín cartel, or Cali cartel, or Italian Mafia."

Zuñiga was stopping for no one, no matter what. His next attempt at eloquence was to quote several passages from the play *A Man for All Seasons,* by Robert Bolt. He ended with: "This country's planted thick with laws from coast to coast. Man's laws, not God's. And if you cut them down, do you really think that you could stand upright in the winds that would blow then? Yes, I give the devil the benefit of law for my own safety's sake.

"Pardon my emotion," he pleaded, "but that's really what we're talking about. You giving these men the benefit of the law. Not condemning them because the idiots involved themselves in something we all hate. If we could, we'd all hit them—we'd all beat them. But we can't do that. We're here to use the law. I ask that you use it and that you acquit them. Thank you."

How do you follow a performance like that, Fink thought. It was like asking the Carpenters to follow Madonna.

Fink began his rebuttal by telling the jury he was going to address his fellow attorneys' allegations, not by criticizing them as individuals but rather the content of the presentations. "Mr. Moore spoke with you about an hour and a half and said he was going to meet the facts head-on. Then he launched into a diatribe of about an hour and a half against Fraley and the other witnesses." Fink retrieved a stack of papers and held it in his hand in plain view. "This is a transcript of the New York meeting in which his client participated. It's 139 pages. Any time during his closing argument, did he try to explain to you what his client was saying in this meeting? This is two hours, composed of, largely, his client's speeches. He never once tried to explain to you what his client was saying if it wasn't to arrange for distribution of a cocaine transaction.

"Mr. Zuñiga just spoke to you for perhaps two hours. He indicated that he was going to meet the evidence head-on. His client's statements are contained in perhaps four volumes of transcripts of tapes. Tapes and transcripts in which his client is assisting, facilitating in the importation of two tons of cocaine. How many times during his closing argument did he address the content of his client's conversations in those tapes?

"Mr. Black spoke for roughly an hour and how many times did he try to explain to you why his client, Frank Díaz, came here to Phoenix in October to discuss a smuggling plan with Leo Fraley? It wasn't the U.S. government who solicited him to come here. It wasn't Leo Fraley. No one even knew who his client was."

"Excuse me," said Black to the judge, "Just note our objection to that, Your Honor, please."

"Overruled. Proceed." Broomfield didn't even raise his eyes above his glasses.

Fink continued: "There's something interesting you should note about that defense as it's being asserted here. Lawyer's love to speak with both hands. We love to say, on the one hand, on the other hand," he said making the appropriate gestures. "And what you have are defense counsel who are telling you, we're asserting the defense of entrapment. But on the other hand my client didn't do it. My client's not guilty. My client didn't have the requisite criminal intent to commit this crime. My client didn't conspire with other people. But if you don't believe that, if that's not true, then he was entrapped. On the one hand he didn't do it, on the other hand, if he did it he was entrapped. They're inconsistent arguments."

He went on to explain elements of entrapment, such as "predisposition."

"It's not entrapment for the government to offer the opportunity to people to commit crimes who have already been involved in that type of criminal activity. And it is not entrapment for the government to offer the opportunity to people that commit a crime who stood eager and ready and willing and able to commit the crimes. People are entrapped if they are otherwise innocent persons. They have to be complete rookies, amateurs, novices, criminal virgins, so to speak."

"Objection," Moore interrupted, "That's not an accurate statement of the law, Your Honor."

"The court will instruct the jury as to the law. Proceed."

"One of the things that you look for is whether or not someone ever expressed any reluctance to commit a crime. Mr. Zuñiga played the tape of Mr. Spicer, one of Mr. Fraley's former workers. Spicer said no. He said 'I'm not in. Count me out.' You heard that on the tape." He told the jury about another associate who also said 'Count me out.' " After that, Fink explained, it was the end of the conversation.

"Did you hear any of these defendants say on any of these tapes—wait a minute, I want out? Do any of you seriously believe that defendant Rico-Pinsón had no prior experience in drug trafficking? It defies all credibility to believe that someone in their first drug transaction would be involved in distributing two tons of cocaine, an *astronomical* amount of cocaine. That's like saying someone who's just come out of boot camp in the Army was put in a position of leading the Fifth Army in the Sinai Desert."

Fink went on to address the issue raised by all three defense attorneys: the government's use of criminals as witnesses. "The government did not go out and say, let's go out and find the dirtiest criminal we can find to come in and help build the case to bring this evidence to court. We didn't make him a witness against these defendants, they made him a witness against themselves. They were doing business with him long before we were. The government takes its witnesses as it finds them. He's in a position to come in here and testify against them about his dealings with them because they put him in that position."

When Fink finished his rebuttal Moore told the judge his client had been "severely prejudiced by the linkage with the other two defendants," and that his client was entitled to a mistrial. Then he asked for a mistrial based on "remarks made by Mr. Zuñiga."

"Any other motions?" asked Judge Broomfield. Seeing none, he said, "I will deny all motions." He then explained his basis of denial on Moore's objections and on the issue of entrapment: "Among other reasons, no objection was made with respect to those remarks during the course of the time they were made."

It was up to Zuñiga to attempt one last time to bring a dying horse to life: "I think it was Justice Brandeis who spoke about authority, when it recognizes illegal conduct and accepts it from law enforcement, adds to the degradation of society. Your Honor, if you turn a blind eye to the illegal importation, the illegal distribution . . . The distribution law is that even law enforcement cannot distribute to those who are not members of law enforcement. There's an abuse of authority. It is illegal." Zuñiga's last-ditch effort to paint the government's agents as the real criminals fell on deaf ears.

* * *

The jury deliberated for two days. On November 5, 1990, the twelve men and women who sat in judgment found all three defendants guilty, on all counts.

Leo Fraley had endured three weeks of verbal abuse from the defense attorneys. But most of their characterizations of him and his crimes had some truth laced throughout their dramatic presentations. Personally, some of their verbal cruelties did penetrate his thick skin. In fact, there were many instances where he agreed with the defense attorneys. His entire adult life was consumed in nothing more than committing crimes. They were actions he has never been proud of.

He later told Gately, however, that despite his thirty-year rap sheet, he maintained a strong sense of pride about two things in his life: his commitment to his family and, as he put it, "being a man of your word."

"The jury didn't like me or disbelieve anything they said about me," he said to Gately. "But when you live something and you tell the truth, you just can't beat that."

CHAPTER

13

THE RAT HOUSE

"OKAY, WATCH THIS," Cuffaro said proudly. His audience was a fellow inmate, another high-profile informant known during his heyday for his violence as a Gambino hit man. Cuffaro was showing off his latest in a series of wood-carved replicas of nineteenth century sailing vessels.

"Anyone here can operate the functional parts of this ship by voice command," Cuffaro exclaimed to a growing audience. "The functional parts are the lights, the rudder and the wheel. Who wants to try?"

The mafioso expressed interest and said in his strong Sicilian/Brooklyn accent, "Okay, turn on da lights."

"No, no, no," Cuffaro said. "You have to say: The captain says, turn on the lights."

"Okay, okay," the gangster said anxiously. "Da captain sez, turn on da lights." He smiled, eyes wide, ready to see the miraculous events. As he finished the sentence the lights of the model ship illuminated. The audience gasped collectively and vied for the next opportunity to operate the vessel by voice command.

One after the other, infamous criminals stepped forward to play the game. Soon they began arguing over who would go next. Cuffaro and Fraley heard them say, "I was the boss. I go next."

And the replies: "You shut up . . . Sit down and wait your turn . . . You're no boss in here!"

Cuffaro laughed. And Fraley—standing on the tier above operating the infrared remote control that Cuffaro had devised, much like the kind used to operate a ceiling fan—joined in, almost doubled over. Their "conspiracies" had been perfected during their years at the Rat House,

Cuffaro's beginning in the summer of 1988, Fraley's in January 1990. In the Rat House they watched in amazement as these mafiosi attempted to establish and maintain a hierarchy, even during events of such a trivial nature.

Joe Cuffaro spent much of his time on two well-known Sicilian crafts, wood-carving and clay work. He made intricate scale models of wooden ships, like the one they had rigged up with the remote control, and created the kind of pottery sold in the outdoor seaside markets of Sicily.

Leo Fraley spent time working with animal skins. Much as he did as a kid, in the Ohio Valley, he treated different types of hide and crafted the finished leather into products ranging from belts to briefcases and women's purses. But mostly he spent his time on the job as head clerk. Fraley's ability to organize and work with numbers, and his natural interest in computers made him a shoo-in for the position. Among his duties were processing the paperwork for incoming and departing prisoners, issuing clothes, assigning cells/rooms and doing the inmate payroll.

Each prisoner received a wage for work performed. "Pay Grade 4," the bottom of the wage scale, paid nine cents an hour. Prisoners had the opportunity to work their way up to "Pay Grade 1," which maxed-out at nineteen cents an hour. In addition, a prisoner who performed in an "exemplary" manner could receive a bonus of up to fifty percent of his monthly wages. The cap on a "Pay Grade 1" with bonuses was ninety-six dollars per month. This required putting in twelve- to sixteen-hour days —a schedule Fraley consistently maintained. At the rate he was going he would never save up enough to fill another floor safe; as a matter of fact, he had made more by "stoning scabs" at the steel mills as a preteen. Still, the work helped pass the time and kept his mind and body occupied.

When he wasn't making model ships or pottery items, Cuffaro himself put his culinary skills to work in the prison kitchen. At nineteen cents an hour Cuffaro was the lowest paid Italian chef in the world, but the wages were no measure for the culinary delights he created in the Rat House *cucina*. Many of his specialty dishes fostered a surprisingly tense atmosphere within the unit's walls and often became a source of contention. On one occasion, when Cuffaro made his linguini with clam sauce and there was not enough for all the inmates, a "sit-down" meeting was ordered by a former Philadelphia boss. The mafioso ordered Cuffaro to make enough for his Scarfo crime family of Philadelphia as if he were making his order to a South Philly Italian deli. Fraley was also ordered to coordinate proper distribution of the linguini. The Philly mob enlisted the aid of the "Westies," former members of the murderous Irish West Side New York gang, to enforce the new rule. Another mafioso from the Gambino clan called for a "sit-down" because Cuffaro did not make enough *braciole,* an Italian favorite of rolled and stuffed, thinly sliced beef cooked in tomato sauce. Indeed, Prison officials repeatedly found themselves trying to sort out food disputes among the mob family inmates. One Gambino mafioso became such a disciplinary problem over Cuffaro's dishes that he was finally transferred to another unit.

The displays of ire of the Mafia inmates were not the only instances of heartburn raised over Cuffaro's cooking. When Sciacchitano, Carrara and Diana Fernández came to visit Cuffaro just before the Italian trial, he had prepared a feast for them. The meeting began with service of an *antipasto* dish: four imported cheeses—*mozzarella di bufala, Romano, parmigiano-reggiano* and *provolone*—adorned the china service. Amidst the cheeses were prosciutto ham, pepperoni, fresh tomato slices, a garnish of fresh asparagus and olives. The two Italian magistrates were delighted at the hospitality, but Fernández appeared miffed. The ability of inmates to enjoy this type of fare obviously bothered her, although she made no comment. In spite of her disapproval she did indulge in the main course, a pasta dish also prepared tableside by Cuffaro.

The little farce perpetrated by Cuffaro and Fraley with the remote-controlled ship took just enough time for his Sicilian meat loaf dish to cook.

"So you wanna take bets on who's going to make a complaint today?" Cuffaro asked as he and Fraley ate.

Even though they laughed at the internal Mafia hierarchy games, they had their own measure of status. There were some prisoners in the Rat House who didn't deserve to be there, they felt. They should have been in the general population with the rest because their criminal involvement was so insignificant. What had they done to be in the Witness Protection Program? The significance of Cuffaro's and Fraley's cases, and the magnitude of the trials in which they had participated, was their measuring stick for status. They were considered among the elite.

"You know, I think I missed my calling, Joe," Fraley said seriously, placing his fork back onto the empty plate.

"What do you mean?"

"I think I shoulda been a lawyer. Now that's a goddamn racket right there. I figure the most skill you gotta have is a good memory and a line of bullshit a mile long and I got no problem with that."

"Well, Leo," Cuffaro said seriously, "I don't think that's the only skill you gotta have to be a lawyer. I think even more important than a good memory is showmanship."

"You shoulda come with me to the Gambino trial." Cuffaro continued. He had just returned from testifying against Joe and John Gambino in New York. "You coulda taken lessons from Bruce Cutler." Cutler, he explained, was attorney for the Gambino brothers and had represented the Gambino family boss, John Gotti.

"You got to talk like you are on stage, Leo," Cuffaro said, rising to his feet to take on the Cutler persona. "Mr. Cuffaro," he began, raising his hand toward the sky, "You lied, lie after lie after lie, didn't you?" Then Cuffaro crouched down on the floor, straining his voice in imitation of Cutler's performance: "It was like an ice-cream sundae, where you add the whipping cream, then the nuts and you top it off with the cherry, and pretty soon the plate is so full the whole thing topples over."

He came back to the table. "That's how you gotta do it, Leo, if you wanna be a successful lawyer."

"You're right, Joe. Did I tell you about the one I got?" Fraley stood up to perform his impression of Robert Moore.

"Look into his eyes, ladies and gentlemen, there sits the devil incarnate," he said with piercing eyes, taking slow and very purposeful steps, scanning the lunchroom as if the chairs were the jury. He looked over at Cuffaro. "Well, what do you think?"

"You know, Leo, I think you may have it. You may have yourself a new career." They laughed and raised their glasses to each other in a toast.

Then Cuffaro's face turned serious. Fraley could see the change. "I almost didn't go to the Gambino trial," Joe said.

Cuffaro told Fraley that his wife and family had been visited by two deputy U.S. Marshals, messengers from the agency's "Witsec," or Witness Security unit.

With his oldest daughter translating, they told Cuffaro's wife that the stipend she had been receiving would soon be cut off. This would have effectively ended her ability to support herself and her children. A minimum-wage job working in a domestic situation had been the only income outside the government assistance from the Witness Protection Program. His wife and children told Cuffaro that the deputies told them they could always get on welfare and live in public housing. The news sent her oldest daughter into a panic. The day ended in a rush to the emergency room and an overnight hospital stay.

"When my family told me about it, I called Jim Brown and Diana Fernández. I told them I wouldn't testify in the Gambino trial and continue to help the government if this was the way my family was going to be treated." Besides, he said, the government had plenty of ammunition with the testimony of Sammy "The Bull" Gravano, also scheduled to testify. Cuffaro would implicate them in crimes related to drug trafficking and Gravano would testify about the many murders. Cuffaro reminded them that he had already fulfilled his plea agreement with the

Department of Justice when he had completed his testimony against John Galatolo. Brown and Fernández both attached enough importance to Cuffaro's testimony in the upcoming prosecution of the Gambinos that they again went to bat for him. Almost immediately the Marshals Service restored the stipend and became less callous in their handling of the Cuffaro family.

Fraley too had had his problems with the system. "I called home on my birthday," he told Cuffaro. "When I asked my sister to pass me to my mom, she told me she had died that morning." He told Cuffaro that thirty-one days later his father, who had fought off cancer for a decade, also passed away.

Fraley had reached out to Gately and Fink and asked them to help him get permission to attend the funerals. Fink put in the calls to main Justice in Washington, but the Office of Enforcement Operations would not support a furlough. Gately and the Phoenix agents even offered to replace, assist or augment the Marshals Service if it would change the situation. The response from the DOJ was that the area where his parents lived in Pennsylvania was considered too dangerous. Travel into that area while Fraley was in the program was out of the question. In the end, Fraley grieved his loss from prison. "I was willin' to go in handcuffs and ankle chains and with a bunch a agents. It just ain't right not to pay your respects at your parents' funerals," Fraley said regretfully. "At least Fink and Gately did what they could," he added. In fact, he told Cuffaro, Fink visited him both times and sat with him in prison.

Despite the government's denial for permission to attend his parents' funerals Fraley did testify in another trial.

Less than a month after his parents had died Fraley made a trip to Tampa, Florida, to testify as a state witness for the Florida Department of Law Enforcement. The Florida State's attorney had indicted James Timanere, the young lawyer and former county solicitor who arranged Fraley's payoffs in the video poker business years earlier. Timanere had relocated to Tarpon Springs, Florida, and had been Fraley's frontman during his cocaine-smuggling ventures there.

John Barry and Ben Fannon, Fraley's crew members on the cocaine runs from Belize, had also been charged in the Racketeering and Corrupt Influence drug trafficking conspiracy. Fannon fell first and Timanere and Barry were convicted a few months later. Fraley testified he had paid Timanere more than three hundred thousand dollars to set up the corporations that held Fraley's assets, paid the lease on his house, purchased his smuggling equipment, supplies and vessels. Fraley told the jury that Timanere's law office even housed the facsimile machine with which Fraley communicated his smuggling plans to Velasco and Ortegón in Colombia.

Prison life was definitely depressing. Cuffaro and Fraley had heard attorneys and others refer to their particular prison as "Club Fed" and "Leisure Cell," just because they were segregated from the general population and were primarily among high-profile convicts. But to them prison was still the same, no matter what the conditions or the stature of their fellow inmates. Individual privacy did not exist and, worst of all, they no longer had the single element they had once taken for granted—freedom.

Unlike for other prisoners, visiting hours were only on the weekends. During the last four and a half years Cuffaro had received only one family visit. The lack of visits, however, was a condition he had imposed on himself and the family, rather than bring his wife and children into the prison environment. On that one day he saw his family, it had become a painful, gut-wrenching experience for his children. He had watched as they left in tears to battle the world without their father, and his heart filled with anguish and guilt knowing that his wife and children, even their youngest, had to find jobs to maintain a tiny run-down apartment in the "low-rent" part of town. The knowledge that he was also totally responsible for his family's suffering was almost unbearable. It had been his greed and contempt for the law that had put them in this horrible situation. So he felt he had done enough to tear his family apart. For almost five years his only contact with his wife and children was through letters and infrequent telephone conversations. Most of his extended family, including his brothers, cut off all communication with him. And Joe Cuffaro knew he was to blame. Because of him his brothers had been forced to enter the Witness Protection Program as well, and had lost their homes and businesses in exchange for protection from the United States government. His brother Mario, who had forfeited his job as a paramedic in Florida, was required to sign a document that, unbeknownst to him, stated that he would refuse assistance from the government in the form of licenses and official documents for employment. Shortly after this when Mario was forced to find a new career path and start all over, he cut off communication with his brother Joe.

In the spring of 1993, Cuffaro received a visit from two U.S. customs special agents from Los Angeles. The customs agents were assisting Italian authorities to prepare a case against the money launderers who had helped Cuffaro's contact in Milan, Giuseppe Lottussi. The Italian government was trying to locate his Los Angeles connection, Giancarlo Formichi Moglia.

Moglia had been arrested in Hawaii for money-laundering violations. After his arrest law enforcement officials discovered he was wanted in Italy for his connection in the six-hundred-kilo Mafia-cartel connection.

As Cuffaro walked into the combination visitor/interview/game room, the agents introduced themselves.

"Joe, I'm Bill Gately, assistant special agent in charge of the Los Angeles office. This is Special Agent Mickey Marzigliano."

Cuffaro told Gately he had heard of him through Leo Fraley. After a few minutes of small talk the two agents pumped Cuffaro for information one more time about the Milan–Los Angeles money-laundering connection. As they referred to the transcripts of several depositions, hearings and trials at which Cuffaro had testified and went over the story, Cuffaro couldn't help but think of Lottussi's face pressed up against his office window in Milan as Vincenzo Galatolo threatened him.

Gately told Cuffaro that he and Marzigliano would be meeting Judge Sciacchitano the next week to assist him in Los Angeles and Hawaii. The Italians planned to file extradition papers for Moglia, who had been arrested by customs agents in Honolulu for money-laundering violations.

As the meeting concluded, Fraley entered the room.

"Well, if it isn't my old pal—the guy who arrested me," Fraley said to Gately, extending his hand.

"How are you doing, Leo?" Gately asked.

"Well, you know, just takin' it one day at a time." Fraley always had a way of remaining low-key, regardless of his circumstances. And he held no grudge, understanding not only that Gately had a job to do but that he had, after all, broken the law.

The four men, two convicted criminals and two law enforcement agents, were an odd combination. Nevertheless, they spent a few minutes reminiscing.

"Hey, you guys still have my big-screen TV?" Fraley asked.

"Yeah, Leo, it's still the property of the government. It's in the training room of the Phoenix office," Gately responded.

"I'm sure they're saving it for you, Leo," Cuffaro said jokingly.

"Shit," Fraley responded.

"So where will you take Sciacchitano when he comes to visit Los Angeles?" asked Cuffaro.

"Oh, I thought I'd take him to an American impersonation of an Italian cafe," Gately said. "He wants to see the Hollywood sign up close and Sophia Loren's star on Hollywood Boulevard, as well as Mann's Chinese Theater."

"I'm sure he'll be happy just to walk down the street without bodyguards," Cuffaro mused.

"That's why we plan to take him for an afternoon stroll on the Strand in Manhattan Beach," Gately said. He paused, then he asked "So, Leo . . . What are your plans if one day they let you walk out of here?"

"Well, I won't be deep-sea fishin' in the gulf, and probably can't be a tour guide in the Colombian Amazon. But one thing's for sure."

"Yeah, what's that?" Gately asked.

"I won't be adding another page to that rap sheet of mine. The government may start charging me for the paper." Then Fraley's tone changed. "I'll be damned if I'm ever coming back to the joint. The next time would be a life sentence—I don't care if it's just for another day."

Fraley knew if he ever returned to general population in any prison he would have a snitch jacket, and his life wouldn't be worth spit. More than that, he just wanted the opportunity to live out the rest of his life without looking over his shoulder or fearing reprisal from the people he had turned against. Fraley told Gately it had taken him thirty years to come to the realization that no matter how much money he made as a criminal, he still didn't have a life. His philosophy of "live for today, for tomorrow may never come" had led only to this.

Cuffaro joined in Fraley's musing about the future, and told Gately within a few months he would be released.

"This was my first and last time in prison. I'll never come back," Cuffaro said.

His plans were to use his talents in a productive way. Start a business like he had with Scirocco Fan Company and never turn back to a life of crime.

During the flight back to Los Angeles, his new home since the summer of 1992, Gately thought about Leo Fraley and Joe Cuffaro. He was convinced of two things about Leo Fraley and Joe Cuffaro. They were men of their word and had clearly done everything they said they could do. It was also clear to him that both of them had come to terms with their actions and even felt remorseful—something he had not heard very often during his more than two decades in the business of putting away criminals.

It was almost a year since Gately had transferred to his new position in Los Angeles. The division he directed targeted the money-laundering cells responsible for collecting and returning hundreds of millions of dollars in drug profits to the cartel. Los Angeles had over the years become a "drug warehouse" and a "financial center" for the cartel. Gately's latest case involved an international money-laundering case involving billions of drug dollars.

His last meeting with these men had made him reflect upon the irony of his job. Even though together they had clearly delivered a devastating blow to three criminal organizations, in the overall scheme these two cases seemed only to skim the surface. After twenty-four years on the job the drug cases Gately was involved in were simply growing larger, more complicated, involving more and more cash.

Another day was just beginning.

Epilogue

THE TESTIMONY OF JOSEPH CUFFARO and Leo Fraley helped damage some of the most powerful criminal organizations in the world.

Like that of many turncoats before him, the effects of Cuffaro's testimony were seen immediately as the world witnessed the eventual downfall of not only the Gambino crime family in New York, but twelve of the highest-ranking mafiosi in Sicily. "Iron Tower," as it was known, was not just another case in Italy. Two decades of courage, tenacity and eventually the ultimate sacrifice by anti-Mafia magistrates Giovanni Falcone and Paolo Borsellino served as the platform from which the government would attempt to bring down the thousand-year stronghold of the Mafia in Sicily and dismantle the entrenchment of government corruption bred by the Mafia's power and wealth.

As a former associate of the American Mafia and the Medellín cartel, Leo Fraley's testimony served as impetus for the domino effect that began the end of an era of narco-terrorism by Pablo Escobar's Medellín cartel.

It is important to note that while their actions alone were significant and, some would argue, revolutionary, they were part of a much larger evolving movement of reform in these arenas. The impact of testimony from individuals like Cuffaro and Fraley would not have had any significant effect without government backing. Conversely, the commitment of courageous government officials might not have seen such a dramatic effect without the assistance of turncoats.

During the past five years the Italian government, fueled by the outrage of its citizenry under the leadership of men like Giusto Sciacchitano, has enacted new anti-Mafia and anticorruption legislation.

As chief magistrate and assistant Italian minister of foreign affairs for organized crime, narcotics trafficking and terrorism, Judge Sciacchitano says that the new, powerful alliance between the Mafia and the cartels has had a dramatic effect on Italy: "The year 1992 is a year where too many incredible and serious events took place which touched us very deeply."

Over the years, the judge has seen his colleagues killed by *La Cosa Nostra,* but the violence has not deterred the anti-Mafia efforts. Instead, it has created a stronger solidarity among all the entities that make up the Italian criminal justice system. New and more effective laws, not only advancing the war against drug trafficking, but also money laundering have been legislated. National reform has also occurred, leaving no one above the law in this all-out effort to attack corruption within the criminal justice system, business and government. The lawlessness and indiscriminate slaughter of judges, police and innocent Italian citizens who stood in their path has served only to unite the populace against the Mafia.

"Colombia is the leader in a fight against a problem it has not created and one which has made it its principal victim," says Maj. Gen. Miguel Antonio Gómez Padilla, former director general of the Colombian national police. In a 1991 publication entitled ". . . A Decade of Force," the Colombian national police says it has reached a "high degree" of effectiveness in combating drugs, thanks to the collaboration between the Colombian government, the people of Colombia and solidarity with countries like the United States, Great Britain and France. Padilla, like many other Colombian officials, has taken a strong stand in their own war on drugs, but the price in Colombia is heavy for those who dare to stand against the powerful drug cartels. Most have been mercilessly gunned down or are victims of endless terrorist acts. The majority of the victims are police officers, with hundreds killed each year. General Padilla says he himself never knows if he will make it through the day. He vividly remembers an act of narco-terrorism that took place a few years ago, to wit: the destruction of a fully occupied government office building in Bogotá that killed and injured thousands of people. Only the solidarity of the world community will make their struggle, sacrifices and the results that they have already obtained worthwhile. But before it gets better, General Padilla has warned that it will get worse.

Today the cartels are branching out into what has proven to be a potentially even more profitable crop. In 1990, Colombia's antinarcotics police seized and eradicated over 1,500 hectares (a unit equal to 100 acres) of Colombia's newest endeavor in the drug trade, the cultivation of poppies that will eventually be refined into heroin. In the last year there has been an increase of as much as 500 percent in the amount of refined heroin entering the United States from Colombia.

Much like the North American Free Trade Agreement, OPEC and the economic union of the Western European Countries, criminal organizations like the Mafia and the Colombian drug cartels have joined forces to become a stronger, more powerful global threat. This should serve as impetus for the global law-enforcement community to also join forces to effectively combat such a formidable enemy.

The drug/crime threat however, is not limited to the traditional organized-crime families in the U.S., Italy and Colombia. The decade-old alliance between the Colombians and the Mexican crime families is growing stronger each year and the break up of Eastern-bloc countries is already serving as fertile ground for drug-based crime. Today the Russian Mafia is becoming a truly global criminal force, with ties now reaching far beyond Europe into the United States and South America. The Asian organized-crime syndicates are becoming so tightly knit as the baton of power is passed from generation to generation over the last millenium, it has become virtually impossible to penetrate their infrastructure. They are the undisputed leaders in the world-wide production and distribution of heroin.

With the deaths of Pablo Escobar, José Rodríguez-Gacha and the imprisonment of several of its high-ranking officers, the Medellín cartel was stripped of its lifeline. But even as this was happening a new and more powerful Cali cartel was emerging. This year the Colombian prosecutor general Gustavo de Greiff, is negotiating the "carefully choreographed surrender" of the Cali cartel's kingpins. Many law enforcement officials in the United States view this as nothing more than a "sell-out," allowing them to pass the torch on to a younger, more violent generation. But the Colombians see this as their only alternative to waging a bloody and costly drug war.

The Republic of Italy has waged a formidable fight against the Mafia, despite its virtually annual political upheavals and scandals of corruption. Notwithstanding the arrests of hundreds of mafiosi, including the infamous "Beast," Salvatore Riina, and the virtual obliteration of his crime family by a rival Mafia family, strength prevails among Italy's three principal organized crime gangs—*La Cosa Nostra,* the Neapolitan *Camorra* and the Calabrian *'Ndrangheta.*

In the United States it appears that the administration is shifting its focus away from the interdiction efforts of Customs and the "kingpin" and organized-crime strategies of DEA and FBI toward prevention and, primarily, the treatment of hard-core users. This is a similar administration policy to the one espoused during the heroin epidemic of the late sixties and early seventies. According to newly appointed drug czar Lee Brown, "The principal drug problem lies with hard-core drug users." Hard-core drug use has not been reduced by past antidrug efforts, especially in our inner cities and among the disadvantaged. Brown says that nationwide cocaine medical emergencies reached to nearly 200,000 incidents in 1992, and heroin emergencies totaled 48,000—the highest levels since this type of data was first collected.

No plan devised by any country thus far has deterred traditional organized crime from immersing itself in international drug trafficking. In the end, it has not been the governments of nations, but rather the individual men and women who have committed their lives to combating organized crime and drug trafficking who have truly made a difference.

It is still only a minuscule difference. As long as individuals demand drugs, and as long as they are willing to violate the law by using them, the drug suppliers will stay open for business.

CAST OF CHARACTERS

PRINCIPLE PLAYERS —IN ORDER OF APPEARANCE :

Leo Fraley: Mafia and Medellín cartel associate who became a government witness after his arrest in August 1989. Fraley took the lead role in a government sting that targeted Escobar's organization in Colombia, Belize and New York. It was shortly after Fraley testified that Escobar turned himself in to the Colombian government in exchange for a no-extradition promise. Fraley is currently a federal prisoner in the Witness Protection Program.

Bill Gately: Metropolitan police officer, Washington, D.C.; U.S. Customs Service special agent, San Diego, California and Miami, Florida; and the resident agent in charge in Phoenix, Arizona. Gately was in charge of the investigation that netted Fraley and later became Operation Dead Ringer. He is currently the assistant special agent in charge in Los Angeles, California.

Joseph Cuffaro: Mafia associate with connections in Sicily, Colombia and the United States. Cuffaro was the bridge between the Sicilian Mafia and the Medellín cartel in the unprecedented alliance between these criminal organizations. He became a government witness after his arrest in December 1988. His testimony was directly responsible for more than thirty convictions of some of the highest level criminals of both organizations on three continents. He has served his time, returned to his family and private life.

Jim Brown: FBI special agent, Kansas City, Puerto Rico, Chicago and Miami. Brown was the case agent in the FBI Operation Deadfish. His investigation of John Galatolo led to the arrest of Cuffaro and the unraveling of the Mafia/cartel conspiracy. Special Agent Brown is currently based in the Southwest.

Tom Fink: Assistant United States Attorney, Phoenix, Arizona. Fink was the federal prosecutor in Operation Dead Ringer. His efforts led to the first life sentences for drug traffickers in the Arizona District. Fink has since prosecuted several of the highest profile drug cases in Arizona. He is currently an AUSA in Tucson.

SUPPORTING PLAYERS —IN ORDER OF APPEARANCE :

Bobby DeVitto: Fraley's partner in several criminal enterprises, Mafia associate, marijuana/cocaine smuggler and trafficker.

Albert "Tubby" Figer: Leo Fraley's protégé in the crime business.

Harvey: DeVitto's pilot.

Leon Burrows: fictitious name for the governor of Great Inagua.

Winces Velasco-Peterson: Member of the Medellín cartel and Fraley's mentor/partner in the cocaine business. Velasco is currently a fugitive from the U.S. who faces life imprisonment for smuggling more than two tons of cocaine.

Dominic "The Mad Bomber" Debonis: Original member of Albert Anastasia's "Murder, Inc." and an associate of the Sebastian LaRocca crime family in Pittsburgh, Pennsylvania. Died of old age in 1983.

Ken Ingleby: USCS special agent in charge in San Diego. He is now the resident agent in charge, Salt Lake City, Utah.

Dodge Gallanos: DEA special agent in charge in San Diego. Retired.

George Hardy: AUSA in San Diego. He is now in private practice.

Pete Nunez: Chief of the criminal division at the U.S. Attorney's office in San Diego. He later served as the U.S. Attorney for the Southern District of California and assistant secretary of the treasury for enforcement. He has returned to private life and law practice in San Diego, California.

Gary Trudeau: Fictitious name for a government informant.

John Ward and Gary Schmidt: Kingpins who were done in by Gary Trudeau.

Larry Reynolds: John Ward's attorney and coconspirator.

Karl Waversfeld: Corporal, RCMP drug enforcement section, Vancouver, British Columbia, Canada. Now a sergeant with the RCMP, Burnaby, British Columbia, drug enforcement section.

Martin Gladstone: Cuffaro's partner in the Scirocco Fan Company. Gladstone was arrested the same day as Cuffaro and later became a cooperating government witness. Gladstone has completed his sentence and has returned to private life.

Paul Gambino: Soldier in the Gambino crime family. He was the younger brother of Carlo Gambino "godfather" of the American Mafia.

Carlo D'Arpa: Cuffaro's partner in Joe's Market, in New York. He was a cousin to the Gambinos and married Paul Gambino's daughter.

Paul Castellano: Mafia associate of the Gambinos. He supplied the equipment to Cuffaro at Joe's Market. He later became the boss of the Gambino family after the death of Carlo Gambino. He was murdered in 1985 during a Mafia shootout in front of a New York City steakhouse.

Tomas Masotto: Mafia member of the Gambino crime family. He helped arrange Cuffaro's marriage to obtain his citizenship.

Kathleen Anderson: Hooker who married Cuffaro to help him obtain American citizenship. For several years Cuffaro maintained contact by sending her Christmas cards. He has had no contact with her in more than twenty years.

Pasquale "Patsy" Conti: Ran a rival grocery store in New York. He originally joined the Gambino crime family and later became crime family *capo.*

Thal Brothers: Owners of the trendy, gourmet Epicure Market in Miami Beach, Florida.

Rigo Malpica: Hired by Cuffaro to help organize other Cuban laborers. Malpica became Cuffaro's partner in the Scirocco Fan Company. He was forced out of the partnership by Galatolo.

John Galatolo: A "made member" of the Madonia crime family of the Sicilian Mafia. He became Cuffaro and Gladstone's partner in the cocaine trafficking business. After Cuffaro and Gladstone's arrest, they testified against Galatolo. Galatolo is currently serving a forty-five-year prison sentence.

Richard Markowitz: Hired Cuffaro as his right-hand man in the Key Largo Fan Company. Markowitz went bankrupt after Cuffaro left the business and started Scirocco Fan Company.

Piero Galeazzi: Worked for the Mafia buying and selling stolen gold and gems. Became a legitimate businessman in the U.S. Suffered a heart attack shortly after Galatolo and his crew robbed him. Current whereabouts unknown.

The Gambino Brothers, Joe and John: Distant cousins of Carlo Gambino. They worked for John Gotti's Gambino crime syndicate in New York. In January 1994 the Gambino brothers pled guilty to drug trafficking and are currently serving federal sentences.

John Gotti: Boss of the Gambino crime family. Convicted in 1973 of murder, and in 1992 of murder and racketeering. He was sentenced to life in prison without parole in the maximum-security federal penitentiary in Marion, Illinois.

Luis Mejía: Drug trafficker in Miami who worked for Aponte. He is a fugitive from the United States.

Tyrone Walker: Drug trafficker who supplied the Detroit market. Walker is currently serving a federal sentence for drug trafficking.

Mariela Liggio; Drug trafficker. Tried, convicted and sentenced to prison. Liggio pled guilty but escaped and was captured in New Jersey in 1991. Currently serving a federal criminal sentence.

Anthony Corinella: Married to John Galatolo's sister. Also a Mafia associate, operated a sucessful photo-retouching business in Manhattan. Has completed his sentence and returned to private life.

Paolo LoDuca: Wealthy Mafioso, associated with the American Mafia with loyalties to the Sicilian Mafia. One of four principals who coordinated the cartel/Mafia deal. Sentenced to twenty-five years, in absentia, by the Italian government. He is currently a free man in the U.S., fighting deportation to Italy.

Francesco Madonia: Head of the Madonia Mafia family in Sicily, godfather to John Galatolo. It was Madonia who originally devised the plan to transport cocaine between Colombia, Sicily and the United States. He remains in prison in Italy.

Alexander Schwerter: Multimillionaire, Chilean of German ancestry. Associate of John Galatolo. Cuffaro maintains he was a CIA operative—not corroborated by the FBI. Never charged with a crime.

Steve Minas: USCS special agent, Gately's partner in Miami, Florida. Now the deputy special agent in charge, Arizona.

"Ray:" USCS informant in Operation High Hat.

Jim Schmand: Deputy director Florida joint task group. Retired USCS special agent in Florida.

Bill Rosenblatt: USCS regional director of investigations, Miami, Florida, and later the assistant commissioner for enforcement. He is currently the special agent in charge, USCS, South Florida.

Ed Mederos: USCS special agent. Partner of Gately and Minas in Operation High Hat. He is currently the codirector of the Florida joint task group.

Ken Wagner: USCS internal affairs special agent. Retired.

Mark Schnapp: Prosecutor/AUSA in Operation High Hat. He is in private practice in Miami and has served as cocounsel for such notable defendants as Manuel Noriega and William Kennedy Smith. He is also reported to be a candidate for the U.S. Senate.

Jimmy O'Brien: USCS internal affairs group supervisor. Retired

Carlos LaFaurie: Drug smuggler and money launderer with the Medellín cartel—in charge of the Eastern Airlines smuggling operation.

"Sam:" Fictitious name for the Chibcha Indian who befriended Fraley in the marijuana fields in LaGuajira, Colombia.

The Romero Brothers: Colombian traffickers who worked with Winces Velasco-Peterson.

José Rodríguez-Gacha: Known as "the Mexican," Gacha was a high-ranking member of the Medellín cartel. Killed in December 1989.

Pablo Escobar: Arguably the most famous or infamous cartel drug lord,

Escobar was gunned down in Colombia in a bloody shootout with soldiers and police on December 2, 1993.

Bobby Povich: Fraley's former partner in crime.

Ian Stephenstown: Fictitious name for the chief of police in Great Inagua.

Don Pedro Ortegón: Considered to be the highest-ranking member of the Medellín cartel. Ortegón is a fugitive who faces life imprisonment in the U.S.

Salvatore "Toto" Riina: Known as "The Beast." He was the head of the Corleonese family in Sicily. He is accused of ordering the deaths of numerous individuals, including mob rival boss Stefano Bontade, during the Great Mafia War in the late 1970s. For years Riina was a fugitive until his capture recently in Sicily. Riina is curently serving a life sentence for the assassination of anti-Mafia judge Giovanni Falcone.

Dominic Mannino: Head of the Castellammarese family in Philadelphia. Mannino is currently a fugitive.

Waldo Aponte: A member of the Medellín cartel who was instrumental in the six-hundred-kilo Sicilian Mafia/Medellín cartel connection. He is now a fugitive from the U.S. and Italy. He faces life imprisonment if captured.

Angel Sánchez: Aponte's partner. Sánchez is also a fugitive facing life imprisonment in the U.S. and Italy.

Allen "Brito" Knox: Captain of the sea vessel *Big John* who transported the cocaine from Colombia to Italy. Knox is a fugitive from Italy who faces life imprisonment.

Rosana: Fictitious name. Joe Cuffaro's wife.

Luis Miguel: Haitian drug dealer who worked with Galatolo as a distributor. He died in Metropolitan Correction Center, Miami, of heart failure after his conviction and prior to sentencing.

George Linares: Associate of John Galatolo—one of his "henchmen." He is now serving a federal sentence.

Tomaso Buscetta: Sicilian boss who lost most of his family and *soldati* to Riina's Corleonese. After his arrest in New York he became one of the first "turncoats." Buscetta testified in the "Pizza Connection" trial in 1986. He is still a protected witness.

Tony Fasulo: One of Galatolo's soldiers. Last known to be living in New York City and a suspect in several murders.

Rosario Naimo: One of the principals in putting together the six-hundred-kilo shipment. He has been a fugitive since his indictment in New York.

Vincenzo Galatolo: John Galatolo's brother and member of the Madonia crime family. He is currently serving time in an Italian prison for drug smuggling.

Raffaele Galatolo: John Galatolo's brother and member of the Madonia crime family. He is currently serving time in an Italian prison for drug smuggling.

Alduccio "Salvo" Madonia: Representative of the Madonia family during the *Big John* drug deal.

Aldo Madonia: Representative of the Ressuttana family during the *Big John* drug deal.

William "Blue" Logan: USCS regional commissioner, Houston, Texas. Later became deputy special agent in charge, Arizona. He is currently the resident agent in charge in Fort Myers, Florida.

Stephen MacNamee: United States Attorney, District of Arizona. He is now a federal judge in Phoenix, Arizona.

William Von Raab: USCS commissioner. He has returned to private life and private law practice.

Tom McDermott: Special agent in charge, Arizona, and later the director of domestic operations. He is currently the customs attaché in London, England.

Dave Hayes: Resident agent in charge in Nogales, Arizona. Transferred to headquarters as the Southwest desk officer. Currently deputy special agent in charge in El Paso, Texas.

Ben Fannon, John Barry, Buck Spicer: Fraley's smuggling crew.

Petie Sanson and Joe Timanier: Fraley's partners in the video poker business.

Roger Mannhalter: USCS special agent in Phoenix, Arizona. One of the co-case agents in Operation Dead Ringer.

Lee Atwood: USCS special agent in Phoenix, Arizona. Group supervisor in Operation Dead Ringer.

Sal Rina: Sicilian Mafia associate and an associate of the Gambino crime family of the U.S. and associate of Galatolo. Arrested in the first phase of the operation known as Dead Fish along with Cuffaro and Gladstone. Remains in prison.

Charles "Chick" McDevitt: FBI special agent in Miami, Florida. James Brown's partner in Operation Dead Fish. Transferred to "office of preference" on the West Coast.

Bill Kane: Informant who worked for the FBI in a sting against the Gambino crime family.

Giuseppe Lottussi: Italian money launderer from Milan who worked for the Medellín cartel.

Bill Meglen: USCS deputy assistant commissioner for enforcement. He has also served as the special agent in charge, San Diego, California; director, office of intelligence, special agent in charge, Newark, New

Jersey; and the customs attaché, Montevideo, Uruaguay. He is currently the special agent in charge in Los Angeles.

Michael Modrak: USCS acting director of special investigations in headquarters. Assistant special agent in charge in Washington, D.C., field office.

Carlos Salazar: USCS special agent, who worked undercover in Operation Dead Ringer.

José Restrepo: Coconspirator in Dead Ringer. Winces Velasco-Peterson's nephew. Sentenced to more than thirty years in prison.

Lazaro "Vicente" Rico-Pinsón: Coconspirator in Dead Ringer. He was sentenced to life without parole. He is serving his time in a maximum-security federal prison.

Fausto "Frank" Diaz: Coconspirator in Dead Ringer. He is serving a twenty-year prison term.

Armando Grijales: Coconspirator in Dead Ringer. Fugitive, facing life in prison.

John Martelli: USCS senior special agent in Phoenix, Arizona. Co-case agent in Dead Ringer.

Sarge Reyes: Coconspirator in Dead Ringer, Grijales's partner. Fugitive facing life in prison.

Rich Bailey: USCS senior special agent in Phoenix, Arizona. Case agent in Dead Ringer.

Ron Meyers: FBI special agent in Phoenix, Arizona. FBI case agent in Dead Ringer.

Dave Rippa: USCS assistant regional commissioner for enforcement, New York City. Currently the deputy special agent in charge, Newark, New Jersey.

James Fox: FBI assistant director in New York City. He is retired and currently serves as the director of security at an internationally known cosmetic company.

Marty Ficke: USCS assistant special agent in charge, Newark, New Jersey.

Angelo Fontana: John Galatolo's son-in-law. He was acquitted.

Sammy "The Bull" Gravano: Gambino crime family member. He has become a protected witness.

Judge Giovanni Falcone: The best-known Italian anti-Mafia magistrate in Sicily. Partner with Borsellino. Assassinated in 1992.

Judge Paolo Borsellino: Italian anti-Mafia judge. Assassinated in 1992, two months after Falcone.

Magistrate Giusto Sciacchitano: Succeeded his partners Borsellino and Falcone. Prosecutor in the Italian trial of Operation Iron Tower. Currently the assistant minister of foreign affairs, anti-terrorism, organized crime and narcotics.

Magistrate Carmello Carrara: Sciacchitano's prosecutorial partner in the Italian trial.

Diana Fernández: AUSA in the trial of Operation Dead Fish. Appointed court commissioner, representing the interests of the U.S. in the Italian trial. She is currently an AUSA in Fort Lauderdale, Florida.

Francesco Ingargiola: President of the court in the Italian trial.

Dr. Florestano Cristodaro and Dr. Salvatore Barresi: Judges in the Italian trial for Operation Dead Fish and Operation Iron Tower.

Antonino Mormino, Marco Clementi, Tomaso Farina, Carmelo Cordaro, Orazio Campo, Giuseppe DiPeri, Giuseppe Giannusa: Italian defense attorneys in the trial of Operation Iron Tower.

David Sabio and Boris Sánchez: Represented the interests of the Medellín cartel, as money collectors in the Italian /Colombian transshipment cocaine-smuggling venture. They became government witnesses.

Amparo: Wife of Angel Sánchez.

Giancarlo Formichi Moglia: Coconspirator in the money-laundering portion of the six-hundred-kilo Italian/Colombian shipment. Targeted in Los Angeles through the investigation Polar Cap. Extradited to Italy.

Antonio Zuniga, Robert Moore, Michael Black: Defense attorneys in the trial of Operation Dead Ringer.

Robert Broomfield: U.S. district court judge during Dead Ringer trial.

OPERATIONS:

Dead Ringer: U.S. Customs code name for the investigation of the Medellín cartel's cocaine-smuggling operation between Colombia, Belize, Florida, New York and Arizona.

Dead Fish: The FBI code name for the Miami/New York investigation targeting the Sicilian/Colombian drug-trafficking connection.

Iron Tower: Italian code name for the Sicilian Mafia investigation that targeted the transatlantic drug-trafficking connection.

GLOSSARY OF TERMS

SAC: Special Agent in Charge.

DSAC: Deputy Special Agent in Charge.

ASAC: Assistant Special Agent in Charge.

RAC: Resident Agent in Charge.

AUSA: Assistant United States Attorney.

RCMP: Royal Canadian Mounted Police.

FDLE: Florida Department of Law Enforcement.

FBI: Federal Bureau of Investigation.

USCS: United States Customs Service.

DEA: Drug Enforcement Administration.

ARCE: U.S. Customs Assistant Regional Commissioner, Enforcement. The position no longer exists.

Attaché: The head of a federal law enforcement agency assigned to an American embassy.

ABSCAM: Famous sting that targeted members of the United States Congress.

Irangate: Political scandal surrounding the arms-for-cash conspiracy involving the Reagan White House, the contras and Iran in the 1980s.

Watergate: Political scandal surrounding the bugging of the Democratic National Committee headquarters by the Nixon White House in 1972.

Sting: Long-term, deep-cover operation in which law-enforcement officials pose as criminals. Developed by the Washington Metropolitan Police Department in 1975.

MCC: Metropolitan Correction Center in Miami, Florida.

Guardia di Finanza: Italian federal law-enforcement agency, equivalent to the U.S. Customs.

OEO: Department of Justice Office of Enforcement Operations. This office oversees the Witness Protection Program and the use of federal prisoners as informers/witnesses by federal law-enforcement agencies.

Buy/Bust: The culmination of a drug transaction between undercover officers and the offender, which immediately results in an arrest.

Main Justice: Another name for the Department of Justice (DOJ) headquarters.

Pen Register: Dial Number Recorder. An electronic device that captures the telephone number called or received at a specific location.

CTR: Currency Transaction Report.

Wire: Court-ordered wiretap.

TO: Table of Organization. A term used to describe the human resources allocated to an office and their positions.

Cartel: An international organization formed to regulate prices and products. Also known as a monopoly. Used to describe Colombian drug organizations.

PHRASES IN SPANISH:

"¿Quién es el gringo?": Who is the gringo? "Gringo" is a word used to describe a light-skinned person—Anglos and Americans.

"Un peso por un dólar": One peso for one dollar.

Aguardiente: Popular Colombian drink. Aguardiente is a typical local alcohol flavored with anise.

"Perdón, Don Winces, por favor": Pardon, Don Winces, please.

"Muy despacio": Very slowly.

"Llega el jefe, Don Winces": The boss, Don Winces, arrives.

"¿Quiére una cerveza, senor?": Would you like a beer, sir?

"Baño": Restroom

"Coca Colombiana": Colombian coca

"Marielitos": Colloquialism used to describe the political refugees from Cuba who arrived in South Florida by boat lift in 1981. The term is derived from the port of Mariel, Cuba.

"Puta madre": Motherfucker

"Buenos días señor. Cómo está? Hace calor ¿nerdad?": Good morning, sir. How are you? It's very hot.

"Sí, pero es bueno": Yes, but it's good.

"El Norte": The North. Often used to describe the United States.

"Café con leche": Coffee with milk.

"Puta madre, la policia": Motherfucker, the police.

"Muchas gracias": Thank you very much.

"Estoy lista": I'm ready.

"Mira, vienen los cochinos": Look, here come the pigs.

"¿Cómo están? Les presento al señor Angel Sánchez": How are you? I would like to present to you Mr. Angel Sánchez.

"Mucho gusto": With much pleasure. Pleased to meet you.

"Este es mi jefe": This is my boss.

"Buenas noches señor, estoy en las Islas de Canarias": Good evening sir, I am in the Canary Islands.

"Hasta luego, mi amigo": Until later, my friend. See you later, my friend.

"¿Que pasó, hombre? Estoy ahora en Malta": What's happening, man? I'm in Malta.

"¿Quiere comer?": Do you want to eat?

"Buenas tardes": Good Afternoon

"Bien, ¿Y usted?": Fine, and you?

"Este es señor Peterson. ¿Tienes mis papeles?": This is Mr. Peterson. Do you have my papers?

"Sí, claro. Aquí los tengo": Yes, sure, I have them right here.

"Por favor, venga al Hotel Sheraton Aeropuerto": Please come to the Hotel Sheraton Airport.

"Ve por el Coronel Vargas": Go for Colonel Vargas.

"Perdóname, por favor . . .": Forgive me, please

"Llegamos": We have arrived.

Compadres: Name used to express kinship.

"Estos condenados Cubanos . . . Deberíamos matarlos nosotros mismos . . . ¡Pinchi comunistas!": These goddamned Cubans, we should kill them ourselves. Fucking communists.

"Necesito hablar con Leo—en privado, por favor": I need to speak with Leo—in private, please.

"Buena suerte, mi amigo": Good luck, my friend.

Plata: Money, silver.

"Señor, venga conmigo. Yo le enseño su cuarto": Mister, come with me. I will show you your room.

"¿Cómo se llama?": What is your name?

"Me llamo Graciela": My name is Graciela.

"Buenos días, amigo": Good morning friend.

Nuevo: New

Conquistadores: Conquerers

"Don Pedro, gracias por venir. Estamos aquí para servirle": Don Pedro, thank you for coming. We are here to serve you.

"El placer es mío": The pleasure is mine.

"Departe de nuestros amigos en Cuba": On behalf of our friends in Cuba.

barajas: Cards

"¿Quiere más café, señor?": Do you want more coffee, sir?

Campesinos: Peasants

"Un momento, y se lo paso a Joe": One moment and I will pass you to Joe.

Guayabera: Light-weight, spring/summer shirt worn by men in Latin America.

Rancho: Ranch

Cobarde: Coward

PHRASES IN ITALIAN

Banca di Italia: Bank of Italy

Tizzuni: derogatory word used to describe black people.

Buona sera.: Good evening

Molti grazie: Thank you very much.

Tutto va benissimo: Everything is great

Come stai?: How are you?

Ciao: Goodbye

Buon giorno: Good day. More commonly, Good morning.

Pronto: Hello. Standard form of answering the phone. It literally means "ready."

Coglione: asshole; literally means testicle. Used in Southern Italy and Sicily.

Omertá: Mafia code of silence

pentiti: term used to describe a "turncoat," the literal translation is "repentants."

cucina: kitchen

INDEX

198, 200, 207, 208, 257, 265, 269,
278
"Vicente." *See* Rico-Pinsón, Lazaro
("Vicente")
Video poker business, 152–53
Von Raab, William, 4–5, 140, 142, 303

Wagner, Ken, 86–87, 301
Walker, Tyrone, 66, 123, 180, 300
Ward, John, 43, 73, 299
War on drugs, background to, 1–7
Washington, D.C., 34–35, 244–45
Watergate affair, 2, 44, 306
Waversfeld, Karl, 39, 42, 299

Weapons smuggling, 67–69
"Willie the Fireman" (pseudonym), 70
Witness Protection Program, 222, 224,
245, 287, 290
Wood, Dave, *169*
Woodward, James, 240, 252

Zuniga, Antonio, 254, 255, 256, 261,
262, 275, 278
background, 305
closing argument, 279–81
interrogation of Fraley, 259–60, 265–
67, 270, 272